The Feminist Standpoint Theory Reader

The Feminist Standpoint Theory Reader

Intellectual and Political Controversies

Edited by **Sandra Harding**

ROUTLEDGE
NEW YORK AND LONDON

Published in 2004 by
Routledge
29 West 35th Street
New York, New York 10001
www.routledge-ny.com

Published in Great Britain by
Routledge
11 New Fetter Lane
London EC4P 4EE
www.routledge.co.uk

10   9   8   7   6   5   4   3

Library of Congress Cataloging-in-Publication Data

The feminist standpoint theory reader : intellectual and political
    controversies / edited by Sandra Harding.
        p.   cm.
    Includes bibliographical references and index.
    ISBN 0-415-94500-3 (alk. paper)—ISBN 0-415-94501-1 (pbk. : alk. paper)
    1. Feminist theory.   I. Harding, Sandra G.
HQ1190 .F46313   2003
305 .42′01—dc21

                                                        2003009900

CONTENTS

Acknowledgments

Conversations with Gail Kligman, Nancy Hartsock, Nancy Naples, and Alison Wylie have helped me to conceptualize this collection. The publisher's reviewers gave me useful suggestions. Ilene Kalish at Routledge gave me good advice. My thanks to Tara Watford for her patient assistance in the permission and manuscript preparation process.

Permissions

Sarah Bracke and María Puig de la Bellacasa, "Building Standpoints." Published by permission of authors.

Patricia Hill Collins, "Learning from the Outsider Within: The Sociological Significance of Black Feminist Thought," from *Social Problems, 33,* no. 6 (1986): S14–S32. Copyright © 1986 by *The Society for the Study of Social Problems.* Reprinted by permission of author and *Social Problems,* www.ucpress.edu.

Patricia Hill Collins, "Comment on Hekman's 'Truth and Method: Feminist Standpoint Theory Revisited': Where's the Power?," from *Signs: Journal of Women in Culture and Society, 22,* no. 21 (1997): 375–81. Copyright © 1997. Reprinted by permission of author and The University of Chicago Press.

Fernando J. García Selgas, "Feminist Epistemologies for Critical Social Theory: From Standpoint Theory to Situated Knowledge." Published by permission from author.

Donna Haraway, "Situated Knowledges: The Science Question in Feminism and the Privilege of Partial Perspective" from *Simians, Cyborgs, and Women: The Reinvention of Nature.* Copyright © 1991. Reproduced by permission of author and Routledge, Inc., part of The Taylor and Francis Group.

Sandra Harding, "Rethinking Standpoint Epistemology: What is 'Strong Objectivity'?," from *Feminist Epistemologies,* edited by Linda Alcoff and Elizabeth Potter, pp. 49–82. Copyright © 1993. Excerpted and reproduced by permission of Routledge, Inc., part of The Taylor and Francis Group.

Sandra Harding, "Comment on Hekman's 'Truth and Method: Feminist Standpoint Theory Revisited': Whose Standpoint Needs the Regimes of Truth and Reality?," from *Signs: Journal of Women in Culture and Society, 22,* no. 21 (1997): 382–91. Copyright © 1997. Excerpted and reprinted by permission of The University of Chicago Press.

Nancy C. M. Hartsock, "The Feminist Standpoint: Developing the Ground for a Specifically Feminist Historical Materialism," from *Discovering Reality,* edited by Merrill B. Hintikka and Sandra Harding, pp. 283–310. Copyright ©

1983. Excerpted and reprinted by permission of author and Kluwer Academic Publishers.

Nancy C. M. Hartsock, "Comment on Hekman's 'Truth and Method: Feminist Standpoint Theory Revisited': Truth or Justice?," from *Signs: Journal of Women in Culture and Society,* 22, no. 21 (1997): 367–74. Copyright © 1997. Excerpted and reprinted by permission of author and The University of Chicago Press.

Susan Hekman, "Truth and Method: Feminist Standpoint Theory Revisted," from *Signs: Journal of Women in Culture and Society,* 22, no. 21 (1997): 341–65. Copyright © 1997. Excerpted and reprinted by permission of author and The University of Chicago Press.

Susan Hekman, "Reply to Hartsock, Collins, Harding, and Smith," from *Signs: Journal of Women in Culture and Society,* 22, no. 21 (1997): 399–402. Copyright © 1997. Reprinted by permission of author and The University of Chicago Press.

Nancy J. Hirschmann, "Feminist Standpoint as Postmodern Strategy," from *Politics and Feminist Standpoint Theories,* edited by S. J. Kenney and H. Kinsella, pp. 73–92. Copyright © 1997. Reprinted by permission of the author and The Haworth Press, Inc.

bell hooks, "Choosing the Margin as a Space of Radical Openness," from *Yearning: Race,Gender, and Cultural Politics,* pp. 145–53. Copyright © 1990. Reprinted by permission of South End Press.

Alison M. Jaggar, "Feminist Politics and Epistemology: The Standpoint of Women," excerpted from "Feminist Politics and Epistemology: Justifying Feminist Theory," from *Feminist Politics and Human Nature,* pp. 353–93. Copyright © 1983. Excerpted and reprinted by permission of author and Rowman & Littlefield, Inc.

Fredric Jameson, "*History and Class Consciousness* as an 'Unfinished Project'," from *Rethinking Marxism, 1,* no. 1 (1988): 49–72. Copyright © 1988. Excerpted, revised and reprinted by permission of author and Routledge, Inc., part of The Taylor and Francis Group.

Catharine A. MacKinnon, "Feminism, Marxism, Method, and the State: Toward Feminist Jurisprudence," from *Signs: Journal of Women in Culture and Society, 8,* no. 4 (1983): 635–58. Copyright © 1983. Excerpted and reprinted by permission of the author and The University of Chicago Press.

1

Introduction:
Standpoint Theory as a Site
of Political, Philosophic, and
Scientific Debate

SANDRA HARDING

A Controversial Theory

Standpoint theory has continued to attract both enthusiasts and critics during the three decades of its recent history. Moreover, tensions within and between its texts still generate lively debates in feminist circles, within which it first appeared a full generation ago. Some see this continuing controversiality as a problem to which they set out to provide a definitive solution. This theory can be saved from its controversiality, they hope. Others see such controversiality as a reason to avoid engaging with standpoint issues at all.[1]

Standpoint theory is valuable in many ways, as its defenders argue. I propose that this controversiality is another valuable resource that standpoint theory contributes to feminism as well as to contemporary scientific, philosophic, and political discussions more generally. Standpoint theory's innovations bring into focus fresh perspectives on some of the most difficult and anxiety-producing dilemmas of our era. Here I identify sources of these controversies. I do so through introducing some of standpoint theory's central themes, concepts, and projects as these have developed within feminist thinking.[2]

Standpoint Origins, Projects

Standpoint theory emerged in the 1970s and 1980s as a feminist critical theory about relations between the production of knowledge and practices of power. It was intended to explain the surprising successes of emerging feminist research in a wide range of projects—"surprising" because feminism is a political movement and, according to the conventional view (one that is currently under siege from various quarters, however), politics can only obstruct and damage the production of scientific knowledge. Standpoint theory challenged this assumption. Consequently, it was proposed not just as an explanatory theory, but also prescriptively, as a method or theory of method (a methodology) to guide future feminist research.

1

Moreover, it expanded conventional horizons of the fields or disciplines mentioned to include normative social theory. Distinctive conceptions of human nature and the ideal society lay behind feminist research. Thus, standpoint theory was both explanatory and normative. Also controversial was the further claim that in this respect standpoint theory was no different from the standard philosophies of science, epistemologies, and methodologies, which persistently obscured their normative features behind a veil of claimed neutrality. Last but not least, standpoint theory was presented as a way of empowering oppressed groups, of valuing their experiences, and of pointing toward a way to develop an "oppositional consciousness," as Patricia Hill Collins (1989) and Chela Sandoval (chapter 14, this volume) put the point. Thus, it was presented by different authors (and sometimes within a single essay) as a philosophy of both natural and social sciences, an epistemology, a methodology (a prescriptive "method of research," as several of its theorists phrased it), and a political strategy. Yet these are fields and projects that conventionally are supposed to be kept separate.

So here are already a number of sources of its controversiality. It set out to explain how certain kinds of politics do not block the growth of knowledge but, rather, can stimulate and guide it. It presented itself as a philosophy of science, an epistemology, and a methodology or method of research, appearing to conflate or even confuse fields standardly kept distinct. It framed these disciplinary projects within a feminist social theory and a political strategy, though standardly it is presumed that these fields can and should be kept immune from social and political elements. It claimed mainstream, purportedly only descriptive and explanatory, theories about science and even within science were also—perhaps always—normative, and that this was so even when they achieved maximally accurate description and explanation.

Additionally, implicitly it insisted that feminist concerns could not be restricted to what are usually regarded as only social and political issues, but instead must be focused on every aspect of natural and social orders, including the very standards for what counts as knowledge, objectivity, rationality, and good scientific method. Thus, feminist issues could not be pigeon-holed and ignored as only women's issues, but instead had to be seen as valuably informing theoretical, methodological, and political thought in general.[3]

Two further aspects of feminist standpoint theory's origins deserve mention here, for each has occasioned significant controversy. Standpoint theory had an earlier history in Marxian thought, upon which most of the early feminist theorists explicitly drew. For those disaffected by Marxian thought and practice, this legacy was bad enough. Some criticize standpoint theory for this legacy and even try to sanitize it by reframing it in empiricist or radical poststructuralist terms. Others, whether from ignorance of or hostility to Marxian insights, ignore this framework, often thereby attributing features to standpoint theory that its framers neither intended nor desired. Yet, as Fredric Jameson argues, it is only the feminist theorists who have succeeded in overcoming fatal flaws in the earlier standpoint projects and thus have been able to give this important aspect of the Marxian legacy a viable future.[4] Moreover, feminist theorists do so just as the last of the governments inspired by the Marxian legacy decline and disappear, and the promise of Marxian thought otherwise seems primarily an archaic relic of a bygone and failed utopian moment. Of course some Marxists disagree with the uses to which feminists have put standpoint theory. For others, however, that it should be feminists who succeed at such a project has been disquieting. Thus feminist standpoint theory revives, improves, and disseminates an important Marxian project and does so at an otherwise inauspicious moment for such an achievement.

During the same period standpoint themes—the "logic of a standpoint"— also appeared in the thinking of a wide array of other prodemocratic social movements, which did not overtly claim the Marxian legacy, standpoint terminology, or, often, feminism. Race, ethnicity-based, anti-imperial, and Queer social justice movements routinely produce standpoint themes.[5] This phenomenon suggests that standpoint theory is a kind of organic epistemology, methodology, philosophy of science, and social theory that can arise whenever oppressed peoples gain public voice. "The social order looks different from the perspective of our lives and our struggles," they say. Thus standpoint theory has both an explicit and implicit history. It has a distinctive intellectual history and also a popular or "folk" history visible in its apparently spontaneous appeal to groups around the world seeking to understand themselves and the world around them in ways blocked by the conceptual frameworks dominant in their culture.[6] Philosophers and science theorists do not take kindly to being asked to think that such a "folk philosophy" or "folk science" has something to teach them.[7] In the modern West, though not in other cultures, philosophy and science are virtually always positioned precisely against such "folk thought."

These sources of contention are by no means the only features of standpoint theory that have made it a valuable site for thoughtful researchers, scholars, and students to reflect on and debate some of the most challenging scientific, political, and intellectual issues of our era. Significantly, in spite of continuing criticisms, it just doesn't go away. Moreover, as a methodology, practitioners seem to think that it works to explain kinds of accounts of nature and social relations not otherwise accessible—accounts that provide valuable resources to social justice movements. And it helps to produce oppositional and shared consciousnesses in oppressed groups—to create oppressed peoples as collective "subjects" of research rather than only as objects of others' observation, naming, and management, as a number of the contributors here argue. Uses and discussions of it by now have appeared in most disciplines and in many policy contexts. Indeed, as several of the essayists here note, in the last few years interest in it has surged ahead in dozens and dozens of articles explaining it again to new audiences, puzzling anew over the issues it raises, or exerting considerable effort to challenge its usefulness in any context at all.[8]

The sections that follow in this introduction pursue further central standpoint themes and concepts and the ways these stimulate valuable controversies at this moment in history.

Knowledge for Oppressed Groups?

Standpoint theorists, like their critics, have differing views of what standpoint theory is and can do. Here we can set the stage for these accounts by noting, first, that women's movements needed knowledge that was *for* women. Women, like members of other oppressed groups, had long been the object of the inquiries of their actual or would-be rulers. Yet the research disciplines and the public policy institutions that depended upon them permitted no conceptual frameworks in which women as a group—or, rather, as groups located in different class, racial, ethnic, and sexual locations in local, national, and global social relations— became the subjects—the authors—of knowledge. Could women (in various diverse collectivities) become subjects of knowledge?

Of course individual women have often managed to "speak" in public. The issue here is a different and controversial one: whether women as culturally diverse collectivities could produce knowledge that answered *their* questions about nature and social relations. The implied "speaker" of scientific (sociological, economic, philosophic, etc.) sentences was never women. It was supposed to be humanity in general. As Donna Haraway famously put the point (chapter 6, this volume), the subject of knowledge claims was to be an idealized agent who performed the "God trick" of speaking authoritatively about everything in the world from no particular location or human perspective at all.

The idea that the very best research, no less than the worst, does and should "speak" from particular, historically specific, social locations has been out of the question for standard research norms. As noted earlier, the whole point of scientific knowledge in the modern West, in contrast to "folk knowledge," is supposed to be that its adequacy should transcend the particular historical projects that produce it or, at any given moment, happen to find it useful. Moreover, to repeat, that it could be the social location of women or other oppressed groups that could be the source of illuminating knowledge claims not only about themselves but also the rest of nature and social relations has remained an arrogant, outrageous, and threatening proposal for conventionalists.

Yet feminist researchers were identifying how the conceptual frameworks of the disciplines and of public policy never achieved the desired political and cultural neutrality that their scientific methods and related administrative procedures had been claimed to promise. The problem was not prejudiced and biased individuals, or other kinds of cases of "bad science," as the Liberal, empiricist (or "positivist") philosophies of science proclaimed. (Not that such individuals and cases didn't exist—alas.) Rather, it was a different kind of obstacle that these researchers encountered. The conceptual frameworks themselves promoted historically distinctive institutional and cultural interests and concerns, which ensured that the knowledge produced through them was always socially situated, in Haraway's phrase (chapter 6, this volume). All too often these interests and concerns were not only not women's but, worse, counter to women's needs and desires. The disciplines were complicitous with sexist and androcentric agendas of public institutions.

Worst of all, the sciences' commitment to social neutrality disarmed the scientifically productive potential of politically engaged research on behalf of oppressed groups and, more generally, the culturally important projects of all but the dominant Western, bourgeois, white-supremacist, androcentric, heteronormative culture. Commitment to an objectivity defined as maximizing social neutrality was not itself socially neutral in its effects (MacKinnon, chapter 12, Harding, chapter 8, this volume). To be sure, politics and culture often function as "prisonhouses" of knowledge, as conventional wisdom points out. Yet they can and often do also function as "toolboxes," enabling new perspectives and new ways of seeing the world to enlarge the horizons of our explanations, understandings, and yearnings for a better life.[9] The feminist research projects, which were guided by politics and thus also socially situated, often succeeded in producing empirically more accurate accounts as well as expanding the horizons of human knowledge. The "goodness" of "good science," feminist or not, was inadequately understood by mainstream philosophy of science, epistemology, and methodology standpoint theorists argued.[10]

Androcentric, economically advantaged, racist, Eurocentric, and heterosexist conceptual frameworks ensured systematic ignorance and error about not only the lives of the oppressed, but also about the lives of their oppressors and thus about how nature and social relations in general worked. In the dominant androcentric accounts it remained mysterious through what processes women's life choices became so restricted. How did it come about that violence against women in every class and race, often committed by men women trusted from within their own social groups, was interpreted persistently by the legal system as women "asking for it" and only "deviant" men doing it? . . . or, as the duty of husbands or slave owners. Who benefits from only one form of "the family" being regarded as normal and desirable, and all others, in which live the vast majority of the citizens of North America and the rest of the world, devalued as deviant and undesirable? How did it occur that a double day of work, one day of which was unpaid, was regarded as normal and necessary for women but not for men? Why were women who were menstruating, birthing, or going through menopause treated by the medical profession as if they were sick? Who benefits when standards for rationality are restricted to the instrumental rationality of those sciences and public institutions from the design and management of which women, the poor, and people of non-Western descent are barred? What social processes made reasonable the belief that women made no contributions to human evolution? The answers to these questions required research about the dominant institutions, and their customs and practices, including, especially, their conceptual practices.

The remedy for the inadequate philosophies of science, epistemologies, and methodologies justifying and guiding mainstream research, and the social theories that informed them, according to these theorists, was to start off thought and research from women's experiences, lives, and activities (or labor) and from the emerging collective feminist discourses. That is, researchers were to avoid taking their research problems, concepts, hypotheses, and background assumptions from the conceptual frameworks of the disciplines or of the social institutions that they served (the legal, welfare, health, education, economic, military, and other institutions). Thus standpoint projects would be "outside the realm of the true" from the perspective of those disciplines and institutions. Moreover, such projects were not intended to end in ethnographies of women's worlds (as some observers have assumed), though often such work became a necessary preliminary step. Rather, women needed to understand the conceptual practices of power, in Dorothy E. Smith's felicitous phrase, through which their oppression was designed, maintained, and made to seem natural and desirable to everyone. Thus standpoint projects must "study up"; they must be part of critical theory, revealing the ideological strategies used to design and justify the sex-gender system and its intersections with other systems of oppression, in the case of feminist projects.

As science, standpoint projects were to see "beneath" or "behind" the dominant sexist and androcentric ideologies that shaped everyone's lives to the relations between, on the one hand, the actualities of women's everyday lives and, on the other hand, the conceptual practices of powerful social institutions, especially including research disciplines. Yet such sciences could not occur without political struggles. Political engagement, rather than dispassionate neutrality, was necessary to gain access to the means to do such research—the research training, jobs in research institutions, research funding, and publication. It was also needed to create women's collective, group consciousnesses that would enable women's groups to design, and to value and engage in, the kinds of research that could enable women to transform their consciousness into an oppositional one and to begin see the possibility of ending their oppression. Last but not least, political struggle itself produced insight. The more value-neutral a conceptual framework appears, the more likely it is to advance the hegemonous interests of dominant groups, and the less likely it is to be able to detect important actualities of social relations (as Smith, Harding, and MacKinnon argue in different ways in this volume). We need not—indeed, must not—choose between "good politics" and "good science," standpoint theorists argued, for the former can produce the latter.

Yet such standpoint projects raise further troubling issues for standpoint theorists themselves as well as for their critics. One continuing theme has focused on whether it is women's experiences, women's social locations, or feminist discourses that are to provide the origin of knowledge projects. Clearly the experiences of oppressed groups can become an important source of critical insight. Moreover mainstream research always draws on distinctive social experience and scientific experience, as recent histories, sociologies, and ethnographies of science argue, so it cannot be that experience is in itself the problem. Indeed, the very best human knowledge of the empirical world is supposed to be grounded in human experience. Yet some critics ask if standpoint theory's focus on the importance of the experience of women and other oppressed groups ensures that it has abandoned the epistemological uses of concepts of truth, objectivity, and good method. And if so, would it not thereby have lost the solid grounding, the epistemological foundations, that any political movement needs to make its claims plausible to dominant groups, and to be useful in political struggle? Relatedly, critics ask if women's experiences and discourses gain automatic epistemic privilege in standpoint theory. Moreover, aren't consciousnesses only individual? So what is a "collective group consciousness"? Furthermore, how does and should standpoint theory account for and engage with differences between women? Can feminist discourses be legitimate if some women cannot agree to them on the basis of their particular experiences? Who are these "women" whose experiences, social locations, and discourses are to ground feminist knowledge? Are they only the women privileged to speak and write from the dominant universities, research institutes, and national and international institutions and agencies? What is the relation between the standpoints of different groups of women? This entangled set of issues arises in the essays here. We can begin to sort them out by focusing first on the scientific and epistemological value of differences between women.

How Can Differences in Oppression Become Political and Scientific Resources?

Let us begin with the claim that knowledge is always socially situated. Thus, to the extent that an oppressed group's situation is different from that of the dominant group, its dominated situation enables the production of distinctive kinds of knowledge. (And let us not forget that dominant groups have always insisted on maintaining different material conditions for themselves and those whose labor makes possible their dominance, and they have insisted that those they dominate do not and could not achieve their own exalted level of consciousness.) After all, knowledge is supposed to be based on experiences, and so different experiences should enable different perceptions of ourselves and our environments.

However, more than this social situatedness is at issue for standpoint theorists. Each oppressed group can learn to identify its distinctive opportunities to turn an oppressive feature of the group's conditions into a source of critical insight about how the dominant society thinks and is structured. Thus, standpoint theories map how a social and political disadvantage can be turned into an epistemological, scientific, and political advantage. With this second claim, a standpoint can not be thought of as an ascribed position with its different perspective that oppressed groups can claim automatically. Rather, a standpoint is an achievement, something for which oppressed groups must struggle, something that requires both science and politics, as Nancy Hartsock put the point.[11] Here the term becomes a technical one in the sense that it is no longer simply another word for viewpoint or perspective, but rather makes visible a different, somewhat hidden phenomenon that we must work to grasp. For an achieved standpoint, science and politics turn out to be internally linked, contrary to the standard Liberal, empiricist, Enlightenment view. Empowerment requires a distinctive kind of knowledge (knowledge *for* one's projects), and that kind of knowledge can emerge only through political processes.

Now we come to the issue of differences. Not all women have the same conditions or experiences. Standpoint theory has often been accused of the very same kind of "centered" and "essentialist" ontology that feminists criticize in androcentric accounts. The Marxian ontology originally borrowed by standpoint theorists shared the Enlightenment tendency to envision only one kind of homogenous, oppressed, heroic, ideal knower, and agent of history versus a homogenized, ideology-producing, economically and politically powerful ignoramus: the idealized proletarian knower versus the ignorant bourgeoisie. Differences between nonbourgeoisie, whether or not they were industrial workers—gender, racial, ethnic differences, for example—were noted in Marxian accounts but not of theoretical interest. Indeed, no theoretical framework was created within classical Marxism to explore the distinctive forms of oppression and sources of resistance that might characterize different such groups.

From its beginnings feminist standpoint theorists have had to struggle, along with other feminists and members of other social justice movements, to create a different kind of *decentered subject* of knowledge and of history than was envisioned either by Enlightenment or Marxian accounts. The work of women of color has been especially important here in developing notions of "intersectional" social locations where oppressive hierarchical structures of gender, class, race and other antidemocratic projects intersect in different ways for different groups. And women of color have led the way in envisioning coalitions of such decentered subjects of knowledge and history whose common experiences are both discovered and forged through shared political projects.[12]

What are these distinctive aspects of oppression that scientific and political projects can turn into epistemic and scientific resources? Dorothy Smith points to women's responsibility for daily life as a source of valuable critical questions and insights about the dominant institutions and the "conceptual practices of power" that the discipline of sociology provides for them. Hilary Rose argues that women's responsibility for their bodies and for emotional labor gives women a distinctive perspective on their own bodies and on the sciences. Patricia Hill Collins argues that Black women's distinctive activities in slavery, in the kinds of work Black women are assigned today, and in their ongoing struggles to support their families and communities gives them powerful critical perspectives on the limitations of mainstream sociology and the social institutions it services.

Other authors focus on other resource-producing oppressive situations and practices: Sara Ruddick on mothering, bell hooks on marginality, Catharine A. MacKinnon on violence against women, Kathi Weeks on women's labor, and Maria Mies and Vandana Shiva on the "subsistence" (survival) activities of women in the Third World. And Chela Sandoval argues that the very exclusion of women of color from the kinds of subjectivity favored in the main forms of white women's feminist theory has in itself provided a distinctive resource for women of color's innovative theorizing.[13] My point here is that this kind of account enables us to understand how each oppressed group will have its own critical insights about nature and the larger social order to contribute to the collection of human knowledge. Because different groups are oppressed in different ways, each has the possibility (not the certainty) of developing distinctive insights about systems of social relations in general in which their oppression is a feature.

When women refuse to assent to some particular claim made in the name of feminism, that is always a good reason to seek to identify the different situations and experiences that support such dissent. Feminism has a long history of association with bourgeois Liberal rights movements, racially and ethnically discriminatory projects, heteronormative understandings, and other theoretical "luxuries" available to women from the dominant groups. Feminist projects often have been too conservative to appeal to the wide range of women they imagine as their eager audience. Moreover, the dominant intellectual projects against which standpoint theory is positioned in Europe and North America today can take other forms in other cultures, leaving standpoint projects positioned against women's interests. (See, for example, the accounts by Uma Narayan [chapter 15, this volume], and by Maria Mies and Vandana Shiva [chapter 26, this volume].) It cannot be overemphasized that the epistemic privilege oppressed groups possess is by no means automatic. The "moment of critical insight" is one that comes only through political struggle, for it is blocked and its understandings obscured by the dominant, hegemonous ideologies and the practices that they make appear normal and even natural. That oppressed groups are indeed capable of precisely the forms of rationality so highly valued by logicians, scientists, and in law courts cannot become visible so long as those groups are denied access to the educations and practices it takes to make logicians, scientists, and lawyers. That women are physically inferior to men appears obvious as long as ideals of womanliness require women to appear weak and frail, to be discouraged from athletic training, to be encouraged to wear clothing that restricts their movement, and as long as athletic performances such as ballet and modern dance are treated as mere entertainment.

Standpoint theory's focus on the historical and social locatedness of knowledge projects and on the way collective political and intellectual work can transform a source of oppression into a source of knowledge and potential liberation, makes a distinctive contribution to social justice projects as well as to our understanding of preconditions for the production of knowledge.

There are yet other sources of standpoint theory's controversiality that have not been addressed by this discussion. Here we take up just two more of them.

Relativism?

Critics often accuse standpoint theory of committing or even embracing a damaging epistemological relativism since standpoint theorists argue that all knowledge claims are socially located, and that some such locations are preferable as possible sources of knowledge. What is and is not at issue here?

Let us begin by noting that while ethical relativism is a very old issue for Western thinkers, the possibility of epistemological relativism is relatively new. Different cultures seem to have not just different moral practices, but different standards—different ethical principles—for what counts as a desirable kind of moral practice. So on what culture-neutral grounds could one decide between competing moral or ethical claims? Attempts to identify a universally valid standard that could fairly adjudicate between competing local practices seem invariably to be confronted with the challenge that the standard proposed—egoism or altruism, utilitarianism, Kantian or Rawlsian rationalism—is not in fact culturally neutral. So the issues of moral and ethical relativism are not new. But until the emergence of post–World War II social studies of science, claims to knowledge about nature, and (their authors hoped) social relations appeared to escape such relativist charges.

Knowledge claims certified by modern Western sciences were assumed to be grounded in reality in ways that claims without such a pedigree were not. Non-Western cultures' knowledge systems were, at best, merely technologies, speculative claims, or prescientific elements of traditional thought. At worst, they were dogma, magic, superstition, and even the "products of the savage mind," in French anthropologist E. G. Lucien Levy-Bruhl's (1926) memorable phrase (see Harding, 1998b). However, with the appearance of Thomas S. Kuhn's 1962 *The Structure of Scientific Revolutions*, the horrifying possibility of epistemological relativism emerged. Kuhn had argued that even the most admired moments in the history of modern science had an "integrity with their era"; that is, they were somehow permeated by historically and culturally local values and interests. Revolutionary changes in science were not a matter of linear progress, but rather of a scientific community simply moving into a different conceptual and research world—a different paradigm, as he put it. The subsequent four decades of the history, philosophy, and social studies of science and technology have had to struggle continuously against charges of a damaging epistemological relativism that, the critics say, threatens to undermine the rationality of preferring modern sciences to other knowledge systems, and thus the legitimacy of these new fields themselves.[14]

Standpoint theory, along with postmodernist and some postcolonial approaches, can seem to share this debilitating relativism because it, too, acknowledges that all knowledge claims are socially situated. Worse, standpoint approaches argue that some kinds of social values can advance the growth of knowledge. Such anxieties require more extended attention than can be given to them here. Yet perhaps relativist fears can be set aside for a while by consideration of the following four points. First, there are familiar research areas where values and interests clearly shape the direction, conceptual frameworks, research methods, and content of research, and yet this is not considered to deteriorate the empirical or theoretical quality of the research. For example, medical and health research is directed to preserving life, finding a cure for cancer, relieving pain, and other such values. We can easily forget that these are indeed particular cultural values. They are not shared, for example, by some religious groups who think either that this life is a misery to be endured so believers can get to the better afterlife or that one should trust God's mysterious ways rather than modern medical interventions. Yet we do not disqualify the results of searches for a pain reliever because the research was shaped by such a value.

Second, claims of any sort only have meaning in some particular cultural context—that is, relative to some set of cultural practices through which the meaning of the claim is learned and subsequently understood. Claims thus have meaning "relative" to that context of practices.[15] We are often surprised when our communication goes astray in another culture because our words are understood through some other set of assumptions than we intended. But this kind of semantic relativity does not remove grounds for evaluating the empirical adequacy of the claims. Neither does the fact that standpoint projects are designed to produce knowledge that is for women, instead of for the effective management of dominant institutions, remove grounds for evaluating the empirical adequacy of the results of standpoint research. Does it or doesn't it produce a reliable account of some part of reality and an account of what women need to know?

Third, in everyday life we often have to make choices, for example, of health therapies, between value-laden and interested claims (by pharmaceutical companies, physicians, insurance companies, our kin, and friends). We sometimes have to do so in conditions of great urgency with insufficient evidence to feel completely certain about the choice made. Yet we gather all the information we can from every kind of source available, weigh it, and tentatively choose, standing ready to revise our decision if the patient doesn't improve. We would regard as mentally disturbed someone who let himself be paralyzed by relativist considerations in such circumstances.

Last but not least, if in fact all knowledge claims are necessarily socially located, including those of modern sciences, and thus permeated by local values and interests, then it should seem a poor strategy to continue to insist that one particular set of such claims—those credentialed by modern science—are not. Instead, we need to work out an epistemology that can account for both this reality that our best knowledge is socially constructed, and also that it is empirically accurate. The first three remarks above are intended to direct us to such a project.

Disciplinary Debates

Finally, a less obvious source of contention arises from the way standpoint theory has developed independently within debates in several distinct disciplinary contexts, with their different discursive histories and contemporary concerns. Carrying out standpoint projects within disciplines is a crucial task since a main objective of standpoint theory and research is precisely to map the conceptual practices through which particular institutions, such as disciplines, serve oppressive forms of power. As Dorothy E. Smith has pointed out (chapter 2, this volume), ruling in our kinds of modern, bureaucratic societies occurs largely through concepts and symbols, and it is the disciplines that work up and legitimate these particular sociological, economic, historical, jurisprudential, or philosophy of science concepts and symbols. Moreover, as bell hooks insists, writing can be a powerful form of political resistance. Such resistance can be effective within disciplinary discourses. Thus researchers have used the resources of disciplinary debates to develop standpoint projects in directions pertinent to the particular conceptual practices of power of each such discipline. This phenomenon becomes clear if one examines the different concerns of theorists and researchers working in the sociology of knowledge (e.g., Smith, Rose, and Collins), political philosophy (e.g., Hartsock and Jaggar), and the philosophy of natural sciences (e.g., Haraway, Harding, Rouse, and Wylie) in the essays collected here, for example.

One continuing site of dissonance between standpoint theorists themselves has such a source. How should one think about the role of experience in the production of knowledge? Feminist standpoint sociologists think about this differently than do political philosophers and philosophers of science. This is one source of the different emphases on "women's standpoint" versus a "feminist standpoint" in these writings. It may be preferable for this reason, among others, to think of the development of standpoint theories, plural. These share a family resemblance and collectively contrast with dominant epistemologies, methodologies, and philosophies of science, yet importantly differ from each other in other respects.

The disciplinary production of standpoint theories creates other striking phenomena. For example, often theorists in one discipline appear unfamiliar with standpoint writings and arguments from other disciplines, though the latter are relevant to the former. Furthermore, as Dorothy E. Smith points out (chapter 20, this volume), aggregating the work of theorists in these disciplines as "standpoint theorists" in order to map the shared differences between their projects and those of traditional epistemologies and philosophies of science[16] obscures the ways these writers were and remain intensely involved in critical and creative conversations, debates, and projects within their disciplines.

Some further sources of controversy will appear in the essays themselves and the introductions to each section.

The Benefits of Controversy

After all this controversy, what remains notable is that standpoint projects appear to have survived and even to be flourishing anew after more than two decades of contention. Few people exposed to the "logic of the standpoint" remain nonchalant about its potential effects, for, as I have been arguing, it has managed to locate its analyses at the juncture of some of our deepest contemporary anxieties. Disturbing though virtually everyone may find one or another of its claims and projects, standpoint theory apparently is destined to persist at least for a while as a seductively volatile site for reflection and debate about difficult to resolve contemporary dilemmas.

Notes

1. Diverse criticisms of standpoint theory appear in these essays. Additional critical sources can be located through the citations.
2. In the interests of full disclosure, I confess to playing four roles in this collection: as one of the standpoint theorists on whom some of its essays focus; as a standpoint practitioner who has used this approach in my own work on the implications for epistemology and philosophy of science of gender and of race relations and European expansion (for example, in Harding 1998b); as an author and editor who has reported, analyzed, defended, published, and reprinted others standpoint essays in a number of publications over the last two decades; and as the editor of this particular collection, who is—in this introduction—giving my current understanding of these issues. Of course others surely would give (and have given) different accounts of the history, nature, strengths, and limitations of standpoint projects, as the selections that follow reveal.
3. Many of these sources of controversiality originate outside standpoint theory. Other feminists have sometimes been criticized in similar ways. This frequently occurs when critics who are apparently new to feminist epistemology take a caricatured representation of standpoint theory as their model for what is wrong with feminist epistemology in general, or with what they claim is "radical feminism." (See, for example, Walby 2001.)
4. See the essays by Hartsock (chapter 3), Jameson (chapter 9), Pels (chapter 22), and Hirschmann (chapter 25) for accounts of this history, and also Jaggar's full chapter from which the excerpt here is drawn.
5. See, for example, essays here by bell hooks (chapter 10), and by Maria Mies and Vandana Shiva (chapter 26). Michel Foucault's analyses have strong standpoint components, as do many lesbian accounts (Foucault, 1980; Harding, 1991, chapter 10: "Thinking From Lesbian Lives"). See also Pels' (chapter 22, this volume) account of standpoint themes in politically regressive accounts. Manuel Castells (1997) discusses the emergence of standpoint claims (he does not use this language) in the American Militia and Patriot Movement of the 1990s as well as in other religious, land, and ethnicity-based fundamentalist movements whose projects are not well served by either modernity

or the emerging postmodern (postindustrial) economic, political, and cultural social order.

6. No doubt for some of these spontaneous standpoint theorists some form of the Marxian legacy was part of the intellectual world of their thinking. For example, "world systems theory" has become familiar in the perspectives of Third World critiques of Western so-called development policies (see Frank, 1969; Wallerstein, 1974; Sachs, 1992).

7. This is certainly not to imply that the carefully crafted writings of bell hooks, Maria Mies, Dorothy E. Smith, Vandana Shiva and other such highly trained and sophisticated theorists are no different than the complaints and folk wisdom in the less artful speech of people in their everyday lives, insightful as are the latter. Rather, these authors give voice and theoretical support to perspectives and "yearnings," as hooks puts it, which arise in the everyday lives and insights of the oppressed.

8. To give one indication of the dimensions of this dissemination, I considered for this collection over 150 essays that were overtly engaged with standpoint issues (in contrast to the many, many more that simply used standpoint approaches). Many interesting ones could not be included—alas. For those wishing to continue pursuit of these concerns, the citations in the essays here contain excellent guides to the large standpoint literature.

9. See chapters 4 and 6, "Cultures as Toolboxes for Sciences and Technologies" and "Are There Gendered Standpoints on Nature?" of Harding 1998b for further discussion of this point.

10. Standpoint theory emerged alongside the post-Kuhnian (1962) postpositivist social studies of science and technology, which took up similar criticisms of mainstream philosophy, history, and sociology of the natural sciences. Standpoint theorists who worked on the natural sciences were influenced by this work but have not much succeeded in influencing it. See Joseph Rouse's discussion of how this is far more than an issue of missing gender-awareness (chapter 28, this volume), and also the essays by Hilary Rose, Donna Haraway, Sandra Harding, and Alison Wylie.

11. Readers will notice that while most of the essays in this reader restrict the term "standpoint" to its technical use as an achieved (versus ascribed) collective identity or consciousness, one for which oppressed groups must struggle, a few of the authors use it colloquially, as a synonym for a viewpoint or perspective, and to refer to dominant perspectives as well as those of oppressed groups. They sometimes use the term this way even while otherwise insisting on the importance of "science and politics" in oppressed groups' struggles to understand nature and social relations. This is confusing. (The term has this double usage also within the Marxian tradition in which it originated.) I will continue to use it here in the restricted, technical sense indicated.

12. Women of color frequently refer to value-systems that existed prior to the colonization of their peoples and that survive through colonization, imperialism, or slavery in contemporary postcolonization communities (post- at least formal colonization!). See, for example, Collins' (1989) discussion of this phenomenon.

13. See these essays in Sections I and II below. Marxists referred to this phenomenon as the "moment of truth" for an oppressed group. (See Jameson chapter 9, this volume.) My own position these days is to avoid such "truth language" (except in everyday discourse and formal logic) since it is unnecessary (it claims more than the situation requires), and it seems virtually impossible, in scholarly and scientific as well as popular discourses, to pry it away from the old "unity of science" argument for one world, one "truth" (empirically adequate, coherent statement) about it, and one ideal science capable of representing that "truth." (And, of course, one ideal knower capable of creating that science.) Claims to truth seem to me often to be intended to shut down further critical examination of the knowledge claimed. At any rate, when truth and power supposedly issue from the same social site, we are always entitled to be suspicious. See Harding, 1998a.

14. This kind of issue is at the base of the recent "science wars". See Gross and Levitt, 1994, for example.

15. One important discussion of this issue appears in Ian Hacking's (1983) and Joseph Rouse's (1996) call for conceptualizing scientific activity as fundamentally intervention in rather than as representation of nature.

16. As I did initially in my 1986 and have continued to do.

References

Castells, Manuel. 1997. *The Power of Identity.* Volume II of *The Information Age: Economy, Society & Culture.* Oxford: Blackwell.

Collins, Patricia Hill. 1989. "The Social Construction of Black Feminist Thought." *Signs: Journal of Women in Culture and Society* 14:4, 745–73.

Foucault, Michel. 1980. *Power/Knowledge: Selected Interviews and Other Writings, 1972–77.* Trans. Colin Gordon, Leo Marshall, John Mepham, and Kate Soper. New York: Random House.

Frank, Andre Gunder. 1969. *Capitalism and Underdevelopment in Latin America.* New York: Monthly Review Press.

Gross, Paul R., and Norman Levitt. 1994. *Higher Superstition: The Academic Left and Its Quarrels with Science.* Baltimore: Johns Hopkins University Press.

Hacking, Ian. 1983. *Representing and Intervening.* Cambridge: Cambridge University Press.

Haraway, Donna. 1997. "Modest_Witness@Second_Millenium," in *Modest_Witness@Second_Millenium.FemaleMan_Meets_OncoMouse: Feminism and Technoscience.* New York: Routledge.

Harding, Sandra. 1986. *The Science Question in Feminism.* Ithaca, N.Y.: Cornell University Press.

———. 1991. *Whose Science? Whose Knowledge? Thinking From Women's Lives.* Ithaca, N.Y.: Cornell University Press.

———, ed. 1993. *The 'Racial' Economy of Science: Toward a Democratic Future.* Bloomington: Indiana University Press.

———. 1998a. "Are Truth Claims Dysfunctional?" In *Philosophy of Language: The Big Questions,* ed. Andrea Nye. New York: Blackwell.

———. 1998b. *Is Science Multicultural? Postcolonialisms, Feminisms, and Epistemologies.* Bloomington: Indiana University Press.

———. 2002. "After Objectivism vs. Relativism." In *Toward a Feminist Philosophy of Economics,* ed. Drucilla K. Barker and Edith Kuiper. New York: Routledge.

Jaggar, Alison M. 1983. "Feminist Politics and Epistemology: Justifying Feminist Theory," in *Feminist Politics and Human Nature.* Rowman and Littlefield, Inc.

Kuhn, Thomas S. 1962. *The Structure of Scientific Revolutions.* 2nd edition 1970. Chicago: University of Chicago Press.

Levy-Bruhl, E. G. Lucien. 1926. *How Natives Think.* London: Allen and Unwin. Trans. from *Les Fonctions Mentales dans les societies inferieures.* Paris: Presses Universitaires de France, 1910.

Rouse, Joseph. 1996. *Engaging Science.* Ithaca, N.Y.: Cornell University Press.

Sachs, Wolfgang, ed. 1992. *The Development Dictionary: A Guide to Knowledge as Power.* Atlantic Highlands, N.J.: Zed Press.

Walby, Sylvia. 2001. "Against Epistemological Chasms: The Science Question in Feminism Revisited." *Signs: Journal of Women in Culture and Society* 26:2: 485–510. See also responses in the same issue by Joey Sprague and Sandra Harding, and Walby's reply: 511–540.

Wallerstein, Immanuel. 1974. *The Modern World-System.* Vol. 1. New York: Academic Press.

1
The Logic of a Standpoint

Introduction

The Introduction to this collection briefly described the history of standpoint theory and some of its central themes. This first section contains widely known accounts of its main features presented in chronological order.

Dorothy E. Smith's essay (chapter 2) was originally presented in 1972 at the Western meetings of the American Association for the Advancement of Science. She is concerned with the way the favored conceptual frameworks of sociology have a suspiciously good fit with, on the one hand, the ways men tend to understand social life and, on the other hand, the categories and explanations of social relations that administrators and managers of social institutions (the law, economic and welfare institutions, health and educational systems, militaries, etc.) need in order to succeed at their work. Thus sociology, in working up daily life into such conceptual frameworks, is complicitous with the projects of dominant groups. Learning to be a sociologist is learning to substitute the concerns of an administrator's world for the concerns people have in everyday life. Women's perspective can discredit sociology's claim to produce objective knowledge that is independent of the sociologist's situation. Whatever sociologists may intend, their projects have been situated in ways that advantage administrative rule and disadvantage the life possibilities of those who must obey institutional rules and practices. By 1979 Smith had written several more essays providing standpoint analyses; her work was featured that year in a review essay in the *Harvard Educational Review*.[1]

The next three essays appeared in 1983. Hartsock's and Rose's were developed independently of each other and without knowledge of Smith's continuing standpoint work. Hartsock approaches standpoint issues from the perspective of concerns in political philosophy.[2] She emphasizes how a standpoint is an achievement that requires political struggle as well as empirical inquiry ("science"). Moreover, such standpoints in turn offer resources for liberatory struggles. Notice that it is a feminist standpoint, not a standpoint of women, as in Smith's account, which Hartsock proposes. What is at issue in this distinction? (See general introduction.) In Hartsock's essay one can clearly perceive the way feminist standpoint theory was conceptualized on the model of earlier analyses of the effects of class relations on the production of knowledge.

The excerpt here by political philosopher Alison M. Jaggar (chapter 4) is from a study of the various philosophic theories that guided leading versions of feminist activism as these existed in the late 1970s and early 1980s.[3] Or, at least, as Chela Sandoval points out (in chapter 14), Jaggar presents feminist theory as it existed in the minds of most theorists of European origin. Note, however, that Jaggar, like Hartsock, is perfectly aware of differences in women's conditions. Yet the borrowed standpoint framework does not in these first feminist uses lend itself to the "decentered" and "intersectional" analyses that will become crucial subsequently. The excerpt here is from Jaggar's last chapter, where she shows how each such feminist political philosophy, with its distinctive theory of human nature, and of the causes of and remedies for women's oppressed conditions, also includes a theory of knowledge: how to get it and how to evaluate competing knowledge claims. Thus she contrasted the epistemologies of Liberal, classical Marxist, and Radical Feminisms with the then newly developing Socialist Feminist standpoint epistemology. Jaggar's book provided a comprehensive background for the way courses introducing students to feminist theory often were organized and taught in the 1970s and throughout the 1980s. She co-edited a widely used anthology of feminist writings organized in accordance with this kind of familiar philosophic account.[4]

In chapter 5, British sociologist of science Hilary Rose takes as her project developing a feminist standpoint epistemology that is specifically for the natural sciences.[5] Rose, like most (perhaps all) of the other early standpoint authors, had been active in New Left political movements and the emerging women's movement of the 1960s and 1970s. She had already co-edited an influential collection of New Left essays on the natural sciences.[6] In her essay here, Rose traces the history of orthodox Marxian critiques of science and then of those emerging from the (prefeminist) radical social movements of the 1970s. She argues that in one way the latter critiques are indistinguishable from the sociobiology they vigorously oppose: they think of emotional work, the labor of caring for others, often assigned primarily to women, as part of the natural. Thus this division of labor is responsible for some of the partial and distorted understandings that can be found in the medical and health sciences, she claims. Rose argues that sciences and epistemologies for women have emerged from the practices of the women's movements rather than from the science labs.

These four early accounts opened a path for feminist research and theory to escape the individualism and voluntarism of the standard empiricist criticisms of researchers' "biases" that were said to cause sexist and androcentric knowledge claims. It was the systematic structural oppression of women, supported by widespread ideologies of women's inferiority, rather than individuals' biases or prejudices, that led to sexist and androcentric conceptual frameworks and their resulting distorted knowledge claims in both research disciplines and the social institutions that they served. Thus these accounts refused the standard attribution of sexist and androcentric claims merely to "bad science." It was "good science," at least as its defenders would evaluate it, that standpoint theorists claimed was responsible for these problems. That claim has remained furiously contested

In the late 1970s Donna Haraway had provided a critical account of the field of primatology, which traced the links between the sexist, racist, and imperial ways this field had been conceptualized at its formation, on the one hand, and the administrative and managerial challenges faced by leaders in early twentieth-century industry and government, on the other hand. She had been "studying up" the conceptual practices of power from the standpoint of those in oppressed classes, races, and genders, people whose lives became "managed" by others through techniques learned in primatology projects. She later went on to show how very different national social agendas had shaped the goals and practices of primatology in Japan, India, and Africa.[7] No matter how international it was, even the cognitive, technical core of primatology, at least, clearly had been constituted within national, racial, and gendered social projects. Readers may want to reflect on the difference between an international science and a value-free one.

Here she charts an epistemological path that appreciates feminist uses of social constructivist accounts of "situated knowledges," and yet also retains the realist tendencies which many perceive to be important for feminist projects.[8] She argues (chapter 6) that the problem for feminists "is how to have *simultaneously* an account of radical historical contingency for all knowledge claims and knowing subjects, a critical practice for recognizing our own 'semiotic technologies' for making meanings, *and* a no-nonsense commitment to faithful accounts of a 'real' world...." One of several strategies she proposes requires conceptualizing the objects of knowledge not as passive resources for imperial projects or as "masks for interests," but rather as active agents or actors with whom sciences have "conversations." In this way, she suggests, we can give up ideals of mastering nature while continuing to search for fidelity to it.

Sociologist Patricia Hill Collins notes that Black women intellectuals, such as herself, have been socialized into white intellectual and academic life, and yet as Blacks and as women remain marginalized to it. She points out that this position is much like that of African American women more generally, who have long worked in white households and workplaces where they remain marginalized in low-paid (or, in slavery, unpaid) and menial work. She argues that Black women intellectuals can learn to use their "stranger" status within sociology and other sites of intellectual work to provide insights unavailable to what sociologist Robert Merton referred to as "white male insiderism." Such a project uses this "outsider/within" status to rethink from the standpoint of Black women's lives the fundamental social elements of society to be studied and how central sociological concepts may not be adequate to such projects. Such a standpoint provides resources for Black women in their struggles for social justice. Collins' account has been especially forceful in drawing attention to the "intersectionality" of gender, class, and race and the necessity to theorize multiple standpoints of the oppressed.[9]

Appeals to objectivity have often been used to discredit women's perceptions and feminist analyses. Consequently many feminists have supposed that the concept and the practices it legitimates are too strong and can offer no resources for their knowledge projects. In a kind of reverse discourse, some have openly called for subjective voices and relativist accounts. In contrast, in chapter 8 philosopher Sandra Harding argues that it is not the strength but the weakness—the incompetence—of the conventional standards for objectivity that poses a problem.[10] After all, they have not been capable of identifying so many sexist, racist, class-based, heteronormative, and other cultural assumptions that frame research projects. Nor have they been able to recognize the positive role that politics, culture, and values can at times play in advancing the growth of knowledge. Standpoint epistemology calls for stronger standards that can detect and eliminate sexist and androcentric assumptions and that can take on the task of distinguishing productive from unproductive interests in knowledge. The essay contrasts standpoint with feminist empiricist epistemology and distinguishes standpoint claims from others with which it is often conflated. It proposes linkages between feminist and other liberatory movements through the kinds of self-consciously intersectional subjects of knowledge each must empower in order to achieve its own goals.

Notes

1. Marcia Westkott, "Feminist Criticism of the Social Sciences," *Harvard Educational Review* 49 (1979).
2. Another version of this essay appeared the same year in Hartsock's own book: *Money, Sex, and Power: Toward a Feminist Historical Materialism* (Boston: Northeastern University Press, 1985).
3. *Feminist Politics and Human Nature* (Totowa, N.J.: Rowman and Allenheld, 1983).
4. *Feminist Frameworks.* New York: McGraw-Hill, 1978, 1984.
5. Though this is perhaps the first feminist standpoint account specifically focused on the natural sciences, standards of objectivity, rationality, and "good science" originating in the natural sciences were a critical focus in the critiques of sociology, political philosophy, and epistemology also.
6. *The Political Economy of Science: Ideology of/in the Natural Sciences,* ed. H. Rose and S. Rose (Cambridge, Mass.: Schenkman, 1976).
7. "The Bio-politics of a Multicultural Field," in *Primate Visions: Gender, Race and Nature in the World of Modern Science* (New York: Routledge, Chapman and Hall, 1989).
8. This essay originated as a comment on Sandra Harding's *The Science Question in Feminism* (Ithaca, N.Y.: Cornell University Press, 1986) at a 1987 Pacific Division meeting of the American Philosophical Association.
9. See also Collins' subsequent influential study of sociology from the standpoint of Black women's lives: *Black Feminist Thought: Knowledge, Consciousness, and the Politics of Empowerment* (New York: Routledge, 1991).
10. This essay explicitly addresses themes that appeared in a less organized way in her earlier standpoint work.

2

Women's Perspective as a Radical Critique of Sociology

DOROTHY E. SMITH

1. The women's movement has given us a sense of our right to have women's interests represented in sociology, rather than just receiving as authoritative the interests traditionally represented in a sociology put together by men. What can we make of this access to a social reality that was previously unavailable, was indeed repressed? What happens as we begin to relate to it in the terms of our discipline? We can of course think, as many do, merely of the addition of courses to the existing repertoire—courses on sex roles, on the women's movement, on women at work, on the social psychology of women and perhaps somewhat different versions of the sociology of the family. But thinking more boldly or perhaps just thinking the whole thing through a little further might bring us to ask first how a sociology might look if it began from the point of view of women's traditional place in it and what happens to a sociology which attempts to deal seriously with that. Following this line of thought, I have found, has consequences larger than they seem at first.

From the point of view of "women's place" the values assigned to different aspects of the world are changed. Some come into prominence while other standard sociological enterprises diminish. We might take as a model the world as it appears from the point of view of the afternoon soap opera. This is defined by (though not restricted to) domestic events, interests, and activities. Men appear in this world as necessary and vital presences. It is not a women's world in the sense of excluding men. But it is a women's world in the sense that it is the relevances of the women's place that govern. Men appear only in their domestic or private aspects or at points of intersection between public and private as doctors in hospitals, lawyers in their offices discussing wills and divorces. Their occupational and political world is barely present. They are posited here as complete persons, and they are but partial—as women appear in sociology predicated on the universe occupied by men.

But it is not enough to supplement an established sociology by addressing ourselves to what has been left out, overlooked, or by making sociological issues of the relevances of the world of women. That merely extends the authority of the existing sociological procedures and makes of a women's sociology an addendum. We cannot rest at that because it does not account for the separation

between the two worlds and it does not account for or analyze for us the relation between them. (Attempts to work on that in terms of biology operate
within the existing structure as a fundamental assumption and are therefore
straightforwardly ideological in character.)

The first difficulty is that how sociology is thought—its methods, conceptual
schemes, and theories—has been based on and built up within the male social
universe (even when women have participated in its doing). It has taken for
granted not just that scheme of relevances as an itemized inventory of issues
or subject matters (industrial sociology, political sociology, social stratification,
etc.) but the fundamental social and political structures under which these
become relevant and are ordered. There is a difficulty first then of a disjunction
between how women find and experience the world beginning (though not
necessarily ending up) from their place and the concepts and theoretical schemes
available to think about it in. Thus in a graduate seminar last year, we discussed
on one occasion the possibility of a women's sociology and two graduate students
told us that in their view and their experience of functioning in experimental
group situations, theories of the emergence of leadership in small groups, etc.,
just did not apply to what was happening as they experienced it. They could not
find the correlates of the theory in their experiences.

A second difficulty is that the two worlds and the two bases of knowledge
and experience don't stand in an equal relation. The world as it is constituted
by men stands in authority over that of women. It is that part of the world
from which our kind of society is governed and from which what happens to us
begins. The domestic world stands in a dependent relation to that other and its
whole character is subordinate to it.

The two difficulties are related to one another in a special way. The effect
of the second interacting with the first is to impose the concepts and terms in
which the world of men is thought as the concepts and terms in which women
must think their world. Hence in these terms women are alienated from their
experience.

The profession of sociology is predicated on a universe which is occupied by
men and is itself still largely appropriated by men as their "territory." Sociology
is part of the practice by which we are all governed and that practice establishes
its relevances. Thus the institutions which lock sociology into the structures
occupied by men are the same institutions which lock women into the situations
in which they find themselves oppressed. To unlock the latter leads logically to
an unlocking of the former. What follows then, or rather what then becomes
possible—for it is of course by no means inevitable—is less a shift in the subject
matter than a different conception of how it is or might become relevant as a
means to understand our experience and the conditions of our experience (both
women's and men's) in corporate capitalist society.

2. When I speak here of governing or ruling I mean something more general
than the notion of government as political organization. I refer rather to that

total complex of activities differentiated into many spheres, by which our kind of society is ruled, managed, administered. It includes that whole section which in the business world is called "management." It includes the professions. It includes of course government more conventionally defined and also the activities of those who are selecting, training, and indoctrinating those who will be its governors. The last includes those who provide and elaborate the procedures in which it is governed and develop methods for accounting for how it is done and predicting and analyzing its characteristic consequences and sequences of events, namely the business schools, the sociologists, the economists, etc. These are the institutions through which we are ruled and through which we, and I emphasize this we, participate in ruling.

Sociology then I conceive as much more than ideology, much more than a gloss on the enterprise which justifies and rationalizes it, and, at the same time as much less than "science." The governing of our kind of society is done in concepts and symbols. The contribution of sociology to this is that of working up the conceptual procedures, models, and methods by which the immediate and concrete features of experience can be read into the conceptual mode in which the governing is done. What is actually observed or what is systematically recovered by the sociologist from the actualities of what people say and do, must be transposed into the abstract mode. Sociology thus participates in and contributes to the formation and facilitation of this mode of action and plays a distinctive part in the work of transposing the actualities of people's lives and experiences into the conceptual currency in which it is and can be governed.

Thus the relevances of sociology are organized in terms of a perspective on the world which is a view from the top and which takes for granted the pragmatic procedures of governing as those which frame and identify its subject matter. Issues are formulated as issues which have become administratively relevant not as they are significant first in the experience of those who live them. The kinds of facts and events which are facts for us have already been shaped up and given their character and substance as facts, as relations, etc., by the methods and practice of governing. Mental illness, crimes, riots, violence, work satisfaction, neighbors and neighborhoods, motivation, etc., these are the constructs of the practice of government. In many instances, such as mental illness, crimes, neighborhoods, etc., they are constituted as discrete phenomena primarily by administrative procedures and others arise as problems in relation to the actual practice of government, as for example concepts of motivation, work satisfaction, etc.

The governing processes of our society are organized as social entities constituted externally to those persons who participate in and perform them. The managers, the bureaucrats, the administrators, are employees, are people who are *used*. They do not own the enterprises or otherwise appropriate them. Sociologists study these entities under the heading of formal organization. They are put together as objective structures with goals, activities, obligations, etc., other than those which its employees can have as individuals. The academic professions are also set up in a mode which externalizes them as entities vis-à-vis their practitioners. The body of knowledge which its members accumulate is appropriated by the discipline as its body. The work of members aims at contributing to that body of knowledge.

As graduate students learning to become sociologists, we learn to think sociology as it is thought and to practice it as it is practiced. We learn that some topics are relevant and some are not. We learn to discard our experienced world as a source of reliable information or suggestions about the character of the world; to confine and focus our insights within the conceptual frameworks and relevances which are given in the discipline. Should we think other kinds of thoughts or experience the world in a different way or with edges and horizons that pass beyond the conceptual, we must practice a discipline which discards them or find some procedure which makes it possible to sneak them in. We learn a way of thinking about the world which is recognizable to its practitioners as the sociological way of thinking.

We learn to practice the sociological subsumption of the actualities of ourselves and of other people. We find out how to treat the world as instances of a sociological body of knowledge. The procedure operates as a sort of conceptual imperialism. When we write a thesis or a paper, we learn that the first thing to do is to latch it on to the discipline at some point. This may be by showing how it is a problem within an existing theoretical and conceptual framework. The boundaries of inquiry are thus set within the framework of what is already established. Even when this becomes, as it happily often does, a ceremonial authorization of a project which has little to do with the theory used to authorize it, we still work within the vocabularies and within the conceptual boundaries of what we have come to know as "the sociological perspective."

An important set of procedures which serve to constitute the body of knowledge of the discipline as something which is separated from its practitioners are those known as "objectivity." The ethic of objectivity and the methods used in its practice are concerned primarily with the separation of the knower from what he knows and in particular with the separation of what is known from any interests, "biases," etc., which he may have which are not the interests and concerns authorized by the discipline. I must emphasize that being interested in knowing something doesn't invalidate what is known. In the social sciences the pursuit of objectivity makes it possible for people to be paid to pursue a knowledge to which they are otherwise indifferent. What they feel and think about society can be taken apart from and kept out of what they are professionally or academically interested in.

3. The sociologist enters the conceptually ordered society when he goes to work. He enters it as a member and he enters it also as the mode in which he investigates it. He observes, analyzes, explains, and examines as if there were no problem in how that world becomes observable to him. He moves among

the doings of organizations, governmental processes, bureaucracies, etc., as a person who is at home in that medium. The nature of that world itself, how it is known to him and the conditions of its existence or his relation to it are not called into question. His methods of observation and inquiry extend into it as procedures which are essentially of the same order as those which bring about the phenomena with which he is concerned, or which he is concerned to bring under the jurisdiction of that order. His perspectives and interests may differ, but the substance is the same. He works with facts and information which have been worked up from actualities and appear in the form of documents which are themselves the product of organizational processes, whether his own or administered by him, or of some other agency. He fits that information back into a framework of entities and organizational processes which he takes for granted as known, without asking how it is that he knows them or what are the social processes by which the phenomena which correspond to or provide the empirical events, acts, decisions, etc., of that world, may be recognized. He passes beyond the particular and immediate setting in which he is always located in the body (the office he writes in, the libraries he consults, the streets he travels, the home he returns to) without any sense of having made a transition. He works in the same medium as he studies.

But like everyone else he also exists in the body in the place in which it is. This is also then the place of his sensory organization of immediate experience, the place where his coordinates of here and now before and after are organized around himself as center; the place where he confronts people face to face in the physical mode in which he expresses himself to them and they to him as more and other than either can speak. It is in this place that things smell. The irrelevant birds fly away in front of the window. Here he has indigestion. It is a place he dies in. Into this space must come as actual material events, whether as the sounds of speech, the scratchings on the surface of paper which he constitutes as document, or directly, anything he knows of the world. It has to happen here somehow if he is to experience it at all.

Entering the governing mode of our kind of society lifts the actor out of the immediate local and particular place in which he is in the body. He uses what becomes present to him in this place as a means to pass beyond it to the conceptual order. This mode of action creates then a bifurcation of consciousness, a bifurcation of course which is there for all those who participate in this mode of action. It establishes two modes of knowing and experiencing and doing, one located in the body and in the space which it occupies and moves into, the other which passes beyond it. Sociology is written in and aims at this second mode. Vide Bierstedt:

> Sociology can liberate the mind from time and space themselves and remove it to a new and transcendental realm where it no longer depends upon these Aristotelian categories. (1966)

Even observational work aims at its description in the categories and hence conceptual forms of the "transcendental realm."

4. Women are outside and subservient to this structure. They have a very specific relation to it which anchors them into the local and particular phase of the bifurcated world. For both traditionally and as a matter of occupational practices in our society, the governing conceptual mode is appropriated by men and the world organized in the natural attitude, the home, is appropriated by (or assigned to) women (Smith, 1973).

It is a condition of a man's being able to enter and become absorbed in the conceptual mode that he does not have to focus his activities and interests upon his bodily existence. If he is to participate fully in the abstract mode of action, then he must be liberated also from having to attend to his needs, etc., in the concrete and particular. The organization of work and expectations in managerial and professional circles both constitutes and depends upon the alienation of man from his bodily and local existence. The structure of work and the structure of career take for granted that these matters are provided for in such a way that they will not interfere with his action and participation in that world. Providing for the liberation from the Aristotelian categories of which Bierstedt speaks, is a woman who keeps house for him, bears and cares for his children, washes his clothes, looks after him when he is sick, and generally provides for the logistics of his bodily existence.

The place of women then in relation to this mode of action is that where the work is done to create conditions which facilitate his occupation of the conceptual mode of consciousness. The meeting of a man's physical needs, the organization of his daily life, even the consistency of expressive background, are made maximally congruent with his commitment. A similar relation exists for women who work in and around the professional and managerial scene. They do those things which give concrete form to the conceptual activities. They do the clerical work, the computer programming, the interviewing for the survey, the nursing, the secretarial work. At almost every point women mediate for men the relation between the conceptual mode of action and the actual concrete forms in which it is and must be realized, and the actual material conditions upon which it depends.

Marx's concept of alienation is applicable here in a modified form. The simplest formulation of alienation posits a relation between the work an individual does and an external order which oppresses her, such that the harder she works the more she strengthens the order which oppresses her. This is the situation of women in this relation. The more successful women are in mediating the world of concrete particulars so that men do not have to become engaged with (and therefore conscious of) that world as a condition to their abstract activities, the more complete man's absorption in it, the more effective the authority of that world and the more total women's subservience to it. And also the more complete the dichotomy between the two worlds, and the estrangement between them.

5. Women sociologists stand at the center of a contradiction in the relation of our discipline to our experience of the world. Transcending that contradiction means setting up a different kind of relation than that which we discover in the routine practice of our worlds.

The theories, concepts, and methods of our discipline claim to account for, or to be capable of accounting for and analyzing the same world as that which we experience directly. But these theories, concepts, and methods have been organized around and built up out of a way of knowing the world which takes for granted the boundaries of an experience in the same medium in which it is constituted. It therefore takes for granted and subsumes without examining the conditions of its existence. It is not capable of analyzing its own relation to its conditions because the sociologist as an actual person in an actual concrete setting has been cancelled in the procedures which objectify and separate him from his knowledge. Thus the linkage which points back to its conditions is lacking.

For women those conditions are central as a direct practical matter, to be somehow solved in the decision to take up a sociological career. The relation between ourselves as practicing sociologists and ourselves as working women is continually visible to us, a central feature of experience of the world, so that the bifurcation of consciousness becomes for us a daily chasm which is to be crossed, on the one side of which is this special conceptual activity of thought, research, teaching, administration, and on the other the world of concrete practical activities in keeping things clean, managing somehow the house and household and the children, a world in which the particularities of persons in their full organic immediacy (cleaning up the vomit, changing the diapers, as well as feeding) are inescapable. Even if we don't have that as a direct contingency in our lives, we are aware of that as something that our becoming may be inserted into as a possible predicate.

It is also present for us to discover that the discipline is not one which we enter and occupy on the same terms as men enter and occupy it. We do not fully appropriate its authority, i.e., the right to author and authorize the acts and knowing and thinking which are the acts and knowing and thinking of the discipline as it is thought. We cannot therefore command the inner principles of our action. That remains lodged outside us. The frames of reference which order the terms upon which inquiry and discussion are conducted originate with men. The subjects of sociological sentences (if they have a subject) are male. The sociologist is "he." And even before we become conscious of our sex as the basis of an exclusion (*they* are not talking about *us*), we nonetheless do not fully enter ourselves as the subjects of its statements, since we must suspend our sex, and suspend our knowledge of who we are as well as who it is that in fact is speaking and of whom. Therefore we do not fully participate in the declarations and formulations of its mode of consciousness. The externalization of sociology as a profession which I have described above becomes for women a double estrangement.

There is then for women a basic organization of their experience which displays for them the structure of the bifurcated consciousness. At the same time it attenuates their commitment to a sociology which aims at an externalized body of knowledge based on an organization of experience which excludes theirs and excludes them except in a subordinate relation.

6. An alternative approach must somehow transcend this contradiction without re-entering Bierstedt's "transcendental realm" (1966). Women's perspective, as I have analyzed it here, discredits sociology's claim to constitute an objective knowledge independent of the sociologist's situation. Its conceptual procedures, methods, and relevances are seen to organize its subject matter from a determinate position in society. This critical disclosure becomes, then, the basis for an alternative way of thinking sociology. If sociology cannot avoid being situated, then sociology should take that as its beginning and build it into its methodological and theoretical strategies. As it is now, these separate a sociologically constructed world from that which is known in direct experience and it is precisely that separation which must be undone.

I am not proposing an immediate and radical transformation of the subject matter and methods of the discipline nor the junking of everything that has gone before. What I am suggesting is more in the nature of a re-organization which changes the relation of the sociologist to the object of her knowledge and changes also her problematic. This reorganization involves first placing the sociologist where she is actually situated, namely at the beginning of those acts by which she knows or will come to know; and second, making her direct experience of the everyday world the primary ground of her knowledge.

We would reject, it seems to me, a sociology aimed primarily at itself. We would not be interested in contributing to a body of knowledge the uses of which are not ours and the knowers of whom are who knows whom, but generally male—particularly when it is not at all clear what it is that is constituted as knowledge in that relation. The professional sociologist's practice of thinking it as it is thought would have to be discarded. She would be constrained by the actualities of how it happens in her direct experience. Sociology would aim at offering to anyone a knowledge of the social organization and determinations of the properties and events of their directly experienced world. Its analyses would become part of our ordinary interpretations of the experienced world, just as our experience of the sun's sinking below the horizon is transformed by our knowledge that the world turns. (Yet from where we are it seems to sink and that must be accounted for.)

The only way of knowing a socially constructed world is knowing it from within. We can never stand outside it. A relation in which sociological phenomena are objectified and presented as external to and independent of the observer is itself a special social practice also known from within. The relation of observer and object of observation, of sociologist to "subject," is a specialized social relationship. Even to be a stranger is to enter a world constituted from within as strange. The strangeness itself is the mode in which it is experienced.

When Jean Briggs (1970) made her ethnographic study of the ways in which an Eskimo people structure and express emotion, what she learned and observed emerged for her in the context of the actual developing relations between her and the family with whom she lived and other members of the group. Her account situates her knowledge in the context of those relationships. Affections, tensions, and quarrels were the living texture in which she learnt what she describes. She makes it clear how this context structured her learning and how what she learnt and can speak of became observable to her. Briggs tells us what is normally discarded in the anthropological or sociological telling. Although sociological inquiry is necessarily a social relation, we have learned to disattend our own part in it. We recover only the object of its knowledge as if that stood all by itself and of itself. Sociology does not provide for seeing that there are always two terms to this relation. An alternative sociology must be reflexive (Gouldner, 1971), i.e., one that preserves in it the presence, concerns, and experience of the sociologist as knower and discover.

To begin from direct experience and to return to it as a constraint or "test" of the adequacy of a systematic knowledge is to begin from where we are located bodily. The actualities of our everyday world are already socially organized. Settings, equipment, "environment," schedules, occasions, etc., as well as the enterprises and routines of actors are socially produced and concretely and symbolically organized prior to our practice. By beginning from her original and immediate knowledge of her world, sociology offers a way of making its socially organized properties first observable and then problematic.

Let me make it clear that when I speak of "experience" I do not use the term as a synonym for "perspective." Nor in proposing a sociology grounded in the sociologist's actual experience, am I recommending the self-indulgence of inner exploration or any other enterprise with self as sole focus and object. Such subjectivist interpretations of "experience" are themselves an aspect of that organization of consciousness which bifurcates it and transports us into mind country while stashing away the concrete conditions and practices upon which it depends. We can never escape the circles of our own heads if we accept that as our territory. Rather the sociologist's investigation of our directly experienced world as a problem is a mode of discovering or rediscovering the society from within. She begins from her own original but tacit knowledge and from within the acts by which she brings it into her grasp in making it observable and in understanding how it works. She aims not at a reiteration of what she already (tacitly) knows, but at an exploration through that of what passes beyond it and is deeply implicated in how it is.

7. Our knowledge of the world is given to us in the modes in which we enter into relations with the object of knowledge. But in this case the object of our

knowledge is or originates in a "subject." The constitution of an objective sociology as an authoritative version of how things are is done from a position and as part of the practices of ruling in our kind of society. It has depended upon class and sex bases which make it possible for sociology to evade the problem that our kind of society is known and experienced rather differently from different positions within it. Our training teaches us to ignore the uneasiness at the junctures where transitional work is done—for example, the ordinary problems respondents have of fitting their experience of the world to the questions in the interview schedule. It is this exclusion which the sociologist who is a woman cannot so easily preserve, for she discovers, if she will, precisely that uneasiness in her relation to her discipline as a whole. The persistence of the privileged sociological version (or versions) relies upon a substructure which has already discredited and deprived of authority to speak, the voices of those who know the society differently. The objectivity of a sociological version depends upon a special relation with others which makes it easy for the sociologist to remain outside the other's experience and does not require her to recognize that experience as a valid contention.

Riding a train not long ago in Ontario I saw a family of Indians, woman, man, and three children standing together on a spur above a river watching the train go by. There was (for me) that moment—the train, those five people seen on the other side of the glass. I saw first that I could tell this incident as it was, but that telling as a description built in my position and my interpretations. I have called them a family; I have said they were watching the train. My understanding has already subsumed theirs. Everything may have been quite other for them. My description is privileged to stand as what actually happened, because theirs is not heard in the contexts in which I may speak. If we begin from the world as we actually experience it, it is at least possible to see that we are located and that what we know of the other is conditional upon that location as part of a relation comprehending the other's location also. There are and must be different experiences of the world and different bases of experience. We must not do away with them by taking advantage of our privileged speaking to construct a sociological version which we then impose upon them as their reality. We may not rewrite the other's world or impose upon it a conceptual framework which extracts from it what fits with ours. Our conceptual procedures should be capable of explicating and analyzing the properties of their experienced world rather than administering it. Their reality, their varieties of experience must be an unconditional datum.

8. My experience on the train epitomizes a sociological relation. The observer is already separated from the world as it is experienced by those she observes. That separation is fundamental to the character of that experience. Once she becomes aware of how her world is put together as a practical everyday matter and of how her relations are shaped by its concrete conditions (even in so simple a matter as that she is sitting in the train and it travels, but those people standing

on the spur do not) the sociologist is led into the discovery that she cannot understand the nature of her experienced world by staying within its ordinary boundaries of assumption and knowledge. To account for that moment on the train and for the relation between the two experiences (or more) and the two positions from which those experiences begin involves positing a total socio-economic order "in back" of that moment. The coming together which makes the observation possible as well as how we were separated and drawn apart as well as how I now make use of that here—these properties are determined elsewhere than in that relation itself.

Further, how our knowledge of the world is mediated to us becomes a problem. It is a problem in knowing how that world is organized for us prior to our participation as knowers in that process. As intellectuals we ordinarily receive it as a media world, of documents, images, journals, books, talk, as well as in other symbolic modes. We discard as an essential focus of our practice other ways of knowing. Accounting for that mode of knowing and the social organization which sets it up for us again leads us back into an analysis of the total socio-economic order of which it is part. It is not possible to account for one's directly experienced world or how it is related to the worlds which others directly experience who are differently placed by remaining within the boundaries of the former.

If we address the problem of the conditions as well as the perceived forms and organization of immediate experience, we should include in it the events as they actually happen or the ordinary material world which we encounter as a matter of fact—the urban renewal project which uproots 400 families; how it is to live on welfare as an ordinary daily practice; cities as the actual physical structures in which we move; the organization of academic occasions such as that in which this paper originated. When we examine them, we find that there are many aspects of how these things come about of which we have little as sociologists to say. We have a sense that the events which enter our experience originate somewhere in a human intention, but we are unable to track back to find it and to find out how it got from there to here. Or take this room in which I work or that room in which you are reading and treat that as a problem. If we think about the conditions of our activity here, we could track back to how it is that there are chairs, table, walls, our clothing, our presence; how these places (yours and mine) are cleaned and maintained, etc. There are human activities, intentions, and relations which are not apparent as such in the actual material conditions of our work. The social organization of the setting is not wholly available to us in its appearance. We bypass in the immediacy of the specific practical activity, a complex division of labor which is an essential precondition to it. Such preconditions are fundamentally mysterious to us and present us with problems in grasping social relations in our kind of society with which sociology is ill equipped to deal. Our experience of the world is of one which is largely incomprehensible beyond the limits of what is known in a common sense. No amount of observation of face-to-face relations, no amounts of analysis of commonsense knowledge of everyday life, will take us beyond our essential ignorance of how it is put together. Our direct experience of it constitutes it (if we will) as a problem, but it does not offer any answers. The matrix of direct experience as that from which sociology might begin discloses that beginning as an "appearance" the determinations of which lie beyond it.

We might think of the "appearances" of our direct experience as a multiplicity of surfaces, the properties and relations among which are generated by a social organization which is not observable in its effects. The structures which underlie and generate the characteristics of our own directly experienced world are social structures and bring us into unseen relations with others. Their experience is necessarily different from ours. Beginning from our experienced world and attempting to analyze and account for how it is, necessitates positing others whose experience is different.

Women's situation in sociology discloses to her a typical bifurcate structure with the abstracted conceptual practices on the one hand and the concrete realizations, the maintenance routines, etc., on the other. Taking each for granted depends upon being fully situated in one or the other so that the other does not appear in contradiction to it. Women's direct experience places her a step back where we can recognize the uneasiness that comes in sociology from its claim to be about the world we live in and its failure to account for or even describe its actual features as we find them in living them. The aim of an alternative sociology would be to develop precisely that capacity from that beginning so that it might be a means to anyone of understanding how the world comes about for her and how it is organized so that it happens to her as it does in her experience.

9. Though such a sociology would not be exclusively for or done by women it does begin from the analysis and critique originating in their situation. Its elaboration therefore depends upon a grasp of that which is prior to and fuller than its formulation. It is a little like the problem of making a formal description of the grammar of a language. The linguist depends and always refers back to the competent speakers' sense, etc. In her own language she depends to a large extent upon her own competence. Women are native speakers of this situation and in explicating it or its implications and realizing them conceptually, they have that relation to it of knowing it before it has been said.

The incomprehensibility of the determinations of our immediate local world is for women a particularly striking metaphor. It recovers an inner organization in common with their typical relation to the world. For women's activities and existence are determined outside them and beyond the world which is their "place." They are oriented by their training and by the daily practices which confirm it, toward the demands and initiations and authority of others. But more than that, the very organization of the world which has been assigned to them as the primary locus of their being is determined by and subordinate to the corporate organization of society (Smith, 1973). Thus, as I have expressed her relation to sociology, its logic lies elsewhere. She lacks the inner principle of her own activity. She does not grasp how it is put together because it is determined elsewhere than where she is. As a sociologist then the grasp and exploration of her own experience as a method of discovering society restores to her a center which in this enterprise at least is wholly hers.

Note

This paper was originally prepared for the meetings of the American Academy for the Advancement of Science (Pacific Division) Eugene, Oregon, June, 1972. The original draft of this paper was typed by Jane Lemke and the final version by Mildred Brown. I am indebted to both of them.

References

Bierstedt, Robert. 1966. "Sociology and general education." In Charles H. Page (ed.), *Sociology and Contemporary Education*. New York: Random House.

Briggs, Jean L. 1970. *Never in Anger*. Cambridge, Mass.: Harvard University Press.

Gouldner, Alvin. 1971. *The Coming Crisis in Western Sociology*. London: Heinemann Educational Books.

Smith, Dorothy E. 1973. "Women, the family and corporate capitalism." In M. L. Stephenson (ed.), *Women in Canada*. Toronto: Newpress.

3

The Feminist Standpoint: Developing the Ground for a Specifically Feminist Historical Materialism*

NANCY C. M. HARTSOCK

The power of the Marxian critique of class domination stands as an implicit suggestion that feminists should consider the advantages of adopting a historical materialist approach to understanding phallocratic domination. A specifically feminist historical materialism might enable us to lay bare the laws of tendency which constitute the structure of patriarchy over time and to follow its development in and through the Western class societies on which Marx's interest centered. A feminist materialism might in addition enable us to expand the Marxian account to include all human activity rather than focussing on activity more characteristic of males in capitalism. The development of such a historical and materialist account is a very large task, one which requires the political and theoretical contributions of many feminists. Here I will address only the question of the epistemological underpinnings such a materialism would require. Most specifically, I will attempt to develop, on the methodological base provided by Marxian theory, an important epistemological tool for understanding and opposing all forms of domination—a feminist standpoint.

Despite the difficulties feminists have correctly pointed to in Marxian theory, there are several reasons to take over much of Marx's approach. First, I have argued elsewhere that Marx's method and the method developed by the contemporary women's movement recapitulate each other in important ways.[1] This makes it possible for feminists to take over a number of aspects of Marx's method. Here, I will adopt his distinctions between appearance and essence, circulation and production, abstract and concrete, and use these distinctions between dual levels of reality to work out the theoretical forms appropriate to each level when viewed not from the standpoint of the proletariat but from a specifically feminist standpoint. In this process I will explore and expand the Marxian argument that socially mediated interaction with nature in the process of production shapes both human beings and theories of knowledge. The Marxian category of labor, including as it does both interaction with other humans and with the natural

35

world, can help to cut through the dichotomy of nature and culture, and, for feminists, can help to avoid the false choice of characterizing the situation of women as either "purely natural" or "purely social." As embodied humans we are of course inextricably both natural and social, though feminist theory to date has, for important strategic reasons, concentrated attention on the social aspect. . . .

Feminist Marxists and materialist feminists more generally have argued that the position of women is structurally different from that of men, and that the lived realities of women's lives are profoundly different from those of men.[2] They have not yet, however, given sustained attention to the epistemological consequences of such a claim. Faced with the depth of Marx's critique of capitalism, feminist analysis, as Iris Young has correctly pointed out, often

> accepts the traditional Marxian theory of production relations, historical change, and analysis of the structure of capitalism in basically unchanged form. It rightly criticizes that theory for being essentially gender-blind, and hence seeks to supplement Marxist theory of capitalism with feminist theory of a system of male domination. Taking this route, however, tacitly endorses the traditional Marxian position that "the woman question" is auxiliary to the central questions of a Marxian theory of society.[3]

By setting off from the Marxian meta-theory I am implicitly suggesting that this, rather than his critique of capitalism, can be most helpful to feminists. I will explore some of the epistemological consequences of claiming that women's lives differ structurally from those of men. In particular, I will suggest that like the lives of proletarians according to Marxian theory, women's lives make available a particular and privileged vantage point on male supremacy, a vantage point which can ground a powerful critique of the phallocratic institutions and ideology which constitute the capitalist form of patriarchy. . . . I will suggest that the sexual division of labor forms the basis for such a standpoint and will argue that on the basis of the structures which define women's activity as contributors to subsistence and as mothers one could begin, though not complete, the construction of such an epistemological tool. I hope to show how just as Marx's understanding of the world from the standpoint of the proletariat enabled him to go beneath bourgeois ideology, so a feminist standpoint can allow us to understand patriarchal institutions and ideologies as perverse inversions of more humane social relations.

The Nature of a Standpoint

A standpoint is not simply an interested position (interpreted as bias) but is interested in the sense of being engaged. It is true that a desire to conceal real social relations can contribute to an obscurantist account, and it is also true that the ruling gender and class have material interests in deception. A standpoint, however, carries with it the contention that there are some perspectives on society from which, however well-intentioned one may be, the real relations of humans with each other and with the natural world are not visible. This contention should be sorted into a number of distinct epistemological and political claims: (1) Material life (class position in Marxist theory) not only structures but sets limits on the understanding of social relations. (2) If material life is structured in fundamentally opposing ways for two different groups, one can expect that the vision of each will represent an inversion of the other, and in systems of domination the vision available to the rulers will be both partial and perverse. (3) The vision of the ruling class (or gender) structures the material relations in which all parties are forced to participate, and therefore cannot be dismissed as simply false. (4) In consequence, the vision available to the oppressed group must be struggled for and represents an achievement which requires both science to see beneath the surface of the social relations in which all are forced to participate, and the education which can only grow from struggle to change those relations. (5) As an engaged vision, the understanding of the oppressed, the adoption of a standpoint exposes the real relations among human beings as inhuman, points beyond the present, and carries a historically liberatory role.

The concept of a standpoint structures epistemology in a particular way. Rather than a simple dualism, it posits a duality of levels of reality, of which the deeper level or essence both includes and explains the "surface" or appearance, and indicates the logic by means of which the appearance inverts and distorts the deeper reality. In addition, the concept of a standpoint depends on the assumption that epistemology grows in a complex and contradictory way from material life. Any effort to develop a standpoint must take seriously Marx's injunction that "all mysteries which lead theory to mysticism find their rational solution in human practice and in the comprehension of this practice."[4] Marx held that the source both for the proletarian standpoint and the critique of capitalism it makes possible is to be found in practical activity itself. The epistemological (and even ontological) significance of human activity is made clear in Marx's argument not only that persons are active but that reality itself consists of "sensuous human activity, practice."[5] Thus Marx can speak of products as crystallized or congealed human activity or work, of products as conscious human activity in another form. He can state that even plants, animals, light, etc., constitute theoretically a part of human consciousness, and a part of human life and activity.[6] As Marx and Engels summarize their position.

> As individuals express their life, so they are. What they are, therefore, coincides with their production, both with *what* they produce and with *how* they produce. The nature of individuals thus depends on the material conditions determining their production.[7]

This starting point has definite consequences for Marx's theory of knowledge. If humans are not what they eat but what they do, especially what they do in the course of production of subsistence, each means of producing subsistence should be expected to carry with it *both* social relations *and* relations to the world of nature which express the social understanding contained in that mode of production. And in any society with systematically divergent practical activities, one should expect the growth of logically divergent world-views. That is, each division of labor, whether by gender or class, can be expected to have consequences for knowledge. Class society, according to Marx, does produce this dual vision in the form of the ruling class vision and the understanding available to the ruled.

On the basis of Marx's description of the activity of commodity exchange in capitalism, the ways in which the dominant categories of thought simply express the mystery of the commodity form have been pointed out. These include a dependence on quantity, duality, and opposition of nature to culture, a rigid separation of mind and body, intention and behavior.[8] From the perspective of exchange, where commodities differ from each other only quantitatively, it seems absurd to suggest that labor power differs from all other commodities. The sale and purchase of labor power from the perspective of capital is simply a contract between free agents, in which "the agreement [the parties] come to is but the form in which they give legal expression of their common will." It is a relation of equality,

> because each enters into relation with the other, as with a simple owner of commodities, and they exchange equivalent for equivalent.... The only force that brings them together and puts them in relation with each other, is the selfishness, the gain and the private interests of each. Each looks to himself only, and no one troubles himself about the rest, and just because they do so, do they all, in accordance with the pre-established harmony of things, or under the auspices of an all shrewd providence, work together to their mutual advantage, for the common weal and in the interest of all.

This is the only description available within the sphere of circulation or exchange of commodities, or as Marx might put it, at the level of appearance. But at the level of production, the world looks far different. As Marx puts it,

> On leaving this sphere of simple circulation or of exchange of commodities.... we can perceive a change in the physiognomy of our *dramatis personae*. He who before was the money-owner, now strides in front as capitalist; the possessor of labor-power follows as his laborer. The one with an air of importance, smirking, intent on business; the other timid and holding back, like one who is bringing his own hide to market and has nothing to expect but—a hiding.[9]

This is a vastly different account of the social relations of the buyer and seller of labor power. Only by following the two into the realm of production and adopting the point of view available to the worker could Marx uncover what is really involved in the purchase and sale of labor power, i.e.—uncover the process by which surplus value is produced and appropriated by the capitalist, and the means by which the worker is systematically disadvantaged.[10]

If one examines Marx's account of the production and extraction of surplus value, one can see in it the elaboration of each of the claims contained in the concept of a standpoint. First, the contention that material life structures understanding points to the importance of the epistemological consequences of the opposed models of exchange and production. It is apparent that the former results in a dualism based on both the separation of exchange from use, and on the positing of exchange as the only important side of the dichotomy. The epistemological result if one follows through the implications of exchange is a series of opposed and hierarchical dualities—mind/body, ideal/material, social/natural, self/other—even a kind of solipsism—replicating the devaluation of use relative to exchange. The proletarian and Marxian valuation of use over exchange on the basis of involvement in production, in labor, results in a dialectical rather than dualist epistemology: the dialectical and interactive unity (distinction within a unity) of human and natural worlds, mind and body, ideal and material, and the cooperation of self and other (community).

As to the second claim of a standpoint, a Marxian account of exchange vs. production indicates that the epistemology growing from exchange not only inverts that present in the process of production but in addition is both partial and fundamentally perverse. The real point of the production of goods and services is, after all, the continuation of the species, a possibility dependent on their use. The epistemology embodied in exchange then, along with the social relations it expresses, not only occupies only one side of the dualities it constructs, but also reverses the proper ordering of any hierarchy in the dualisms: use is primary, not exchange.

The third claim for a standpoint indicates a recognition of the power realities operative in a community, and points to the ways the ruling group's vision may be *both* perverse *and* made real by means of that group's power to define the terms for the community as a whole. In the Marxian analysis, this power is exercised in both control of ideological production, and in the real participation of the worker in exchange. The dichotomous epistemology which grows from exchange cannot be dismissed either as simply false or as an epistemology relevant to only a few: the worker as well as the capitalist engages in the purchase and sale of commodities, and if material life structures consciousness, this cannot fail to have an effect. This leads into the fourth claim for a standpoint—that it is achieved rather than obvious, a mediated rather than immediate understanding. Because the ruling group controls the means of mental as well as physical production, the production of ideals as well as goods, the standpoint of the oppressed represents an achievement both of science (analysis) and of political struggle on the basis of which this analysis can be conducted.

Finally, because it provides the basis for revealing the perversion of both life and thought, the inhumanity of human relations, a standpoint can be the basis for moving beyond these relations. In the historical context of Marx's theory, the engaged vision available to the producers, by drawing out the potentiality available in the actuality, that is, by following up the possibility of abundance capitalism creates, leads toward transcendence. Thus, the proletariat is the only class which has the possibility of creating a classless society. It can do this simply (!) by generalizing its own condition, that is, by making society itself a propertyless producer.[11]

These are the general characteristics of the standpoint of the proletariat. What guidance can feminists take from this discussion? I hold that the powerful vision of both the perverseness and reality of class domination made possible by Marx's adoption of the standpoint of the proletariat suggests that a specifically feminist standpoint could allow for a much more profound critique of phallocratic ideologies and institutions than has yet been achieved. The effectiveness of Marx's critique grew from its uncompromising focus on material life activity, and I propose here to set out from the Marxian contention that not only are persons active, but that reality itself consists of "sensuous human activity, practice." But rather than beginning with men's labor, I will focus on women's life activity and on the institutions which structure that activity in order to raise the question of whether this activity can form the ground for a distinctive standpoint, that is, to determine whether it meets the requirements for a feminist standpoint. (I use the term, "feminist" rather than "female" here to indicate both the achieved character of a standpoint and that a standpoint by definition carries a liberatory potential.)

Women's work in every society differs systematically from men's. I intend to pursue the suggestion that this division of labor is the first and in some societies the only division of labor, and moreover, that it is central to the organization of social labor more generally. On the basis of an account of the sexual division of labor, one should be able to begin to explore the oppositions and differences between women's and men's activity and their consequences for epistemology. While I cannot attempt a complete account, I will put forward a schematic and simplified account of the sexual division of labor and its consequences for epistemology.... My focus is on institutionalized social practices and on the specific epistemology and ontology manifested by the institutionalized sexual division of labor. Individuals, as individuals, may change their activity in ways which move them outside the outlook embodied in these institutions, but such a move can be significant only when it occurs at the level of society as a whole.

I will discuss the "sexual division of labor" rather than the "gender division of labor" to stress, first my belief that the division of labor between women and men cannot be reduced to purely social dimensions. One must distinguish between what Sara Ruddick has termed "invariant and *nearly* unchangeable" features of human life, and those which despite being "*nearly* universal" are "certainly changeable."[12] Thus, the fact that women and not men *bear* children is not (yet) a social choice, but that women and not men rear children in a society structured by compulsory heterosexuality and male dominance is clearly a societal choice. A second reason to use the term "sexual division of labor" is to keep hold of the bodily aspect of existence—perhaps to grasp it over-firmly in an effort to keep it from evaporating altogether. There is some biological, bodily component to human existence. But its size and substantive content will remain unknown until at least the certainly changeable aspects of the sexual division of labor are altered....

On the basis of a schematic account of the sexual division of labor, I will begin to fill in the specific content of the feminist standpoint and begin to specify how women's lives structure an understanding of social relations, that is, begin to follow out the epistemological consequences of the sexual division of labor. In addressing the institutionalized sexual division of labor, I propose to lay aside the important differences among women across race and class boundaries and instead search for central commonalities. I take some justification from the fruitfulness of Marx's similar strategy in constructing a simplified two class, two man model in which everything was exchanged at its value.... Still, I adopt this strategy with some reluctance, since it contains the danger of making invisible the experience of lesbians or women of color.[13] At the same time, I recognize that the effort to uncover a feminist standpoint assumes that there are some things common to all women's lives in Western class societies.

The feminist standpoint which emerges through an examination of women's activities is related to the proletarian standpoint, but deeper going. Women and workers inhabit a world in which the emphasis is on change rather than stasis, a world characterized by interaction with natural substances rather than separation from nature, a world in which quality is more important than quantity, a world in which the unification of mind and body is inherent in the activities performed. Yet, there are some important differences, differences marked by the fact that the proletarian (if male) is immersed in this world only during the time his labor power is being used by the capitalist. If, to paraphrase Marx, we follow the worker home from the factory, we can once again perceive a change in the *dramatis personae.* He who before followed behind as the worker, timid and holding back, with nothing to expect but a hiding, now strides in front while a third person, not specifically present in Marx's account of the transaction between capitalist and worker (both of whom are male) follows timidly behind, carrying groceries, baby, and diapers.

The Sexual Division of Labor

Women's activity as institutionalized has a double aspect—their contribution to subsistence, and their contribution to childrearing. Whether or not all of us do both, women as a sex are institutionally responsible for producing both goods and human beings and all women are forced to become the kinds of people who can do both. Although the nature of women's contribution to subsistence varies immensely over time and space, my primary focus here is on capitalism, with a secondary focus on the Western class societies which preceded it.[14] In capitalism, women contribute both production for wages and production of goods in the home, that is, they like men sell their labor power and produce both commodities and surplus value, and produce use-values in the home. Unlike men, however, women's lives are institutionally defined by their production of use-values in the home.[15] And here we begin to encounter the narrowness of the Marxian concept of production. Women's production of use-values in the home has not been well understood by socialists. It is no surprise to feminists that Engels, for example, simply asks how women can continue to do the work in the home and also work in production outside the home. Marx too takes for granted women's responsibility for household labor. He repeats, as if it were his own, the question of a Belgian factory inspector: If a mother works for wages, "how will [the household's] internal economy be cared for; who will look after the young children; who will get ready the meals, do the washing and mending?"[16]

Let us trace both the outlines and the consequences of women's dual contribution to subsistence in capitalism. Women's labor, like that of the male worker, is contact with material necessity. Their contribution to subsistence, like that of the male worker, involves them in a world in which the relation to nature and to concrete human requirements is central, both in the form of interaction with natural substances whose quality, rather than quantity is important to the production of meals, clothing, etc., and in the form of close attention to the natural changes in these substances. Women's labor both for wages and even more in household production involves a unification of mind and body for the purpose of transforming natural substances into socially defined goods. This too is true of the labor of the male worker.

There are, however, important differences. First, women as a group work more than men. We are all familiar with the phenomenon of the "double day," and with indications that women work many more hours per week than men.[17] Second, a larger proportion of women's labor time is devoted to the production of use-values than men's. Only some of the goods women produce are commodities (however much they live in a society structured by commodity production and exchange). Third, women's production is structured by repetition in a different way than men's. While repetition for both the woman and the male worker may take the form of production of the same object, over and over—whether apple pies or brake linings—women's work in housekeeping involves a repetitious cleaning.[18]

Thus, the male worker in the process of production is involved in contact with necessity, and interchange with nature as well as with other human beings, but the process of production or work does not consume his whole life. The activity of a woman in the home as well as the work she does for wages keeps her continually in contact with a world of qualities and change. Her immersion in the world of use—in concrete, many-qualited, changing material processes— is more complete than his. And if life itself consists of sensuous activity, the vantage point available to women on the basis of their contribution to subsistence represents an intensification and deepening of the materialist world-view and consciousness available to the producers of commodities in capitalism, an intensification of class consciousness. The availability of this outlook to even non-working-class women has been strikingly formulated by Marilyn French in *The Women's Room.*

> Washing the toilet used by three males, and the floor and walls around it, is, Mira thought, coming face to face with necessity. And that is why women were saner than men, did not come up with the mad, absurd schemes men developed; they were in touch with necessity, they had to wash the toilet bowl and floor.[19]

The focus on women's subsistence activity rather than men's leads to a model in which the capitalist (male) lives a life structured completely by commodity exchange and not at all by production, and at the furthest distance from contact with concrete material life. The male worker marks a way station on the path to the other extreme of the constant contact with material necessity in women's contribution to subsistence. There are of course important differences along the lines of race and class. For example, working class men seem to do more domestic labor than men higher up in the class structure—car repairs, carpentry, etc. And until very recently, the wage work done by most women of color replicated the housework required by their own households. Still, there are commonalities present in the institutionalized sexual division of labor which make women responsible for both housework and wage work.

The female contribution to subsistence, however, represents only a part of women's labor. Women also produce/reproduce men (and other women) on both a daily and a long-term basis. This aspect of women's "production" exposes the deep inadequacies of the concept of production as a description of women's activity. One does not (cannot) produce another human being in anything like the way one produces an object such as a chair. Much more is involved, activity which cannot easily be dichotomized into play or work. Helping another to develop, the gradual relinquishing of control, the experience of the human limits of one's action—all these are important features of women's activity as mothers. Women as mothers even more than as workers, are institutionally involved in processes of change and growth, and more than workers, must understand the importance of avoiding excessive control in order to help others grow.[20] The activity involved is far more complex than the instrumental working with others to transform objects. (Interestingly, much of women's wage work—nursing, social work, and some secretarial jobs in particular—requires and depends on the relational and interpersonal skills women learned by being mothered by someone of the same sex.)

This aspect of women's activity too is not without consequences. Indeed, it is in the production of men by women and the appropriation of this labor and women themselves by men that the opposition between feminist and masculinist experience and outlook is rooted, and it is here that features of the proletarian vision are enhanced and modified for the woman and diluted for the man. The female experience in reproduction represents a unity with nature which goes beyond the proletarian experience of interchange with nature. As another theorist has put it, "reproductive labor might be said to combine the functions of the arthitect and the bee: like the architect, parturitive woman knows what she is doing; like the bee, she cannot help what she is doing." And just as the worker's acting on the external world changes both the world and the worker's nature, so too "a new life changes the world and the consciousness of the woman."[21] In addition, in the process of producing human beings, relations with others may take a variety of forms with deeper significance than simple cooperation with others for common goals—forms which range from a deep unity with another through the many-leveled and changing connections mothers experience with growing children. Finally, the female experience in bearing and rearing children involves a unity of mind and body more profound than is possible in the worker's instrumental activity....

Abstract Masculinity and the Feminist Standpoint

... The differential male and female life activity in class society leads on the one hand toward a feminist standpoint and on the other toward an abstract masculinity.

Because the problem for the boy is to distinguish himself from the mother and to protect himself against the real threat she poses for his identity, his conflictual and oppositional efforts lead to the formation of rigid ego boundaries. The way Freud takes for granted the rigid distinction between the "me and not-me" makes the point well: "Normally, there is nothing of which we are more certain than the feeling of ourself, of our own ego. This ego appears to us as something autonomous and unitary, marked off distinctly from everything else." At least toward the outside, "the ego seems to maintain clear and sharp lines of demarcation."[22] Thus, the boy's construction of self in opposition to unity with the mother, his construction of identity as differentiation from the other, sets a hostile and combative dualism at the heart of both the community men construct and the masculinist world-view by means of which they understand their lives.

I do not mean to suggest that the totality of human relations can be explained by psychoanalysis. Rather I want to point to the ways male rather than female experience and activity replicates itself in both the hierarchical and dualist institutions of class society and in the frameworks of thought generated by this experience. It is interesting to read Hegel's account of the relation of self and other as a statement of male experience: the relation of the two consciousnesses takes the form of a trial by death. As Hegel describes it, "each seeks the death of the other."

> Thus, the relation of the two self-conscious individuals is such that they provide themselves and each other through a life-and-death struggle. They must engage in this struggle, for they must raise their certainty *for themselves* to truth, both in the case of the other and in their own case.[23]

The construction of the self in opposition to another who threatens one's very being reverberates throughout the construction of both class society and the masculinist world-view and results in a deepgoing and hierarchical dualism. First, the male experience is characterized by the duality of concrete versus abstract. Material reality as experienced by the boy in the family provides no model, and is unimportant in the attainment of masculinity. Nothing of value to the boy occurs with the family, and masculinity becomes an abstract ideal to be achieved over the opposition of daily life.[24] Masculinity must be attained by means of opposition to the concrete world of daily life, by escaping from contact with the female world of the household into the masculine world of public life. This experience of two worlds, one valuable, if abstract and deeply unattainable, the other useless and demeaning, if concrete and necessary, lies at the heart of a series of dualisms—abstract/concrete, mind/body, culture/nature, ideal/real, stasis/change. And these dualisms are overlaid by gender: only the first of each pair is associated with the male.

... Abstract masculinity, then, can be seen to have structured Western social relations and the modes of thought to which these relations give rise at least since the founding of the *polis*. ...

Interestingly enough the epistemology and society constructed by men suffering from the effects of abstract masculinity have a great deal in common with that imposed by commodity exchange. The separation and opposition of social and natural worlds, of abstract and concrete, of permanence and change, the effort to define only the former of each pair as important, the reliance on a series of counter factual assumptions—all this is shared with the exchange abstraction. Abstract masculinity shares still another of its aspects with the exchange abstraction: it forms the basis for an even more problematic social synthesis. Hegel's analysis makes clear the problematic social relations available to the self which maintains itself by opposition: each of the two subjects struggling for recognition risks its own death in the struggle to kill the other, but if the other is killed the subject is once again alone.[25] In sum, then, the male experience when replicated as epistemology leads to a world conceived as, and (in fact) inhabited by, a number of fundamentally hostile others whom one comes to know by means of opposition (even death struggle) and yet with whom one must construct a social relation in order to survive.

The female construction of self in relation to others leads in an opposite direction—toward opposition to dualisms of any sort, valuation of concrete, everyday life, sense of a variety of connectednesses and continuities both with other persons and with the natural world. If material life structures consciousness, women's relationally defined existence, bodily experience of boundary challenges, and activity of transforming both physical objects and human beings must be expected to result in a world-view to which dichotomies are foreign. ...

That this is indeed women's experience is documented in both the theory and practice of the contemporary women's movement and needs no further development here.[26] The more important question here is whether female experience and the world-view constructed by female activity can meet the criteria for a standpoint. If we return to the five claims carried by the concept of a standpoint, it seems clear that women's material life activity has important epistemological and ontological consequences for both the understanding and construction of social relations. Women's activity, then, does satisfy the first requirement of a standpoint.

I can now take up the second claim made by a standpoint: that the female experience not only inverts that of the male, but forms a basis on which to expose abstract masculinity as both partial and fundamentally perverse, as not only occupying only one side of the dualities it has constructed, but reversing the proper valuation of human activity. The partiality of the masculinist vision and of the societies which support this understanding is evidenced by its confinement of activity proper to the male to only one side of the dualisms. Its perverseness, however, lies elsewhere. Perhaps the most dramatic (though not the only) reversal of the proper order of things characteristic of the male experience is the substitution of death for life.

The substitution of death for life results at least in part from the sexual division of labor in childrearing. The self-surrounded by rigid ego-boundaries, certain of what is inner and what is outer, the self experienced as walled city, is discontinuous with others. Georges Bataille has made brilliantly clear the ways in which death emerges as the only possible solution to this discontinuity and has followed the logic through to argue that reproduction itself must be understood not as the creation of life, but as death. The core experience to be understood is that of discontinuity and its consequences. As a consequence of this experience of discontinuity and aloneness, penetration of ego-boundaries, or fusion with another is experienced as violent. Thus, the desire for fusion with another can take the form of domination of the other. In this form, it leads to the only possible fusion with a threatening other: when the other ceases to exist as a separate, and for that reason, threatening being. Insisting that another submit to one's will is simply a milder form of the destruction of discontinuity in the death of the other since in this case one is no longer confronting a discontinuous and opposed will, despite its discontinuous embodiment. This is perhaps one source of the links between sexual activity, domination, and death.

Bataille suggests that killing and sexual activity share both prohibitions and religious significance. Their unity is demonstrated by religious sacrifice since the latter:

> is intentional like the act of the man who lays bare, desires and wants to penetrate his victim. The lover strips the beloved of her identity no less than the bloodstained priest his human or animal victim. The woman in the hands of her assailant is despoiled of her being ... loses the firm barrier that once separated her from others ... is brusquely laid open to the violence of the sexual urges set loose in the organs of reproduction; she is laid open to the impersonal violence that overwhelms her from without.[27]

Note the use of the term "lover" and "assailant" as synonyms and the presence of the female as victim.

The importance of Bataille's analysis lies in the fact that it can help to make clear the links between violence, death, and sexual fusion with another, links which are not simply theoretical but actualized in rape and pornography. Images of women in chains, being beaten, or threatened with attack carry clear social messages, among them that "the normal male is sexually aggressive in a brutal and demeaning way."[28] Bataille's analysis can help to understand why "men advertise, even brag, that their movie is the 'bloodiest thing that ever happened in front of a camera'."[29] The analysis is supported by the psychoanalyst who suggested that although one of the important dynamics of pornography is hostility, "one can raise the possibly controversial question whether in humans (especially males) powerful sexual excitement can ever exist without brutality also being present."[30]

Bataille's analysis can help to explain what is erotic about "snuff" films, which not only depict the torture and dismemberment of a woman, but claim that the actress is *in fact* killed. His analysis suggests that perhaps she is a sacrificial victim whose discontinuous existence has been succeeded in her death by "the organic continuity of life drawn into the common life of the beholders."[31] Thus, the pair "lover-assailant" is not accidental. Nor is the connection of reproduction and death.

"Reproduction," Bataille argues, "implies the existence of *discontinuous* beings." This is so because, "Beings which reproduce themselves are distinct from one another, and those reproduced are likewise distinct from each other, just as they are distinct from their parents. Each being is distinct from all others. His birth, his death, the events of his life may have an interest for others, but he alone is directly concerned in them. He is born alone. He dies alone. Between one being and another, there is a *gulf*, a discontinuity."[32] (Clearly it is not just a gulf, but is better understood as a chasm.) In reproduction, sperm and ovum unite to form a new entity, but they do so from the death and disappearance of two separate beings. Thus, the new entity bears within itself "the transition to continuity, the fusion, fatal to both, of two separate beings."[33] Thus, death and reproduction are intimately linked, yet Bataille stresses that "it is only death which is to be identified with continuity." Thus, despite the unity of birth and death in this analysis, Bataille gives greater weight to a "tormenting fact: the urge towards love, pushed to its limit, is an urge toward death."[34] Bataille holds to this position despite his recognition that reproduction is a form of growth. The growth, however, he dismisses as not being "ours," as being only "impersonal."[35] This is not the female experience in which reproduction is hardly impersonal, nor experienced as death. It is, of course, in a literal sense, the sperm which is cut off from its source, and lost. No wonder, then, at the masculinist preoccupation with death, and the feeling that growth is "impersonal," not of fundamental concern to oneself. But this complete dismissal of the experience of another bespeaks a profound lack of empathy and refusal to recognize the very being of another. It is a manifestation of the chasm which separates each man from every other being and from the natural world, the chasm which both marks and defines the problem of community.

The preoccupation with death instead of life appears as well in the argument that it is the ability to kill (and for centuries, the practice) which sets humans above animals. Even Simone de Beauvoir has accepted that "it is not in giving life but in risking life that man is raised above the animal: that is why superiority has been accorded in humanity not to the sex that brings forth but to that which kills."[36] That superiority has been accorded to the sex which kills is beyond doubt. But what kind of experience and vision can take reproduction, the creation of new life, and the force of life in sexuality, and turn it into death—not just in theory but in the practice of rape, pornography, and sexual murder? Any why give pride of place to killing? This is not only an inversion of the proper order of things, but also a refusal to recognize the real activities in which men as well as women are engaged. The producing of goods and the reproducing of human beings are certainly life-sustaining activities. And even the deaths of the ancient heroes in search of undying fame were pursuits of life, and represented the attempt to avoid death by attaining immortality. The search for life, then, represents the deeper reality which lies beneath the glorification of death and destruction.

Yet one cannot dismiss the substitution of death for life as simply false. Men's power to structure social relations in their own image means that women too must participate in social relations which manifest and express abstract masculinity. The most important life activities have consistently been held by the powers that be to be unworthy of those who are fully human most centrally because of their close connections with necessity and life: motherwork (the rearing of children), housework, and until the rise of capitalism in the West, any work necessary to subsistence. In addition, these activities in contemporary capitalism are all constructed in ways which systematically degrade and destroy the minds and bodies of those who perform them.[37]

... This brings me to the fourth claim for a standpoint—its character as an achievement of both analysis and political struggle occurring in a particular historical space.... Feminists have only begun the process of revaluing female experience, searching for common threads which connect the diverse experiences of women, and searching for the structural determinants of the experiences.... A feminist standpoint may be present on the basis of the common threads of female experience, but it is neither self-evident nor obvious.

Finally, because it provides a way to reveal the perverseness and inhumanity of human relations, a standpoint forms the basis for moving beyond these relations.... The articulation of a feminist standpoint based on women's relational self-definition and activity exposes the world men have constructed and the self-understanding which manifests these relations as partial and perverse.

More importantly, by drawing out the potentiality available in the actuality and thereby exposing the inhumanity of human relations, it embodies a distress which requires a solution. The experience of continuity and relation—with others, with the natural world, of mind with body—provides an ontological base for developing a non-problematic social synthesis, a social synthesis which need not operate through the denial of the body, the attack on nature, or the death struggle between the self and other, a social synthesis which does not depend on any of the forms taken by abstract masculinity.

What is necessary is the generalization of the potentiality made available by the activity of women—the defining of society as a whole as propertyless producer both of use-values and of human beings. To understand what such a transformation would require we should consider what is involved in the partial transformation represented by making the whole of society into propertyless producers of use-values—i.e., socialist revolution. The abolition of the division between mental and manual labor cannot take place simply by means of adopting worker-self-management techniques, but instead requires the abolition of private property, the seizure of state power, and lengthy post-revolutionary class struggle. Thus, I am not suggesting that shared parenting arrangements can abolish the sexual division of labor. Doing away with this division of labor would of course require institutionalizing the participation of both women and men in childrearing; but just as the rational and conscious control of the production of goods and services requires a vast and far-reaching social transformation, so the rational and conscious organization of reproduction would entail the transformation both of *every* human relation, and of human relations to the natural world....

Conclusion

An analysis which begins from the sexual division of labor...could form the basis for an analysis of the real structures of women's oppression, an analysis which would not require that one sever biology from society, nature from culture, an analysis which would expose the ways women both participate in and oppose their own subordination. The elaboration of such an analysis cannot but be difficult. Women's lives, like men's, are structured by social relations which manifest the experience of the dominant gender and class.... Feminist theorists must demand that feminist theorizing be grounded in women's material activity and must as well be a part of the political struggle necessary to develop areas of social life modeled on this activity. The outcome could be the development of a political economy which included women's activity as well as men's, and could as well be a step toward the redefining and restructuring of society as a whole on the basis of women's activity.

Generalizing the activity of women to the social system as a whole would raise, for the first time in human history, the possibility of a fully human community, a community structured by connection rather than separation and opposition.

One can conclude then that women's life activity does form the basis of a specifically feminist materialism, a materialism which can provide a point from which both to critique and to work against phallocratic ideology and institutions.

My argument here opens a number of avenues for future work. Clearly, a systematic critique of Marx on the basis of a more fully developed understanding of the sexual division of labor is in order. ... A second avenue for further investigation is the relation between exchange and abstract masculinity. An exploration of Mauss's *The Gift* would play an important part in this project, since he presents the solipsism of exchange as an overlay on and substitution for a deeper going hostility, the exchange of gifts as an alternative to war. We have seen that the necessity for recognizing and receiving recognition from another to take the form of a death struggle memorializes the male rather than female experience of emerging as a person in opposition to a woman in the context of a deeply phallocratic world. If the community of exchangers (capitalists) rests on the more overtly and directly hostile death struggle of self and other, one might be able to argue that what underlies the exchange abstraction is abstract masculinity. One might then turn to the question of whether capitalism rests on and is a consequence of patriarchy. Perhaps then feminists can produce the analysis which could amend Marx to read: "Though class society appears to be the source, the cause of the oppression of women, it is rather its consequence." Thus, it is "only at the last culmination of the development of class society [that] this, its secret, appear[s] again, namely, that on the one hand it is the *product* of the oppression of women, and that on the other it is the *means* by which women participate in and create their own oppression."[38]

Notes

* I take my title from Iris Young's call for the development of a specifically feminist historical materialism. See "Socialist Feminism and the Limits of Dual Systems Theory," in *Socialist Review* 10, 2/3 (March-June, 1980). My work on this paper is deeply indebted to a number of women whose ideas are incorporated here, although not always used in the ways they might wish. My discussions with Donna Haraway and Sandra Harding have been intense and ongoing over a period of years. I have also had a number of important and useful conversations with Jane Flax, and my project here has benefitted both from these contacts, and from the opportunity to read her paper, "Political Philosophy and the Patriarchal Unconscious: A Psychoanalytic Perspective on Epistemology and Metaphysics." In addition I have been helped immensely by collective discussions with Annette Bickel, Sarah Begus, and Alexa Freeman. All of these people (along with Iris Young and Irene Diamond) have read and commented on drafts of this paper. I would also like to thank Alison Jaggar for continuing to question me about the basis on which one could claim the superiority of a feminist standpoint and for giving me the opportunity to deliver the paper at the University of Cincinnati Philosophy Department Colloquium; and Stephen Rose for taking the time to read and comment on a rough draft of the paper at a critical point in its development.

1. See my "Feminist Theory and the Development of Revolutionary Strategy," in Zillah Eisenstein, ed., *Capitalist Patriarchy and the Case for Socialist Feminism* (New York: Monthly Review, 1978).

2. The recent literature on mothering is perhaps the most detailed on this point. See Dorothy Dinnerstein, *The Mermaid and the Minotaur* (New York: Harper and Row, 1976); Nancy Chodorow, *The Reproduction of Mothering* (Berkeley: University of California Press, 1978).

3. Iris Young, "Socialist Feminism and the Limits of Dual Systems Theory" in *Socialist Review* 10, 2/3 (March–June 1980), p. 100.

4. Eighth Thesis on Feuerbach, in Karl Marx, "Theses on Feuerbach," in *The German Ideology*, C. J. Arthur, ed. (New York: International Publishers, 1970), p. 121.

5. Ibid. Conscious human practice, then, is at once both an epistemological category and the basis for Marx's conception of the nature of humanity itself. To put the case even more strongly, Marx argues that human activity has both an ontological and episte- mological status, that human feelings are not "merely anthropological phenomena," but are "truly ontological affirmations of being." See Karl Marx, *Economic and Philo- sophic Manuscripts of 1844*, Dirk Struik, ed. (New York: International Publishers, 1964), pp. 113, 165, 188.

6. Marx, *1844*, p. 112. Nature itself, for Marx, appears as a form of human work, since he argues that humans duplicate themselves actively and come to contemplate themselves in a world of their own making. (Ibid., p. 114.) On the more general issue of the relation of natural to human worlds see the very interesting account by Alfred Schmidt, *The Concept of Nature in Marx*, tr. Ben Foukes (London: New Left Books, 1971).

7. Marx and Engels, *The German Ideology*, p. 42.

8. See Alfred Sohn-Rethel, *Intellectual and Manual Labor: A Critique of Epistemology* (London: Macmillan, 1978). I should note that my analysis both depends on and is in tension with Sohn-Rethel's. Sohn-Rethel argues that commodity exchange is a char- acteristic of all class societies—one which comes to a head in capitalism or takes its most advanced form in capitalism. His project, which is not mine, is to argue that (a) commodity exchange, a characteristic of all class societies, is an original source of abstraction, (b) that this abstraction contains the formal element essential for the cognitive faculty of conceptual thinking, and (c) that the abstraction operating in ex- change, an abstraction in practice, is the source of the ideal abstraction basic to Greek philosophy and to modern science. (See Ibid., p. 28.) In addition to a different purpose, I should indicate several major differences with Sohn-Rethel. First, he treats the pro- ductive forces as separate from the productive relations of society and ascribes far too much autonomy to them. (See, for example, his discussions on pp. 84–86, 95.) I take the position that the distinction between the two is simply a device used for purposes of analysis rather than a feature of the real world. Second, Sohn-Rethel characterizes the period preceding generalized commodity production as primitive communism. (See p. 98.) This is however an inadequate characterization of tribal societies.

9. Karl Marx, *Capital*, I (New York: International Publishers, 1967), p. 176.

10. I have done this elsewhere in a systematic way. For the analysis, see my discussion of the exchange abstraction in *Money, Sex, and Power: An Essay on Domination and Community* (New York: Longman, Inc., 1983).

11. This is Iris Young's point. I am indebted to her persuasive arguments for taking what she terms the "gender differentiation of labor" as a central category of analysis (Young, "Dual Systems Theory," p. 185). My use of this category, however, differs to some extent from hers. Young's analysis of women in capitalism does not seem to include marriage as a part of the division of labor. She is more concerned with the division of labor in the productive sector.

12. See Sara Ruddick, "Maternal Thinking," *Feminist Studies* 6, 2 (Summer, 1980), p. 364.

13. See, for discussions of this danger, Adrienne Rich, "Disloyal to Civilization: Feminism, Racism, Gynephobia," in *On Lies, Secrets, and Silence* (New York: W. W. Norton & Co., 1979), pp. 275–310; Elly Bulkin, "Racism and Writing: Some Implications for White Lesbian Critics," in *Sinister Wisdom*, No. 6 (Spring, 1980).

14. Some cross-cultural evidence indicates that the status of women varies with the work they do. To the extent that women and men contribute equally to subsistence, women's status is higher than it would be if their subsistence work differed profoundly from that of men; that is, if they do none or almost all of the work of subsistence, their status remains low. See Peggy Sanday, "Female Status in the Public Domain," in Michelle Rosaldo and Louise Lamphere, eds., *Women, Culture, and Society* (Stanford: Stanford University Press, 1974), p. 199. See also Iris Young's account of the sexual division of labor in capitalism, mentioned above.

15. It is irrelevant to my argument here that women's wage labor takes place under different circumstances than men's—that is, their lower wages, their confinement to only a few occupational categories, etc. I am concentrating instead on the formal, structural

features of women's work. There has been much effort to argue that women's domestic labor is a source of surplus value, that is, to include it within the scope of Marx's value theory as productive labor, or to argue that since it does not produce surplus value it belongs to an entirely different mode of production, variously characterized as domestic or patriarchal. My strategy here is quite different from this. See, for the British debate, Mariarosa Dalla Costa and Selma James, *The Power of Women and the Subversion of the Community* (Bristol: Falling Wall Press, 1975); Wally Secombe, "The Housewife and Her Labor Under Capitalism," *New Left Review* 83 (January-February, 1974); Jean Gardiner, "Women's Domestic Labour," *New Left Review* 89 (March, 1975); and Paul Smith, "Domestic Labour and Marx's Theory of Value," in Annette Kuhn and Ann Marie Wolpe, eds., *Feminism and Materialism* (Boston: Routledge and Kegal Paul, 1978). A portion of the American debate can be found in Ira Gerstein, "Domestic Work and Capitalism," and Lisa Vogel, "The Earthly Family," *Radical America* 7, 4/5 (July-October, 1973); Ann Ferguson, "Women as a New Revolutionary Class," in Pat Walker, ed., *Between Labor and Capital* (Boston: South End Press, 1979).

16. Frederick Engels, *Origins of the Family, Private Property and the State* (New York: International Publishers, 1942); Karl Marx, *Capital*, Vol. I. p. 671. Marx and Engels have also described the sexual division of labor as natural or spontaneous. See Mary O'Brien, "Reproducing Marxist Man," in Lorenne Clark and Lynda Lange, eds., *The Sexism of Social and Political Theory: Women and Reproduction from Plato to Nietzsche* (Toronto: University of Toronto Press, 1979).

17. For a discussion of women's work, see Elise Boulding, "Familial Constraints on Women's Work Roles," in Martha Blaxall and B. Reagan, eds., *Women and the Workplace* (Chicago: University of Chicago Press, 1976), esp. the charts on pp. 111, 113. An interesting historical note is provided by the fact that even Nausicaa, the daughter of a Homeric king, did the household laundry. (See M. I. Finley, *The World of Odysseus* [Middlesex, England: Penguin, 1979], p. 73.) While aristocratic women were less involved in actual labor, the difference was one of degree. And as Aristotle remarked in *The Politics*, supervising slaves is not a particularly uplifting activity. The life of leisure and philosophy, so much the goal for aristocratic Athenian men, then, was almost unthinkable for any woman.

18. Simone de Beauvoir holds that repetition has a deeper significance and that women's biological destiny itself is repetition. (See *The Second Sex*, tr. H. M. Parshley [New York: Knopf, 1953], p. 59.) But see also her discussion of housework in Ibid., pp. 434ff. There her treatment of housework is strikingly negative. For de Beauvoir, transcendence is provided in the historical struggle of self with other and with the natural world. The oppositions she sees are not really stasis vs. change, but rather transcendence, escape from the muddy concreteness of daily life, from the static, biological, concrete repetition of "placid femininity."

19. Marilyn French, *The Women's Room* (New York: Jove, 1978), p. 214.

20. Sara Ruddick, "Maternal Thinking," presents an interesting discussion of these and other aspects of the thought which emerges from the activity of mothering. Although I find it difficult to speak the language of interests and demands she uses, she brings out several valuable points. Her distinction between maternal and scientific thought is very intriguing and potentially useful (see esp. pp. 350–353).

21. O'Brien, "Reproducing Marxist Man," p. 115, n.11.

22. Sigmund Freud, *Civilization and Its Discontents* (New York: Norton, 1961), pp. 12–13.

23. Hegel, *Phenomenology of Spirit* (New York: Oxford University Press, 1979), trans. A. V. Miller, p. 114. See also Jessica Benjamin's very interesting use of this discussion in "The Bonds of Love: Rational Violence and Erotic Domination," *Feminist Studies* 6, 1 (June, 1980).

24. Alvin Gouldner has made a similar argument in his contention that the Platonic stress on hierarchy and order resulted from a similarly learned opposition to daily life which was rooted in the young aristocrat's experience of being taught proper behavior by slaves who could not themselves engage in this behavior. See *Enter Plato* (New York: Basic Books, 1965), pp. 351–355.

25. See Benjamin, "Bonds of Love," p. 152. The rest of her analysis goes in a different direction than mine, though her account of *The Story of O* can be read as making clear the problems for any social synthesis based on the Hegelian model.

26. My arguments are supported with remarkable force by both the theory and practice of the contemporary women's movement. In theory, this appears in different forms

in the work of Dorothy Riddle, "New Visions of Spiritual Power," *Quest; a Feminist Quarterly* 1, 3 (Spring, 1975); Susan Griffin, *Woman and Nature,* esp. Book IV: "The Separate Rejoined": Adrienne Rich, *Of Woman Born,* esp. pp. 62–68; Linda Thurston, "On Male and Female Principle," *The Second Wave* 1, 2 (Summer, 1971). In feminist political organizing, this vision has been expressed as an opposition of leadership and hierarchy, as an effort to prevent the development of organizations divided into leaders and followers. It has also taken the form of an insistence on the unity of the personal and the political, a stress on the concrete rather than on abstract principles (an opposition to theory), and a stress on the politics of everyday life. For a fascinating and early example, see Pat Mainardi, "The Politics of Housework," in Leslie Tanner, ed., *Voices of Women's Liberation* (New York: New American Library, 1970).

27. George Bataille, *Death and Sensuality* (New York: Arno Press, 1977), p. 90.
28. *Women Against Violence Against Women Newsletter,* June, 1976, p. 1.
29. *Aegis: A Magazine on Ending Violence Against Women,* November/December, 1978, p. 3.
30. Robert Stoller, *Perversion: The Erotic Form of Hatred* (New York: Pantheon, 1975), p. 88.
31. Bataille, *Death and Sensuality,* p. 91. See pp. 91ff. for a more complete account of the commonalities of sexual activity and ritual sacrifice.
32. Ibid., p. 12 (italics mine). See also de Beauvoir's discussion in *The Second Sex,* pp. 135, 151.
33. Bataille, *Death and Sensuality,* p. 14.
34. Ibid., p. 42. While Adrienne Rich acknowledges the violent feelings between mothers and children, she quite clearly does not put these at the heart of the relation (*Of Woman Born*).
35. Bataille, *Death and Sensuality,* pp. 95–96.
36. *The Second Sex,* p. 58. It should be noted that killing and risking life are ways of indicating one's contempt for one's body, and as such are of a piece with the Platonic search for disembodiment.
37. Consider, for example, Rich's discussion of pregnancy and childbirth, Chs. VI and VII, *Of Woman Born.* And see also Charlotte Perkins Gilman's discussion of domestic labor in *The Home* (Urbana, Ill.: The University of Illinois Press, 1972).
38. See Marx, *1844,* p. 117.

4

Feminist Politics and Epistemology: The Standpoint of Women

ALISON M. JAGGAR

There are many ways of being a feminist. Contemporary feminists are united in their opposition to women's oppression, but they differ not only in their views of how to combat that oppression, but even in their conception of what constitutes women's oppression in contemporary society. Liberal feminists, as we have seen, believe that women are oppressed insofar as they suffer unjust discrimination; traditional Marxists believe that women are oppressed in their exclusion from public production; radical feminists see women's oppression as consisting primarily in the universal male control of women's sexual and procreative capacities; while socialist feminists characterize women's oppression in terms of a revised version of the Marxist theory of alienation. Each of these analyses of women's oppression reflects a distinctive feminist perspective on contemporary society and each of them is associated with a characteristic conception of human nature. While these distinctive feminist perspectives have been in some ways cross-fertile, they are ultimately incompatible with each other. In other words, one cannot view contemporary society simultaneously from more than one of these perspectives. The question then arises which perspective one should choose. What are the reasons for preferring one feminist theory to another?

... I shall argue that the most politically appropriate and theoretically illuminating interpretations of theoretical desiderata are those associated with socialist feminism....

Socialist Feminism and the Standpoint of Women

The socialist feminist theory of human nature is structurally identical with that of traditional Marxism and so, consequently, is the structure of its epistemology. Like both traditional Marxists and radical feminists, socialist feminists view knowledge as a social and practical construct and they believe that conceptual frameworks are shaped and limited by their social origins. They believe that, in any historical period, the prevailing world-view will reflect the interests and values of the dominant class. Consequently, they recognize that the establishment of a less mystified and more reliable world-view will require not only scientific

55

struggle and intellectual argument but also the overthrow of the prevailing system of social relations.

Where social feminist differs from traditional Marxist epistemology is in its assertion that the special social or class position of women gives them a special epistemological standpoint which makes possible a view of the world that is more reliable and less distorted than that available either to capitalist or to working-class men. Socialist feminists believe, therefore, that a primary condition for the adequacy of a feminist theory, indeed for the adequacy of any theory, is that it should represent the world from the standpoint of women. A number of theorists are working to develop this insight, although they do not all use the terminology of women's standpoint or even mean quite the same thing by it when they do. These theorists include Elizabeth Fee, Jane Flax, Sandra Harding, Nancy Hartsock, Evelyn Fox Keller, and Dorothy Smith.[1]

Both liberal and Marxist epistemologists consider that, in order to arrive at an adequate representation of reality, it is important to begin from the proper standpoint. Within liberal epistemology, the proper standpoint is the standpoint of the neutral, disinterested observer, a so-called Archimedean standpoint somewhere outside the reality that is being observed. Marxist epistemology, by contrast, recognizes that there is no such standpoint: that all systems of conceptualization reflect certain social interests and values. In a society where the production of knowledge is controlled by a certain class, the knowledge produced will reflect the interests and values of that class. In other words, in class societies the prevailing knowledge and science interpret reality from the standpoint of the ruling class. Because the ruling class has an interest in concealing the way in which it dominates and exploits the rest of the population, the interpretation of reality that it presents will be distorted in characteristic ways. In particular, the suffering of the subordinate classes will be ignored, redescribed as enjoyment or justified as freely chosen, deserved, or inevitable.

Because their class position insulates them from the suffering of the oppressed, many members of the ruling class are likely to be convinced by their own ideology; either they fail to perceive the suffering of the oppressed or they believe that it is freely chosen, deserved, or inevitable. They experience the current organization of society as basically satisfactory and so they accept the interpretation of reality that justifies that system of organization. They encounter little in their daily lives that conflicts with that interpretation. Oppressed groups, by contrast, suffer directly from the system that oppresses them. Sometimes the ruling ideology succeeds in duping them into partial denial of their pain or into accepting it temporarily, but the pervasiveness, intensity, and relentlessness of their suffering constantly push oppressed groups toward a realization that something is wrong with the prevailing social order. Their pain provides them with a motivation for finding out what is wrong, for criticizing accepted interpretations of reality, and for developing new and less distorted ways of understanding the world. These new systems of conceptualization will reflect the interests and values of the oppressed groups and so constitute a representation of reality from an alternative to the dominant standpoint.

The standpoint of the oppressed is not just different from that of the ruling class; it is also epistemologically advantageous. It provides the basis for a view of reality that is more impartial than that of the ruling class and also more comprehensive. It is more impartial because it comes closer to representing the interests of society as a whole; whereas the standpoint of the ruling class reflects the interests only of one section of the population, the standpoint of the oppressed represents the interests of the totality in that historical period. Moreover, whereas the condition of the oppressed groups is visible only dimly to the ruling class, the oppressed are able to see more clearly the ruled as well as the rulers and the relation between them. Thus, the standpoint of the oppressed includes and is able to explain the standpoint of the ruling class.

The political economy of socialist feminism establishes that, in contemporary society, women suffer a special form of exploitation and oppression. Socialist feminist epistemologists argue that this distinctive social or class position provides women with a distinctive epistemological standpoint. From this standpoint, it is possible to gain a less biased and more comprehensive view of reality than that provided either by established bourgeois science or by the male-dominated leftist alternatives to it. An adequate understanding of reality must be undertaken from the standpoint of women. As socialist feminists conceive it, however, the standpoint of women is not expressed directly in women's naive and unreflective world-view. We have seen earlier that socialist feminists recognize that women's perceptions of reality are distorted both by male-dominant ideology and by the male-dominated structure of everyday life. The standpoint of women, therefore, is not something that can be discovered through a survey of women's existing beliefs and attitudes—although such a survey should identify certain commonalities that might be incorporated eventually into a systematic representation of the world from women's perspective. Instead, the standpoint of women is discovered through a collective process of political and scientific struggle. The distinctive social experience of women generates insights that are incompatible with men's interpretations of reality and these insights provide clues to how reality might be interpreted from the standpoint of women. The validity of these insights, however, must be tested in political struggle and developed into a systematic representation of reality that is not distorted in ways that promote the interests of men above those of women. . . .

Within contemporary capitalism, the society with which they are concerned primarily, socialist feminist theorists remind us that the sexual division of labor assigns to women work that is very different from that of men. Dorothy Smith argues that women's work is primarily in what she calls "the bodily mode"; it focuses on the transformation of the immediate and concrete world. Men's work, by contrast, is in what Smith calls "the abstracted conceptual mode" which is the ruling mode in industrial society. The rulers are able to operate in the conceptual mode, abstracting from the concrete realities of daily existence, only because they participate in a system of social organization which assigns bodily work to others—others who also "produce the invisibility of that work."[2]

> The place of women, then, ... is where the work is done to facilitate man's occupation of the conceptual mode of action. Women keep house, bear and care for children, look after him when he is sick, and in general provide for the logistics of his bodily existence. But this marriage aspect of women's work is only one side of a more general relation. Women work in and around the professional managerial scene in analogous ways. They do those things which give concrete form to the conceptual activities. They do the clerical work, giving material form to the words or thoughts of the boss. They do the routine computer work, the interviewing for the survey, the nursing, the secretarial work. At almost every point women mediate for men the relation between the conceptual mode of action and the actual concrete forms on which it depends. Women's work is interposed between the abstracted modes and the local and particular actualities in which they are necessarily anchored. *Also, women's work conceals from men acting in the abstract mode just this anchorage*[3] (my italics).

Nancy Hartsock provides a similar account of women's work in contemporary capitalism. She too points out that women's domestic work mediates much of men's contact with natural substances; women cook the food that men eat and wash the toilet bowls that men use. This sexual division of labor hardly permits women to think in abstractions, such as the abstraction of human beings from the non-human world, and instead requires women to focus on the sensuous and ever-changing qualities of the material world. Women's child-rearing work further discourages abstraction and instrumentalism. Many studies have shown that children cannot thrive on bread alone; they must also receive love and affection. To rear children successfully, women must concentrate on the quality rather than the quantity of the relation, they must be sensitive to the changing needs of the child and they cannot remain emotionally detached from their work. Finally, Hartsock claims that the intimate involvement of women's bodies in pregnancy, childbirth, and lactation has epistemological consequences:

> The unity of mental and manual labor and the directly sensuous nature of women's work leads to a more profound unity of mental and manual labor, social and natural worlds, than is experienced by the male worker in capitalism. The unity grows from the fact that women's bodies, unlike men's, can be themselves instruments of production: in pregnancy, giving birth or lactation, arguments about a division of mental from manual labor are fundamentally foreign.[4] ...

Although feminist psychoanalysis is currently popular among socialist feminists as an explanation of the psychological mechanism through which gendered conceptual frameworks emerge from the sexual division of labor in childrearing, socialist feminist epistemology does not stand or fall with feminist psychoanalysis. Socialist feminist epistemology claims that the social experience of women is so different from that of men that it shapes and limits their vision

in substantially different ways—in other words, that women's position in society provides the basis for an autonomous epistemological standpoint. Socialist
feminist epistemology is not committed, however, to any specific account of
the psychological relation between the sexual division of labor and the gender
structuring of knowledge; it is quite compatible with socialist feminism for the
gender-structured adult experience of women and men to be more influential than their infant experience in shaping their world-view. Whenever and
however this shaping occurs, growing empirical evidence shows that women
tend to conceive the world differently from men and have different attitudes
toward it.[5] The discovery of the precise nature and causes of these differences
is a task for feminist psychologists and sociologists of knowledge. The task for
feminist scientists and political theorists is to build on women's experience and
insights in order to develop a systematic account of the world, together with its
potentialities for change, as it appears from the standpoint of women.

As we saw earlier, women are far from creating systematic alternatives to
the prevailing male-dominant ways of conceptualizing reality. Even to imagine
what such alternatives might be like is, as Elizabeth Fee says, "rather like asking a
medieval peasant to imagine the theory of genetics or the production of a space
capsule; our images are, at best, likely to be sketchy and insubstantial."[6] Socialist
feminist theorists claim, however, that women's experience has generated at
least the outline of a distinctive world-view, even though this outline is, as Fee
predicts, sketchy and insubstantial. Nancy Hartsock provides this outline:

> The female construction of self in relation to others, leads ... toward opposition
> to dualisms of any sort, valuation of concrete, everyday life, sense of a variety of
> connectednesses and continuities both with other persons and with the natural
> world. If material life structures consciousness, women's relationally defined
> existence, bodily experience of boundary challenges, and activity of transforming
> both physical objects and human beings must be expected to result in a world
> view to which dichotomies are foreign.[7]

The standpoint of women generates an ontology of relations and of continual
process.

The basic structure of the world, as Hartsock claims that it appears from the
standpoint of women, bears a strong resemblance to the world as described by
radical feminism. Indeed, my characterization of several of the theorists mentioned above as socialist rather than radical feminist is perhaps presumptuous
and may not be in accord with their own definition of themselves. The writings
of Sandra Harding, Nancy Hartsock, and Dorothy Smith could all be described
as radical feminist insofar as they all seem to suggest that the sexual division of labor has more causal primacy than other divisions and so generates a deeper and
more permanent division in knowledge. An additional radical feminist element
in Hartsock's work is her discussion of procreation, where she seems to suggest
that the difference between women's and men's world-views is partly rooted

in certain of women's experiences that she calls "inherent in the female physiology." Specifically, she mentions "menstruation, coitus, pregnancy, childbirth and lactation."[8] The claim that certain distinctive differences between women and men's perceptions of reality are rooted in "inherent" biological differences rather than in a sexual division of labor is more typical of radical feminism than of socialist feminism, as I have characterized these positions. My criterion for identifying all these theorists as socialist feminist, however, is that all of them adhere in principle to a historical materialist approach for understanding social reality. Hartsock explicitly commits herself to this method, and so she is precluded from regarding even physiology as a pre-social given and must see it ultimately as socially constructed, although certainly less immediately susceptible to social alteration than some other aspects of human life. In general, the work of all those theorists whom I have characterized as socialist feminist is clearly a development of radical feminist insights and shows how great is the debt that socialist feminism owes to radical feminism.

In spite of this debt, the socialist feminist concept of the standpoint of women is rather different from the superficially similar concept that is assumed in the writing of many popular American radical feminists. In the next section, I shall focus on the contrasts between radical and socialist feminist epistemology and also on the contrasts between socialist feminist epistemology and the epistemology of liberalism and of traditional Marxism.

. . . Any theory that claims to express the standpoint of women must be able to explain why it is itself rejected by the vast majority of women. Radical feminist epistemology suggests an answer to this question in terms of the dominance of patriarchal culture. Socialist feminist epistemology, however, is explicitly historical materialist and so is able to explain why this culture is dominant and to link the anti-feminist consciousness of many women with the structure of their daily lives. At the same time, the socialist feminist account preserves the apparently contradictory claim that women occupy a distinctive epistemological standpoint that offers unique insight into certain aspects of reality.

According to the socialist feminist conception, a standpoint is a position in society from which certain features of reality come into prominence and from which others are obscured. Although a standpoint makes certain features of reality visible, however, it does not necessarily reveal them clearly nor in their essential interconnections with each other. The daily experience of oppressed groups provides them with an immediate awareness of their own suffering but they do not perceive immediately the underlying causes of this suffering nor even necessarily perceive it as oppression. Their understanding is obscured both by the prevailing ideology and by the very structure of their lives. . . .

In addition to the mystifications created by the dominant ideology and by the structure of our lives, Jane Flax claims that women face another obstacle as they seek to develop a systematic feminist alternative to the masculine modes of conceiving the world. This obstacle is the typically feminine set of attitudes and modes of perception that have been imposed on women in a male-dominated society. While this set of attitudes and modes of perception provides part of the basis for an alternative to the masculine view, it cannot be the only basis of such an alternative. Flax writes:

> Women's experience, which has been excluded from the realm of the known, of the rational, is not in itself an adequate ground for theory. As the other pole of the dualities, it must be incorporated and transcended. Women, in part because of their own history as daughters, have problems with differentiation and the development of a true self and reciprocal relations.[9]

In other words, while women's experience of subordination puts them in a uniquely advantageous position for reinterpreting reality, it also imposes on them certain psychological difficulties which must themselves be the focus of self-conscious struggle.

Simply to be a woman, then, is not sufficient to guarantee a clear understanding of the world as it appears from the standpoint of women. As we saw earlier, the standpoint of women is not discovered by surveying the beliefs and attitudes of women under conditions of male dominance, just as the standpoint of the proletariat is not discovered by surveying the beliefs and attitudes of workers under capitalism. . . . In the end, an adequate representation of the world from the standpoint of women requires the material overthrow of male domination. Donna Haraway writes:

> A socialist-feminist science will have to be developed in the process of constructing different lives in interaction with the world. Only material struggle can end the logic domination. . . . It is a matter for struggle. I do not know what life science would be like if the historical structure of our lives minimized domination. I do know that the history of biology convinces me that basic knowledge would reflect and reproduce the new world, just as it has participated in maintaining our old one.[10]

Even though we do not yet know how the world looks from the standpoint of women, I think that the socialist feminist concept of women's standpoint constitutes a valuable epistemological device for identifying certain necessary conditions of theoretical adequacy. It provides a politically appropriate and theoretically illuminating interpretation of such generally acknowledged conditions as impartiality, objectivity, comprehensiveness, verifiability, and usefulness.

First, the concept of women's standpoint presupposes that all knowledge reflects the interests and values of specific social groups. Since this is so, objectivity cannot be interpreted to mean destitute of values, and impartiality cannot be interpreted to mean neutrality between conflicting interests. If these interpretations are ruled out, and given that we want to preserve the conditions of objectivity and impartiality, the question for epistemology becomes the following: if claims to knowledge are to be objective and impartial, whose interests should they reflect? Socialist feminists answer that they should reflect the interests of women. Women's subordinate status means that, unlike men, women do not have an interest in mystifying reality and so are likely to develop a clearer and more trustworthy understanding of the world. A representation of reality from the standpoint of women is more objective and unbiased than the prevailing representations that reflect the standpoint of men.

The concept of women's standpoint also provides an interpretation of what it is for a theory to be comprehensive. It asserts that women's social position offers them access to aspects or areas of reality that are not easily accessible to men. For instance, to use one of Hartsock's examples, it is only from the standpoint of women that household labor becomes visible as work rather than as a labor of love. The same might be said of socializing children, of empathizing with adults and even, often, of engaging in sexual relations. Thus the standpoint of women provides the basis for a more comprehensive representation of reality than the standpoint of men. Certain areas or aspects of the world are not excluded. The standpoint of women reveals more of the universe, human and non-human, than does the standpoint of men.

Every epistemological tradition requires that genuine claims to knowledge be verified in some way and several of them require that genuine knowledge be useful. The socialist feminist conception of women's standpoint specifies certain interpretations of verification and of usefulness. It asserts that knowledge is useful if it contributes to a practical reconstruction of the world in which women's interests are not subordinate to those of men. Whether or not knowledge is useful in this way is verified in the process of political and scientific struggle to build such a world, a world whose maintenance does not require illusions.

The concept of women's standpoint is not theory-neutral. Like every epistemology, it is conceptually linked to a certain ontology: its model of how knowledge is achieved necessarily presupposes certain general features of human nature and human social life. Whether or not one accepts socialist feminist epistemology thus depends in part on whether or not one accepts the general view of reality on which it rests. One thing that may be said in favor of the concept of women's standpoint, however, is that it is itself more comprehensive than the other interpretations of theoretical adequacy that have been examined already. It explains not only why prevailing representations of reality are systematically male-biased but even why the conditions of theoretical adequacy themselves have been interpreted in characteristically male-biased ways. Thus it provides the basis for a new historical materialist critique of epistemology. It also offers at least a method for discovering the material reasons for its own emergence in this particular historical period.[11]

The concept of women's standpoint is not entirely unproblematic and in the next section I shall discuss one important problem with it. Even so, I think that this concept shows us how to construct a standard for judging the adequacy not just of feminist theory but of all claims to knowledge....

Identifying the Standpoint of Women

Liberal political theory speaks of human rights; Marxist political theory speaks of class conflict. Feminist theorists have used the concept of women's standpoint as a way of criticizing the abstractness and overinclusiveness of such male-generated categories that conceal the special nature of women's oppression. As Sandra Bartky has pointed out, however, the concept of women's standpoint is itself overinclusive and abstract if it presupposes that all or most women share a common social location.[12] From what I have said so far, it may seem as though socialist feminism, whose political analysis stresses the differences in women's social experience, is developing an epistemology that obscures those differences. If socialist feminist epistemology is accepted, then knowledge must be reconstructed from the standpoint of women. But do all women really occupy the same standpoint? And if they do not, which women occupy the standpoint that is most advantageous?

Until recently, socialist feminist theorists have been preoccupied primarily with establishing that women indeed have a distinct epistemological standpoint. Occasionally they have shown some awareness that women's different experiences generate perceptions of reality that differ significantly from each other as well as sharing certain common features. Dorothy Smith, for instance, remarks: "To begin from (women's) standpoint does not imply a common viewpoint among women. What we have in common is that organization of social relations which has accomplished our exclusion."[13] Only very recently, however, have socialist feminist theorists begun considering seriously the epistemological consequences of the differences as well as the commonalities in women's lives.

Sandra Harding points out that "We theory-makers are our own subject/objects but not a very historically representative part of 'women.'"[14] She suggests that contemporary feminist theory is likely to be biased itself by its predominantly white, middle-class origins. White, middle-class women, for instance, are likely to experience their family life as a source of oppression and to make generalizations about "the family" that are quite incongruent with the experience of women in "cultures of resistance," for whom the family may be a source of individual and collective strength. Harding suggests, however, that the differences in women's experience need not be a source of division and weakness. If we learn how to use them, she claims, these differences can be a "scientific and political resource" for feminism. Her idea is not that feminist theory should reflect only the experience of a single group of women, presumably of the most oppressed; for instance, feminist theory does not have to be grounded only on the experience of physically challenged Jewish lesbians of color. Women's oppression is constantly changing in form and these forms cannot be ranked. Consequently, we cannot identify the standpoint of women with the standpoint of physically challenged women, or of lesbian women, or of women of color, or of colonized or immigrant women. For each of these overlapping groups of women, some aspects of reality may be clearly visible and others may be blurred. A representation of reality from the standpoint of women must draw on the variety of all women's experience.

In order to do this, a way must be found in which all groups of women can participate in building theory. Historically, working-class women and women of color have been excluded from intellectual work. This exclusion must be challenged. Working-class women, women of color, and other historically silenced women must be enabled to participate as subjects as well as objects in feminist theorizing. At first it may be impossible for such women to work collectively with middle-class white/Anglo women. Maria Lugones writes: "We cannot talk to you in our language because you do not understand it. . . . The power of white/Anglo women vis-à-vis Hispanas and Black women is in inverse proportion to their working knowledge of each other."[15]

Because of their ignorance, white/Anglo women who try to do theory with women of color inevitably disrupt the dialogue. Before they can contribute to a collective dialogue, they need to "know the text," to have become familiar with an alternative way of viewing the world. To acquire such understanding is not easy:

> You need to learn to become unintrusive, unimportant, patient to the point of tears, while at the same time open to learning any possible lessons. You will also have to come to terms with the sense of alienation, of not belonging, of having your world thoroughly disrupted, having it criticized and scrutinized from the point of view of those who have been harmed by it, having important concepts central to it dismissed, being viewed with mistrust, being seen as of no consequence except as an object of mistrust.[16]

As we saw earlier, the construction of a systematic theoretical alternative to prevailing ways of interpreting the world is an achievement linked inseparably with a transformation of power relations. Only when women are free from domination will they have access to the resources necessary to construct a systematic and fully comprehensive view of the world from the standpoint of women. In the meantime, within a class-divided and racist society, different groups of women inevitably have unequal opportunities to speak and to be heard. For this reason, the goal that women should begin to theorize together is itself a political goal and to succeed in collective theorizing would be itself a political achievement. Women who can theorize together can work together politically; indeed, in theorizing together they are already doing one kind of political work.

In beginning the scientific reconstruction of the world from their own standpoint, women must draw on the experiences of all women. As they do so, their representation of reality will become increasingly adequate—and its adequacy will be tested constantly by its usefulness in helping women to transform that reality. Since women cannot transform reality alone, they must also find ways to work politically with men without being dominated by them and men may even be able to contribute to women's theoretical work. To do so. however, men will have to learn women's "text," a process that will require at least as much humility and commitment as that needed by white/Anglo women to understand the experience of women of color. Even when men contribute to the construction of a systematic alternative to the dominant world-view, it is still accurate to describe this alternative as a representation of reality from the standpoint of women. As we have seen, the socialist feminist conception of the standpoint of women does not refer to a perspective that is immediately available to all and only to women. Instead, it refers to a way of conceptualizing reality that reflects women's interests and values and draws on women's own interpretation of their own experience. Women's standpoint offers a perspective on reality that is accessible in principle to men as well as to women, although a materialist epistemology predicts that men will find it more difficult than women to comprehend this perspective and that widespread male acceptance of it will require political as well as theoretical struggle....

Socialist feminism shows that to reconstruct reality from the standpoint of women requires a far more total transformation of our society and of ourselves than is dreamt of by a masculinist philosophy.

Notes

1. Elizabeth Fee, "Is Feminism a Threat to Scientific Objectivity?" *International Journal of Women's Studies* 4, pp. 378–392. Jane Flax, "Political Philosophy and the Patriarchal Unconscious: A Psychoanalytic Perspective on Epistemology and Metaphysics," in M. Hintikka and S. Harding, eds., *Discovering Reality: Feminist Perspectives on Epistemology, Metaphysics, Methodology and the Philosophy of Science* (Dordrecht: Reidel, 1983). Sandra Harding, "The Norms of Social Inquiry and Masculine Experience," in P. D. Asquith and R. N. Giere, eds., *PSA 1980*, Vol. II (East Lansing, Mich.: Philosophy of Science Association); "Why Has the Sex/Gender System Become Visible Only Now?" in Hintikka and Harding, eds., *Discovering Reality*; "Is Gender a Variable in Conceptions of Rationality? A Survey of the Issues," *Dialectica* 36, nos. 2–3 (1982), reprinted in C. Gould, ed., *Beyond Domination: New Perspectives on Women and Philosophy* (Totowa, N.J.: Rowman & Allanheld) "Towards a Reflexive Feminist Theory" (unpublished). Nancy Hartsock, "Social Life and Social Science: The Significance of the Naturalist/Intentionalist Dispute," *PSA 1980*; "The Feminist Standpoint: Developing the Ground for a Specifically Feminist Historical Materialism," in Hintikka and Harding, eds., *Discovering Reality*. Evelyn Fox Keller, "Gender and Science," *Psychoanalysis and Contemporary Thought*, reprinted in Hintikka and Harding, eds., *Discovering Reality*; "Feminism and Science" (unpublished, 1981). Dorothy Smith, "Women's Perspective as a Radical Critique of Sociology," *Sociological Inquiry* 44 (1974); "Some Implications of a Sociology for Women," in N. Glazer and H. Waehrer, eds., *Woman in a Manmade World: A Socioeconomic Handbook* (Chicago: Rand-McNally, 1977); "A Sociology for Women," in *The Prism of Sex: Essays in the Sociology of Knowledge* (Madison: University of Wisconsin Press, 1979).
2. Smith, "A Sociology for Women," p. 166.
3. Ibid., p. 168.
4. Hartsock, "The Feminist Standpoint," p. 24 of typescript.
5. See the essays in Julia A. Sherman and Evelyn Torton Beck, eds., *The Prism of Sex: Essays in the Sociology of Knowledge* (Madison: University of Wisconsin Press, 1977); Marcia Millman and Rosabeth Moss Kanter, eds., *Another Voice: Feminist Perspectives on Social Life and Social Science* (New York: Anchor Books, 1975); Shirley Ardener, ed., *Perceiving Women* (New York: Halstead Press, 1975). A less academic account is Anne Wilson Schaef's *Women's Reality: An Emerging Female System in the White Male Society* (Minneapolis: Winston Press, 1981).

6. Fee, "Is Feminism a Threat to Scientific Objectivity?," p. 389.
7. Hartsock, "The Feminist Standpoint," p. 23.
8. Ibid., p. 17.
9. Flax, "Political Philosophy and the Patriarchal Unconscious," p. 37.
10. Haraway, "The Biological Enterprise: Sex, Mind, and Profit from Human Engineering to Sociobiology," in *Radical History Review* 20 (1979), pp. 232–33.
11. Sandra Harding suggests that the distinctive insights of contemporary feminism became possible only with the recent emergence of what she provisionally calls "wage-laboring mothers." Only these insights could generate the concept of the standpoint of women. Harding, "Towards a Reflexive Feminist Theory."
12. Sandra Bartky, private correspondence. Maria Lugones and E. V. Spelman make a similar criticism of prevailing interpretations of the concept of speaking in "the woman's voice," a concept closely related to the concept of women's standpoint. See Lugones and Spelman, "Have We Got a Theory for You! Feminist Theory, Cultural Imperialism and the Woman's Voice," paper read to the Tenth Anniversary Conference of the Eastern Division of the Society for Women in Philosophy, Northampton, Massachusetts, October 1982. Alan Soble is another critic of the concept of women's standpoint or the perspective of women because he claims that it reifies women. He argues that reification can be avoided only by taking into account the variety of "racial ethnic, political, geographical and religious factors" that distinguish women from each other. Once this is done, he argues, we shall see that "there is no such thing as 'the perspective of women.'" Alan Soble, "Feminist Epistemology and Women Scientists," *Metaphilosophy* vol. 14, no 3 & 4 (1983), pp. 291–307.
13. Smith, "A Sociology for Women," p. 163.
14. Harding, "Towards a Reflexive Feminist Theory," p. 17 of typescript.
15. Lugones and Spelman, "Have We Got a Theory for You!," pp. 7, 20 of typescript.
16. Ibid., p. 22.

5

Hand, Brain, and Heart: A Feminist Epistemology for the Natural Sciences

HILARY ROSE

Science it would seem is not sexless; she is a man, a father and infected too.

[Virginia Woolf, *Three Guineas*]

This paper starts from the position that the attitudes dominant within science and technology must be transformed, for their telos is nuclear annihilation. It first examines the achievements during the 1970s of those who sought to analyze and critique capitalist science's existing forms and systems of knowledge and goes on to argue that their critiques (which may well have been developed with a conscious opposition to sexism) are theoretically sex blind. Their analysis of the division of labor stops short at the distinction between the manual and mental labor associated with production. Indifferent to the second system of production—reproduction—the analysis excludes the relationship of science to patriarchy, to the sexual division of labor in which caring labor is primarily allocated to women in both unpaid and paid work. Transcendence of this division of labor set up among hand, brain, and heart makes possible a new scientific knowledge and technology that will enable humanity to live in harmony rather than in antagonism with nature, including human nature. The necessity and magnitude of the task must be recognized.

The Need for a New Science

Over the past dozen years the critique of science and technology has focused attention on the ways in which existing science and technology are locked into capitalism and imperialism as a system of domination. This denunciation has served two functions. Negatively, it has facilitated the growth of an antipathy to science that rejects all scientific investigation carried out under any conditions and at any historical time. More positively, it has set itself the difficult task of constructing, in a prefigurative way, both the forms and the content of a different, alternative science—one that anticipates the science and technology possible in a new society and, at the same time, contributes through innovatory practice to the realization of that society. This paper aligns itself with such a venture, while recognizing that—with its false starts as well as real achievements, its perilous balancing between atheoretical activism and abstract theoreticism—the project is not without its contradictions and difficulties. Feminism is just beginning to recapture the full force of Virginia Woolf's insight: science it would seem— to rephrase her—is neither sexless nor classless; she is a man, bourgeois, and infected too.

The trouble with science and technology from a feminist perspective is that they are integral not only to a system of capitalist domination but also to one of patriarchal domination; yet to try to discuss science under both these systems of domination is peculiarly difficult.[1] Historically, it has been women outside science, such as the novelist and essayist Virginia Woolf, or the ex-scientist, now writer, Ruth Wallsgrove, or the sociologist Liliane Stéhélin who have dared to speak of science as male, as part of a phallocentric culture.[2] For women inside science, protest has been much more difficult. Numbers are few and developing the network among isolated women is intractable work. Yet as we enter the eighties an invisible college of feminist scientists is beginning to assemble.[3] One of the new voices breaking through from within the laboratory is that of Rita Arditti, who, having worked in the competitive and macho world of genetics, was radicalized by the antiwar movement.[4] She became a feminist through this experience and now argues that nothing less than a new science will serve.

Apart from a handful who wrote pioneering papers, feminists in the early days of the movement avoided the discussion of science, often retreating into a total rejection of science as the monolithic enemy. Doing science became an activity in which no serious feminist would engage. But there arose a growing political threat as, during the 1970s, a new wave of biological determinism sought to renaturalize women. It has required women biologists—or women who will enter the terrain of biological knowledge—to contest its claims. Doing biology is thus no longer seen as hostile but as helpful to women's interests, and increasingly it is possible to go forward from this essentially defensive purpose to the much more positive goal of seeking to show how a feminist knowledge of the natural world offers an emancipatory rather than an exterminatory science. The task of developing a feminist critique of existing science and of moving toward an as yet unrealized feminist natural science is at once more difficult and more exciting than the academically respectable activity of making descriptive reports on women's position within science. There is a watershed between work carried out within a transformative view of women's destiny and projects shaped by the main variants of structural functionalism still extant. For feminist analysis, unlike developed Marxist theory—though like early Marxism—calls for interpretation constantly tested not simply against the demands of theory, but always and incessantly against the experience of the specific oppression of women.

Here I shall first, briefly, set out the theoretical achievements of the radical critique of science, making plain the weaknesses that stem from its one-sided materialism. Second, drawing on the fast-developing feminist analysis of the links between women's paid and unpaid labor, I shall suggest not only why women are by and large excluded from science, but also what kind of science the exclusion produces. Last, and most tentatively, I pick out some of the examples of a new science that have been developed through the feminist movement.

The Radical Critique of Science

The critique of science was to explode into practice and to struggle into theory during the radical movement of the late 1960s and early 1970s. The numerous issues contained in the class and social struggles of the movement were frequently narrowed and constrained as the theoreticians filtered the wealth of lived experience through the abstract categories of theory. From an early rhetoric that attacked with a certain evenhandedness the class society, imperialism, racism, and sexism (those who were black, colonized, or women might well have had doubts about their equal prioritization in practice as well as in rhetoric), the theoreticians were to develop two main lines of analysis. The first considered the political economy of science, and the second took up the relationship between science and ideology. While the two are linked at many points, work in political economy was more coherently developed; work on the debate over science and ideology was and remains more problematic. The need to reply immediately to the ideological attacks of a racist or sexist science accelerated as the crisis deepened; it was difficult simultaneously to resist the attack and to analyze the issues. Indeed, the hostility to science within the movement so conflated science and ideology that it aided the growth of attitudes that rejected science altogether.[5]

The socialist tradition, at least up to the sixties, believed that the advances of science would automatically create problems that capitalist society could not solve; hence in some way science was at least "neutral," at best allied to those working for a new and socially just society. Such a neutral science was seen as uninfluenced by class, race, gender, nationality, or politics; it was the abstract accumulation of knowledge—of facts, theories, and techniques—which could be "used" or "abused" by society. The experiences of the sixties and seventies overthrew such notions of science. What the sixties' radicals discovered in their campaigns against an abused, militarized, and polluting science was that those in charge of neutral science were overwhelmingly white, male, and privileged occupants of positions in advanced industrialized society. The antihuman technologies that science generated were being used for the profit of some and the distress of many. Thus, the politics of experience brought the radical movement's attitudes toward science into a confrontation with the orthodox Marxist analysis of science.

The latter had claimed that there was an inevitable contradiction between the productive forces unleashed by science and the capitalist order. Hence, science could not be used to its full creative potential within capitalism, and attempts to control the forces of technological innovation would ultimately lead to the destruction of capital. Embodied in Bernalism (though perhaps exaggerated there from what is strictly to be found in the work of John Desmond Bernal), this old belief of the Left that science, technology, and socialism have a necessary relationship was, in time, abandoned, but no critical alternative to bourgeois science was set in its place. Hope for that lay buried in the cupboard of the Lysenko affair, and fashioning a critique of science has been carried out in relative isolation from the mainstream of Marxist scholarship.[6]

The Lysenko affair epitomizes the period from the 1930s to the 1940s in the Soviet Union during which there was an attempt to develop a specifically proletarian interpretation of all culture, including the natural sciences. Against the more cautious views of geneticists, Trofim Lysenko advanced the thesis that acquired characteristics are inherited. He set his social origins as a peasant (and thus his experimental knowledge) against the aristocratic origins (and therefore abstract knowledge) of his leading opponent, Nikolai I. Vavilov. The debate was resolved by Lysenko's falsified statistics on the amounts of grain produced according to his theory and this resolution was sustained by the imposition of Stalinist terror. In 1940 Vavilov was arrested and Lysenko set in his place as director of the Institute of Genetics.[7]

Marxist scholarship shrank from analyzing the circumstances and implications of this failed cultural revolution and retreated to the position that there is only one science—by implication, bourgeois science. Thus, when the radical movement turned to Marxist analysis of the natural sciences, it found embarrassed silences. Nor was the movement helped by the special status of science within Marxism as a body of thought—from Marx's and Engels's claims for a scientific socialism, to Lenin's enthusiasm for Frederick Taylor's application of scientific methods to the production process, to Louis Althusser's influential project to depersonalize Marxist analysis so as to make it truly scientific.

The Myth of the Neutrality of Science

While here I have deliberately focused on the writing of those who have been influential within the radical science movement, over the last decade or so there has also been a dramatic shift in the history, philosophy, and sociology of science. A sophisticated form of externalism holding the thesis that scientific knowledge is structured through its social genesis has become common to all three, so that research is aimed at demonstrating how interests fashion knowledge.[8] Thus, while Thomas Kuhn's work marked the beginnings of the thaw for an age that seemed forever frozen in the timeless certainties of positivism and the Vienna circle, it was a mathematician, historian of science, and political radical—Jerome Ravetz—who posed the question of why and how science is a social problem.[9] To answer this, Ravetz examined the circumstances in which scientists actually produce scientific knowledge. Abandoning the heady and very abstract Popperian theory of "bold conjectures and refutation,"[10] he asked: What do scientists actually do? Through an examination of the production of science from the seventeenth to the nineteenth century he argued that, whereas in the early period science was considered a craft, it increasingly adopted industrialized methods of production as it entered the twentieth century. Where the craft worker had labored alone, or with a couple of apprentices, the new system required substantial capital, a large group of scientists, a clear division of labor between them, and common goals to be set and managed by a scientific director.

Ravetz held that this industrialization of science has produced its uncritical character. In an essentially romantic and libertarian political response, he called for the deinstitutionalization of science. When tied to the state and industry, science must inevitably lose its critical force and become an agent of oppression. If a true science is to reachieve the liberating role it had in the time, say, of Galileo, it must, like Galileo, once more stand in opposition to institutionalized science. It must become critical. The problem with Ravetz's position is that it is idealist in both senses. Although we have seen the welcome development of a handful of deinstitutionalized scientific ventures, it would be unrealistic to consider their contribution a sign of the restructuring of science, since their access to the means of scientific production is minimal.[11]

Less attracted than Ravetz by alternatives outside science, and more oriented toward contesting existing science, others within the radical science movement were nonetheless pursuing the same theoretical concerns. They were revolted by the genocidal science that the United States employed in the war in Southeast Asia and by the expanding new technologies of urban repression at home. They asked, How can science claim to be ideologically pure, value-free, and above all neutral, when even a well-regarded text entitled *The Scientific Method* offers as an example of scientific development the making and testing of napalm on a university playing field, without any references to ethical or political problems? From the "use and abuse" model, in which science remained fundamental, basic, and pure, though possibly abused by political others, the New Left—to the equal concern of both the scientific establishment and the Old Left—had laid siege to the myth of the neutrality of science itself.[12]

A new political economy of science, associated with the physicist Marxists Marcello Cini, Michelangelo de Maria, and Giovanni Cicotti,[13] was to argue that bringing science into the capitalist mode of production meant that knowledge itself, as the product of scientific labor, had been made a commodity. In this analysis, scientific knowledge is no longer timeless but has value only at a particular time and a particular place. For industry the patent laws already encompassing physics and chemistry and presently reaching into the burgeoning area of biotechnology are designed to police ownership patterns.[14] For the basic sciences the rewards go to those who publish the knowledge first. The very process of diffusion reduces the value of the knowledge (typically produced in the elite institutions of the metropolitan countries) by the time it is transferred to the nonelite institutions in the periphery. The value of the knowledge as it passes from the center of production to the periphery declines as surely as that of a car as it moves from second to third hand.

The change in the mode of scientific production, its loss of criticality, and its subjugation to the laws of commodity production are features of the sciences most closely integrated with the reproduction of social and economic power. The physical sciences, above all physics itself, are at once the most arcane and the most deeply implicated in the capitalist system of domination. At the same time, the physical sciences more or less successfully exclude any more than small numbers of women. These industrialized sciences would appear to be highly resistant to feminist reconceptualization, not least because the success of feminist theory has lain in areas such as history, philosophy, and sociology—all characterized by little capital equipment per worker and by craft methods of production.

The Social Origins of Science as Alienated Knowledge

While many within the radical science movement were influenced by the writings of the Frankfurt school, it was Alfred Sohn-Rethel, as part of that tradition, who was to seek to explain the social origins of the highly abstract and alienated character of scientific knowledge.[15] Drawing on historical material, he suggested that abstraction arises with the circulation of money; but he went on to argue that the alienated and abstract character of scientific knowledge has its roots in the profound division of intellectual and manual labor integral to the capitalist social formation. Scientific knowledge and its production system are of a piece with the abstract and alienated labor of the capitalist mode of production itself. The Cultural Revolution, with its project of transcending the division of mental and manual labor, was seen by Sohn-Rethel and indeed by many or most of the New Left as offering a model of immense historical significance. They saw within this movement not only the possibility of transcending hierarchical and antagonistic social relations, but also the means for creating a new science and technology not directed toward the domination of nature or of humanity as part of nature. Especially at present, when assessment of the experience of the Cultural Revolution is problematic, it is important to affirm our need of the project it undertook.

In a world where the alienation of science and technology confronts us in the pollution of the seas, the cities, the countryside—and in the fear of nuclear holocaust—such a longing cannot be dismissed as merely romantic. Its realization may rather be a guarantor of our survival. Certainly aerospace workers in Britain—not easily equated with romantic intellectuals—have in their practice come to conclusions very similar to those of Sohn-Rethel. Beginning with their opposition to the threat of redundancy and with a moral distaste for being so deeply involved in the manufacture of war technology, the workers went on to design, and in some cases to make, socially useful technologies such as the road-rail bus. In this they have simultaneously both contested the division of mental and manual labor in the production of technology and through the unity of hand and brain, begun the long struggle to transform the commodity itself.[16]

The Second System of Domination

Despite the advances made through the critique of science pursued during the 1970s, the critique is, in a theoretical sense, sex blind. It is not that the critics have been insensitive to the problems of sexism and racism; many have honorable records in trying to contest them. It is rather that the theoretical categories make it impossible for them to explain why science is not only bourgeois but male. For it is unequivocally clear that the elite of science—its managers and the constructors of its ideology—are men. Within science, as within all other aspects of production, women occupy subordinate positions, and the exceptional women who make it in this man's world only prove the rule. Yet this exclusion of half of humanity means that the 1970s' critics of science, while they grappled with the structuring of science and technology under capitalism, failed to grasp the significance of—or even to recognize—the structuring under patriarchy, that second and pervasive system of domination. Indeed the radical science movement itself was to reflect in its practice much of the sexism of the social order it opposed. Nonetheless, the critique laid successful siege to claims that science and technology transcend history, and made plain as well the class character of science within a capitalist social formation. Science as an abstraction came to be analyzed as an ideology having a specific historical development within the making of capitalism. Demystifying science exposed the myths that had served to integrate science and mask its internal contradictions and external functions.

Yet within the radical critique of science there remained a disjuncture between actual struggle, on one hand, and theorizing, on the other. Looking back over the writing of the sixties and early seventies, it is difficult not to feel that, as the critical work became more theoretical, more fully elaborated, so women and women's interests receded. Thus, this writing gives no systematic explanation of the gender division of labor within science, nor, despite its denunciation of scientific sexism, does it explain why science so often works to benefit men. By attributing the exclusion of women to ideology, it ignores the possibility that there is a materialist explanation, nowhere hazarding the suggestion that it is in the interests of men to subordinate women within, as well as without, the production system of science. It is taken for granted that the domination/subordination, oppressor/oppressed relationship between men and women is either irrelevant or is explained by the production process.

Feminism as Materialism

Yet this prioritization of the production process ignores that other materialist necessity of history—reproduction. The preoccupation with production as a social process with a corresponding social division of labor and the neglect of reproduction as an analogous process with its division of labor perpetuates a one-sided materialism. It cannot help us understand our circumstances, let alone transcend them.

Reproduction has, meanwhile, been a central focus of the feminist movement in both pragmatic social struggle and theoretical explanation. It is not by chance that the movement has been concerned with abortion, birth control, sexuality, housework, child care—indeed, with all those matters that had been trivialized into silence in the long period since an earlier wave of feminism. Even though now most Left journals will find space occasionally or even regularly for articles by feminists, the exercise remains relatively tokenistic, as the "important" articles dealing with the present crisis show few signs of integrating feminist theory. More than ever, feminists must insist on the significance of the division of labor and prevent the "renaturalization" of women's labor. Economic, political, and ideological pressures can make it seem only right to restore woman to her "natural" place. Science as the great legitimator is, as usual, offering its services.

The Labor of Love

If we are to understand the character of a science denied the input of women's experiences, feminists must return to the sexual division of labor within the household, which, in science as elsewhere, finds its ironic echo in paid labor. Women's work is of a particular kind—whether menial or requiring the sophisticated skills involved in child care, it always involves personal service. Perhaps to make the nature of this caring, intimate, emotionally demanding labor clear, we should use the ideologically loaded term "love." For without love, without close interpersonal relationships, human beings, and it would seem especially small human beings, cannot survive. This emotionally demanding labor requires that women give something of themselves to the child, to the man. The production of people is thus qualitatively different from the production of things. It requires caring labor—the labor of love.

If we return to Sohn-Rethel's emancipatory project of overcoming the division between mental and manual labor, the significance of woman's caring labor for the production of science becomes clear. He saw the division of labor which lies between men, yet took for granted the allocation of caring labor to women. For while intellectual labor is allocated to a minority of men, the majority are assigned manual, highly routine labor. For women, the division of labor is structured along different lines: even those few who become intellectuals are, in the first instance, assigned domestic labor in which caring informs every act. Both the emancipatory theoretical project of Sohn-Rethel and the emancipatory practice of the aerospace workers seek to overcome the division of labor and urge a new science and a new technology; nonetheless their projects still lie within the production of commodities. They seek the unity of hand and brain but exclude the heart. A theoretical recognition of caring labor as critical for the production of *people* is necessary for any adequate materialist analysis of science and is a crucial precondition for an alternative epistemology and method that will help us construct a new science and a new technology. Thus, while Sohn-Rethel's proposal seeks to overcome capitalist social relations, it leaves untouched the patriarchal relations between the sexes. In the production of knowledge, this limitation carries within it the implication that, even if knowledge thus produced were less abstract and its reification overcome, it would still reflect only the historically masculine concern with production. The historically feminine concern with reproduction would remain excluded.

Sohn-Rethel's neglect of the caring labor of women means that the theorist of the transcendence of the division of labor implicitly has joined forces with the far-from-emancipatory program of sociobiology, which argues that woman's destiny is in her genes. The sociobiological thesis that women are genetically programmed for monogamous heterosexual-relationships and motherhood receives tacit endorsement through the androcentric preoccupation of Marxist thought. If we return to Marx's vision of the postrevolutionary society—where we fish and hunt before dinner and make social criticism after the dinner—it is clear that Sohn-Rethel, like Marx, has made the tacit assumption that the usual invisible laborer cooks the meal.[17]

Nor is it enough merely to add a female dimension to a basically productionist argument by bringing in the caring contribution of women. Such an additive process runs the danger of denying the social genesis of women's caring skills, which are extracted from them by men primarily within the home but also in the work place. It moves toward the essentialist thought that women are "naturally" more caring. The problem for materialists is to admit biology—that is, a constrained essentialism—while giving priority to social construction, without concluding at the same time that human beings are infinitely malleable. The dialectical relationship between both systems of production—the production of things and the production of people—holds the explanation not only of why there are so few women in science, but also, and equally or even more importantly, of why the knowledge produced by science is so abstract and depersonalized. . . .

Women Scientists in the Men's Laboratories

Women who manage to get jobs in science have to handle a peculiar contradiction between the demands on them as caring laborers and as abstract mental laborers. Many resolve this by withdrawing or letting themselves be excluded from science; others become essentially honorary men, denying that being a woman creates any problems at all.[18] This sex blindness is particularly evident in the autobiographical accounts of successful women in the sciences, such as those in the 1965 symposium entitled *Women in the Scientific Professions*. It has taken Anne Sayre's passionate defense of Rosalind Franklin to demystify this sexlessness and to insist that the woman scientist is always working in the men's laboratory.[19]

Evelyn Fox Keller, writing of her experiences as a student physicist and later as a research worker, echoes this theme—the continuous, subtle, and not-so-subtle exclusion mechanisms deployed against women scientists. She writes that as a student, she had to be careful to enter a lecture room with or after other students; if she entered first and sat down, men students found it threatening to sit near this low-status person—a woman student—and she was often surrounded by a "sea of seats." On one occasion when she solved a mathematical problem the male university teacher was so incredulous that Keller, like Naomi Weisstein in a similar situation, was quite gently asked who (i.e., which man) did it for her, or where she got (i.e., stole) the solution. Keller's experiences are not, however, unique; what is new is that they are discussed.[20]

Thus a woman scientist is cut in two. Her involvement with the abstraction of scientific practice as it has developed under capitalism and patriarchy, on one hand, is in painful contradiction with her caring labor, on the other. As Ruth Wallsgrove writes, "A woman, especially if she has any ambition or education, receives two kinds of messages: the kind that tells her what it is to be a successful person; and the kind that tells her what it is to be a 'real' woman."[21] Small wonder that women, let alone feminists, working in natural science and engineering are rarities. It is difficult enough to suppress half of oneself to pursue knowledge of the natural world as a woman; it is even more difficult to develop a feminist epistemology.[22] Part of that feminist epistemology involves creation of a practice of feeling, thinking, and writing that opposes the abstraction of male and bourgeois scientific thought.

Reconceptualizing Science

Feminist theorizing about science is of a piece with feminist theoretical production. Unlike the alienated abstract knowledge of science, feminist methodology seeks to bring together subjective and objective ways of knowing the world. It begins with and constantly returns to the subjective shared experience of oppression. It is important to stress *shared* experience, since the purely personal account of oppression, while casting some brilliant insights, may tell us more about the essentially idiosyncratic character of individual experience than about the general experience of all or even most women. Nonetheless, within feminist theoretical production, experience, the living participating "I," is seen as a dimension that must be included in an adequate analysis.[23] The very fact that women are, by and large, shut out of the production system of scientific knowledge, with its ideological power to define what is and what is not objective knowledge, paradoxically has offered feminists a fresh page on which to write.[24] Largely ignored by the oppressors and their systems of knowledge, feminists have necessarily theorized from practice and returned theory to practice.

While it would be false to suggest that all work claiming to be feminist achieves this dialectical synthesis, there is a sense in which theoretical writing looks and must look to the women's movement rather than to the male academy. Working from the experience of the specific oppression of women fuses the personal, the social, and the biological. It is not surprising that, within the natural sciences, it has been in biology and medicine that feminists have sought to defend women's interests and advance feminist interpretations. To take an example: menstruation, which so many women experience as distressing or at best uncomfortable, has generated a tremendous amount of collective discussion, study, and writing. A preeminent characteristic of these investigations lies in their fusing of subjective and objective knowledge in such a way as to make new knowledge. Cartesian dualism, biological determinism, and social constructionism fade when faced with the necessity of integrating and interpreting the personal experience of bleeding, pain, and tension.

Many of the slogans as well as titles of books and pamphlets arising from the movement speak to this necessary fusion. "A woman's right to choose" makes immediate sense to women. It is the demand for women to recover the control over their own bodies, a control that male-dominated medical professions and the profit motive have appropriated. Self-examination and self-health-care groups not only offer prefigurative social forms of health care, but also prefigurative forms of knowledge about natural science. The rightly best-selling book *Our Bodies, Ourselves* seeks to reclaim our sense of wholeness—the experiential unity of personal identity. In a similar vein, *For Her Own Good* not only affirms woman's capacities to understand her interests, but also exposes the male professionalization of medicine in which alienated forms of both knowledge and care have driven out nonalienated female forms.[25] In this situation a feminist biology does not attempt to be objective and external to the female biological entity; it attempts to make over biological knowledge in order to overcome women's alienation from our own bodies, our own selves.

Here I can only pick out particular texts, but any reading of the abundant literature of the movement, particularly at the grass-roots level, reveals a feminism seeking to understand and contest the alienated forms of caring labor and to transform them into nonalienated forms. These moments, in which skill-sharing and skill-enhancing work collectively replaces the private drudgery and sexual servicing of the wife-mother, can only be fragmentary within a society that is systematically capitalist and patriarchal. Even the concept of prefigurative forms is too definite for the fragile but infinitely precious anticipations of the future such moments offer. Nonetheless the future is dialectically contained within the present—that is, insofar as humanity has a future, a prospect that can by no means be taken for granted in the eighties.

The creative energy of the women's movement in simultaneously fashioning new organizational forms and new knowledge is almost taken for granted by the movement itself. It makes fresh syntheses of theoretical significance for reconceptualizing the natural, as well as the social, sciences with the disarming charm of Molière's hero who discovered that he had been speaking prose all his life. While feminist theoreticians are increasingly exploring the epistemological transformations of feminist work in the social sciences, the implications for the natural sciences are only beginning to be articulated.[26] Yet because of the significance of science and technology as major instruments of both ideological and material oppression, the need for a feminist science is increasingly acute.[27] Socialist critical thought of the seventies explored the division of mental and manual labor and its implications for alienated knowledge in the production of things. Feminism points to the third and hidden division of caring labor in the alienated reproduction of human beings themselves. Bringing caring labor and the knowledge that stems from participation in it to the analysis becomes critical for a transformative program equally within science and within society. The baby socks, webs of wool, photos, and flowers threaded into wire fences by the thousands of women peace activists ringing Greenham Common speak for this knowledge of the integration of hand, brain, *and* heart.

Notes

I would like to thank the editorial collective of *donnawomanfemme* for publishing an earlier version of this essay as "Dominio ed Esclusione" (see issue 17 [1981]: 9–28). Too many members of the invisible college of feminist scientists have provided encouragement and helpful comments for me to list them here.

1. Since this paper was written, the debate concerning the possibility of moving beyond dualism has sharpened with the publication of Lydia Sargent's edited collection *Women and Revolution: A Discussion of the Unhappy Marriage of Marxism and Feminism* (Boston: South End Press, 1981). While I am attracted to the theoretical project of a unified explanation, as elaborated within this collection, e.g., by Iris Young, the political and theoretical conditions for its achievement seem to me to be premature. The fruitful analysis of gender, class, and ethnic divisions of labor is likely to continue in both dualistic and unitary forms. See, e.g., the special issue entitled "Development and the Sexual Division of Labor," *Signs: Journal of Women in Culture and Society*, vol. 7, no. 2 (Winter 1981).
2. Ruth Wallsgrove, "The Masculine Face of Science," in *Alice through the Looking Glass*, ed. Brighton Women and Science Group (London: Virago, 1980); Liliane Stéhélin, "Sciences, Women and Ideology," in *The Radicalisation of Science*, ed. Hilary Rose and Steven Rose (London: Macmillan Publishers, 1976); also Hilary Rose and Steven Rose, eds., *Ideology of/in the Sciences* (Boston: Schenkman Publishing Co., 1979).
3. See, e.g., Ann Arbor Science for the People Collective, eds., *Sociobiology as a Social Weapon* (Minneapolis: Burgess Publishing Co., 1977); Susan Griffin, *Woman and Nature: The Roaring Inside Her* (New York: Harper & Row Publishers, 1978); Lila Leibowitz, *Females, Males and Families: A Biosocial Approach* (North Scituate, Mass.: Duxbury Press, 1978); Ethel Tobach and Betty Rosoff, eds., *Genes and Gender I: On Hereditarianism and Women* (New York: Gordian Press, 1978); Ruth Hubbard and Marian Lowe, eds., *Genes and Gender II: Pitfalls in Research on Sex and Gender* (New York: Gordian Press, 1979); Ethel Tobach and Betty Rosoff, eds., *Genes and Gender III: Genetic Determinism and Children* (New York: Gordian Press, 1980); *Signs: Journal of Women in Culture and Society* (special issue entitled "Women, Science, and Society," esp. the papers by Donna Haraway, Adrienne Zihlman, Helen Lambert, Marian Lowe, and Ruth Bleier), vol. 4, no. 1 (Autumn 1978); Carolyn Merchant, *The Death of Nature: Women, Ecology and the Scientific Revolution* (San Francisco: Harper & Row Publishers, 1980); Ruth Hubbard, Mary Sue Henifin, and Barbara Fried, eds., *Women Look at Biology Looking at Women* (Cambridge, Mass.: Schenkman Publishing Co., 1979); Janet Sayers, *Biological Politics: Feminist and Anti-Feminist Perspectives* (London: Tavistock Publications, 1982).
4. Rita Arditti, "Feminism and Science," in *Science and Liberation*, ed. Rita Arditti, Pat Brennan, and Steve Cavrak (Boston: South End Press, 1979); James Watson's *The Double*

Helix (New York: Atheneum Publishers, 1968) was to provide an even more demystified account of how science really gets done—one more honest (not least in its acceptance of machismo) than perhaps he himself had intended.

5. Hilary Rose, "Hyper-reflexivity: A New Danger for the Countermovements," in *Countermovements in the Sciences: Sociology of Science Yearbook*, ed. Helga Nowotny and Hilary Rose (Dordrecht: Reidel, 1979); and Hilary Rose and Steven Rose, "Radical Science and Its Enemies," in *Socialist Register*, ed. Ralph Miliband and John Saville (Atlantic Highlands, N.J.: Humanities Press, 1979).

6. The writings of John Desmond Bernal were central among socialist scientists of the thirties, esp. *The Social Functions of Science* (London: Routledge & Kegan Paul, 1939). Bernalist ideas remain only in old Left theories—whether those of official communism or of the Trotskyist faction—extending as it were from the Soviet academician Mikhail Millionshchikov to the fourth international theorist Ernest Mandel. See Mikhail Millionshchikov in *The Scientific and Technological Revolution*, ed. Robert Daglish (Moscow: Progress Publishers, 1972), pp. 13–18; and Ernest Mandel, *Late Capitalism* (London: New Left Books, 1975).

7. The Lysenko affair was neglected for almost thirty years by Marxists. In the mid-seventies the American biologists Richard Lewontin and Richard Levins and the French philosopher Dominique Lecourt broke the long silence. Lewontin and Levins, "The Problem of Lysenkoism," in *Ideology of/in the Sciences* (n.2 above); Lecourt, *Proletarian Science? The Case of Lysenko* (London: New Left Books, 1977).

8. This project has been particularly associated with the Edinburgh school and the "strong" program in the sociology of knowledge, and would include the work of Barry Barnes, David Bloor, and Donald McKenzie. Ultimately epistemologically problematic, the approach has facilitated a critical view of science. For a feminist use of a sophisticated externalism that avoids the excesses of the strong program, see Elizabeth Fee, "Nineteenth-Century Craniology: The Study of the Female Skull," *Bulletin of the History of Medicine* 53 (1980): 415–33; Donna Haraway, "Animal Sociology and the Natural Economy of the Body Politic Part I," and "Part II," *Signs: Journal of Women in Culture and Society* 4, no. 1 (1978): 21–60.

9. Jerome R. Ravetz, *Scientific Knowledge and Its Social Problems* (New York: Oxford University Press, 1971).

10. Karl R. Popper, *Conjectures and Refutations: The Growth of Scientific Knowledge* (London: Routledge & Kegan Paul, 1963).

11. These ventures are documented primarily in alternative magazines, particularly those associated with anarchism, but see also Nowotny and Rose, eds. (n.5 above).

12. Hilary Rose and Steven Rose, "The Myth of the Neutrality of Science," in Arditti, Brennan, and Cavrak, eds. (n.4 above).

13. Giovanni Cicotti, Marcello Cini, and Michelangelo de Maria, "The Production of Science in Advanced Capitalist Countries," in *The Political Economy of Science*, ed. Hilary Rose and Steven Rose (London: Macmillan Publishers, 1976). (This essay unfortunately is not included in the American edition, published by G. K. Hall in 1979.)

14. David Noble, *America by Design* (Cambridge, Mass.: MIT University Press, 1979).

15. Alfred Sohn-Rethel, *Intellectual and Manual Labour* (London: Macmillan Publishers, 1978).

16. Mike Cooley, *Architect or Bee?* (Slough, England: Hand and Brain Press, 1980); Dave Elliot and Hilary Wainwright, *The Lucas Plan: A New Trade Unionism in the Making* (London: Allison & Bushy, 1982).

17. Mary O'Brien's feminist rendering of the vision proposes child care as one of the daytime activities. See *The Politics of Reproduction* (London: Routledge & Kegan Paul, 1981).

18. This view is held by most of the women natural scientists contributing to either the New York symposium of 1965 or the more recent one held by UNESCO. However, it is my impression that, in private discussion, distinguished women scientists often have another interpretation; they thus perhaps hold public and private accounts according to which domain they are in. See *Women in the Scientific Professions* (New York: New York Academy of Science, 1965). Alice Rossi's paper in this otherwise ideologically "correct" collection contains a remarkable pioneering discussion.

19. Anne Sayre, *Rosalind Franklin and D.N.A.: A Vivid View of What It Is Like to Be a Gifted Woman in an Especially Male Profession* (New York: W. W. Norton & Co., 1975).

20. Evelyn Fox Keller, "The Anomaly of a Woman in Physics," in *Working It Out: 23 Women, Writers, Scientists and Scholars Talk about Their Lives,* ed. Sara Ruddick and Pamela Daniels (New York: Pantheon Books, 1977); Naomi Weisstein, "Adventures of a Woman in Science," in *Working It Out.*
21. Wallsgrove (n.2 above), p. 237.
22. Feminism has been quick to spell out its methodology, but slower when it comes to epistemology; see, e.g., Helen Roberts, ed., *Feminist Methodology* (London: Routledge & Kegan Paul, 1981).
23. See Ruth Hubbard's discussion of evolutionary theory as an example; Hubbard, Henifin, and Fried, eds. (n.3 above), pp. 7–36.
24. Elizabeth Fee's "Is Feminism a Threat to Scientific Objectivity" (paper presented at the American Association for the Advancement of Science meeting, Toronto, January 4, 1981) pursues parallel themes.
25. Boston Women's Health Care Collective, *Our Bodies, Ourselves* (New York: Random House, 1971); Barbara Ehrenreich and Deirdre English, *For Her Own Good: 150 Years of the Experts' Advice to Women* (Garden City, N.Y.: Doubleday, Anchor Press, 1978).
26. In this emerging debate some, such as Griffin (n.3 above), seek to replace men's objectivity with women's subjectivity; others, such as Rose ("Hyper-reflexivity" [n.5 above]) and Evelyn Fox Keller ("Feminism and Science," *Signs: Journal of Women in Culture and Society* 7, no. 3 [Spring 1982]: 589–602), seek a synthesis combining subjective and objective ways of knowing the natural world.
27. Though it is beyond the scope of this article, the need for a specifically feminist technology is beginning to be expressed particularly in connection with the "new technology." Feminist collectives working on computing and word processing are increasingly evident. See, e.g., a recent issue of *Scarlet Woman*, vol. 14 (1982), available c/o 177 St. Georges Rd., N. Fitzroy, Victoria 3068, Australia.

6

Situated Knowledges: The Science Question in Feminism and the Privilege of Partial Perspective[1]

DONNA HARAWAY

Academic and activist feminist enquiry has repeatedly tried to come to terms with the question of what *we* might mean by the curious and inescapable term "objectivity." We have used a lot of toxic ink and trees processed into paper decrying what *they* have meant and how it hurts *us*. The imagined "they" constitute a kind of invisible conspiracy of masculinist scientists and philosophers replete with grants and laboratories; and the imagined "we" are the embodied others, who are not allowed *not* to have a body, a finite point of view, and so an inevitably disqualifying and polluting bias in any discussion of consequence outside our own little circles, where a "mass"-subscription journal might reach a few thousand readers composed mostly of science-haters. At least, I confess to these paranoid fantasies and academic resentments lurking underneath some convoluted reflections in print under my name in the feminist literature in the history and philosophy of science. We, the feminists in the debates about science and technology, are the Reagan era's "special interest groups" in the rarefied realm of epistemology, where traditionally what can count as knowledge is policed by philosophers codifying cognitive canon law. Of course, a special interest group is, by Reaganoid definition, any collective historical subject which dares to resist the stripped-down atomism of Star Wars, hypermarket, postmodern, media-simulated citizenship. Max Headroom doesn't have a body; therefore, he alone *sees* everything in the great communicator's empire of the Global Network. No wonder Max gets to have a naïve sense of humour and a kind of happily regressive, pre-oedipal sexuality, a sexuality which we ambivalently—and dangerously incorrectly—had imagined was reserved for lifelong inmates of female and colonized bodies, and maybe also white male computer hackers in solitary electronic confinement.

It has seemed to me that feminists have both selectively and flexibly used and been trapped by two poles of a tempting dichotomy on the question of objectivity. Certainly I speak for myself here, and I offer the speculation that

there is a collective discourse on these matters. On the one hand, recent social studies of science and technology have made available a very strong social
constructionist argument for *all* forms of knowledge claims, most certainly and
especially scientific ones.[2] In these tempting views, no insider's perspective is
privileged, because all drawings of inside–outside boundaries in knowledge are
theorized as power moves, not moves toward truth. So, from the strong social
constructionist perspective, why should we be cowed by scientists' descriptions
of their activity and accomplishments; they and their patrons have stakes in
throwing sand in our eyes. They tell parables about objectivity and scientific
method to students in the first years of their initiation, but no practitioner of
the high scientific arts would be caught dead *acting on* the textbook versions.
Social constructionists make clear that official ideologies about objectivity and
scientific method are particularly bad guides to how scientific knowledge is actually *made*. Just as for the rest of us, what scientists believe or say they do and
what they really do have a very loose fit.

The only people who end up actually *believing* and, goddess forbid, acting
on the ideological doctrines of disembodied scientific objectivity enshrined in
elementary textbooks and technoscience booster literature are non-scientists,
including a few very trusting philosophers. Of course, my designation of this
last group is probably just a reflection of residual disciplinary chauvinism from
identifying with historians of science and too much time spent with a microscope
in early adulthood in a kind of disciplinary pre-oedipal and modernist poetic
moment when cells seemed to be cells and organisms, organisms. *Pace*, Gertrude
Stein. But then came the law of the father and its resolution of the problem of
objectivity, solved by always already absent referents, deferred signifieds, split
subjects, and the endless play of signifiers. Who wouldn't grow up warped?
Gender, race, the world itself—all seem just effects of warp speeds in the play
of signifiers in a cosmic force field. All truths become warp speed effects in a
hyper-real space of simulations. But we cannot afford these particular plays on
words—the projects of crafting reliable knowledge about the "natural" world
cannot be given over to the genre of paranoid or cynical science fiction. For
political people, social constructionism cannot be allowed to decay into the
radiant emanations of cynicism.

In any case, social constructionists could maintain that the ideological doctrine of scientific method and all the philosophical verbiage about epistemology
were cooked up to distract our attention from getting to know the world *effectively* by practising the sciences. From this point of view, science—the real game
in town, the one we must play—is rhetoric, the persuasion of the relevant social
actors that one's manufactured knowledge is a route to a desired form of very
objective power. Such persuasions must take account of the structure of facts and
artefacts, as well as of language-mediated actors in the knowledge game. Here,
artefacts and facts are parts of the powerful art of rhetoric. Practice is persuasion,
and the focus is very much on practice. All knowledge is a condensed node in

an agonistic power field. The strong programme in the sociology of knowledge joins with the lovely and nasty tools of semiology and deconstruction to insist on the rhetorical nature of truth, including scientific truth. History is a story Western culture buffs tell each other; science is a contestable text and a power field; the content is the form.[3] Period. The form in science is the artefactual-social rhetoric of crafting the world into effective objects. This is a practice of world-changing persuasions that take the shape of amazing new objects—like microbes, quarks, and genes.

But whether or not they have the structure and properties of rhetorical objects, late twentieth-century scientific entities—infective vectors (microbes), elementary particles (quarks), and biomolecular codes (genes)—are not Romantic or modernist objects with internal laws of coherence.[4] They are momentary traces focused by force fields, or they are information vectors in a barely embodied and highly mutable semiosis ordered by acts of recognition and misrecognition. Human nature, encoded in its genome and its other writing practices, is a vast library worthy of Umberto Eco's imagined secret labyrinth in *The Name of the Rose* (1980). The stabilization and storage of this text of human nature promise to cost more than its writing. This is a terrifying view of the relationship of body and language for those of us who would still like to talk about *reality* with more confidence than we allow the Christian right's discussion of the Second Coming and their being raptured out of the final destruction of the world. We would like to think our appeals to real worlds are more than a desperate lurch away from cynicism and an act of faith like any other cult's, no matter how much space we generously give to all the rich and always historically specific mediations through which we and everybody else must know the world.

So, the further I get with the description of the radical social constructionist programme and a particular version of postmodernism, coupled to the acid tools of critical discourse in the human sciences, the more nervous I get. Like all neuroses, mine is rooted in the problem of metaphor, that is, the problem of the relation of bodies and language. For example, the force field imagery of moves in the fully textualized and coded world is the matrix for many arguments about socially negotiated reality for the postmodern subject. This world-as-code is, just for starters, a high-tech military field, a kind of automated academic battlefield, where blips of light called players disintegrate (what a metaphor!) each other in order to stay in the knowledge and power game. Technoscience and science fiction collapse into the sun of their radiant (ir)reality—war.[5] It shouldn't take decades of feminist theory to sense the enemy here. Nancy Hartsock (1983b) got all this crystal clear in her concept of abstract masculinity.

I, and others, started out wanting a strong tool for deconstructing the truth claims of hostile science by showing the radical historical specificity, and so contestability, of *every* layer of the onion of scientific and technological constructions, and we end up with a kind of epistemological electro-shock therapy, which far from ushering us into the high stakes tables of the game of contesting public truths, lays us out on the table with self-induced multiple personality disorder. We wanted a way to go beyond showing bias in science (that proved too easy anyhow), and beyond separating the good scientific sheep from the bad goats of bias and misuse. It seemed promising to do this by the strongest possible constructionist argument that left no cracks for reducing the issues to bias versus objectivity, use versus misuse, science versus pseudo-science. We unmasked the doctrines of objectivity because they threatened our budding sense of collective historical subjectivity and agency and our "embodied" accounts of the truth, and we ended up with one more excuse for not learning any post-Newtonian physics and one more reason to drop the old feminist self-help practices of repairing our own cars. They're just texts anyway, so let the boys have them back. Besides these textualized postmodern worlds are scary, and we prefer our science fiction to be a bit more utopic, maybe like *Woman on the Edge of Time* or even *Wanderground*.

Some of us tried to stay sane in these disassembled and dissembling times by holding out for a feminist version of objectivity. Here, motivated by many of the same political desires, is the other seductive end of the duplicitous objectivity problem. Humanistic Marxism was polluted at the source by its structuring ontological theory of the domination of nature in the self-construction of man and by its closely related impotence to historicize anything women did that didn't qualify for a wage. But Marxism was still a promising resource in the form of epistemological feminist mental hygiene that sought our own doctrines of objective vision. Marxist starting points offered tools to get to our versions of standpoint theories, insistent embodiment, a rich tradition of critiques of hegemony without disempowering positivisms and relativisms, and nuanced theories of mediation. Some versions of psychoanalysis aided this approach immensely, especially anglophone object relations theory, which maybe did more for US socialist-feminism for a time than anything from the pen of Marx or Engels, much less Althusser or any of the late pretenders to sonship treating the subject of ideology and science.[6]

Another approach, "feminist empiricism," also converges with feminist uses of Marxian resources to get a theory of science which continues to insist on legitimate meanings of objectivity and which remains leery of a radical constructivism conjugated with semiology and narratology (Harding, 1986, pp. 24–26, 161–62). Feminists have to insist on a better account of the world; it is not enough to show radical historical contingency and modes of construction for everything. Here, we, as feminists, find ourselves perversely conjoined with the discourse of many practising scientists, who, when all is said and done, mostly believe they are describing and discovering things *by means of* all their constructing and arguing. Evelyn Keller has been particularly insistent on this fundamental matter, and Harding calls the goal of these approaches a "successor science." Feminists have stakes in a successor science project that offers a more adequate, richer, better account of a world, in order to live in it well and in critical, reflexive relation to our own as well as others' practices of domination and the unequal parts of privilege and oppression that make up all positions. In traditional philosophical categories, the issue is ethics and politics perhaps more than epistemology.

So, I think my problem and "our" problem is how to have *simultaneously* an account of radical historical contingency for all knowledge claims and knowing subjects, a critical practice for recognizing our own "semiotic technologies" for making meanings, *and* a no-nonsense commitment to faithful accounts of a "real" world, one that can be partially shared and friendly to earth-wide projects of finite freedom, adequate material abundance, modest meaning in suffering, and limited happiness. Harding calls this necessary multiple desire a need for a successor science project and a postmodern insistence on irreducible difference and radical multiplicity of local knowledges. *All* components of the desire are paradoxical and dangerous, and their combination is both contradictory and necessary. Feminists don't need a doctrine of objectivity that promises transcendence, a story that loses track of its mediations just where someone might be held responsible for something, and unlimited instrumental power. We don't want a theory of innocent powers to represent the world, where language and bodies both fall into the bliss of organic symbiosis. We also don't want to theorize the world, much less act within it, in terms of Global Systems, but we do need an earth-wide network of connections, including the ability partially to translate knowledges among very different—and power-differentiated—communities. We need the power of modern critical theories of how meanings and bodies get made, not in order to deny meaning and bodies, but in order to live in meanings and bodies that have a chance for a future.

Natural, social, and human sciences have always been implicated in hopes like these. Science has been about a search for translation, convertibility, mobility of meanings, and universality—which I call reductionism, when one language (guess whose) must be enforced as the standard for all the translations and conversions. What money does in the exchange orders of capitalism, reductionism does in the powerful mental orders of global sciences: there is finally only one equation. That is the deadly fantasy that feminists and others have identified in some versions of objectivity doctrines in the service of hierarchical and positivist orderings of what can count as knowledge. That is one of the reasons the debates about objectivity matter, metaphorically and otherwise. Immortality and omnipotence are not our goals. But we could use some enforceable, reliable accounts of things not reducible to power moves and agonistic, high status games of rhetoric or to scientistic, positivist arrogance. This point applies whether we are talking about genes, social classes, elementary particles, genders, races, or texts; the point applies to the exact, natural, social, and human sciences, despite the slippery ambiguities of the words *objectivity* and *science* as we slide around the discursive terrain. In our efforts to climb the greased pole leading to a usable doctrine of objectivity, I and most other feminists in the objectivity debates have alternatively, or even simultaneously, held on to both ends of the dichotomy, which Harding describes in terms of successor science projects versus postmodernist accounts of difference and I have sketched in this chapter as radical constructivism versus feminist critical empiricism. It is, of course, hard to climb when you are holding on to both ends of a pole, simultaneously or alternately. It is, therefore, time to switch metaphors.

The Persistence of Vision[7]

I would like to proceed by placing metaphorical reliance on a much maligned sensory system in feminist discourse: vision. Vision can be good for avoiding binary oppositions. I would like to insist on the embodied nature of all vision, and so reclaim the sensory system that has been used to signify a leap out of the marked body and into a conquering gaze from nowhere. This is the gaze that mythically inscribes all the marked bodies, that makes the unmarked category claim the power to see and not be seen, to represent while escaping representation. This gaze signifies the unmarked positions of Man and White, one of the many nasty tones of the world *objectivity* to feminist ears in scientific and technological, late industrial, militarized, racist and male dominant societies, that is, here, in the belly of the monster, in the United States in the late 1980s. I would like a doctrine of embodied objectivity that accommodates paradoxical and critical feminist science projects: feminist objectivity means quite simply *situated knowledges.*

The eyes have been used to signify a perverse capacity—honed to perfection in the history of science tied to militarism, capitalism, colonialism, and male supremacy—to distance the knowing subject from everybody and everything in the interests of unfettered power. The instruments of visualization in multinationalist, postmodernist culture have compounded these meanings of dis-embodiment. The visualizing technologies are without apparent limit; the eye of any ordinary primate like us can be endlessly enhanced by sonography systems, magnetic resonance imaging, artificial intelligence-linked graphic manipulation systems, scanning electron microscopes, computer-aided tomography scanners, colour enhancement techniques, satellite surveillance systems, home and office VDTs, cameras for every purpose from filming the mucous membrane lining the gut cavity of a marine worm living in the vent gases on a fault between continental plates to mapping a planetary hemisphere elsewhere in the solar system. Vision in this technological feast becomes unregulated gluttony; all perspective gives way to infinitely mobile vision, which no longer seems just mythically about the god-trick of seeing everything from nowhere, but to have put the myth into ordinary practice. And like the god-trick, this eye fucks the world to make techno-monsters. Zoe Sofoulis (1988) calls this the cannibal-eye of masculinist extra-terrestrial projects for excremental second birthing.

A tribute to this ideology of direct, devouring, generative, and unrestricted vision, whose technological mediations are simultaneously celebrated and presented as utterly transparent, the volume celebrating the 100th anniversary of

the National Geographic Society closes its survey of the magazine's quest literature, effected through its amazing photography, with two juxtaposed chapters.
The first is on "Space," introduced by the epigraph, "The choice is the universe—
or nothing" (Bryan, 1987, p. 352). Indeed. This chapter recounts the exploits
of the space race and displays the colour-enhanced "snapshots" of the outer
planets reassembled from digitalized signals transmitted across vast space to
let the viewer "experience" the moment of discovery in immediate vision of
the "object."[8] These fabulous objects come to us simultaneously as indubitable
recordings of what is simply there and as heroic feats of techno-scientific production. The next chapter is the twin of outer space: "Inner Space," introduced
by the epigraph, "The stuff of stars has come alive" (Bryan, 1987, p. 454). Here,
the reader is brought into the realm of the infinitesimal, objectified by means
of radiation outside the wavelengths that "normally" are perceived by hominid
primates, i.e., the beams of lasers and scanning electron microscopes, whose signals are processed into the wonderful full-colour snapshots of defending T cells
and invading viruses.

But of course that view of infinite vision is an illusion, a god-trick. I would
like to suggest how our insisting metaphorically on the particularity and embodiment of all vision (though not necessarily organic embodiment and including
technological mediation), and not giving in to the tempting myths of vision as
a route to disembodiment and second-birthing, allows us to construct a usable,
but not an innocent, doctrine of objectivity. I want a feminist writing of the
body that metaphorically emphasizes vision again, because we need to reclaim
that sense to find our way through all the visualizing tricks and powers of modern sciences and technologies that have transformed the objectivity debates.
We need to learn in our bodies, endowed with primate colour and stereoscopic
vision, how to attach the objective to our theoretical and political scanners in
order to name where we are and are not, in dimensions of mental and physical
space we hardly know how to name. So, not so perversely, objectivity turns out
to be about particular and specific embodiment, and definitely not about the
false vision promising transcendence of all limits and responsibility. The moral
is simple: only partial perspective promises objective vision. This is an objective
vision that initiates, rather than closes off, the problem of responsibility for the
generativity of all visual practices. Partial perspective can be held accountable
for both its promising and its destructive monsters. All Western cultural narratives about objectivity are allegories of the ideologies of the relations of what
we call mind and body, of distance and responsibility, embedded in the science
question in feminism. Feminist objectivity is about limited location and situated
knowledge, not about transcendence and splitting of subject and object. In this
way we might become answerable for what we learn how to see.

These are lessons which I learned in part walking with my dogs and won-
dering how the world looks without a fovea and very few retinal cells for colour
vision, but with a huge neural processing and sensory area for smells. It is a

lesson available from photographs of how the world looks to the compound eyes of an insect, or even from the camera eye of a spy satellite or the digitally transmitted signals of space probe-perceived differences "near" Jupiter that have been transformed into coffee table colour photographs. The "eyes" made available in modern technological sciences shatter any idea of passive vision; these prosthetic devices show us that all eyes, including our own organic ones, are active perceptual systems, building in translations and specific *ways* of seeing, that is, ways of life. There is no unmediated photograph or passive camera obscure in scientific accounts of bodies and machines; there are only highly specific visual possibilities, each with a wonderfully detailed, active, partial way of organizing worlds. All these pictures of the world should not be allegories of infinite mobility and interchangeability, but of elaborate specificity and difference and the loving care people might take to learn how to see faithfully from another's point of view, even when the other is our own machine. That's not alienating distance; that's a *possible* allegory for feminist versions of objectivity. Understanding how these visual systems work, technically, socially, and psychically ought to be a way of embodying feminist objectivity.

Many currents in feminism attempt to theorize grounds for trusting especially the vantage points of the subjugated; there is good reason to believe vision is better from below the brilliant space platforms of the powerful (Hartsock, 1983a; Sandoval, n.d.; Harding, 1986; Anzaldúa, 1987). Linked to this suspicion, this chapter is an argument for situated and embodied knowledges and against various forms of unlocatable, and so irresponsible, knowledge claims. Irresponsible means unable to be called into account. There is a premium on establishing the capacity to see from the peripheries and the depths. But here lies a serious danger of romanticizing and/or appropriating the vision of the less powerful while claiming to see from their positions. To see from below is neither easily learned nor unproblematic, even if "we" "naturally" inhabit the great underground terrain of subjugated knowledges. The positionings of the subjugated are not exempt from critical re-examination, decoding, deconstruction, and interpretation; that is, from both semiological and hermeneutic modes of critical enquiry. The standpoints of the subjugated are not "innocent" positions. On the contrary, they are preferred because in principle they are least likely to allow denial of the critical and interpretative core of all knowledge. They are savvy to modes of denial through repression, forgetting, and disappearing acts—ways of being nowhere while claiming to see comprehensively. The subjugated have a decent chance to be on to the god-trick and all its dazzling—and, therefore, blinding—illuminations. "Subjugated" standpoints are preferred because they seem to promise more adequate, sustained, objective, transforming accounts of the world. But *how* to see from below is a problem requiring at least as much skill with bodies and language, with the mediations of vision, as the "highest" techno-scientific visualizations.

Such preferred positioning is as hostile to various forms of relativism as to the most explicitly totalising versions of claims to scientific authority. But the alternative to relativism is not totalization and single vision, which is always finally the unmarked category whose power depends on systematic narrowing and obscuring. The alternative to relativism is partial, locatable, critical knowledges sustaining the possibility of webs of connections called solidarity in politics and shared conversations in epistemology. Relativism is a way of being nowhere while claiming to be everywhere equally. The "equality" of positioning is a denial of responsibility and critical enquiry. Relativism is the perfect mirror twin of totalization in the ideologies of objectivity; both deny the stakes in location, embodiment, and partial perspective; both make it impossible to see well. Relativism and totalization are both "god-tricks" promising vision from everywhere and nowhere equally and fully, common myths in rhetorics surrounding science. But it is precisely in the politics and epistemology of partial perspectives that the possibility of sustained, rational, objective enquiry rests.

So, with many other feminists, I want to argue for a doctrine and practice of objectivity that privileges contestation, deconstruction, passionate construction, webbed connections, and hope for transformation of systems of knowledge and ways of seeing. But not just any partial perspective will do; we must be hostile to easy relativisms and holisms built out of summing and subsuming parts. "Passionate detachment" (Kuhn, 1982) requires more than acknowledged and self-critical partiality. We are also bound to seek perspective from those points of view, which can never be known in advance, which promise something quite extraordinary, that is, knowledge potent for constructing worlds less organized by axes of domination. In such a viewpoint, the unmarked category would *really* disappear—quite a difference from simply repeating a disappearing act. The imaginary and the rational—the visionary and objective vision—hover close together. I think Harding's plea for a successor science and for postmodern sensibilities must be read to argue that this close touch of the fantastic element of hope for transformative knowledge and the severe check and stimulus of sustained critical enquiry are jointly the ground of any believable claim to objectivity or rationality not riddled with breath-taking denials and repressions. It is even possible to read the record of scientific revolutions in terms of this feminist doctrine of rationality and objectivity. Science has been utopian and visionary from the start; that is one reason "we" need it.

A commitment to mobile positioning and to passionate detachment is dependent on the impossibility of innocent "identity" politics and epistemologies as strategies for seeing from the standpoints of the subjugated in order to see well. One cannot "be" either a cell or molecule—or a woman, colonized person, labourer, and so on—if one intends to see and see from these positions critically. "Being" is much more problematic and contingent. Also, one cannot relocate in any possible vantage point without being accountable for that movement.

Vision is *always* a question of the power to see—and perhaps of the violence implicit in our visualizing practices. With whose blood were my eyes crafted? These points also apply to testimony from the position of "oneself." We are not immediately present to ourselves. Self-knowledge requires a semiotic-material technology linking meanings and bodies. Self-identity is a bad visual system. Fusion is a bad strategy of positioning. The boys in the human sciences have called this doubt about self-presence the "death of the subject," that single ordering point of will and consciousness. That judgement seems bizarre to me. I prefer to call this generative doubt the opening of non-isomorphic subjects, agents, and territories of stories unimaginable from the vantage point of the cyclopian, self-satiated eye of the master subject. The Western eye has fundamentally been a wandering eye, a travelling lens. These peregrinations have often been violent and insistent on mirrors for a conquering self—but not always. Western feminists also *inherit* some skill in learning to participate in revisualizing worlds turned upside down in earth-transforming challenges to the views of the masters. All is not to be done from scratch.

The split and contradictory self is the one who can interrogate positionings and be accountable, the one who can construct and join rational conversations and fantastic imaginings that change history.[9] Splitting, not being, is the privileged image for feminist epistemologies of scientific knowledge. "Splitting" in this context should be about heterogeneous multiplicities that are simultaneously necessary and incapable of being squashed into isomorphic slots or cumulative lists. This geometry pertains within and among subjects. The topography of subjectivity is multi-dimensional; so, therefore, is vision. The knowing self is partial in all its guises, never finished, whole, simply there and original; it is always constructed and stitched together imperfectly, and *therefore* able to join with another, to see together without claiming to be another. Here is the promise of objectivity: a scientific knower seeks the subject position not of identity, but of objectivity; that is, partial connection. There is no way to "be" simultaneously in all, or wholly in any, of the privileged (subjugated) positions structured by gender, race, nation, and class. And that is a short list of critical positions. The search for such a "full" and total position is the search for the fetishized perfect subject of oppositional history, sometimes appearing in feminist theory as the essentialized Third World Woman (Mohanty, 1984). Subjugation is not grounds for an ontology; it might be a visual clue. Vision requires instruments of vision; an optics is a politics of positioning. Instruments of vision mediate standpoints; there is no immediate vision from the standpoints of the subjugated. Identity, including self-identical, unmarked, disembodied, unmediated, transcendent, born again. It is unfortunately possible for the subjugated to lust for and even scramble into that subject position—and then disappear from view. Knowledge from the point of view of the unmarked is truly fantastic, distorted, and so irrational. The only position from which objectivity could not possibly be practised and honoured is the standpoint of the master, the Man, the One God, whose

Eye produces, appropriates, and orders all difference. No one ever accused the God of monotheism of objectivity, only of indifference. The god-trick is self-identical, and we have mistaken that for creativity and knowledge, omniscience even.

Positioning is, therefore, the key practice grounding knowledge organized around the imagery of vision, as so much Western scientific and philosophic discourse is organized. Positioning implies responsibility for our enabling practices. It follows that politics and ethics ground struggles for the contests over what may count as rational knowledge. That is, admitted or not, politics and ethics ground struggles over knowledge projects in the exact, natural, social, and human sciences. Otherwise, rationality is simply impossible, an optical illusion projected from nowhere comprehensively. Histories of science may be powerfully told as histories of the technologies. These technologies are ways of life, social orders, practices of visualization. Technologies are skilled practices. How to see? Where to see from? What limits to vision? What to see for? Whom to see with? Who gets to have more than one point of view? Who gets blinkered? Who wears blinkers? Who interprets the visual field? What other sensory powers do we wish to cultivate besides vision? Moral and political discourse should be the paradigm of rational discourse in the imagery and technologies of vision. Sandra Harding's claim, or observation, that movements of social revolution have most contributed to improvements in science might be read as a claim about the knowledge consequences of new technologies of positioning. But I wish Harding had spent more time remembering that social and scientific revolutions have not always been liberatory, even if they have always been visionary. Perhaps this point could be captured in another phrase: the science question in the military. Struggles over what will count as rational accounts of the world are struggles over *how* to see. The terms of vision: the science question in colonialism; the science question in exterminism (Sofoulis, 1988); the science question in feminism.

The issue in politically engaged attacks on various empiricisms, reductionisms, or other versions of scientific authority should not be relativism, but location. A dichotomous chart expressing this point might look like this:

universal rationality	ethnophilosophies
common language	heteroglossia
new organon	deconstruction
unified field theory	oppositional positioning
world system	local knowledges
master theory	webbed accounts

But a dichotomous chart misrepresents in a critical way the positions of embodied objectivity which I am trying to sketch. The primary distortion is the illusion of symmetry in the chart's dichotomy, making any position appear, first, simply alternative and, second, mutually exclusive. A map of tensions and resonances between the fixed ends of a charged dichotomy better represents the potent politics and epistemologies of embodied, therefore accountable, objectivity. For example, local knowledges have also to be in tension with the productive structurings that force unequal translations and exchanges—material and semiotic—within the webs of knowledge and power. Webs *can* have the property of systematicity, even of centrally structured global systems with deep filaments and tenacious tendrils into time, space, and consciousness, the dimensions of world history. Feminist accountability requires a knowledge tuned to resonance, not to dichotomy. Gender is a field of structured and structuring difference, where the tones of extreme localization, of the intimately personal and individualized body, vibrate in the same field with global high tension emissions. Feminist embodiment, then, is not about fixed location in a reified body, female or otherwise, but about nodes in fields, inflections in orientations, and responsibility for difference in material-semiotic fields of meaning. Embodiment is significant prosthesis; objectivity cannot be about fixed vision when what counts as an object is precisely what world history turns out to be about.

How should one be positioned in order to see in this situation of tensions, resonances, transformations, resistances, and complicities? Here, primate vision is not immediately a very powerful metaphor or technology for feminist political-epistemological clarification, since it seems to present to consciousness already processed and objectified fields; things seem already fixed and distanced. But the visual metaphor allows one to go beyond fixed appearances, which are only the end products. The metaphor invites us to investigate the varied apparatuses of visual production, including the prosthetic technologies interfaced with our biological eyes and brains. And here we find highly particular machineries for processing regions of the electro-magnetic spectrum into our pictures of the world. It is in the intricacies of these visualization technologies in which we are embedded that we will find metaphors and means for understanding and intervening in the patterns of objectification in the world, that is, the patterns of reality for which we must be accountable. In these metaphors, we find means for appreciating simultaneously *both* the concrete, "real" aspect and the aspect of semiosis and production in what we call scientific knowledge.

I am arguing for politics and epistemologies of location, positioning, and situating, where partiality and not universality is the condition of being heard to make rational knowledge claims. These are claims on people's lives; the view from a body, always a complex, contradictory, structuring and structured body, versus the view from above, from nowhere, from simplicity. Only the god-trick is forbidden. Here is a criterion for deciding the science question in militarism, that dream science/technology of perfect language, perfect communication, final order.

Feminism loves another science: the sciences and politics of interpretation, translation, stuttering, and the partly understood. Feminism is about the sciences of the multiple subject with (at least) double vision. Feminism is about a

critical vision consequent upon a critical positioning in inhomogeneous gendered social space.[10] Translation is always interpretative, critical, and partial.
Here is a ground for conversation, rationality, and objectivity—which is power-
sensitive, not pluralist, "conversation." It is not even the mythic cartoons of
physics and mathematics—incorrectly caricatured in anti-science ideology as
exact, hyper-simple knowledges—that have come to represent the hostile other
to feminist paradigmatic models of scientific knowledge, but the dreams of the
perfectly known in high-technology, permanently militarized scientific productions and positionings, the god-trick of a Star Wars paradigm of rational knowledge. So location is about vulnerability; location resists the politics of closure,
finality, or, to borrow from Althusser, feminist objectivity resists "simplification
in the last instance." That is because feminist embodiment resists fixation and is
insatiably curious about the webs of differential positioning. There is no single
feminist standpoint because our maps require too many dimensions for that
metaphor to ground our visions. But the feminist standpoint theorists' goal
of an epistemology and politics of engaged, accountable positioning remains
eminently potent. The goal is better accounts of the world, that is, "science."

Above all, rational knowledge does not pretend to disengagement: to be
from everywhere and so nowhere, to be free from interpretation, from being
represented, to be fully self-contained or fully formalizable. Rational knowledge
is a process of ongoing critical interpretation among "fields" of interpreters and
decoders. Rational knowledge is power-sensitive conversation (King, 1987a):

> knowledge:community::knowledge:power
> hermeneutics:semiology::critical interpretation:codes.

Decoding and transcoding plus translation and criticism; all are necessary. So
science becomes the paradigmatic model not of closure, but of that which is
contestable and contested. Science becomes the myth not of what escapes human
agency and responsibility in a realm above the fray, but rather of accountability
and responsibility for translations and solidarities linking the cacophonous
visions and visionary voices that characterize the knowledges of the subjugated.
A splitting of senses, a confusion of voice and sight, rather than clear and distinct
ideas, becomes the metaphor for the ground of the rational. We seek not the
knowledges ruled by phallogocentrism (nostalgia for the presence of the one true
Word) and disembodied vision, but those ruled by partial sight and limited voice.
We do not seek partiality for its own sake, but for the sake of the connections
and unexpected openings situated knowledges make possible. The only way to
find a larger vision is to be somewhere in particular. The science question in
feminism is about objectivity as positioned rationality. Its images are not the
products of escape and transcendence of limits, i.e., the view from above, but
the joining of partial views and halting voices into a collective subject position
that promises a vision of the means of ongoing finite embodiment, of living
within limits and contradictions, i.e., of views from somewhere.

Objects as Actors: The Apparatus of Bodily Production

Throughout this reflection on "objectivity," I have refused to resolve the ambiguities built into referring to science without differentiating its extraordinary range of contexts. Through the insistent ambiguity, I have foregrounded a field of commonalities binding exact, physical, natural, social, political, biological, and human sciences; and I have tied this whole heterogeneous field of academically (and industrially, for example, in publishing, the weapons trade, and pharmaceuticals) institutionalized knowledge production to a meaning of science that insists on its potency in ideological struggles. But, partly in order to give play to both the specificities and the highly permeable boundaries of meanings in discourse on science, I would like to suggest a resolution to one ambiguity. Throughout the field of meanings constituting science, one of the commonalities concerns the status of any object of knowledge and of related claims about the faithfulness of our accounts to a "real world," no matter how mediated for us and no matter how complex and contradictory these worlds may be. Feminists, and others who have been most active as critics of the sciences and their claims or associated ideologies, have shied away from doctrines of scientific objectivity in part because of the suspicion that an "object" of knowledge is a passive and inert thing. Accounts of such objects can seem to be either appropriations of a fixed and determined world reduced to resource for the instrumentalist projects of destructive Western societies, or they can be seen as masks for interests, usually dominating interests.

For example, "sex" as an object of biological knowledge appears regularly in the guise of biological determinism, threatening the fragile space for social constructionism and critical theory, with their attendant possibilities for active and transformative intervention, called into being by feminist concepts of gender as socially, historically, and semiotically positioned difference. And yet, to lose authoritative biological accounts of sex, which set up productive tensions with its binary pair, gender, seems to be to lose too much; it seems to be to lose not just analytic power within a particular Western tradition, but the body itself as anything but a blank page for social inscriptions, including those of biological discourse. The same problem of loss attends a radical "reduction" of the objects of physics or of any other sciences to the ephemera of discursive production and social construction.[11]

But the difficulty and loss are not necessary. They derive partly from the analytical tradition, deeply indebted to Aristotle and to the transformative history of "White Capitalist Patriarchy" (how may we name this scandalous Thing?) that turns everything into a resource for appropriation, in which an object of knowledge is finally itself only matter for the seminal power, the act, of the knower. Here, the object both guarantees and refreshes the power of the knower, but any status as *agent* in the productions of knowledge must be denied the object. It—the world—must, in short, be objectified as thing, not as an agent; it must be matter for the self-formation of the only social being in the productions of knowledge, the human knower. Zoe Sofoulis (1988) identified the structure of this mode of knowing in technoscience as "resourcing"—the second-birthing of Man through the homogenizing of all the world's body into resource for his perverse projects. Nature is only the raw material of culture, appropriated, preserved, enslaved, exalted, or otherwise made flexible for disposal by culture in the logic of capitalist colonialism. Similarly, sex is only the matter to the act of gender; the productionist logic seems inescapable in traditions of Western binarisms. This analytical and historical narrative logic accounts for my nervousness about the sex/gender distinction in the recent history of feminist theory. Sex is "resourced" for its re-presentation as gender, which "we" can control. It has seemed all but impossible to avoid the trap of an appropriationist logic of domination built into the nature/culture binarism and its generative lineage, including the sex/gender distinction.

It seems clear that feminist accounts of objectivity and embodiment—that is, of a world—of the kind sketched in this chapter require a deceptively simple manoeuvre within inherited Western analytical traditions, a manoeuvre begun in dialectics, but stopping short of the needed revisions. Situated knowledges require that the object of knowledge be pictured as an actor and agent, not a screen or a ground or a resource, never finally as slave to the master that closes off the dialectic in his unique agency and authorship of "objective" knowledge. The point is paradigmatically clear in critical approaches to the social and human sciences, where the agency of people studied itself transforms the entire project of producing social theory. Indeed, coming to terms with the agency of the "objects" studied is the only way to avoid gross error and false knowledge of many kinds in these sciences. But the same point must apply to the other knowledge projects called sciences. A corollary of the insistence that ethics and politics covertly or overtly provide the bases for objectivity in the sciences as a heterogeneous whole, and not just in the social sciences, is granting the status of agent/actor to the "objects" of the world. Actors come in many and wonderful forms. Accounts of a "real" world do not, then, depend on a logic of "discovery," but on a power-charged social relation of "conversation." The world neither speaks itself nor disappears in favour of a master decoder. The codes of the world are not still, waiting only to be read. The world is not raw material for humanization; the thorough attacks on humanism, another branch of "death of the subject" discourse, have made this point quite clear. In some critical sense that is crudely hinted at by the clumsy category of the social or of agency, the world encountered in knowledge projects is an active entity. In so far as a scientific account has been able to engage this dimension of the world as object of knowledge, faithful knowledge can be imagined and can make claims on us. But no particular doctrine of representation or decoding or discovery guarantees anything. The approach I am recommending is not a version of "realism," which has proved a rather poor way of engaging with the world's active agency.

My simple, perhaps simple-minded, manoeuvre is obviously not new in Western philosophy, but it has a special feminist edge to it in relation to the science question in feminism and to the linked questions of gender as situated difference and of female embodiment. Ecofeminists have perhaps been most insistent on some version of the world as active subject, not as resource to be mapped and appropriated in bourgeois, Marxist, or masculinist projects. Acknowledging the agency of the world in knowledge makes room for some unsettling possibilities, including a sense of the world's independent sense of humour. Such a sense of humour is not comfortable for humanists and others committed to the world as resource. Richly evocative figures exist for feminist visualizations of the world as witty agent. We need not lapse into an appeal to a primal mother resisting becoming resource. The Coyote or Trickster, embodied in American Southwest Indian accounts, suggests our situation when we give up mastery but keep searching for fidelity, knowing all the while we will be hoodwinked. I think these are useful myths for scientists who might be our allies. Feminist objectivity makes room for surprises and ironies at the heart of all knowledge production; we are not in charge of the world. We just live here and try to strike up non-innocent conversations by means of our prosthetic devices, including our visualization technologies. No wonder science fiction has been such a rich writing practice in recent feminist theory. I like to see feminist theory as a reinvented coyote discourse obligated to its enabling sources in many kinds of heterogeneous accounts of the world.

Another rich feminist practice in science in the last couple of decades illustrates particularly well the "activation" of the previously passive categories of objects of knowledge. The activation permanently problematizes binary distinctions like sex and gender, without however eliminating their strategic utility. I refer to the reconstructions in primatology, especially but not only women's practice as primatologists, evolutionary biologists, and behavioural ecologists, of what may count as sex, especially as female sex, in scientific accounts (Haraway, 1989b). The *body,* the object of biological discourse, itself becomes a most engaging being. Claims of biological determinism can never be the same again. When female "sex" has been so thoroughly re-theorized and revisualized that it emerges as practically indistinguishable from "mind," something basic has happened to the categories of biology. The biological female peopling current biological behavioural accounts has almost no passive properties left. She is structuring and active in every respect; the "body" is an agent, not a resource. Difference is theorized *biologically* as situational, not intrinsic, at every level from gene to foraging pattern, thereby fundamentally changing the biological politics of the body. The relations between sex and gender have to be categorically reworked within these frames of knowledge. I would like to suggest this trend in explanatory strategies in biology as an allegory for interventions faithful to projects of feminist objectivity. The point is not that these new pictures of the biological female are simply true or not open to contestation and conversation. Quite the opposite. But these pictures foreground knowledge as situated conversation at every level of its articulation. The boundary between animal and human is one of the stakes in this allegory, as well as that between machine and organism.

So I will close with a final category useful to a feminist theory of situated knowledges: the apparatus of bodily production. In her analysis of the production of the poem as an object of literary value, Katie King offers tools that clarify matters in the objectivity debates among feminists. King suggests the term "apparatus of literary production" to highlight the emergence of what is embodied as literature at the intersection of art, business, and technology. The apparatus of literary production is a matrix from which "literature" is born. Focusing on the potent object of value called the "poem," King applies her analytic frame to the relation of women and writing technologies (King, 1987b). I would like to adapt her work to understanding the generation—the actual production and reproduction—of bodies and other objects of value in scientific knowledge projects. At first glance, there is a limitation to using King's scheme inherent in the "facticity" of biological discourse that is absent from literary discourse and its knowledge claims. Are biological bodies "produced" or "generated" in the same strong sense as poems? From the early stirrings of Romanticism in the late eighteenth century, many poets and biologists have believed that poetry and organisms are siblings. *Frankenstein* may be read as a meditation on this proposition. I continue to believe in this potent proposition, but in a postmodern and not a Romantic manner of belief. I wish to translate the ideological dimensions of "facticity" and "the organic" into a cumbersome entity called a "material-semiotic actor." This unwieldy term is intended to highlight the object of knowledge as an active, meaning-generating axis of the apparatus of bodily production, without *ever* implying immediate presence of such objects or, what is the same thing, their final or unique determination of what can count as objective knowledge at a particular historical juncture. Like King's objects called "poems," which are sites of literary production where language also is an actor independent of intentions and authors, bodies as objects of knowledge are material-semiotic generative nodes. Their *boundaries* materialize in social interaction. Boundaries are drawn by mapping practices; "objects" do not pre-exist as such. Objects are boundary projects. But boundaries shift from within; boundaries are very tricky. What boundaries provisionally contain remains generative, productive of meanings and bodies. Siting (sighting) boundaries is a risky practice.

Objectivity is not about dis-engagement, but about mutual *and* usually unequal structuring, about taking risks in a world where "we" are permanently mortal, that is, not in "final" control. We have, finally, no clear and distinct ideas. The various contending biological bodies emerge at the intersection of biological research and writing, medical and other business practices, and technology, such as the visualization technologies enlisted as metaphors in this chapter. But also invited into that node of intersection is the analogue to the lively languages that actively intertwine in the production of literary value: the coyote and pro-tean embodiments of a world as witty agent and actor. Perhaps the world resists being reduced to mere resource because it is—not mother/matter/mutter—but coyote, a figure for the always problematic, always potent tie of meaning and bodies. Feminist embodiment, feminist hopes for partiality, objectivity and sit-uated knowledges, turn on conversations and codes at this potent node in fields of possible bodies and meanings. Here is where science, science fantasy, and science fiction converge in the objectivity question in feminism. Perhaps our hopes for accountability, for politics, for ecofeminism, turn on revisioning the world as coding trickster with whom we must learn to converse.

Notes

1. This chapter originated as a commentary on Harding (1986), at the Western Division meetings of the American Philosophical Association, San Francisco, March 1987. Sup-port during the writing of this paper was generously provided by the Alpha Fund of the Institute for Advanced Study, Princeton, New Jersey. Thanks especially to Joan Scott, Rayna Rapp, Judy Newton, Judy Butler, Lila Abu-Lughod, and Dorinne Kondo.

2. For example, see Knorr-Cetina and Mulkay (1983); Bijker et al. (1987); and especially, Latour (1984, 1988). Borrowing from Michel Tournier's *Vendredi* (1967), Latour's bril-liant and maddening aphoristic polemic against all forms of reductionism makes the essential point for feminists: "Méfiez-vous de la pureté; c'est le vitriol de l'âme" (Latour, 1984, p. 171). Latour is not otherwise a notable feminist theorist, but he might be made into one by readings as perverse as those he makes of the laboratory, that great machine for making significant mistakes faster than anyone else can, and so gaining world-changing power. The laboratory for Latour is the railroad industry of epistemology, where facts can only be made to run on the tracks laid down from the laboratory out. Those who control the railroads control the surrounding territory. How could we have forgotten? But now it's not so much the bankrupt railroads we need as the satellite network. Facts run on lightbeams these days.

3. For an elegant and very helpful elucidation of a non-cartoon version of this argument, see White (1987). I still want more; and unfulfilled desire can be a powerful seed for changing the stories.

4. In her analysis exploring the fault line between modernism and postmodernism in ethnography and anthropology—in which the high stakes are the authorization or prohibition to craft *comparative* knowledge across "cultures," from some epistemolog-ically grounded vantage point *either* inside, outside, or in dialogical relation with any unit of analysis—Marilyn Strathern (1987) made the crucial observation that it is not the written ethnography that is parallel to the work of art as object-of-knowledge, but the *culture*. The Romantic and modernist natural-technical objects of knowledge, in science and in other cultural practice, stand on one side of this divide. The postmod-ernist formation stands on the other side, with its "anti-aesthetic" of permanently split, problematized, always systems, selves, and cultures. "Objectivity" in a postmodern frame cannot be about unproblematic objects; it must be about specific prosthesis and translation. Objectivity, which at root has been about crafting *comparative* knowledge (how to name things to be stable and to be like each other), becomes a question of the politics of redrawing of boundaries in order to have non-innocent conversations and connections. What is at stake in the debates about modernism and postmodernism is the pattern of relationships between and within bodies and language.

5. Zoe Sofoulis (1988) has produced a dazzlingly (she will forgive me the metaphor) theoretical treatment of technoscience, the psychoanalysis of science fiction culture, and the metaphorics of extra-terrestrialism, including a wonderful focus on the ideologies and philosophies of light, illumination, and discovery in Western mythics of science and technology. My essay was revised in dialogue with Sofoulis's arguments and metaphors in her Ph.D. dissertation.

6. Crucial to this discussion are Harding (1986), Keller (1985), Hartsock (1983a, 1983b), Flax (1983, 1987), Keller and Grontkowski (1983), II. Rose (1986), Haraway (1985), and Petchesky (1987).

7. John Varley's science fiction short story called "The Persistence of Vision" is part of the inspiration for this section. In the story, Varley constructs a utopian community designed and built by the deaf-blind. He then explores these people's technologies and other mediations of communication and their relations to sighted children and visitors (Varley, 1978). In "Blue Champagne," Varley (1986) transmutes the theme to interrogate the politics of intimacy and technology for a paraplegic young woman whose prosthetic device, the golden gypsy, allows her full mobility. But since the infinitely costly device is owned by an intergalactic communications and entertainment empire for which she works as a media star making "feelies," she may keep her technological, intimate, enabling, other self only in exchange for her complicity in the commodification of all experience. What are her limits to the reinvention of experience for sale? Is the personal political under the sign of simulation? One way to read Varley's repeated investigations of finally always limited embodiments, differently abled beings, prosthetic technologies, and cyborgian encounters with their finitude despite their extraordinary transcendence of "organic" orders is to find an allegory for the personal and political in the historical mythic time of the late twentieth century, the era of techno-biopolitics. Prosthesis becomes a fundamental category for understanding our most intimate selves. Prosthesis is semiosis, the making of meanings and bodies, not for transcendence but for power-charged communication.

8. I owe my understanding of the experience of these photographs to Jim Clifford, University of California at Santa Cruz, who identified their "land ho!" effect on the reader.

9. Joan Scott reminded me that Teresa de Lauretis (1986, pp. 14–15) put it like this:

> Differences among women may be better understood as differences within women.... But once understood in their constitutive power—once it is understood, that is, that these differences not only constitute each woman's consciousness and subjective limits but all together define the *female subject of feminism* in its very specificity, its inherent and at least for now irreconcilable contradiction—these differences, then, cannot be again collapsed into a fixed identity, a sameness of all women as Woman, or a representation of Feminism as a coherent and available image.

10. Harding (1986, p. 18) suggested that gender has three dimensions, each historically specific: gender symbolism, the social-sexual division of labour, and processes of constructing individual gendered identity. I would enlarge her point to note that there is no reason to expect the three dimensions to co-vary or co-determine each other, at least not directly. That is, extremely steep gradients between contrasting terms in gender symbolism may very well not correlate with sharp social-sexual divisions of labour or social power, but may be closely related to sharp racial stratification or something else. Similarly, the processes of gendered subject formation may not be directly illuminated by knowledge of the sexual division of labour or the gender symbolism in the particular historical situation under examination. On the other hand, we should expect mediated relations among the dimensions. The mediations might move through quite different social axes of organization of both symbols, practice, and identity, such as race. And vice versa. I would suggest also that science, as well as gender or race, might usefully be broken up into such a multi-part scheme of symbolism, social practice, and subject position. More than three dimensions suggest themselves when the parallels are drawn. The different dimensions of, for example, gender, race, and science might mediate relations among dimensions on a parallel chart. That is, racial divisions of labour might mediate the patterns of connection between symbolic connections and formation of individual subject position on the science or gender chart. Or formations of gendered or racial subjectivity might mediate the relations between scientific social division of labour and scientific symbolic patterns.

The chart below begins an analysis by parallel dissections. In the chart (and in reality?), both gender and science are analytically asymmetrical; i.e., each term contains and obscures a structuring hierarchicalized binarism, sex/gender and nature/science. Each binarism orders the silent term by a logic of appropriation, as resource to product, nature to culture, potential to actual. Both poles of the binarism are constructed and structure each other dialectically. Within each voiced or explicit term, further asymmetrical splittings can be excavated, as from gender, masculine to feminine, and from science, hard sciences to soft sciences. This is a point about remembering how a particular analytical tool works, willy nilly, intended or not. The chart reflects common ideological aspects of discourse on science and gender and may help as an analytical tool to crack open mystified units like Science or Woman.

Gender	Science
symbolic system	symbolic system
social division of labour	social division of labour
(by sex, by race, etc.)	(by craft, industrial, or post-industrial logics)
individual identity/subject position	individual identity/subject position
(desiring/desired;	(knower/known;
autonomous/relational)	scientist/other)
material culture	material culture
(gender paraphernalia and daily gender technologies: the narrow tracks on which sexual difference runs)	(laboratories: the narrow tracks on which facts run)
dialectic of construction and discovery	dialectic of construction and discovery

11.   Evelyn Keller (1987) insists on the important possibilities opened up by the construction of the intersection of the distinction between sex and gender, on the one hand, and nature and science, on the other. She also insists on the need to hold to some nondiscursive grounding in "sex" and "nature," perhaps what I am calling the "body" and "world."

References

Anzaldúa, Gloria. (1987). *Borderlands/La Frontera*. San Francisco: Spinsters/Aunt Lute.
Bijker, Wiebe E., Hughes, Thomas, P., and Pinch, Trevor, eds. (1987). *The Social Construction of Technological Systems*. Cambridge, MA: MIT Press.
Bryan, C. D. B. (1987). *The National Geographic Society: 100 Years of Adventure and Discovery*. New York: Abrams.
de Lauretis, Teresa. (1986). "Feminist studies/critical studies: issues, terms, and contexts," in de Lauretis, ed., *Feminist Studies/Critical Studies*. Bloomington: Indiana University Press, pp. 1–19.
Eco, Umberto. (1980). *Il nome della rosa*. Milano: Bompiani.
Flax, Jane. (1983). "Political philosophy and the patriarchal unconscious: a psychoanalytic perspective on epistemology and metaphysics," in Harding and Hintikka (1983), pp. 245–82.
———. (1987). "Postmodernism and gender relations in feminist theory," *Signs* 12(4): 621–43.
Haraway, Donna J. (1985). "Manifesto for cyborgs: science, technology, and socialist feminism in the 1980s," *Socialist Review* 80: 65–108. (This vol. pp. 149–81.)
———. (1989). *Primate Visions: Gender, Race, and Nature in the World of Modern Science*. New York: Routledge.
Harding, Sandra. (1986). *The Science Question in Feminism*. Ithaca: Cornell University Press.
——— and Hintikka, Merill, eds. (1983). *Discovering Reality: Feminist Perspectives on Epistemology, Metaphysics, Methodology, and Philosophy of Science*. Dordrecht: Reidel.
Hartsock, Nancy. (1983a). "The feminist standpoint: developing the ground for a specifically feminist historical materialism," in Harding and Hintikka (1983), pp. 283–310.
———. (1983b). *Money, Sex, and Power*. New York: Longman; Boston: Northeastern University Press, 1984.
Keller, Evelyn Fox. (1985). *Reflections on Gender and Science*. New Haven: Yale University Press.
———. (1987). "The gender/science system: or, is sex to gender as nature is to science?" *Hypatia* 2(3): 37–49.
——— and Grontkowski, Christine. (1983). "The mind's eye," in Harding and Hintikka (1983), pp. 207–24.

King, Katie. (1987a). "Canons without innocence." University of California at Santa Cruz PhD thesis
———. (1987b). *The Passing Dreams of Choice... Once Before and After: Audre Lorde and the Apparatus of Literary Production,* book prospectus, University of Maryland at College Park.
Knorr-Cetina, Karin and Mulkay, Michael, eds. (1983). *Science Observed: Perspectives on the Social Study of Science.* Beverly Hills: Sage.
Kuhn, Annette. (1982). *Women's Pictures: Feminism and Cinema.* London: Routledge & Kegan Paul.
Latour, Bruno. (1984). *Les microbes, guerre et paix, suivi des irréductions.* Paris: Métailié.
———. (1988). *The Pasteurization of France, followed by Irreductions: A Politico-Scientific Essay.* Cambridge, MA: Harvard University Press.
Mohanty, Chandra Talpade. (1984). "Under western eyes: feminist scholarship and colonial discourse," *Boundary* 2, 3 (12/13): 333–58.
Petchesky, Rosalind Pollack. (1987). "Fetal images: the power of visual culture in the politics of reproduction," *Feminist Studies* 13(2): 263–92.
Rose, Hilary. (1986). "Women's work: women's knowledge," in Juliet Mitchell and Ann Oakley, eds., *What Is Feminism? A Re-Examination.* New York: Pantheon, pp. 161–83.
Sandoval, Chela. (n.d.). *Yours in Struggle: Women Respond to Racism, a Report on the National Women's Studies Association.* Oakland, CA: Center for Third World Organizing.
Sofoulis, Zoe. (1988). "Through the lumen: Frankenstein and the optics of re-origination," University of California at Santa Cruz, PhD thesis.
Strathern, Marilyn. (1987). "Out of context: the persuasive fictions of anthropology," *Current Anthropology* 28(3): 251–81.
Tournier, Michel. (1967). *Vendredi.* Paris: Gallimard.
Varley, John. (1978). "The persistence of vision," in *The Persistence of Vision.* New York: Dell, pp. 263–316.
———. (1986). "Blue champagne," in *Blue Champagne.* New York: Berkeley, pp. 17–79.
von Bertalanffy, Ludwig. (1968). *General Systems Theory.* New York: Braziller.
White, Hayden. (1987). *The Content of the Form: Narrative Discourse and Historical Representation.* Baltimore: Johns Hopkins University Press.

7

Learning from the Outsider Within: The Sociological Significance of Black Feminist Thought

PATRICIA HILL COLLINS

Black women have long occupied marginal positions in academic settings. I argue that many Black female intellectuals have made creative use of their marginality— their "outsider within" status—to produce Black feminist thought that reflects a special standpoint on self, family, and society. I describe and explore the sociological significance of three characteristic themes in such thought: (1) Black women's self-definition and self-valuation; (2) the interlocking nature of oppression; and (3) the importance of Afro-American women's culture. After considering how Black women might draw upon these key themes as outsiders within to generate a distinctive standpoint on existing sociological paradigms, I conclude by suggesting that other sociologists would also benefit by placing greater trust in the creative potential of their own personal and cultural biographies.

Afro-American women have long been privy to some of the most intimate secrets of white society. Countless numbers of Black women have ridden buses to their white "families," where they not only cooked, cleaned, and executed other domestic duties, but where they also nurtured their "other" children, shrewdly offered guidance to their employers, and frequently became honorary members of their white "families." These women have seen white elites, both actual and aspiring, from perspectives largely obscured from their Black spouses and from these groups themselves.[1]

On one level, this "insider" relationship has been satisfying to all involved. The memoirs of affluent whites often mention their love for their Black "mothers," while accounts of Black domestic workers stress the sense of self-affirmation they experienced at seeing white power demystified—of knowing that it was not the intellect, talent, or humanity of their employers that supported their superior status, but largely just the advantages of racism.[2] But on another level, these same Black women knew they could never belong to their white "families." In spite of their involvement, they remained "outsiders."[3]

This "outsider within" status has provided a special standpoint on self, family, and society for Afro-American women.[4] A careful review of the emerging Black

103

feminist literature reveals that many Black intellectuals, especially those in touch with their marginality in academic settings, tap this standpoint in producing distinctive analyses of race, class, and gender. For example, Zora Neal Hurston's 1937 novel, *Their Eyes Were Watching God,* most certainly reflects her skill at using the strengths and transcending the limitations both of her academic training and of her background in traditional Afro-American community life.[5] Black feminist historian E. Frances White (1984) suggests that Black women's ideas have been honed at the juncture between movements for racial and sexual equality, and contends that Afro-American women have been pushed by "their marginalization in both arenas" to create Black feminism. Finally, Black feminist critic bell hooks captures the unique standpoint that the outsider within status can generate. In describing her small-town, Kentucky childhood, she notes, "living as we did—on the edge—we developed a particular way of seeing reality. We looked both from the outside and in from the inside out . . . we understood both" (1984:vii).

In spite of the obstacles that can confront outsiders within, such individuals can benefit from this status. Simmel's (1921) essay on the sociological signifi-cance of what he called the "stranger" offers a helpful starting point for under-standing the largely unexplored area of Black female outsider within status and the usefulness of the standpoint it might produce. Some of the potential benefits of outsider within status include: (1) Simmel's definition of "objectivity" as "a peculiar composition of nearness and remoteness, concern and indifference"; (2) the tendency for people to confide in a "stranger" in ways they never would with each other; and (3) the ability of the "stranger" to see patterns that may be more difficult for those immersed in the situation to see. Mannheim (1936) labels the "strangers" in academia "marginal intellectuals" and argues that the critical posture such individuals bring to academic endeavors may be essential to the creative development of academic disciplines themselves. Finally, in assess-ing the potentially positive qualities of social difference, specifically marginality, Lee notes, "for a time this marginality can be a most stimulating, albeit often a painful, experience. For some, it is debilitating . . . for others, it is an excitement to creativity" (1973:64).[6]

Sociologists might benefit greatly from serious consideration of the emerg-ing, cross-disciplinary literature that I label Black feminist thought, precisely because, for many Afro-American female intellectuals, "marginality" has been an excitement to creativity. As outsiders within, Black feminist scholars may be one of many distinct groups of marginal intellectuals whose standpoints promise to enrich contemporary sociological discourse. Bringing this group— as well as others who share an outsider within status vis-à-vis sociology—into the center of analysis may reveal aspects of reality obscured by more orthodox approaches.

In the remainder of this essay, I examine the sociological significance of the Black feminist thought stimulated by Black women's outsider within status.

First, I outline three key themes that characterize the emerging cross-disciplinary literature that I label Black feminist thought.[7] For each theme, I summarize its content, supply examples from Black feminist and other works that illustrate its nature, and discuss its importance. Second, I explain the significance these key themes in Black feminist thought may have for sociologists by describing why Black women's outside/within status might generate a distinctive standpoint vis-à-vis existing sociological paradigm. Third, I discuss one general implication of this essay for social scientists: namely, the potential usefulness of identifying and using one's own standpoint in conducting research.

Three Key Themes in Black Feminist Thought

Black feminist thought consists of ideas produced by Black women that clarify a standpoint of and for Black women. Several assumptions underlie this working definition. First, the definition suggests that it is impossible to separate the structure and thematic content of thought from the historical and material conditions shaping the lives of its producers (Berger and Luckmann 1966; Mannheim 1936). Therefore, while Black feminist thought may be recorded by others, it is produced by Black women. Second, the definition assumes that Black women possess a unique standpoint on, or perspective of, their experiences and that there will be certain commonalities of perception shared by Black women as a group. Third, while living life as Black women may produce certain commonalities of outlook, the diversity of class, region, age, and sexual orientation, shaping individual Black women's lives has resulted in different expressions of these common themes. Thus, universal themes included in the Black women's standpoint may be experienced and expressed differently by distinct groups of Afro-American women. Finally, the definition assumes that, while a Black women's standpoint exists, its contours may not be clear to Black women themselves. Therefore, one role for Black female intellectuals is to produce facts and theories about the Black female experience that will clarify a Black woman's standpoint for Black women. In other words, Black feminist thought contains observations and interpretations about Afro-American womanhood that describe and explain different expressions of common themes.

No one Black feminist platform exists from which one can measure the "correctness" of a particular thinker; nor should there be one. Rather, as I defined it above, there is a long and rich tradition of Black feminist thought. Much of it has been oral and has been produced by ordinary Black women in their roles as mothers, teachers, musicians, and preachers.[8] Since the civil rights and women's movements, Black women's ideas have been increasingly documented and are reaching wider audiences. The following discussion of three key themes in Black feminist thought is itself part of this emerging process of documentation and interpretation. The three themes I have chosen are not exhaustive but, in my assessment, they do represent the thrust of much of the existing dialogue.

The Meaning of Self-Definition and Self-Valuation

An affirmation of the importance of Black women's self-definition and self-valuation is the first key theme that pervades historical and contemporary statements of Black feminist thought. Self-definition involves challenging the political knowledge-validation process that has resulted in externally-defined, stereotypical images of Afro-American womanhood. In contrast, self-valuation stresses the content of Black women's self-definitions—namely, replacing externally derived images with authentic Black female images.

Both Mae King's (1973) and Cheryl Gilkes's (1981) analyses of the importance of stereotypes offer useful insights for grasping the importance of Black women's self-definition. King suggests that stereotypes represent externally defined, controlling images of Afro-American womanhood that have been central to the dehumanization of Black women and the exploitation of Black women's labor. Gilkes points out that Black women's assertiveness in resisting the multifaceted oppression they experience has been a consistent threat to the status quo. As punishment, Black women have been assaulted with a variety of externally-defined negative images designed to control assertive Black female behavior.

The value of King's and Gilkes's analyses lies in their emphasis on the function of stereotypes in controlling dominated groups. Both point out that replacing negative stereotypes with ostensibly positive ones can be equally problematic if the function of stereotypes as controlling images remains unrecognized. John Gwaltney's (1980) interview with Nancy White, a 73-year-old Black woman, suggests that ordinary Black women may also be aware of the power of these controlling images in their everyday experiences. In the following passage, Ms. White assesses the difference between the controlling images applied to Afro-American and white women as being those of degree, and not of kind:

> My mother used to say that the black woman is the white man's mule and the white woman is his dog. Now, she said that to say this: we do the heavy work and get beat whether we do it well or not. But the white woman is closer to the master and he pats them on the head and lets them sleep in the house, but he ain't gon' treat neither one like he was dealing with a person (1980:148).

This passage suggests that while both groups are stereotyped, albeit in different ways, the function of the images is to dehumanize and control both groups. Seen in this light, it makes little sense, in the long run, for Black women to exchange one set of controlling images for another even if, in the short run, positive stereotypes bring better treatment.

The insistence on Black female self-definition reframes the entire dialogue from one of determining the technical accuracy of an image, to one stressing the power dynamics underlying the very process of definition itself. Black feminists have questioned not only what has been said about Black women, but the credibility and the intentions of those possessing the power to define. When Black women define themselves, they clearly reject the taken-for-granted assumption that those in positions granting them the authority to describe and analyze reality are entitled to do so. Regardless of the actual content of Black women's self-definitions, the act of insisting on Black female self-definition validates Black women's power as human subjects.

The related theme of Black female self-valuation pushes this entire process one step further. While Black female self-definition speaks to the power dynamics involved in the act of defining images of self and community, the theme of Black female self-valuation addresses the actual content of these self-definitions. Many of the attributes extant in Black female stereotypes are actually distorted renderings of those aspects of Black female behavior seen as most threatening to white patriarchy (Gilkes, 1981; White, 1985). For example, aggressive Afro-American women are threatening because they challenge white patriarchal definitions of femininity. To ridicule assertive women by labeling them Sapphires reflects an effort to put all women in their place. In their roles as central figures in socializing the next generation of Black adults, strong mothers are similarly threatening, because they contradict patriarchal views of family power relations. To ridicule strong Black mothers by labeling them matriarchs (Higginbotham, 1982) reflects a similar effort to control another aspect of Black female behavior that is especially threatening to the status quo.

When Black females choose to value those aspects of Afro-American womanhood that are stereotyped, ridiculed, and maligned in academic scholarship and the popular media, they are actually questioning some of the basic ideas used to control dominated groups in general. It is one thing to counsel Afro-American women to resist the Sapphire stereotype by altering their behavior to become meek, locale, and stereotypically "feminine." It is quite another to advise Black women to embrace their assertiveness, to value their sassiness, and to continue to use these qualities to survive in and transcend the harsh environments that circumscribe so many Black women's lives. By defining and valuing assertiveness and other "unfeminine" qualities as necessary and functional attributes for Afro-American womanhood, Black women's self-valuation challenges the content of externally defined controlling images.

This Black feminist concern—that Black women create their own standards for evaluating Afro-American womanhood and value their creations—pervades a wide range of literary and social science works. For example, Alice Walker's 1982 novel, *The Color Purple,* and Ntozake Shange's 1978 choreopoem, *For Colored Girls Who Have Considered Suicide,* are both bold statements of the necessity for Black female self-definition and self-valuation. Lena Wright Myers's (1980) work shows that Black women judge their behavior by comparing themselves to Black women facing similar situations and thus demonstrates the presence of Black female definitions of Afro-American womanhood. The recent spate of Black female historiography suggests that self-defined, self-valuating Black women have long populated the ranks of Afro-American female leaders (Giddings, 1984; Loewenberg and Bogin, 1976).

Black women's insistence on self-definition, self-valuation, and the necessity for a Black female-centered analysis is significant for two reasons. First, defining and valuing one's consciousness of one's own self-defined standpoint in the face of images that foster a self-definition as the objectified "other" is an important way of resisting the dehumanization essential to systems of domination. The status of being the "other" implies being "other than" or different from the assumed norm of white male behavior. In this mode, powerful white males define themselves as subjects, the true actors, and classify people of color and women in terms of their position vis-à-vis this white male hub. Since Black women have been denied the authority to challenge these definitions, this model consists of images that define Black women as a negative other, the virtual antithesis of positive white male images. Moreover, as Brittan and Maynard (1984:199) point out, "domination always involves the objectification of the dominated; all forms of oppression imply the devaluation of the subjectivity of the oppressed."

One of the best examples of this process is described by Judith Rollins (1985). As part of her fieldwork on Black domestics, Rollins worked as a domestic for six months. She describes several incidents where her employers treated her as if she were not really present. On one occasion while she sat in the kitchen having lunch, her employers had a conversation as if she were not there. Her sense of invisibility became so great that she took out a pad of paper and began writing field notes. Even though Rollins wrote for 10 minutes, finished lunch, and returned to work, her employers showed no evidence of having seen her at all. Rollins notes,

> It was this aspect of servitude I found to be one of the strongest affronts to my dignity as a human being. . . . These gestures of ignoring my presence were not, I think, intended as insults; they were expressions of the employers' ability to annihilate the humanness and even, at times, the very existence of me, a servant and a black woman (1985:209).

Racist and sexist ideologies both share the common feature of treating dominated groups—the "others"—as objects lacking full human subjectivity. For example, seeing Black women as obstinate mules and viewing white women as obedient dogs objectifies both groups, but in different ways. Neither is seen as fully human, and therefore both become eligible for race/gender specific modes of domination. But if Black women refuse to accept their assigned status as the quintessential "other," then the entire rationale for such domination is challenged. In brief, abusing a mule or a dog may be easier than abusing a person who is a reflection of one's own humanness.

A second reason that Black female self-definition and self-valuation are significant concerns their value in allowing Afro-American women to reject internalized, psychological oppression (Baldwin, 1980). The potential damage of internalized control to Afro-American women's self-esteem can be great, even to the prepared. Enduring the frequent assaults of controlling images requires considerable inner strength. Nancy White, cited earlier, also points out how debilitating being treated as less than human can be if Black women are not self-defined. She notes, "Now, you know that no woman is a dog or a mule, but if folks keep making you feel that way, if you don't have a mind of your own, you can start letting them tell you what you are" (Gwaltney, 1980:152). Seen in this light, self-definition and self-valuation are not luxuries—they are necessary for Black female survival.

The Interlocking Nature of Oppression

Attention to the interlocking nature of race, gender, and class oppression is a second recurring theme in the works of Black feminists (Beale, 1970; Davis, 1981; Dill, 1983; hooks, 1981; Lewis, 1977; Murray, 1970; Steady, 1981).[9] While different socio-historical periods may have increased the saliency of one or another type of oppression, the thesis of the linked nature of oppression has long pervaded Black feminist thought. For example, Ida Wells Barnett and Frances Ellen Watkins Harper, two prominent Black feminists of the late 1800s, both spoke out against the growing violence directed against Black men. They realized that civil rights held little meaning for Black men and women if the right to life itself went unprotected (Loewenberg and Bogin, 1976:26). Black women's absence from organized feminist movements has mistakenly been attributed to a lack of feminist consciousness. In actuality, Black feminists have possessed an ideological commitment to addressing interlocking oppression yet have been excluded from arenas that would have allowed them to do so (Davis, 1981).

As Barbara Smith points out, "the concept of the simultaneity of oppression is still the crux of a Black feminist understanding of political reality and . . . is one of the most significant ideological contributions of Black feminist thought" (1983:xxxii). This should come as no surprise since Black women should be among the first to realize that minimizing one form of oppression, while essential, may still leave them oppressed in other equally dehumanizing ways. Sojourner Truth knew this when she stated, "there is a great stir about colored men getting their rights, and not colored women theirs, you see the colored men will be masters over the women, and it will be just as bad as before" (Loewenberg and Bogin, 1976:238). To use Nancy White's metaphors, the Black woman as "mule" knows that she is perceived to be an animal. In contrast, the white woman as "dog" may be similarly dehumanized, and may think that she is an equal part of the family when, in actuality, she is a well-cared-for pet. The significant factor shaping Truth's and White's clearer view of their own subordination than that of Black men or white women is their experience at the intersection of multiple structures of domination.[10] Both Truth and White are Black, female, and poor. They therefore have a clearer view of oppression than other groups who occupy more contradictory positions vis-à-vis white male power—unlike white women, they have no illusions that their whiteness will negate female subordination, and unlike Black men, they cannot use a questionable appeal to manhood to neutralize the stigma of being Black.

The Black feminist attention to the interlocking nature of oppression is significant for two reasons. First, this viewpoint shifts the entire locus of investigation from one aimed at explicating elements of race or gender or class oppression to one whose goal is to determine what the links are among these systems. The first approach typically prioritizes one form of oppression as being primary, then handles remaining types of oppression as variables within what is seen as the most important system. For example, the efforts to insert race and gender into Marxist theory exemplify this effort. In contrast, the more holistic approach implied in Black feminist thought treats the interaction among multiple systems as the object of study. Rather than adding to existing theories by inserting previously excluded variables, Black feminists aim to develop new theoretical interpretations of the interaction itself.

Black male scholars, white female scholars, and more recently, Black feminists like bell hooks, may have identified one critical link among interlocking systems of oppression. These groups have pointed out that certain basic ideas crosscut multiple systems of domination. One such idea is either/or dualistic thinking, claimed by hooks to be "the central ideological component of all systems of domination in Western society" (1984:29).

While hooks's claim may be somewhat premature, there is growing scholarly support for her viewpoint.[11] Either/or dualistic thinking, or what I will refer to as the construct of dichotomous oppositional difference, may be a philosophical lynchpin in systems of race, class, and gender oppression. One fundamental characteristic of this construct is the categorization of people, things, and ideas in terms of their difference from one another. For example, the terms in dichotomies such as black/white, male/female, reason/emotion, fact/opinion, and subject/object gain their meaning only in *relation* to their difference from their oppositional counterparts. Another fundamental characteristic of this construct is that difference is not complementary in that the halves of the dichotomy do not enhance each other. Rather, the dichotomous halves are different and inherently opposed to one another. A third and more important characteristic is that these oppositional relationships are intrinsically unstable. Since such dualities rarely represent different but equal relationships, the inherently unstable relationship is resolved by subordinating one half of each pair to the other. Thus, whites rule Blacks, males dominate females, reason is touted as superior to emotion in ascertaining truth, facts supercede opinion in evaluating knowledge, and subjects rule objects. Dichotomous oppositional differences invariably imply relationships of superiority and inferiority, hierarchical relationships that mesh with political economies of domination and subordination.

The oppression experienced by most Black women is shaped by their subordinate status in an array of either/or dualities. Afro-American women have been assigned the inferior half of several dualities, and this placement has been central to their continued domination. For example, the allegedly emotional, passionate nature of Afro-American women has long been used as a rationale for their sexual exploitation. Similarly, denying Black women literacy—then claiming that they lack the facts for sound judgment—illustrates another case of assigning a group inferior status, then using that inferior status as proof of the group's inferiority. Finally, denying Black women agency as subjects and treating them as objectified "others" represents yet another dimension of the power that dichotomous oppositional constructs have in maintaining systems of domination.

While Afro-American women may have a vested interest in recognizing the connections among these dualities that together comprise the construct of dichotomous oppositional difference, that more women have not done so is not surprising. Either/or dualistic thinking is so pervasive that it suppresses other alternatives. As Dill points out, "the choice between identifying as black or female is a product of the patriarchal strategy of divide-and-conquer, and the continued importance of class, patriarchal, and racial divisions perpetuate such choices both within our consciousness and within the concrete realities of our daily lives" (1983:136). In spite of this difficulty, Black women experience oppression in a personal, holistic fashion and emerging Black feminist perspectives appear to be embracing an equally holistic analysis of oppression.

Second, Black feminist attention to the interlocking nature of oppression is significant in that implicit in this view is an alternative humanist vision of societal organization. This alternative world-view is cogently expressed in the following passage from an 1893 speech delivered by the Black feminist educator, Anna Julia Cooper:

> We take our stand on the solidarity of humanity, the oneness of life, and the unnaturalness and injustice of all special favoritisms, whether of sex, race, country, or condition. . . . The colored woman feels that woman's cause is one and universal; and that . . . not till race, color, sex, and condition are seen as accidents, and not the substance of life; not till the universal title of humanity to life, liberty, and the pursuit of happiness is conceded to be inalienable to all; not till then is woman's lesson taught and woman's cause won—not the white woman's nor the black woman's, nor the red woman's, but the cause of every man and of every woman who has writhed silently under a mighty wrong (Loewenberg and Bogin, 1976:330–31).

I cite the above passage at length because it represents one of the clearest statements of the humanist vision extant in Black feminist thought.[12] Black feminists who see the simultaneity of oppression affecting Black women appear to be more sensitive to how these same oppressive systems affect Afro-American men, people of color, women, and the dominant group itself. Thus, while Black feminist activists may work on behalf of Black women, they rarely project separatist solutions to Black female oppression. Rather, the vision is one that, like Cooper's, takes its "stand on the solidarity of humanity."

The Importance of Afro-American Women's Culture

A third key theme characterizing Black feminist thought involves efforts to redefine and explain the importance of Black women's culture. In doing so, Black feminists have not only uncovered previously unexplored areas of the Black female experience, but they have also identified concrete areas of social relations where Afro-American women create and pass on self-definitions and self-valuations essential to coping with the simultaneity of oppression they experience.

In contrast to views of culture stressing the unique, ahistorical values of a particular group, Black feminist approaches have placed greater emphasis on the role of historically specific political economies in explaining the endurance of certain cultural themes. The following definition of culture typifies the approach taken by many Black feminists. According to Mullings, culture is composed of

> the symbols and values that create the ideological frame of reference through which people attempt to deal with the circumstances in which they find themselves. Culture . . . is not composed of static, discrete traits moved from one locale to another. It is constantly changing and transformed, as new forms are created out of old ones. Thus culture . . . does not arise out of nothing: it is created and modified by material conditions (1986a:13).

Seen in this light, Black women's culture may help provide the ideological frame of reference—namely, the symbols and values of self-definition and self-valuation—that assist Black women in seeing the circumstances shaping race, class, and gender oppression. Moreover, Mullings's definition of culture suggests that the values which accompany self-definition and self-valuation will have concrete, material expression: they will be present in social institutions like church and family, in creative expression of art, music, and dance, and, if unsuppressed, in patterns of economic and political activity. Finally, this approach to culture stresses its historically concrete nature. While common themes may link Black women's lives, these themes will be experienced differently by Black women of different classes, ages, regions, and sexual preferences as well as by Black women in different historical settings. Thus, there is no monolithic Black women's culture—rather, there are socially-constructed Black women's cultures that collectively form Black women's culture.

The interest in redefining Black women's culture has directed attention to several unexplored areas of the Black female experience. One such area concerns the interpersonal relationships that Black women share with each other. It appears that the notion of sisterhood—generally understood to mean a supportive feeling of loyalty and attachment to other women stemming from a shared feeling of oppression—has been an important part of Black women's culture (Dill, 1983:132). Two representative works in the emerging tradition of Black feminist research illustrate how this concept of sisterhood, while expressed differently in response to different material conditions, has been a significant feature of Black women's culture. For example, Debra Gray White (1985) documents the ways Black slave women assisted each other in childbirth, cared for each other's children, worked together in sex-segregated work units when pregnant or nursing children, and depended on one another when married to males living on distant farms. White paints a convincing portrait of Black female slave communities where sisterhood was necessary and assumed. Similarly, Gilkes's (1985) work on Black women's traditions in the Sanctified Church suggests that the sisterhood Black women found had tangible psychological and political benefits.[13]

The attention to Black women's culture has stimulated interest in a second type of interpersonal relationship: that shared by Black women with their biological children, the children in their extended families, and with the Black community's children. In reassessing Afro-American motherhood, Black feminist researchers have emphasized the connections between (1) choices available to Black mothers resulting from their placement in historically-specific political economies, (2) Black mothers' perceptions of their children's choices as compared to what mothers thought those choices should be, and (3) actual strategies employed by Black mothers both in raising their children and in dealing with institutions that affected their children's lives. For example, Janice Hale (1980) suggests that effective Black mothers are sophisticated mediators between the competing offerings of an oppressive dominant culture and a nurturing Black value-structure. Dill's (1980) study of the childrearing goals of Black domestics stresses the goals the women in her sample had for their children and the strategies these women pursued to help their children go further than they themselves had gone. Gilkes (1980) offers yet another perspective on the power of Black motherhood by observing that many of the Black female political activists in her study became involved in community work through their role as mothers. What typically began as work on behalf of their own children evolved into work on behalf of the community's children.

Another dimension of Black women's culture that has generated considerable interest among Black feminists is the role of creative expression in shaping and sustaining Black women's self-definitions and self-valuations. In addition to documenting Black women's achievements as writers, dancers, musicians, artists, and actresses, the emerging literature also investigates why creative expression has been such an important element of Black women's culture.[14] Alice Walker's (1974) classic essay, "In Search of Our Mothers' Gardens," explains the necessity of Black women's creativity, even if in very limited spheres, in resisting objectification and asserting Black women's subjectivity as fully human beings. Illustrating Walker's thesis, Willie Mae Ford Smith, a prominent gospel singer featured in the 1984 documentary, "Say Amen Somebody," describes what singing means to her. She notes, "it's just a feeling within. You can't help yourself. . . . I feel like I can fly away. I forget I'm in the world sometimes. I just want to take off." For Mother Smith, her creativity is a sphere of freedom, one that helps her cope with and transcend daily life.

This third key theme in Black feminist thought—the focus on Black women's culture—is significant for three reasons. First, the data from Black women's culture suggest that the relationship between oppressed people's consciousness of oppression and the actions they take in dealing with oppressive structures may be far more complex than that suggested by existing social theory. Conventional social science continues to assume a fit between consciousness and activity; hence, accurate measures of human behavior are thought to produce accurate portraits of human consciousness of self and social structure (Westkott, 1979). In contrast, Black women's experiences suggest that Black women may overtly conform to the societal roles laid out for them, yet covertly oppose these roles in numerous spheres, an opposition shaped by the consciousness of being on the bottom. Black women's activities in families, churches, community institutions, and creative expression may represent more than an effort to mitigate pressures stemming from oppression. Rather, the Black female ideological frame of reference that Black women acquire through sisterhood, motherhood, and creative expression may serve the added purpose of shaping a Black female consciousness about the workings of oppression. Moreover, this consciousness is shaped not only through abstract, rational reflection, but also is developed through concrete rational action. For example, while Black mothers may develop consciousness through talking with and listening to their children, they may also shape consciousness by how they live their lives, the actions they take on behalf of their children. That these activities have been obscured from traditional social scientists should come as no surprise. Oppressed peoples may maintain hidden consciousness and may not reveal their true selves for reasons of self-protection.[15]

A second reason that the focus on Black women's culture is significant is that it points to the problematic nature of existing conceptualizations of the term "activism." While Black women's reality cannot be understood without attention to the interlocking structures of oppression that limit Black women's lives, Afro-American women's experiences suggest that possibilities for activism exist even within such multiple structures of domination. Such activism can take several forms. For Black women under extremely harsh conditions, the private decision to reject external definitions of Afro-American womanhood may itself be a form of activism. If Black women find themselves in settings where total conformity is expected, and where traditional forms of activism such as voting, participating in collective movements, and officeholding are impossible, then the individual women who in their consciousness choose to be self-defined and self-evaluating are, in fact, activists. They are retaining a grip over their definition as subjects, as full humans, and rejecting definitions of themselves as the objectified "other." For example, while Black slave women were forced to conform to the specific oppression facing them, they may have had very different assessments of themselves and slavery than did the slaveowners. In this sense, consciousness can be viewed as one potential sphere of freedom, one that may exist simultaneously with unfree, allegedly conforming behavior (Westkott,

1979). Moreover, if Black women simultaneously use all resources available to them their roles as mothers, their participation in churches, their support of one another in Black female networks, their creative expression—to be self-defined and self-valuating and to encourage others to reject objectification, then Black women's everyday behavior itself is a form of activism. People who view themselves as fully human, as subjects, become activists, no matter how limited the sphere of their activism may be. By returning subjectivity to Black women, Black feminists return activism as well.

A third reason that the focus on Black women's culture is significant is that an analytical model exploring the relationship between oppression, consciousness, and activism is implicit in the way Black feminists have studied Black women's culture. With the exception of Dill (1983), few scholars have deliberately set out to develop such a model. However, the type of work done suggests that an implicit model paralleling that proposed by Mullings (1986a) has influenced Black feminist research.

Several features pervade emerging Black feminist approaches. First, re-searchers stress the interdependent relationship between the interlocking op-pression that has shaped Black women's choices and Black women's actions in the context of those choices. Black feminist researchers rarely describe Black women's behavior without attention to the opportunity structures shaping their subjects' lives (Higginbotham, 1985; Ladner, 1971; Myers, 1980). Second, the question of whether oppressive structures and limited choices stimulate Black women's behavior characterized by apathy and alienation, or behavior demonstrating subjectivity and activism, is seen as ultimately dependent on Black women's perceptions of their choices. In other words, Black women's consciousness—their analytical, emotional, and ethical perspective of them-selves and their place in society—becomes a critical part of the relationship between the working of oppression and Black women's actions. Finally, this relationship between oppression, consciousness, and action can be seen as a dialectical one. In this model, oppressive structures create patterns of choices which are perceived in varying ways by Black women. Depending on their con-sciousness of themselves and their relationship to these choices, Black women may or may not develop Black-female spheres of influence where they develop and validate what will be appropriate, Black-female sanctioned responses to op-pression. Black women's activism in constructing Black-female spheres of influ-ence may, in turn, affect their perceptions of the political and economic choices offered to them by oppressive structures, influence actions actually taken, and ultimately alter the nature of oppression they experience.

The Sociological Significance of Black Feminist Thought

Taken together, the three key themes in Black feminist thought—the meaning of self-definition and self-valuation, the interlocking nature of oppression, and the importance of redefining culture—have made significant contributions to the task of clarifying a Black women's standpoint of and for Black women. While this accomplishment is important in and of itself, Black feminist thought has potential contributions to make to the diverse disciplines housing its practitioners.

The sociological significance of Black feminist thought lies in two areas. First, the content of Black women's ideas has been influenced by and contributes to on-going dialogues in a variety of sociological specialities. While this area merits attention, it is not my primary concern in this section. Instead, I investigate a second area of sociological significance: the process by which these specific ideas were produced by this specific group of individuals. In other words, I examine the influence of Black women's outsider within status in academia on the actual thought produced. Thus far, I have proceeded on the assumption that it is impossible to separate the structure and thematic content of thought. In this section, I spell out exactly what form the relationship between the three key themes in Black feminist thought and Black women's outsider within status might take for women scholars generally, with special attention to Black female sociologists.

First, I briefly summarize the role sociological paradigms play in shaping the facts and theories used by sociologists. Second, I explain how Black women's outsider within status might encourage Black women to have a distinctive standpoint vis-à-vis sociology's paradigmatic facts and theories. I argue that the thematic content of Black feminist thought described above represents elements of just such a standpoint and give examples of how the combination of sociology's paradigms and Black women's outsider within status as sociologists directed their attention to specific areas of sociological inquiry.

Two Elements of Sociological Paradigms

Kuhn defines a paradigm as the "entire constellation of beliefs, values, techniques, and so on shared by the members of a given community" (1962:175). As such, a paradigm consists of two fundamental elements: the thought itself and its producers and practitioners.[16] In this sense, the discipline of sociology is itself a paradigm—it consists of a system of knowledge shared by sociologists— and simultaneously consists of a plurality of paradigms (e.g., functionalism, Marxist sociology, feminist sociology, existential sociology), each produced by its own practitioners.

Two dimensions of thought itself are of special interest to this discussion. First, systems of knowledge are never complete. Rather, they represent guidelines for "thinking as usual." Kuhn (1962) refers to these guidelines as "maps," while Schutz (1944) describes them as "recipes." As Schutz points out, while "thinking as usual" is actually only partially organized and partially clear, and may contain contradictions, to its practitioners it provides sufficient coherence, clarity, and consistency. Second, while thought itself contains diverse elements, I will focus mainly on the important fact/theory relationship. As Kuhn (1962) suggests, facts or observations become meaningful in the context of theories or interpretations of those observations. Conversely, theories "fit the facts" by transforming previously accessible observations into facts. According to Mulkay, "observation is not separate from interpretation; rather these are two facets of a single process" (1979:49).

Several dimensions of the second element of sociological paradigms—the community formed by a paradigm's practitioners—are of special interest to this discussion. First, group insiders have similar worldviews, aquired through similar educational and professional training, that separate them from everyone else. Insider worldviews may be especially alike if group members have similar social class, gender, and racial backgrounds. Schutz describes the insider worldview as the "cultural pattern of group life"—namely, all the values and behaviors which characterize the social group at a given moment in its history. In brief, insiders have undergone similar experiences, possess a common history, and share taken-for-granted knowledge that characterizes "thinking as usual."

A second dimension of the community of practitioners involves the process of becoming an insider. How does one know when an individual is really an insider and not an outsider in disguise? Merton suggests that socialization into the life of a group is a lengthy process of being immersed in group life, because only then can "one understand the fine-grained meanings of behavior, feeling, and values . . . and decipher the unwritten grammar of conduct and nuances of cultural idiom" (1972:15). The process is analogous to immersion in a foreign culture in order to learn its ways and its language (Merton, 1972; Schutz, 1944). One becomes an insider by translating a theory or worldview into one's own language until, one day, the individual converts to thinking and acting according to that worldview.

A final dimension of the community of practitioners concerns the process of remaining an insider. A sociologist typically does this by furthering the discipline in ways described as appropriate by sociology generally, and by areas of specialization particularly. Normal foci for scientific sociological investigation include: (1) determining significant facts; (2) matching facts with existing theoretical interpretations to "test" the paradigm's ability to predict facts; and (3) resolving ambiguities in the paradigm itself by articulating and clarifying theory (Kuhn, 1962).

Black Women and the Outsider Within Status

Black women may encounter much less of a fit between their personal and cultural experiences and both elements of sociological paradigms than that facing other sociologists. On the one hand, Black women who undergo sociology's lengthy socialization process, who immerse themselves in the cultural pattern of sociology's group life, certainly wish to acquire the insider skills of thinking in and acting according to a sociological worldview. But on the other hand, Black women's experienced realities, both prior to contact and after initiation, may provide them with "special perspectives and insights . . . available to that category of outsiders who have been systematically frustrated by the social system"

(Merton, 1972:29). In brief, their outsider allegiances may militate against their choosing full insider status, and they may be more apt to remain outsiders within.[17]

In essence, to become sociological insiders, Black women must assimilate a standpoint that is quite different than their own. White males have long been the dominant group in sociology, and the sociological worldview understandably reflects the concerns of this group of practitioners. As Merton observes, "white male insiderism in American sociology during the past generations has largely been of the tacit or de facto . . . variety. It has simply taken the form of patterned expectations about the appropriate . . . problems for investigation" (1972:12). In contrast, a good deal of the Black female experience has been spent coping with, avoiding, subverting, and challenging the workings of this same white male insiderism. It should come as no surprise that Black women's efforts in dealing with the effects of interlocking systems of oppression might produce a standpoint quite distinct from, and in many ways opposed to, that of white male insiders.

Seen from this perspective, Black women's socialization into sociology represents a more intense case of the normal challenges facing sociology graduate students and junior professionals in the discipline. Black women become, to use Simmel's (1921) and Schutz's terminology, penultimate "strangers."

> The stranger . . . does not share the basic assumptions of the group. He becomes essentially the man who has to place in question nearly everything that seems to be unquestionable to the members of the approached group. . . . To him the cultural patterns of the approached group do not have the authority of a tested system of recipes . . . because he does not partake in the vivid historical tradition by which it has been formed (Schutz, 1944:502).

Like everyone else, Black women may see sociological "thinking as usual" as partially organized, partially clear, and contradictory, and may question these existing recipes. However, for them, this questioning process may be more acute, for the material that they encounter—white male insider-influenced observations and interpretations about human society—places white male subjectivity at the center of analysis and assigns Afro-American womanhood a position on the margins.

In spite of a lengthy socialization process, it may also be more difficult for Afro-American women to experience conversion and begin totally to think in and act according to a sociological worldview. Indeed, since past generations of white male insiderism has shaped a sociological worldview reflecting this group's concerns, it may be self-destructive for Black women to embrace that worldview. For example, Black women would have to accept certain fundamental and self-devaluing assumptions: (1) white males are more worthy of study because they are more fully human than everyone else; and (2) dichotomous oppositional thinking is natural and normal. More importantly, Black women would have to act in accordance with their place in a white male worldview. This involves accepting one's own subordination or regretting the accident of not being born white and male. In short, it may be extremely difficult for Black women to accept a worldview predicated upon Black female inferiority.

Remaining in sociology by doing normal scientific investigation may also be less complicated for traditional sociologists than for Afro-American women. Unlike Black women, learners from backgrounds where the insider information and experiences of sociology are more familiar may be less likely to see the taken-for-granted assumptions of sociology and may be more prone to apply their creativity to "normal science." In other words, the transition from student status to that of a practitioner engaged in finding significant facts that sociological paradigms deem important, matching facts with existing theories, and furthering paradigmatic development itself may proceed more smoothly for white middle-class males than for working-class Black females. The latter group is much more inclined to be struck by the mismatch of its own experiences and the paradigms of sociology itself. Moreover, those Black women with a strong foundation in Black women's culture (e.g., those that recognize the value of self-definition and self-valuation, and that have a concrete understanding of sisterhood and motherhood) may be more apt to take a critical posture toward the entire sociological enterprise. In brief, where traditional sociologists may see sociology as "normal" and define their role as furthering knowledge about a normal world with taken-for-granted assumptions, outsiders within are liable to see anomalies.

The types of anomalies typically seen by Black female academicians grow directly from Black women's outsider within status and appear central in shaping the direction Black feminist thought has taken thus far. Two types of anomalies are characteristically noted by Black female scholars. First, Black female sociologists typically report the omission of facts or observations about Afro-American women in the sociological paradigms they encounter. As Scott points out, "from reading the literature, one might easily develop the impression that Black women have never played any role in this society" (1982:85). Where white males may take it as perfectly normal to generalize findings from studies of white males to other groups, Black women are more likely to see such a practice as problematic, as an anomaly. Similarly, when white feminists produce generalizations about "women," Black feminists routinely ask "which women do you mean?" In the same way that Rollins (1985) felt invisible in her employer's kitchen, Afro-American female scholars are repeatedly struck by their own invisibility, both as full human subjects included in sociological facts and observations, and as practitioners in the discipline itself. It should come as no surprise that much of Black feminist thought aims to counter this invisibility by presenting sociological analyses of Black women as fully human subjects. For example, the growing research describing Black women's historical and contemporary behavior as mothers, community workers, church leaders, teachers, and employed workers, and Black women's ideas about themselves and their opportunities, reflects an effort to respond to the omission of facts about Afro-American women.

A second type of anomaly typically noted by Black female scholars concerns distortions of facts and observations about Black women. Afro-American women in academia are frequently struck by the difference between their own experiences and sociological descriptions of the same phenomena. For example, while Black women have and are themselves mothers they encounter distorted versions of themselves and their mothers under the mantle of the Black matriarchy thesis. Similarly, for those Black women who confront racial and sexual discrimination and know that their mothers and grandmothers certainly did, explanations of Black women's poverty that stress low achievement motivation and the lack of Black female "human capital" are less likely to ring true. The response to these perceived distortions has been one of redefining distorted images—for example, debunking the Sapphire and Mammy myths.

Since facts or observations become meaningful in the context of a theory, this emphasis on producing accurate descriptions of Black women's lives has also refocused attention on major omissions and distortions in sociological theories themselves. By drawing on the strengths of sociology's plurality of subdisciplines, yet taking a critical posture toward them, the work of Black feminist scholars taps some fundamental questions facing all sociologists. One such question concerns the fundamental elements of society that should be studied. Black feminist researchers' response has been to move Black women's voices to the center of the analysis, to study people, and by doing so, to reaffirm human subjectivity and intentionality. They point to the dangers of omission and distortion that can occur if sociological concepts are studied at the expense of human subjectivity. For example, there is a distinct difference between conducting a statistical analysis of Black women's work, where Afro-American women are studied as a reconstituted amalgam of researcher-defined variables (e.g., race, sex, years of education, and father's occupation), and examining Black women's self-definitions and self-valuations of themselves as workers in oppressive jobs. While both approaches can further sociological knowledge about the concept of work, the former runs the risk of objectifying Black women, of reproducing constructs of dichotomous oppositional difference, and of producing distorted findings about the nature of work itself.

A second question facing sociologists concerns the adequacy of current interpretations of key sociological concepts. For example, few sociologists would question that work and family are two fundamental concepts for sociology. However, bringing Black feminist thought into the center of conceptual analysis raises issues of how comprehensive current sociological interpretations of these two concepts really are. For example, labor theories that relegate Afro-American women's work experiences to the fringe of analysis miss the critical theme of the interlocking nature of Black women as female workers (e.g., Black women's unpaid domestic labor) and Black women as racially-oppressed workers (e.g., Black women's unpaid slave labor and exploited wage labor). Examining the extreme case offered by Afro-American women's unpaid and paid work experiences raises questions about the adequacy of generalizations about work itself. For example, Black feminists' emphasis on the simultaneity of oppression redefines the economic system itself as problematic. From this perspective, all generalizations about the normal workings of labor markets, organizational structure, occupational mobility, and income differences that do not explicitly see oppression as problematic become suspect. In short, Black feminists suggest that all generalizations about groups of employed and unemployed workers (e.g., managers, welfare mothers, union members, secretaries, Black teenagers) that do not account for interlocking structures of group placement and oppression in an economy are simply less complete than those that do.

Similarly, sociological generalizations about families that do not account for Black women's experience will fail to see how the public/private split shaping household composition varies across social and class groupings, how racial/ethnic family members are differentially integrated into wage labor, and how families alter their household structure in response to changing political economies (e.g., adding more people and becoming extended, fragmenting and becoming female-headed, and migrating to locate better opportunities). Black women's family experiences represent a clear case of the workings of race, gender, and class oppression in shaping family life. Bringing undistorted observations of Afro-American women's family experiences into the center of analysis again raises the question of how other families are affected by these same forces.

While Black women who stand outside academia may be familiar with omissions and distortions of the Black female experience, as outsiders to sociology, they lack legitimated professional authority to challenge the sociological anomalies. Similarly, traditional sociological insiders, whether white males or their nonwhite and/or female disciples, are certainly in no position to notice the specific anomalies apparent to Afro-American women, because these same sociological insiders produced them. In contrast, those Black women who remain rooted in their own experiences as Black women—and who master sociological paradigms yet retain a critical posture toward them—are in a better position to bring a special perspective not only to the study of Black women, but to some of the fundamental issues facing sociology itself.

Toward Synthesis: Outsiders Within Sociology

Black women are not the only outsiders within sociology. As an extreme case of outsiders moving into a community that historically excluded them, Black women's experiences highlight the tension experienced by any group of less powerful outsiders encountering the paradigmatic thought of a more powerful insider community. In this sense, a variety of individuals can learn from Black women's experiences as outsiders within: Black men, working-class individuals, white women, other people of color, religious and sexual minorities, and all individuals who, while from social strata that provided them with the benefits of white male insiderism, have never felt comfortable with its taken-for-granted assumptions.

Outsider within status is bound to generate tension, for people who become outsiders within are forever changed by their new status. Learning the subject matter of sociology stimulates a reexamination of one's own personal and cultural experiences; and, yet, these same experiences paradoxically help to illuminate sociology's anomalies. Outsiders within occupy a special place—they become different people, and their difference sensitizes them to patterns that may be more difficult for established sociological insiders to see. Some outsiders within try to resolve the tension generated by their new status by leaving sociology and remaining sociological outsiders. Others choose to suppress their difference by striving to become bonafide, "thinking as usual" sociological insiders. Both choices rob sociology of diversity and ultimately weaken the discipline.

A third alternative is to conserve the creative tension of outsider within status by encouraging and institutionalizing outsider within ways of seeing. This alternative has merit not only for actual outsiders within, but also for other sociologists as well. The approach suggested by the experiences of outsiders within is one where intellectuals learn to trust their own personal and cultural biographies as significant sources of knowledge. In contrast to approaches that require submerging these dimensions of self in the process of becoming an allegedly unbiased, objective social scientist, outsiders within bring these ways of knowing back into the research process. At its best, outsider within status seems to offer its occupants a powerful balance between the strengths of their sociological training and the offerings of their personal and cultural experiences. Neither is subordinated to the other. Rather, experienced reality is used as a valid source of knowledge for critiquing sociological facts and theories, while sociological thought offers new ways of seeing that experienced reality.

What many Black feminists appear to be doing is embracing the creative potential of their outsider within status and using it wisely. In doing so, they move themselves and their disciplines closer to the humanist vision implicit in their work—namely, the freedom both to be different and part of the solidarity of humanity.

Notes

I wish to thank Lynn Weber Cannon, Bonnie Thornton Dill, Alison M. Jaggar, Joan Hartman, Ellen Messer-Davidow, and several anonymous reviewers for their helpful comments about earlier drafts of this paper.

1. In 1940, almost 60 percent of employed Afro-American women were domestics. The 1970 census was the first time this category of work did not contain the largest segment of the Black female labor force. See Rollins (1985) for a discussion of Black domestic work.

2. For example, in *Of Women Born: Motherhood as Experience and Institution*, Adrienne Rich has fond memories of her Black "mother," a young, unstereotypically slim Black woman she loved. Similarly, Dill's (1980) study of Black domestic workers reveals Black

women's sense of affirmation at knowing that they were better mothers than their employers, and that they frequently had to teach their employers the basics about children and interaction in general. Even though the Black domestic workers were officially subordinates, they gained a sense of self-worth at knowing they were good at things that they felt mattered.

3.   For example, in spite of Rich's warm memories of her Black "mother," she had all but forgotten her until beginning research for her book. Similarly, the Black domestic workers in both Dill's (1980) and Rollins's (1985) studies discussed the limitations that their subordinate roles placed on them.

4.   For a discussion of the notion of a special standpoint or point of view of oppressed groups, see Hartsock (1983). See Merton's (1972) analysis of the potential contributions of insider and outsider perspectives to sociology. For a related discussion of outsider within status, see his section "Insiders as 'Outsiders' " (1972:29–30).

5.   Hurston has been widely discussed in Black feminist literary criticism. For example, see selected essays in Walker's (1979) edited volume on Hurston.

6.   By stressing the potentially positive features of outsider within status, I in no way want to deny the very real problem this social status has for large numbers of Black women. American sociology has long identified marginal status as problematic. However, my sense of the "problems" diverge from those espoused by traditional sociologists. For example, Robert Park states, "the marginal man . . . is one whom fate has condemned to live in two societies and in two, not merely different but antagonistic cultures" (1950:373). From Park's perspective, marginality and difference themselves were problems. This perspective quite rationally led to the social policy solution of assimilation, one aimed at eliminating difference, or if that didn't work, pretending it was not important. In contrast, I argue that it is the meaning attached to difference that is the problem. See Lorde (1984:114–23 and passim) for a Black feminist perspective on difference.

7.   In addition to familiarizing readers with the contours of Black feminist thought, I place Black women's ideas in the center of my analysis for another reason. Black women's ideas have long been viewed as peripheral to serious intellectual endeavors. By treating Black feminist thought as central, I hope to avoid the tendency of starting with the body of thought needing the critique—in this case sociology—fitting in the dissenting ideas, and thus, in the process, reifying the very systems of thought one hopes to transform.

8.   On this point, I diverge somewhat from Berger and Luckmann's (1966) definition of specialized thought. They suggest that only a limited group of individuals engages in theorizing and that "pure theory" emerges with the development of specialized legitimating theories and their administration by full-time legitimators. Using this approach, groups denied the material resources to support pure theorists cannot be capable of developing specialized theoretical knowledge. In contrast, I argue that "traditional wisdom" is a system of thought and that it reflects the material positions of its practitioners.

9.   Emerging Black feminist research is demonstrating a growing awareness of the importance of including the simultaneity of oppression in studies of Black women. For example, Paula Giddings's (1984) history of Afro-American women emphasizes the role of class in shaping relations between Afro-American and white women, and among Black women themselves. Elizabeth Higginbotham's (1985) study of Black college women examines race and class barriers to Black women's college attendance. Especially noteworthy is the growing attention to Black women's labor market experiences. Studies such as those by Dill (1980), Rollins (1985), Higginbotham (1983), and Mullings (1986b) indicate a new sensitivity to the interactive nature of race, gender, and class. By studying Black women, such studies capture the interaction of race and gender. Moreover, by examining Black women's roles in capitalist development, such work taps the key variable of class.

10.   The thesis that those affected by multiple systems of domination will develop a sharper view of the interlocking nature of oppression is illustrated by the prominence of Black lesbian feminists among Black feminist thinkers. For more on this, see Smith (1983), Lorde (1984), and White (1984:22–24).

11.   For example, African and Afro-American scholars point to the role dualistic thinking has played in domestic racism (Asante, 1980; Baldwin, 1980; Richards 1980). Feminist scholars note the linkage of duality with conceptualizations of gender in Western

cultures (Chodorow, 1978; Keller, 1983; Rosaldo, 1983). Recently, Brittan and Maynard, two British scholars, have suggested that dualistic thinking plays a major role in linking systems of racial oppression with those of sexual oppression. They note that

> there is an implicit belief in the duality of culture and nature. Men are the creators and mediators of culture—women are the manifestations of nature. The implication is that men develop culture in order to understand and control the natural world, while women being the embodiment of forces of nature, must be brought under the civilizing control of men. . . . This duality of culture and nature . . . is also used to distinguish between so-called higher nations or civilizations, and those deemed to be culturally backward. . . . Non-European peoples are conceived of as being nearer to nature than Europeans. Hence, the justification . . . for slavery and colonialism . . . (1984:193–94).

12. This humanist vision takes both religious and secular forms. For religious statements, see Andrews's (1986) collection of the autobiographies of three nineteenth-century, Black female evangelical preachers. For a discussion of the humanist tradition in Afro-American religion that has contributed to this dimension of Black feminist thought, see Paris (1985). Much of contemporary Black feminist writing draws on this religious tradition, but reframes the basic vision in secular terms.

13. During a period when Black women were widely devalued by the dominant culture, Sanctified Church members addressed each other as "Saints." During the early 1900s, when basic literacy was an illusive goal for many Blacks, Black women in the Church not only stressed education as a key component of a sanctified life, but supported each other's efforts at educational excellence. In addition to these psychological supports, the Church provided Afro-American women with genuine opportunities for influence, leadership, and political clout. The important thing to remember here is that the Church was not an abstract, bureaucratic structure that ministered to Black women. Rather, the Church was a predominantly female community of individuals in which women had prominent spheres of influence.

14. Since much Black feminist thought is contained in the works of Black women writers, literary criticism by Black feminist critics provides an especially fertile source of Black women's ideas. See Tate (1983) and Christian (1985).

15. Audre Lorde (1984:114) describes this conscious hiding of one's self as follows: "In order to survive, those of us for whom oppression is as American as apple pie have always had to be watchers, to become familiar with the language and manners of the oppressor, even sometimes adopting them for some illusion of protection."

16. In this sense, sociology is a special case of the more generalized process discussed by Mannheim (1936). Also, see Berman (1981) for a discussion of Western thought as a paradigm, Mulkay (1979) for a sociology of knowledge analysis of the natural sciences, and Berger and Luckmann (1966) for a generalized discussion of how everyday knowledge is socially constructed.

17. Jackson (1974) reports that 21 of the 145 Black sociologists receiving doctoral degrees between 1945 and 1972 were women. Kulis et al. (1986) report that Blacks comprised 5.7 percent of all sociology faculties in 1984. These data suggest that historically, Black females have not been sociological insiders, and currently, Black women as a group comprise a small portion of sociologists in the United States.

References

Andrews, William L. (ed.). 1986. *Sisters of the Spirit.* Bloomington, IN: Indiana University Press.

Asante, Molefi Kete. 1980. "International/intercultural relations." Pp. 43–58 in Molefi Kete Asante and Abdulai S. Vandi (eds.), *Contemporary Black Thought.* Beverly Hills, CA: Sage.

Baldwin, Joseph A. 1980. "The psychology of oppression." Pp. 95–110 in Molefi Kete Asante and Abdulai S. Vandi (eds.), *Contemporary Black Thought.* Beverly Hills, CA: Sage.

Beale, Frances. 1970. "Double jeopardy: to be Black and female." Pp. 90–110 in Toni Cade (ed.), *The Black Woman.* New York: Signet.

Berger, Peter L. and Thomas Luckmann. 1966. *The Social Construction of Reality.* New York: Doubleday.

Berman, Morris. 1981. *The Reenchantment of the World.* New York: Bantam.

Brittan, Arthur and Mary Maynard. 1984. *Sexism, Racism and Oppression.* New York: Basil Blackwell.

Chodorow, Nancy. 1978. *The Reproduction of Mothering.* Berkeley, CA: University of California Press.

Christian, Barbara. 1985. *Black Feminist Criticism: Perspectives on Black Women Writers.* New York: Pergamon.

Davis, Angela. 1981. *Women, Race and Class.* New York: Random House.

Dill, Bonnie Thornton. 1980. " 'The means to put my children through': child-rearing goals and strategies among Black female domestic servants." Pp. 107–23 in LaFrances Rodgers-Rose (ed.), *The Black Woman.* Beverly Hills, CA: Sage.

———. 1983. "Race, class, and gender: prospects for an all-inclusive sisterhood." *Feminist Studies* 9:131–50.

Giddings, Paula. 1984. *When and Where I Enter... The Impact of Black Women on Race and Sex in America.* New York: William Morrow.

Gilkes, Cheryl Townsend. 1980. " 'Holding back the ocean with a broom': Black women and community work." Pp. 217–31 in LaFrances Rodgers-Rose (ed.), *The Black Woman.* Beverly Hills, CA: Sage.

———. 1981. "From slavery to social welfare: racism and the control of Black women." Pp. 288–300 in Amy Smerdlow and Helen Lessinger (eds.), *Class, Race, and Sex: The Dynamics of Control.* Boston: G.K. Hall.

———. 1985. " 'Together and in harness': women's traditions in the sanctified church." *Signs* 10:678–99.

Gwaltney, John Langston. 1980. *Drylongso, a Self-portrait of Black America.* New York: Vintage.

Hale, Janice. 1980. "The Black woman and child rearing." Pp. 79–88 in LaFrances Rodgers-Rose (ed.), *The Black Woman.* Beverly Hills, CA: Sage.

Hartsock, Nancy M. 1983. "The feminist standpoint: developing the ground for a specifically feminist historical materialism." Pp. 283–310 in Sandra Harding and Merrill Hintikka (eds.), *Discovering Reality.* Boston: D. Reidel.

Higginbotham, Elizabeth. 1982. "Two representative issues in contemporary sociological work on Black women." Pp. 93–98 in Gloria T. Hull, Patricia Bell Scott, and Barbara Smith (eds.), *But Some of Us Are Brave.* Old Westbury, NY: Feminist Press.

———. 1983 "Laid bare by the system: work and survival for Black and Hispanic women." Pp. 200–15 in Amy Smerdlow and Helen Lessinger (eds.), *Class, Race, and Sex: The Dynamics of Control.* Boston: G.K. Hall.

———. 1985. "Race and class barriers to Black women's college attendance." *Journal of Ethnic Studies* 13:89–107.

hooks, bell. 1981. *Ain't I a Woman: Black Women and Feminism.* Boston: South End Press.

———. 1984. *From Margin to Center.* Boston: South End Press.

Jackson, Jacquelyn. 1974. "Black female sociologists." Pp. 267–98 in James E. Blackwell and Morris Janowitz (eds.), *Black Sociologists.* Chicago: University of Chicago Press.

Keller, Evelyn Fox. 1983. "Gender and science." Pp. 187–206 in Sandra Harding and Merrill Hintikka (eds.), *Discovering Reality.* Boston: D. Reidel.

King, Mae. 1973. "The politics of sexual stereotypes." *Black Scholar* 4:12–23.

Kuhn, Thomas S. 1970. *The Structure of Scientific Revolutions.* 2d Edition. Chicago: [1962] University of Chicago Press.

Kulis, Stephen, Karen A. Miller, Morris Axelrod, and Leonard Gordon. 1986. "Minority representation of U.S. departments." *ASA Footnotes* 14:3.

Ladner, Joyce. 1971. *Tomorrow's Tomorrow: The Black Woman.* Garden City, NY: Anchor.

Lee, Alfred McClung. 1973. *Toward Humanist Sociology.* Englewood Cliffs, NJ: Prentice-Hall.

Lewis, Diane. 1977. "A response to inequality: Black women, racism and sexism." *Signs* 3:339–61.

Loewenberg, Bert James and Ruth Bogin (eds.). 1976. *Black Women in Nineteenth-century Life.* University Park, PA: Pennsylvania State University.

Lorde, Audre. 1984. *Sister Outsider.* Trumansburg, NY: The Crossing Press.

Mannheim, Karl. 1954. *Ideology and Utopia: An Introduction to the Sociology of Knowledge [1936].* New York: Harcourt, Brace & Co.

Merton, Robert K. 1972. "Insiders and outsiders: a chapter in the sociology of knowledge." *American Journal of Sociology* 78:9–47.

Mulkay, Michael. 1979. *Science and the Sociology of Knowledge.* Boston: George Allen & Unwin.

Mullings, Leith. 1986a. "Anthropological perspectives on the Afro-American family." *American Journal of Social Psychiatry* 6:11–16.

———. 1986b. "Uneven development: class, race and gender in the United States before 1900." Pp. 41–57 in Eleanor Leacock and Helen Safa (eds.), *Women's Work, Development and the Division of Labor by Gender.* South Hadley, MA: Bergin & Garvey.

Murray, Pauli. 1970. "The liberation of Black women." Pp. 87–102 in Mary Lou Thompson (ed.), *Voices of the New Feminism.* Boston: Beacon Press.

Myers, Lena Wright. 1980. *Black Women: Do They Cope Better?* Englewood Cliffs, NJ: Prentice-Hall.

Paris, Peter J. 1985. *The Social Teaching of the Black Churches.* Philadelphia: Fortress Press.

Park, Robert E. 1950. *Race and Culture.* Glencoe, IL: Free Press.

Rich, Adrienne. 1976. *Of Woman Born: Motherhood as Experience and Institution.* New York: Norton.

Richards, Dona. 1980. "European mythology; the ideology of 'progress'." Pp. 59–79 in Molefi Kete Asante and Abdulai S. Vandi (eds.), *Contemporary Black Thought.* Beverly Hills, CA: Sage.

Rollins, Judith. 1985. *Between Women, Domestics and Their Employers.* Philadelphia: Temple University Press.

Rosaldo, Michelle Z. 1983. "Moral/analytic dilemmas posed by the intersection of feminism and social science." Pp. 76–96 in Norma Hann, Robert N. Bellah, Paul Rabinow, and William Sullivan (eds.), *Social Science as Moral Inquiry.* New York: Columbia University Press.

Schutz, Alfred. 1944. "The stranger: an essay in social psychology." *American Journal of Sociology* 49:499–507.

Scott, Patricia Bell. 1982. "Debunking sapphire: toward a non-racist and non-sexist social science." Pp. 85–92 in Gloria T. Hull, Patricia Bell Scott, and Barbara Smith (eds.), *But Some of Us Are Brave.* Old Westbury, NY: Feminist Press.

Simmel, Georg. 1921. "The sociological significance of the 'stranger'." Pp. 322–27 in Robert E. Park and Ernest W. Burgess (eds.), *Introduction to the Science of Sociology.* Chicago: University of Chicago Press.

Smith, Barbara (ed.). 1983. *Home Girls: A Black Feminist Anthology.* New York: Kitchen Table, Women of Color Press.

Steady, Filomina Chioma. 1981. "The Black woman cross-culturally: an overview." Pp. 7–42 in Filomina Chioma Steady (ed.), *The Black Woman Cross-culturally.* Cambridge, MA: Schenkman.

Tate, Claudia. 1983. *Black Women Writers at Work.* New York: Continuum.

Walker, Alice. 1974. "In search of our mothers' gardens." Pp. 231–43 in *In Search of Our Mothers' Gardens.* New York: Harcourt Brace Jovanovich.

Walker, Alice (ed.). 1979. *I Love Myself When I Am Laughing . . . A Zora Neal Hurston Reader.* Old Westbury, NY: Feminist Press.

Westkott, Marcia. 1979. "Feminist criticism of the social sciences." *Harvard Educational Review* 49:422–30.

White, Deborah Gray. 1985. *Art'n't I a Woman? Female Slaves in the Plantation South.* New York: W.W. Norton.

White, E. Frances. 1984. "Listening to the voices of Black feminism." *Radical America* 18:7–25.

8

Rethinking Standpoint Epistemology: What Is "Strong Objectivity"?

SANDRA HARDING

"Feminist objectivity means quite simply situated knowledges."
—Donna Haraway[1]

Both Ways

For almost two decades, feminists have engaged in a complex and charged conversation about objectivity. Its topics have included which kinds of knowledge projects have it, which don't, and why they don't; whether the many different feminisms need it, and if so why they do; and if it is possible to get it, how to do so.[2] This conversation has been informed by complex and charged prefeminist writings that tend to get stuck in debates between empiricists and intentionalists, objectivists and interpretationists, and realists and social constructionists (including poststructuralists).[3] . . .

Many feminists, like thinkers in the other new social liberation movements, now hold that it is not only desirable but also possible to have that apparent contradiation in terms—socially-situated knowledge. . . . The standpoint epistemologists—and especially the feminists who have most fully articulated this kind of theory of knowledge—have claimed to provide a fundamental map or "logic" for how to do this: "start thought from marginalized lives" and "take everyday life as problematic."[4] However, these maps are easy to misread if one doesn't understand the principles used to construct them. Critics of standpoint writings have tended to refuse the invitation to "have it both ways" by accepting the idea of real knowledge that is socially situated. Instead they have assimilated standpoint claims either to objectivism or some kind of conventional foundationalism or to ethnocentrism, relativism, or phenomenological approaches in philosophy and the social sciences.

Here I shall try to make clear how it really is a misreading to assimilate standpoint epistemologies to those older ones and that such misreadings distort or make invisible the distinctive resources that they offer. . . . Then I shall show why it is reasonable to think that the socially situated grounds and subjects of standpoint epistemologies require and generate stronger standards for objectivity than do those that turn away from providing systematic methods for locating knowledge in history. The problem with the conventional conception of objectivity is not that it is too rigorous or too "objectifying," as some have argued, but that it is *not rigorous or objectifying enough;* it is too weak to accomplish even the goals for which it has been designed, let alone the more difficult projects called for by feminisms and other new social movements. . . .

What Are the Grounds for Knowledge Claims?

Standpoint theories argue for "starting off thought" from the lives of marginalized peoples; beginning in those determinate, objective locations in any social order will generate illuminating critical questions that do not arise in thought that begins from dominant group lives. Starting off research from women's lives will generate less partial and distorted accounts not only of women's lives but also of men's lives and of the whole social order. Women's lives and experiences provide the "grounds" for this knowledge, though these clearly do not provide foundations for knowledge in the conventional philosophical sense. These grounds are the site, the activities, from which scientific questions arise. The epistemologically advantaged starting points for research do not guarantee that the researcher can maximize objectivity in her account; these grounds provide only a necessary—not a sufficient—starting point for maximizing objectivity. It is useful to contrast standpoint grounds for knowledge with four other kinds: the "God-trick," ethnocentrism, relativism, and the unique abilities of the oppressed to produce knowledge.

Standpoint Theories versus the "God-Trick"

First, for standpoint theories, the grounds for knowledge are fully saturated with history and social life rather than abstracted from it. Standpoint knowledge projects do not claim to originate in purportedly universal human problematics; they do not claim to perform the "God-trick."[5] However, the fact that feminist knowledge claims are socially situated does not in practice distinguish them from any other knowledge claims that have ever been made inside or outside the history of Western thought and the disciplines today; all bear the fingerprints of the communities that produce them. All thought by humans starts off from socially determinate lives. As Dorothy Smith puts the point, "women's perspective, as I have analyzed it here, discredits sociology's claim to constitute an objective knowledge independent of the sociologists's situation. Its conceptual procedures, methods, and relevances are seen to organize its subject matter from a determinate position in society."[6]

It is a delusion—and a historical identifiable one—to think that human thought could completely erase the fingerprints that reveal its production process. Conventional conceptions of scientific method enable scientists to be relatively good at eliminating those social interests and values from the results of research that differ *within* the scientific community. . . . But scientific method

provides no rules, procedures, or techniques for even identifying, let alone eliminating, social concerns and interests that are shared by all (or virtually all) of
the observers, nor does it encourage seeking out observers whose social beliefs
vary in order to increase the effectiveness of scientific method. Thus culturewide
assumptions *that have not been criticized within the scientific research process* are
transported into the results of research, making visible the historicity of specific
scientific claims to people at other times, other places, or in other groups in the
very same social order. We could say that standpoint theories not only acknowledge the social situatedness that is the inescapable lot of all knowledge-seeking
projects but also, more importantly, transform it into a systematically available
scientific resource.

Standpoint Theories versus Ethnocentrism

Universalists have traditionally been able to imagine only ethnocentrism and
relativism as possible alternatives to "the view from nowhere" that they assert grounds universal claims, so they think standpoint epistemologies must
be supporting (or doomed to) one or the other of these positions. Is there
any reasonable sense in which the ground for knowledge claimed by feminist
standpoint theory is ethnocentric?

Ethnocentrism is the belief in the inherent superiority of one's own ethnic
group or culture. Do feminist standpoint theorists argue that the lives of *their
own group or culture* is *superior* as a grounds for knowledge?[7] At first glance,
one might think that this is the case if one notices that it is primarily women
who have argued for starting thought from women's lives. However, there are
several reasons why it would be a mistake to conclude from this fact that feminist
standpoint theory is ethnocentric.

First, standpoint theorists themselves all explicitly argue that marginal lives
that are not their own provide better grounds for certain kinds of knowledge.
Thus the claim by women that women's lives provide a better starting point
for thought about gender system is not the same as the claim that *their own*
lives are the best such starting points. They are not denying that their own lives
can provide important resources for such projects, but they are arguing that
other, different (and sometimes oppositional) women's lives also provide such
resources. For example, women who are not prostitutes and have not been raped
have argued that starting thought from women's experiences and activities in
such events reveals that the state is male because it looks at women's lives here
just as men (but not women) do. Dorothy Smith writes of the value of starting to
think about a certain social situation she describes from the perspective of Native
Canadian lives.[8] Bettina Aptheker has argued that starting thought from the everyday lives of women who are holocaust survivors, Chicana cannery workers,
older lesbians, African-American women in slavery, Japanese-American con-
centration camp survivors, and others who have had lives different from hers
increases our ability to understand a great deal about the distorted way the

dominant groups conceptualize politics, resistance, community, and other key history and social science notions.[9] Patricia Hill Collins, an African-American sociologist, has argued that starting thought from the lives of poor and in some cases illiterate African-American women reveals important truths about the lives of intellectuals, both African-American and European-American, as well as about those women.[10] Many theorists who are not mothers (as well as many who are) have argued that starting thought in mother-work generates important questions about the social order. Of course some women no doubt do argue that their own lives provide the one and only best starting point for all knowledge projects, but this is not what standpoint theory holds. Thus, although it is not an accident that so many women have argued for feminist standpoint approaches, neither is it evidence that standpoint claims are committed to ethnocentrism.

Second, and relatedly, thinkers with "center" identities have also argued that marginalized lives are better places from which to start asking causal and critical questions about the social order. After all, Hegel was not a slave, though he argued that the master/slave relationship could be better understood from the perspective of slaves' activities. Marx, Engels, and Lukacs were not engaged in the kind of labor that they argued provided the starting point for developing their theories about class society. There are men who have argued for the scientific and epistemic advantages of starting thought from women's lives, European-Americans who understand that much can be learned about their lives as well as African-American lives if they start their thought from the latter, and so on.[11]

Third, women's lives are shaped by the rules of femininity or womanliness; in this sense they "express feminine culture." Perhaps the critic of standpoint theories thinks feminists are defending femininity and thus "their own culture." But all feminist analyses, including feminist standpoint writings, are in principle ambivalent about the value of femininity and womanliness. Feminists criticize femininity on the grounds that it is fundamentally defined by and therefore part of the conceptual project of exalting masculinity; it is the "other" against which men define themselves as admirably and uniquely human. Feminist thought does not try to substitute loyalty to femininity for the loyalty to masculinity it criticizes in conventional thought. Instead, it criticizes all gender loyalties as capable of producing only partial and distorted results of research. However, it must do this while also arguing that women's lives have been inappropriately devalued. Feminist thought is forced to "speak as" and on behalf of the very notion it criticizes and tries to dismantle—women. In the contradictory nature of this project lies both its greatest challenge and a source of its great creativity. . . .

Fourth, there are many feminisms, and these can be understood to be starting off their analyses from the lives of different historical groups of women. Liberal feminism initially started off its analyses from the lives of women in the eighteenth- and nineteenth-century European and U.S. educated classes; Marxist feminism, from the lives of wage-working women in the nineteenth- and early twentieth-century industrializing or "modernizing" societies; Third World feminism, from the lives of late twentieth-century women of Third World descent—and these different Third World lives produce different feminisms. Standpoint theory argues that each of these groups of women's lives is a good place to start in order to explain certain aspects of the social order. There is no single, ideal woman's life from which standpoint theories recommend that thought start. Instead, one must turn to all of the lives that are marginalized in different ways by the operative systems of social stratification. The different feminisms inform each other; we can learn from all of them and change our patterns of belief.

Last, one can note that from the perspective of marginalized lives, it is the dominant claims that we should in fact regard as ethnocentric. It is relatively easy to see that overtly racist, sexist, classist, and heterosexist claims have the effect of insisting that the dominant culture is superior. But it is also the case that claims to have produced universally valid beliefs—principles of ethics, of human nature, epistemologies, and philosophies of science—are ethnocentric. Only members of the powerful groups in societies stratified by race, ethnicity, class, gender, and sexuality could imagine that their standards for knowledge and the claims resulting from adherence to such standards should be found preferable by all rational creatures, past, present, and future. This is what the work of Smith, Hartsock, and the others discussed earlier shows. Moreover, standpoint theory itself is a historical emergent. There are good reasons why it has not emerged at other times in history; no doubt it will be replaced by more useful epistemologies in the future—the fate of all human products.[12]

Standpoint Theory versus Relativism, Perspectivalism, and Pluralism

If there is no single, transcendental standard for deciding between competing knowledge claims, then it is said that there can be only local historical ones, each valid in its own lights but having no claims against others. The literature on cognitive relativism is by now huge, and here is not the place to review it.[13] However, standpoint theory does not advocate—nor is it doomed to—relativism. It argues against the idea that all social situations provide equally useful resources for learning about the world and against the idea that they all set equally strong limits on knowledge. Contrary to what universalists think, standpoint theory is not committed to such a claim as a consequence of rejecting universalism. Standpoint theory provides arguments for the claim that some social situations are scientifically better than others as places from which to start off knowledge projects, and those arguments must be defeated if the charge of relativism is to gain plausibility.[14]

Judgmental (or epistemological) relativism is anathema to any scientific project, and feminist ones are no exception.[15] It is not equally true as its denial that women's uteruses wander around in their bodies when they take math courses, that only Man the Hunter made important contributions to distinctively human history, that women are biologically programmed to succeed at mothering and fail at equal participation in governing society, that women's preferred modes of moral reasoning are inferior to men's, that targets of rape and battering must bear the responsibility for what happens to them, that the sexual molestation and other physical abuses children report are only their fantasies, and so on—as various sexist and androcentric scientific theories have claimed. Feminist and prefeminist claims are usually not complementary but conflicting, just as the claim that the earth is flat conflicts with the claim that it is round. *Sociological* relativism permits us to acknowledge that different people hold different beliefs, but what is at issue in rethinking objectivity is the different matter of *judgmental* or epistemological relativism. Standpoint theories neither hold nor are doomed to it. . . .

Standpoint Theory versus the Unique Abilities of the Oppressed to Produce Knowledge

This is another way of formulating the charge that standpoint theories, in contrast to conventional theories of knowledge, are ethnocentric. However, in this form the position has tempted many feminists, as it has members of other liberatory knowledge projects.[16] . . . To pursue the issue further, we turn to examine just who is the "subject of knowledge" for standpoint theories. . . .

New Subjects of Knowledge

For empiricist epistemology, the subject or agent of knowledge—that which "knows" the "best beliefs" of the day—is supposed to have a number of distinctive characteristics. First, this subject of knowledge is culturally and historically disembodied or invisible because knowledge is by definition universal. "Science says. . . . " we are told. Whose science, we can ask? The drug and cigarette companies'? The Surgeon General's? The National Institute of Health's? The science of the critics of the NIH's racism and sexism? Empiricism insists that scientific knowledge has no particular historical subject. Second, in this respect, the subject of scientific knowledge is different in kind from the objects whose properties scientific knowledge describes and explains, because the latter are determinate in space and time. Third, though the subject of knowledge for empiricists is transhistorical, knowledge is initially produced ("discovered") by individuals and groups of individuals (reflected in the practice of scientific awards and honors), not by culturally specific societies or subgroups in a society such as a certain class or gender or race. Fourth, the subject is homogeneous and unitary, because knowledge must be consistent and coherent. If the subject of knowledge were permitted to be multiple and heterogeneous, then the knowledge produced by such subjects would be multiple and contradictory and thus inconsistent and incoherent.

The subjects of knowledge for standpoint theories contrast in all four respects. First, they are embodied and visible, because the lives from which thought has started are always present and visible in the results of that thought, This is true even though the way scientific method is operationalized usually succeeds in removing all personal or individual fingerprints from the results of research. But personal fingerprints are not the problem standpoint theory is intended to address. The thought of an age is *of an age,* and the delusion that one's thought can escape historical locatedness is just one of the thoughts that is typical of dominant groups in these and other ages. The "scientific world view" is, in fact, a view of (dominant groups in) modern, Western societies, as the histories of science proudly point out. Standpoint theories simply disagree with the further ahistorical and incoherent claim that the content of "modern and Western" scientific thought is also, paradoxically, not shaped by its historical location.

Second, the fact that subjects of knowledge are embodied and socially located has the consequence that they are not fundamentally different from objects of knowledge. We should assume causal symmetry in the sense that the same kinds of social forces that shape objects of knowledge also shape (but do not determine) knowers and their scientific projects.

This may appear to be true only for the objects of social science knowledge, not for the objects that the natural sciences study. After all, trees, rocks, planetary orbits, and electrons do not constitute themselves as historical actors. What they are does not depend on what they think they are; they do not think or carry on any of the other activities that distinguish human communities from other constituents of the world around us. However, this distinction turns out to be irrelevant to the point here because, in fact, scientists never can study the trees, rocks, planetary orbits, or electrons that are "out there" and untouched by human concerns. Instead, they are destined to study something different (but hopefully systematically related to what is "out there"): *nature as an object of knowledge.* Trees, rocks, planetary orbits, and electrons always appear to natural scientists only as they are already socially constituted in some of the ways that humans and their social groups are already socially constituted for the social scientist. Such objects are already effectively "removed from pure nature" into social life—they are social objects—by, first of all, the contemporary general cultural meanings that these objects have for everyone, including the entire scientific community.[17] They also become socially constituted objects of knowledge through the shapes and meanings these objects gain for scientists because of earlier generations of scientific discussion about them.... Finally, their own interactions with such objects also culturally constitute them; to treat a piece of nature with respect, violence, degradation, curiosity, or indifference is to participate in culturally constituting such an object of knowledge....

Third, consequently, communities and not primarily individuals produce knowledge. For one thing, what I believe that I thought through all by myself (in my mind), which I know, only gets transformed from my personal belief to knowledge when it is socially legitimated. Just as importantly, my society ends up assuming all the claims I make that neither I nor my society critically interrogate. It assumes the eurocentric, androcentric, heterosexist, and bourgeois beliefs that I do not critically examine as part of my scientific research and that, consequently, shape my thought and appear as part of my knowledge claims. These are some of the kinds of features that subsequent ages (and Others today) will say make my thought characteristic of my age, or society, community, race, class, gender, or sexuality. The best scientific thought of today is no different in this respect from the thought of Galileo or Darwin; in all can be found not only brilliant thoughts first expressed by individuals and then legitimated by communities but also assumptions we now regard as false that were distinctive to a particular historical era and not identified as part of the "evidence" that scientists actually used to select the results of research.[18]

Fourth, the subjects/agents of knowledge for feminist standpoint theory are multiple, heterogeneous, and contradictory or incoherent, not unitary, homogeneous, and coherent as they are for empiricist epistemology.[19] Feminist knowledge has started off from women's lives, but it has started off from many different women's lives; there is no typical or essential woman's life from which feminisms start their thought. . . .

However, the subject/agent of feminist knowledge is multiple, heterogeneous, and frequently contradictory in a second way that mirrors the situation for women as a class. It is the thinker whose consciousness is bifurcated, the outsider within, the marginal person now located at the center,[20] the person who is committed to two agendas that are by their nature at least partially in conflict— the liberal feminist, socialist feminist, Sandinista feminist, Islamic feminist, or feminist scientist—who has generated feminist sciences and new knowledge. It is starting off thought from a contradictory social position that generates feminist knowledge. So the logic of the directive to "start thought from women's lives" requires that one start one's thought from multiple lives that are in many ways in conflict with each other, each of which itself has multiple and contradictory commitments. . . .

This logic of multiple subjects leads to the recognition that the subject of liberatory feminist knowledge must also be, in an important if controversial sense, the subject of every other liberatory knowledge project. This is true in the collective sense of "subject of knowledge," because lesbian, poor, and racially marginalized women are all women, and therefore all feminists will have to grasp how gender, race, class, and sexuality are used to construct each other. It will have to do so if feminism is to be liberatory for marginalized women, but also if it is to avoid deluding dominant group women about their/our own situations. If this were not so, there would be no way to distinguish between feminism and the narrow self-interest of dominant group women—just as conventional androcentric thought permits no criterion for distinguishing between "best beliefs" and those that serve the self-interest of men as men. (Bourgeois thought permits no criterion for identifying specifically bourgeois self-interest; racist thought, for identifying racist self-interest; and so on.)

But the subject of every other liberatory movement must also learn how gender, race, class, and sexuality are used to construct each other in order to accomplish their goals. That is, analyses of class relations must look at their agendas from the perspective of women's lives, too. Women, too, hold class positions, and they are not identical to their brothers'. . . . Antiracist movements must look at their issues from the perspective of the lives of women of color, and so forth. Everything that feminist thought must know must also inform the thought of every other liberatory movement, and vice versa. It is not just the women in those other movements who must know the world from the perspective of women's lives. Everyone must do so if the movements are to succeed at their own goals. . . .

However, if every other liberatory movement must generate feminist knowl-edge, it cannot be that women are the unique generators of feminist knowledge. Women cannot claim this ability to be uniquely theirs, and men must not be permitted to claim that because they are not women, they are not obligated to produce fully feminist analyses. Men, too, must contribute distinctive forms of specifically feminist knowledge from their particular social situation. Men's thought, too, will begin first from women's lives in all the ways that feminist theory, with its rich and contradictory tendencies, has helped us all—women as well as men—to understand how to do. It will start there in order to gain the maximally objective theoretical frameworks within which men can begin to de-scribe and explain their own and women's lives in less partial and distorted ways. This is necessary if men are to produce more than the male supremacist "folk belief" about themselves and the world they live in to which female feminists object. Women have had to learn how to substitute the generation of feminist thought for the "gender nativism" androcentric cultures encourage in them, too. Female feminists are made, not born. Men, too must learn to take historic responsibility for the social position from which they speak. . . .

Far from licensing European-Americans to appropriate African-American thought or men to appropriate women's thought, this approach challenges mem-bers of dominant groups to make themselves "fit" to engage in collaborative, democratic, community enterprises with marginal peoples. Such a project re-quires learning to listen attentively to marginalized people; it requires educating oneself about their histories, achievements, preferred social relations, and hopes for the future; it requires putting one's body on the line for "their" causes un-til they feel like "our" causes; it requires critical examination of the dominant institutional beliefs and practices that systematically disadvantage them; it re-quires critical self-examination to discover how one unwittingly participates in generating disadvantage to them . . . and more. Fortunately, there are plenty of models available to us not only today but also through an examination of the history of members of dominant groups who learned to think from the lives of marginalized people and to act on what they learned. We can choose which historical lineage to claim as our own.

To conclude this section, we could say that since standpoint analyses explain how and why the subject of knowledge always appears in scientific accounts of nature and social life as part of the object of knowledge of those accounts, standpoint approaches have had to learn to use the social situatedness of subjects of knowledge systematically as a resource for maximizing objectivity. They have made the move from declaiming as a problem or acknowledging as an inevitable fact to theorizing as a *systematically accessible* resource for maximizing objectivity the inescapable social situatedness of knowledge claims.

Standards for Maximizing Objectivity

We are now in a position to draw out of this discussion of the innovative grounds and subject of knowledge for feminist standpoint theories the stronger standards for maximizing objectivity that such theories both require and generate. Strong objectivity requires that the subject of knowledge be placed on the same critical, causal plane as the objects of knowledge. Thus, strong objectivity requires what we can think of as "strong reflexivity." This is because culturewide (or nearly culturewide) beliefs function as evidence at every stage in scientific inquiry: in the selection of problems, the formation of hypotheses, the design of research (including the organization of research communities), the collection of data, the interpretation and sorting of data, decisions about when to stop research, the way results of research are reported, and so on. The subject of knowledge—the individual and the historically located social community whose unexamined beliefs its members are likely to hold "unknowingly," so to speak—must be considered as part of the object of knowledge from the perspective of scientific method. All of the kinds of objectivity-maximizing procedures focused on the nature and/or social relations that are the direct object of observation and reflection must also be focused on the observers and reflectors—scientists and the larger society whose assumptions they share. But a maximally critical study of scientists and their communities can be done only from the perspective of those whose lives have been marginalized by such communities. Thus, strong objectivity requires that scientists and their communities be integrated into democracy-advancing projects for scientific and epistemological reasons as well as moral and political ones.

From the perspective of such standpoint arguments, empiricism's standards appear weak; empiricism advances only the "objectivism" that has been so widely criticized from many quarters.[21] Objectivism impoverishes its attempts at maximizing objectivity when it turns away from the task of critically identifying all of those broad, historical social desires, interests, and values that have shaped the agendas, contents, and results of the sciences much as they shape the rest of human affairs.

Consider, first, how objectivism too narrowly operationalizes the notion of maximizing objectivity.[22] The conception of value-free, impartial, dispassionate research is supposed to direct the identification of all social values and their elimination from the results of research, yet it has been operationalized to identify and eliminate only those social values and interests that differ among the researchers and critics who are regarded by the scientific community as competent to make such judgments. If the community of "qualified" researchers and critics systematically excludes, for example, all African-Americans and women of all races and if the larger culture is stratified by race and gender and lacks powerful critiques of this stratification, it is not plausible to imagine that racist and sexist interests and values would be identified within a community of scientists composed entirely of people who benefit—intentionally or not—from institutionalized racism and sexism. This kind of blindness is advanced by the conventional belief that the truly scientific part of knowledge seeking—the part controlled by methods of research—occurs only in the context of justification. The context of discovery, in which problems are identified as appropriate for scientific investigation, hypotheses are formulated, key concepts are defined— this part of the scientific process is thought to be unexaminable within science by rational methods. Thus "real science" is restricted to those processes controllable by methodological rules. The methods of science—or rather, of the special sciences—are restricted to procedures for the testing of already formulated hypotheses. Untouched by these methods are those values and interests entrenched in the very statement of what problem is to be researched and in the concepts favored in the hypotheses that are to be tested. Recent histories of science are full of cases in which broad social assumptions stood little chance of identification or elimination through the very best research procedures of the day. Thus objectivism operationalizes the notion of objectivity in much too narrow a way to permit the achievement of the value-free research that is supposed to be its outcome.

But objectivism also conceptualizes the desired value-neutrality of objectivity too broadly. Objectivists claim that objectivity requires the elimination of *all* social values and interests from the research process and the results of research. It is clear, however, that not all social values and interests have the same bad effects upon the results of research. Democracy-advancing values have systematically generated less partial and distorted beliefs than others.

Objectivism's rather weak standards for maximizing objectivity make objectivity a mystifying notion, and its mystificatory character is largely responsible for its usefulness and its widespread appeal to dominant groups. It offers hope that scientists and science institutions, themselves admittedly historically located, can produce claims that will be regarded as objectively valid without having to examine critically their own historical commitments from which— intentionally or not—they actively construct their scientific research. It permits scientists and science institutions to be unconcerned with the origins or consequences of their problematics and practices or with the social values and interests that these problematics and practices support. . . . In contrast, standpoint approaches require the strong objectivity that can take the subject as well as the object of knowledge to be a necessary object of critical, causal— scientific!—social explanations. This program of strong reflexivity is a resource for objectivity, in contrast to the obstacle that *de facto* reflexivity has posed to weak objectivity.

Some feminists and thinkers from other liberatory knowledge projects have thought that the very notion of objectivity should be abandoned. They say that it is hopelessly tainted by its use in racist, imperialist, bourgeois, homophobic, and androcentric scientific projects. Moreover, it is tied to a theory of representation and concept of the self or subject that insists on a rigid barrier between subject and object of knowledge—between self and Other—which feminism and other new social movements label as distinctively androcentric or eurocentric. Finally, the conventional notion of objectivity institutionalizes a certain kind of lawlessness at the heart of science, we could say, by refusing to theorize any criteria internal to scientific goals for distinguishing between scientific method, on the one hand, and such morally repugnant acts as torture or ecological destruction, on the other. Scientists and scientific institutions disapprove of, engage in political activism against, and set up special committees to screen scientific projects for such bad consequences, but these remain ad hoc measures, extrinsic to the conventional "logic" of scientific research.

However, there is not just one legitimate way to conceptualize objectivity, any more than there is only one way to conceptualize freedom, democracy, or science. The notion of objectivity has valuable political and intellectual histories; as it is transformed into "strong objectivity" by the logic of standpoint epistemologies, it retains central features of the older conceptions. In particular, might should not make right in the realm of knowledge production any more than in matters of ethics. Understanding ourselves and the world around us requires understanding what others think of us and our beliefs and actions, not just what we think of ourselves and them.[23] Finally, the appeal to objectivity is an issue not only between feminist and prefeminist science and knowledge projects but also within each feminist and other emancipatory research agenda. There are many feminisms, some of which result in claims that distort the racial, class, sexuality, and gender relationships in society. Which ones generate less or more partial and distorted accounts of nature and social life? The notion of objectivity is useful in providing a way to think about the gap that should exist between how any individual or group wants the world to be and how in fact it is.[24] . . .

Can the new social movements "have it both ways"? Can they have knowledge that is fully socially situated? We can conclude by putting the question another way: if they cannot, what hope is there for anyone else to maximize the objectivity of *their* beliefs?

Notes

1. "Situated Knowledges: *The Science Question in Feminism* and the Privilege of Partial Perspective," *Feminist Studies* 14, 3 (1988): 581. Reprinted and revised in Donna J. Haraway, *Simians, Cyborgs, and Women* (New York: Routledge, 1991). I thank Linda Alcoff and Elizabeth Potter for helpful comments on an earlier draft.

2.	Important works here include Susan Bordo, *The Flight to Objectivity: Essays on Carte-sianism & Culture* (Albany: SUNY Press, 1987); Anne Fausto-Sterling, *Myths of Gender* (New York: Basic Books, 1985); Elizabeth Fee, "Women's Nature and Scientific Ob-jectivity," in *Woman's Nature: Rationalizations of Inequality,* ed. Marion Lowe and Ruth Hubbard (New York: Pergamon Press, 1981); Donna Haraway, cited in note 1 and *Primate Visions: Gender, Race and Nature in the World of Modern Science* (New York: Routledge, 1989); Ruth Hubbard, *The Politics of Women's Biology* (New Brunswick: Rutgers University Press, 1990); Evelyn Keller, *Reflections on Gender and Science* (New Haven: Yale University Press, 1984); Helen Longino, *Science as Social Knowledge* (Princeton, N.J.: Princeton University Press, 1990); and Lynn Hankinson Nelson, *Who Knows: From Quine to a Feminist Empiricism* (Philadelphia: Temple Uni-versity Press, 1990). These are just *some* of the important works on the topic; many other authors have made contributions to the discussion. I have addressed these issues in *The Science Question in Feminism* (Ithaca: Cornell University Press, 1986) and *Whose Science? Whose Knowledge? Thinking From Women's Lives* (Ithaca: Cornell University Press, 1991); see also the essays in Sandra Harding and Merrill Hintikka, eds., *Dis-covering Reality: Feminist Perspectives on Epistemology, Metaphysics, Methodology and the Philosophy of Science* (Dordrecht: Reidel, 1983). An interesting parallel discussion occurs in the feminist jurisprudence literature in the course of critiques of conventional conceptions of what "the rational man" would do, "the objective observer" would see, and "the impartial judge" would reason; see, for example many of the essays in the special issue of the *Journal of Legal Education* on *Women in Legal Education—Pedagogy, Law, Theory, and Practice* 39, 1–2 (1988), ed. Carrie Menkel-Meadow, Martha Minow, and David Vernon; and Katharine T. Bartlett, "Feminist Legal Methods," *Harvard Law Review* 103, 4 (1990).

3.	This literature is by now huge. For a sampling of its concerns, see Richard Bernstein, *Beyond Objectivism and Relativism* (Philadelphia: University of Pennsylvania Press, 1983); Martin Hollis and Steven Lukes, eds., *Rationality and Relativism* (Cambridge, Mass.: Harvard University Press, 1982); Michael Krausz and Jack Meiland, eds., *Rela-tivism: Cognitive and Moral* (Notre Dame, Ind.: University of Notre Dame Press, 1982); and Stanley Aronowitz, *Science and Power: Discourse and Ideology in Modern Society* (Minneapolis: University of Minnesota Press, 1988).

4.	Dorothy Smith, *The Everyday World as Problematic: A Feminist Sociology* (Boston: Northeastern University Press, 1987) and *The Conceptual Practices of Power: A Feminist Sociology of Knowledge* (Boston: Northeastern University Press, 1990); Nancy Hartsock, "The Feminist Standpoint: Developing the Ground for a Specifically Feminist His-torical Materialism," in Harding and Hintikka, eds., *Discovering Reality;* Hilary Rose, "Hand, Brain and Heart: A Feminist Epistemology of the Natural Sciences," *Signs* 9, 1 (1983); and my discussion of these writings in chapter 6 of *The Science Question in Feminism.* Alison Jaggar also developed an influential account of standpoint episte-mology in chapter 11 of *Feminist Politics and Human Nature* (Totowa, N.J.: Rowman & Allenheld, 1983). For more recent developments of standpoint theory see Patricia Hill Collins, chapters 10 and 11 of *Black Feminist Thought: Knowledge, Consciousness and the Politics of Empowerment* (Boston: Unwin Hyman, 1990) and chapters 5, 6, 7, and 11 of my *Whose Science? Whose Knowledge?*

5.	This is Donna Haraway's phrase in "Situated Knowledges" cited in note 1.

6.	Smith, "Women's Perspective as a Radical Critique of Sociology," in *Feminism and Methodology,* 91.

7.	Of course a gender is not an ethnicity. Yet historians and anthropologists write of women's cultures, so perhaps it does not stretch the meaning of ethnicity too far to think of women's cultures this way. Certainly some of the critics of standpoint theory have done so.

8.	"Women's Perspective," cited in note 6.

9.	Bettina Aptheker, *Tapestries of Life: Women's Work, Women's Consciousness, and the Meaning of Daily Life* (Amherst: University of Massachusetts Press, 1989).

10.	*Black Feminist Thought,* cited in note 4.

11.	The preceding citations contain many examples of such cases.

12.	What are the material limits of standpoint theories? Retroactively, we can see that they require the context of scientific culture; that is, they center claims about greater objectivity, the possibility and desirability of progress, the value of causal accounts

140 • Sandra Harding

for social projects, and so on. They also appear to require that the barriers between dominant and dominated be not absolutely rigid; there must be some degree of social mobility. Some marginal people must be able to observe what those at the center do, some marginal voices must be able to catch the attention of those at the center, and some people at the center must be intimate enough with the lives of the marginalized to be able to think how social life works from the perspective of their lives. A totalitarian system would be unlikely to breed standpoint theories. So a historical move to antiscientific or to totalitarian systems would make standpoint theories less useful. No doubt there are other historical changes that would limit the resources standpoint theories can provide.

13. See the citations in note 3.
14. All of the feminist standpoint theorists and science writers insist on distinguishing their positions from relativist ones. I have discussed the issue of relativism in several places, most recently in chapters 6 and 7 of *Whose Science? Whose Knowledge?*
15. See S. P. Mohanty, "Us and Them: On the Philosophical Bases of Political Criticism," *Yale Journal of Criticism*, 2, 2 (1989); and Donna Haraway's "Situated Knowledges" for especially illuminating discussions of why relativism can look attractive to many thinkers at this moment in history, but why it should nevertheless be resisted.
16. Critics of standpoint theories usually attribute this position to standpoint theorists. Within the array of feminist theoretical approaches, the claim that only women can produce knowledge is most often made by Radical Feminists.
17. For example, mechanistic models of the universe had different meanings for Galileo's critics than they have had for modern astronomers or, later, for contemporary ecologists, as Carolyn Merchant and other historians of science point out. See Carolyn Merchant, *The Death of Nature: Women, Ecology and the Scientific Revolution* (New York: Harper & Row, 1980). To take another case, "wild animals" and, more generally, "nature" are defined differently by Japanese, Indian, and Anglo-American primatologists, as Donna Haraway points out in *Primate Visions* (cited in note 2). The cultural character of nature as an object of knowledge has been a consistent theme in Haraway's work.
18. Longino and Nelson's arguments are particularly telling against the individualism of empiricism. See Nelson's "Who Knows," chapter 6 in *Who Knows*, and Longino's discussion of how the underdetermination of theories by their evidence insures that "background beliefs" will function as if they were evidence in many chapters of *Science as Social Knowledge* (cited in note 2) but especially in chapters 8, 9, and 10.
19. See Elizabeth Spelman, *Inessential Woman: Problems of Exclusion in Feminist Thought* (Boston: Beacon Press, 1988) for a particularly pointed critique of essentialist tendencies in feminist writings. Most of the rest of this section appears also in "Subjectivity, Experience and Knowledge: An Epistemology from/for Rainbow Coalition Politics," in *Questions of Authority: The Politics of Discourse and Epistemology in Feminist Thought*, ed. Judith Roof and Robyn Wiegman. I have also discussed these points in several other places.
20. These ways of describing this kind of subject of knowledge appear in the writings of, respectively, Smith ("Women's Perspective"), Collins (*Black Feminist Thought*) and bell hooks, *Feminist Theory From Margin to Center* (Boston: South End Press, 1983).
21. See the citations in note 3. The term "objectivism" has been used to identify the objectionable notion by Bernstein, Keller, and Bordo (see earlier citations), among others.
22. The following arguments are excerpted from pp. 143–48 in my *Whose Science? Whose Knowledge?*
23. David Mura puts the point this way in "Strangers in the Village," in *The Graywolf Annual Five: Multi-cultural Literacy*, ed. Rick Simonson and Scott Walker (St. Paul: Graywolf Press, 1988), 152.
24. These arguments for retaining the notion of objectivity draw on ones I have made several times before, most recently in *Whose Science? Whose Knowledge?*, pp. 157–61.

II
Identifying Standpoints

Introduction

What is it about the oppression women experience, or the forms of oppression experienced by other groups, that can be turned into scientific and epistemic resources? Critics of standpoint theory have had a hard time answering this question, and standpoint theorists have themselves revised and rearticulated their answers to this question. (See, for example, Susan Hekman's essay, the responses to it, and the discussion of it in Alison Wylie's essay.)

Of course there is the mere difference of women's activities and experiences from men's, where it exists, that can provide resources for knowledge. Yet the distinctive standpoint move brings into focus another kind of resource: exploited and dominated peoples have been able to turn "an oppressive restriction . . . into a capacity for new kinds of experience and for seeing features and dimensions of the world and of history masked to other social actors," as Fredric Jameson puts the point. And because each group is oppressed and exploited in different ways, each has the possibility (not the certainty) of bringing distinctive resources to everyone's understandings of nature and social relations.[1] Of course a standpoint theorist must provide examples of the content of thought of an oppressed group to make clear the argument. But it is the process of obtaining from the experience of a concrete and ideological oppression a critical insight about the dominant group, its institutions, practices, and culture, that distinguishes a standpoint. Jameson proposes three features of women's experience that provided valuable epistemological possibilities for feminism: a distinctive experience of the body, a "capacity for non-reified consciousness," and the experience of a collective consciousness that is different from the consciousness created through working-class experience.

In the standpoint analyses of Part I are a number of proposals for the contents of distinctive experiences of oppression within which lie the possibility of developing critical epistemic and scientific insights into the workings of social relations, nature, and history. Smith focused on women's responsibility for everyday life. Hartsock focused on the women's work that transforms "raw nature" into social or cultural objects—animals of our species into our children, the products of the hunt into food, and so on. Rose focused on women's experiences of their bodies and on their responsibility for emotional labor. Collins focused on the experiences of being an "outsider within," of racial oppression, and of being always "named" by others.

In the essays in Part II additional distinctive women's conditions are identified as the starting point for developing critical, potentially liberatory accounts of nature, social relations, and history. Cultural critic bell hooks points to the importance for each oppressed group to identify, choose, and invent forms of marginality that enable them to survive by developing oppositional worldviews. She recalls the way she learned such a resistance strategy from her Black American family and friends in the small Kentucky town where she grew up. Philosopher Sara Ruddick explains how the standpoint of mothering activities (regardless of who does them) enables critical insights into the dominant institutions of mothering. The dissemination of such critical insights could, she hopes, help recruit women into anti-militarist projects. Philosopher of law Catharine A. MacKinnon identifies women's experiences of sexual and domestic violence as enabling women to see how "the state is male" insofar as it understands violence against women just the way its perpetrators do rather than in the way it is understood by its victims. Thus, she argues, from the standpoint of women's experience of rape and domestic abuse, the law's purported objectivity is indistinguishable from what is distinctively men's ways of thinking. Political philosopher Kathi Weeks focuses on women's oppression in labor as the activity permitting the emergence of feminist subjectivity.

Chela Sandoval identifies the continual exclusion and silencing of Third World women in North American white feminist movements as an important site enabling both critical examination of the conceptual practices of power of white feminist theory of the 1970s and 1980s, and the emergence of a "differential oppositional consciousness." This standpoint does not deny the value of the white feminist theoretical approaches, but it does challenge the claim of each to be the one and only valuable feminist conceptual framework. A "differential oppositional consciousness" permits a mobile, tactical feminism for Third World women (and the rest of us) that uses the resources each feminism provides for the contexts in which they are useful. In other sections are identified additional features of women's oppression that provide the potential for liberatory knowledge that is *for* women. For example, in Part IV, Maria Mies and Vandana Shiva identify the subsistence standpoint (which they elsewhere refer to as "the survival standpoint") of poor women and peasants in the Third World, and what can be learned about Western development policies for the Third World by starting off from such a standpoint.

Note

1. To the extent that one side of a "mere difference" is devalued and oppressed by the other, it has the possibility of being turned into a resource for a full-fledged, achieved standpoint. However, "mere differences" alone also provide resources on which multicultural science and technology movements, for example, have focused. See a framework for thinking about the resource that differences provide in "Cultures as Toolboxes for Sciences and Technologies" (chapter 4) and "Are There Gendered Standpoints on Nature?" (chapter 6) in my *Is Science Multicultural? Postcolonialisms, Feminisms, and Epistemologies* (Bloomington: Indiana University Press, 1998).

9

History and Class Consciousness as an "Unfinished Project"

FREDRIC JAMESON

... *History and Class Consciousness* [by Georg Lukács] was, ... one of the earliest explicit proposals (in what was to become the so-called Western Marxist tradition) for a new and more complexly mediated theory of ideology.[1] ...

What is argued in this text is essentially an *epistemological* priority of a particular social group or class in advanced society. Whatever the group or class identified and "privileged" by such an argument, therefore, the form of the argument is itself unusual and demands attention in its own right, since in its very structure it seeks to relate a truth claim to the social structure and phenomenological experience of a specific collectivity. Epistemology thus passes over into social phenomenology in a way that cannot but be felt as scandalous, and as a kind of "category mistake," by those for whom these levels correspond to distinct academic disciplines and their strictly differentiated methodologies. Since such differentiation—epistemology, economics, sociology as three autonomous fields of study—corresponds to Lukács's previous diagnosis of the reification of bourgeois thought, his very argument here—and the polemic against such specialization, in the form of the conceptual adversary or hostile reader—is itself a kind of "unity of theory and practice" and dramatized in the text the conceptual content of his position.

But the inverse form of formulating the issue of "priority" is no less misleading. It is, for example, tempting to suppose that if the matter of the practical balance of forces in alliance politics is not here immediately at stake, then the argument must somehow be a "metaphysical" one, that is, an argument about ultimate grounds or foundations, or about what the Marxist tradition notoriously calls "ultimately determining instances." The shape of a metaphysical argument of this kind comes immediately into view when one replaces Lukács's designation of the working class by a classification of its abstract concept, namely, *social class*. At that point, one concludes that Lukács is arguing the explanatory priority of the concept of *class* over competing concepts or "ultimately determining instances"—mostly, in the contemporary situation, sorted out according to race or gender or some related social concept on the one hand, or according to language or some related "dimensional" concept on the other. The polemic, thus conceived, becomes a two-front struggle. On one hand, "Marxism" (in the person of Lukács) wages a battle against feminism and race- or ethnic-based ideologies (or even against the more general prioritization of the "new social movements" or of "marginality"). On the other hand, it responds to the philosophical threat of various language-based "structuralisms" in the largest sense (Umberto Eco's defense of the sign,[2] for example, or Habermas's communicational model). This is, however, to recast Lukács's arguments in terms of what each side replies by reiterating its own "absolute presupposition," after the fashion of the older disputes (also still with us, however) over whether human nature is essentially good or essentially bad.

What is more significant is that this way of restaging the fundamental issue at stake in this moment of "Reification and the Consciousness of the Proletariat" omits not only what was its most original feature but also the very "move" or "step" on which the whole argument turned: namely the insistence, not on abstract concepts such as "class" or "production," but rather on group experience. The omission characterizes Lukács's defenders fully as much as his various adversaries to the point where, today, one has the feeling that the most authentic descendency of Lukács's thinking is to be found, not among the Marxists, but within a certain feminism, where the unique conceptual move of *History and Class Consciousness* has been appropriated for a whole program, now renamed (after Lukács's own usage) *standpoint theory*.[3]

These path-breaking texts now allow us to return to Lukács's argument in a new way, which opens a space of a different kind for polemics about the epistemological priority of the experience of various groups or collectivities (most immediately, in this case, the experience of women as opposed to the experience of the industrial working class). For the argument of standpoint theory now enables a principled relativism, in which the epistemological claims of the various groups can be inspected (and respected) for their "truth content" (Adorno's *Wahrheitsgehalt*) or their respective "moments of truth" (to use another convenient contemporary German expression). The presupposition is that, owing to its structural situation in the social order and to the specific forms of oppression and exploitation unique to that situation, each group lives the world in a phenomenologically specific way that allows it to see, or better still, that makes it unavoidable for that group to see and to know, features of the world that remain obscure, invisible, or merely occasional and secondary for other groups.

This way of describing the argument has, incidentally, the additional merit of cutting across that most notorious of all Lukács's secondary qualifications, namely the seemingly last-minute distinction between the actual experience and thinking of working-class people and their "imputed consciousness" *(zugerechnetes Bewusstsein)*.[4] This distinction opens the wedge through which Lukács's various adversaries (on the extreme left as well as on the right) glimpse the wolf-in-sheep's-clothing of the Party or the Intellectual, who now conveniently get substituted for a sociological working class that needs them to find out what it "really" thinks. But it should also be juxtaposed against the other crucial qualification of Lukács (shared, one would think, by all forms of Marxism), that the "subject" in question here is not, as in the bourgeois epistemologies, an *individual* one, but is the result of "the abolition of the isolated individual."[5]

> The bourgeoisie always perceives the subject and object of the historical process and of social reality in a double form: in terms of his consciousness the single individual is a perceiving subject confronting the overwhelming objective necessities imposed by society of which only minute fragments can be comprehended. But in reality it is precisely the conscious activity of the individual that is to be found on the object-side of the process, while the subject (the class) cannot be awakened into consciousness and this activity must always remain beyond the consciousness of the (apparent) subject, the individual.[6]

The temptations of the centered subject, therefore—including the optical illusion that scientific truth could somehow be the experience and spiritual property of an individual consciousness (of Lacan's "sujet supposé savoir," for example)—are a socially generated (but "objective") mirage projected by a properly bourgeois experience of social fragmentation and monadization.

The opposite of this monadic conception of individual consciousness is not, however, some doubtful, mystical or mystified, notion of *collective* consciousness. In my view, indeed, the stirring slogan so often taken to be the climax of *History and Class Consciousness*—the proletariat as "the identical subject-object of history"[7]—is rather the local thematic climax of Lukács's intermittent engagement throughout this text with the central motifs of German idealism from Fichte to Hegel. The passing phrase marks the "solution" to those specific traditional contradictions, in their own specific language or code, which is no longer our own. It is preferable, in our own linguistic and intellectual climate, to retranslate the perspectival and subject-oriented figure of the "standpoint" into the structural notion of the positioning of a given class or class fraction in the social totality.

At that point, it becomes clear that the epistemological "priority" of "proletarian consciousness," as a class or collective phenomenon, has to do with the *conditions of possibility* of new thinking inherent in this particular class position. It is not a matter of the scientific aptitude of individual workers (although Sartre quite properly underscores the qualitative difference in thought mode of people who work with machines as opposed, for example, to peasants or shopkeepers), still less of the mystical properties of some collective proletarian "world view." The conception of "conditions of possibility" then has the advantage of stressing, not the content of scientific thought, but its prerequisites, its preparatory requirements, that without which it cannot properly develop. It is a conception that includes the diagnosis of blocks and limits to knowledge (reification as what suppresses the ability to grasp totalities) as well as the enumeration of positive new features (the capacity to think in terms of process).[8]

Contemporary feminist standpoint theory was able to restore and to make again visible this fundamental line of Lukács's argument (often effaced or distorted by generations of "faithful" as well as hostile commentators), because of the central importance, it gives to the problem of Western science itself and of scientific knowledge. Lukács's work had rarely been seen in this context for two reasons: first, because of his own anti-scientific and Viconian bias, inherited by so-called Western Marxism as a whole,[9] and second, because developments in the history and philosophy of science were in the past never so propitious for the posing of such questions as they are in the effervescence of the post-Kuhnian moment of this sub-discipline, when stereotypes of Lysenko have been displaced by a new speculative willingness to grasp scientific facts and scientific knowledge as a human construct and as praxis.[10] But it is precisely only within that radically different framework—science as construction and invention, rather than science as discovery and as the passive contemplation of external law—that such Lukácsean issues as the class preconditions of the possible forms of scientific praxis become meaningful and even urgent.

Meanwhile, the feminist appropriation of Lukács also allows for a productive and comparative inquiry into the epistemological potentialities of the various social groups which is very different in spirit from that sterile metaphysical quarrel about "ultimately determining instances" to which reference has already been made. And this is also the moment in which the conception of a "moment of truth" in the various competing types of group experience becomes crucial, since it is not some abstract evaluation applied from the outside and after the fact to this new kind of epistemological and sociological description, but is rather immanent and inherent in this last. Lukács himself, for example, first characterized the phenomenological experience of the industrial working class in terms of a new capacity to see the world historically and in terms of process, which that class very specifically owed to its concrete situation as the ultimate, but very unique, commodity in the system of capitalist production. Its structural destiny, therefore, on this formulation, lay in its experience of itself as wage labor, or in other words as the commodification of labor power, a form of *negative* constraint and violence which now dialectically produces the unexpectedly *positive*, new content of its experience as "the self-consciousness of the commodity."[11] In his 1967 Preface to the book—a mature autocritique which can no longer be supposed to be motivated by any of the Galilean ambiguities of his earlier recantation—Lukács proposes a reformulation of this epistemological "exceptionality" of the industrial working class in terms of labor and praxis[12] (whether the transformation in contemporary production and machinery, the new dynamics of the cybernetic in late capitalism, modifies or enriches this descriptive option remains to be seen). Meanwhile, other forms of Marxism have thematized the uniqueness of working-class experience in further, distinct categories, such as that of a specific experience of cooperative or collective action.

If one wants to be consequent about Lukács's model, however, it seems clear that *History and Class Consciousness* must also be read, or must be rewritten, as including a description of the specific epistemological capacities of the bourgeoisie itself, the very originator of "Western science" in its current form. At that point, it will be very precisely the dynamics of reification as a social and phenomenological experience that constitute the "moment of truth" of the extraordinary disciplinary and specializing developments of "positivist" research. Those developments comprise a long and incomparably productive period which now seems to have touched its structural limits, if the unparalleled intensity of contemporary critiques of Western "rationality," of the dynamics of the physical sciences, and of the historical and structural closure of the various disciplines, is to be believed.

Feminist "standpoint theory," which has generated some of the most acute of those critiques, now stages the specific phenomenological experience of women in the patriarchal social order as an equally "exceptional" but very different structural submission to negative constraint from that of the working class. That experience generates new and positive epistemological possibilities which are thematically distinct from those enumerated by the Marxist tradition. The emphases here—whose relationship varies according to the description, in this theory currently in full elaboration—include an experience of the body radically distinct from that of men, or even of male workers (even though what is presupposed is that this is an experience of the deeper truth of all bodily experience, generally masked from men's consciousness). They also include a capacity for non-reified consciousness, generally negatively characterized in the caricatured attributes of feeling or of "intuition," but which itself "leaps over" a certain historical stage of the psychic division of labor to which men have historically had to submit. Finally, feminist "standpoint theory" emphasizes an experience of the collective which is different from the active collective praxis of workers and already constitutively experienced as that community and cooperation, which for the working-class movement still lies in the future.[13]

The Black experience has its "priority" in something like a combination of both of these distinct "moments of truth" (that attributed to workers and that attributed to women), but a combination which is qualitatively distinct from both, including not merely an experience of reification deeper than the commodity form, but also the historic link, by way of imperialism and the plunder of what was to become the Third World, with the older stage of capitalist accumulation. These kinds of unique epistemological priorities are surely presupposed in all Black theory as it emerged from the 1960s and the Black Power movement; but their fundamental theorization goes back, famously, to the immense figure of DuBois and his notion of a "double-consciousness": "this sense of always looking at one's self through the eyes of others, of measuring one's soul by the tape of a world that looks on in amused contempt and pity."[14]

Meanwhile, despite the development of a Jewish-Studies industry since the first printing of this essay, it seems appropriate to add a word about this specific social and epistemological situation as well, so intimately related to the development of Marxism and of dialectical thought. We are in fact often tempted, as intellectuals, to stress the obvious formal analogies between the Talmudic tradition and its exegetical relationship to sacred texts and the intricacies of modern dialectical reading and writing. But these analogies pre-suppose a cultural transmission which remains obscure, and which may well be very problematical indeed in the case of assimilated urban Jews whose interest in the tradition (one thinks of Walter Benjamin) was purely intellectual and a development in later adult life. The "moment of truth" of the Central European Jewish situation seems to me very different from this, and cannot go unnoticed by any reader of the work of Adorno, and in particular of *Dialectic of Enlightenment*. This is not first and foremost the formal and aesthetic stress on pain and suffering, on dissonance and the negative, everywhere present in Adorno, but rather a more primary experience, namely that of *fear* and of vulnerability—the primal fact, for Adorno and Horkheimer, of human history itself and of that "dialectic of Englightenment," that scientific domination of nature and the self, which constitutes the internal machine of Western civilization. But this experience of fear, in all its radicality, which cuts across class and gender to the point of touching the bourgeois in the very isolation of his town houses of sumptuous Berlin apartments, is surely the very "moment of truth" of ghetto life itself, as the Jews and so many other ethnic groups have had to live it: the helplessness of the village community before the perpetual and unpredictable imminence of the lynching or the pogrom, the race riot. Other groups' experience of fear is occasional, rather than constitutive: standpoint analysis specifically demands a differentiation between the various negative experiences of constraint, between the *exploitation* suffered by workers and the *oppression* suffered by women and continuing on through the distinct structural forms of exclusion and alienation characteristic of other kinds of group experience.

Those clearly include the heterosexist life-worlds that inspire queer theory; as well as a variety of other ethnic or even national situations; but it is important that such comparison of the "wounds" should not degenerate into a pluralist or multi-cultural aesthetic delectation on the order of the older historicism, even though history is a better way to approach the singular structure of the collective experience in question than the much abused pseudoconcept of "culture" as such. Deleuze offers a productive version of standpoint theory when he recommends that we think of it in terms of the absence of a "people"—"le peuple, c'est ce qui manque, c'est ce qui n'est pas là";[15] rather than in terms of a power to achieve or which is already achieved. Such analysis is finally not complete until the identification of the "moment of truth" of group experience—itself negative and positive all at once, an oppressive restriction which turns into a capacity for new kinds of experience and for seeing features and dimensions of the world and of history masked to other social actors is prolonged by an epistemological articulation that translates such experience into new possibilities of thought and knowledge. That such new possibilities can also be thought of in aesthetic and formal ways, alongside these scientific and epistemological ones, must now be recalled and emphatically stressed, since it was in terms of this very interrelationship between the formal possibilities of "realism" and of standpoint knowledge that we argued for the deeper continuity between the Lukács of *History and Class Consciousness* and the later theoretician of the realist novel.

What emerges from the feminist project, and from the speculations it inspires, is an "unfinished project": namely the differentiation of all those situations of what I have tried neutrally to characterize as "constraint," which are often monolithically subsumed under single-shot political concepts such as "domination" or "power"; economic concepts such as "exploitation"; social concepts such as "oppression"; or philosophical concepts such as "alienation." These reified concepts and terms, taken on their own as meaningful starting points, encourage the revival of what I have characterized above as an essentially metaphysical polemic about the ultimate priority of the political, say (the defense of the primacy of "domination"), versus that of the economic (the counter-primacy of the notion of "exploitation").

What seems more productive is to dissolve this conceptuality once again back into the concrete situations from which it emerged: to make an inventory of the variable structures of "constraint" lived by the various marginal, oppressed, or dominated groups—the so-called "new social movements" fully as much as the working classes—with this difference, that each form of privation is acknowledged as producing its own specific "epistemology," its own specific view from below, and its own specific and distinctive truth claim. It is a project that will sound like "relativism" or "pluralism" only if the identity of the absent common object of such "theorization" from multiple "standpoints" is overlooked—what one therefore does not exactly have the right to call (but let it stand as contradictory short-hand) "late capitalism."

As for the "workerism" of *History and Class Consciousness*, I have tried to suggest that it is also not an end point, not a "solution" or a final position on matters of group consciousness and praxis, but rather the beginning of work yet to be done, and of a task or project which is not that of ancient history, but of our present. Toward the end of his life, in an interview conducted in the late 1960s, Lukács had this to say about the utopian romanticism of that now bygone era:

> Today, in arousing the subjective factor, we cannot recreate and continue the 1920s, we have instead to proceed on the basis of a new beginning, with all the experience that we have from the earlier workers' movement and from Marxism. We must be clear about this, however, that the problem is to begin anew; to use an analogy, we are not now in the twenties of the twentieth century, but in a certain

sense at the beginning of the nineteenth century, when the workers' movement slowly began to take shape in the wake of the French revolution. I believe that this idea is very important for theorists, for despair can very rapidly set in if the assertion of certain truths only finds a very weak resonance. Don't forget that certain things that Saint-Simon and Fourier spoke about had at the time an extraordinarily weak resonance, and it was only in the thirties and forties of the nineteenth century that a revival of the workers' movement got underway.[16]

The Communist Manifesto, in other words, let alone Lenin and the Soviet revolution, are not behind us somewhere in time; they have yet to come into being. In some new way we are called on to achieve them through the slow and intricate resistances of historical time. Something like this is also what I would have liked to say about Lukács himself. History and Class Consciousness is a work whose prodigious intellectual deductions had an incomparable effect on several generations of revolutionary intellectuals. In that sense, to be sure, it is alive in the past and a perpetually fascinating object of historical mediation, among those very special dead which it is the mission of the historian, à la Michelet or Benjamin, to summon back to life. I think that it would be better, however, to consider that, like the Manifesto, it has yet to be written, it lies ahead of us in historical time. Our task, as political intellectuals, is to lay the groundwork for that situation in which it can again appear, with all the explosive freshness of the Novum, as though for the first time in which it can, once again, become both real and true.

Notes

1. Geschichte und Klassenbewusstsein (Neuwied: Luchterhand, 1977), 387–393; History and Class Consciousness, trans. Rodney Livingstone (Cambridge: MIT Press, 1971), 199–204. Hereafter page references will designate both editions, the German preceding the English. Re-edited, with additions, by the author.
2. As for example in The Theory of Semiotics (Bloomington: Indiana University Press, 1976).
3. See Nancy Hartsock, Money, Sex and Power (New York: Longman, 1983): Sandra Harding, The Science Question in Feminism (Ithaca: Cornell University Press, 1986); and Alison M. Jaggar, Feminist Politics and Human Nature (Totowa: Rowman and Allanheld, 1983).
4. The term is not used in the major essay on which we have drawn here, "Reification and the Consciousness of the Proletariat," but rather in the essay entitled "Class Consciousness" (History and Class Consciousness, op. cit., 223–224/51). The fateful sentence reads as follows: "Class consciousness consists in the fact of the appropriate and rational actions 'imputed' to a particular typical position in the process of production." That the word "rational" specifically mobilizes Weber's theory of rationalization may not be particularly evident in the English-language context, but obviously moves Lukács's thinking much closer to Weber's theory of "ideal types."
5. History and Class Consciousness, op. cit., 356/171.
6. Ibid., 350/165.
7. Ibid., 385/197.
8. These are of course the central features of Lukács's socio-economic description of reification in the first section of "Reification and the Consciousness of the Proletariat" and of his philosophical description in the second section.
9. See Perry Anderson, Considerations on Western Marxism (London: Verso, 1976), 56; on the orientation to epistemology, 52–53. Vico's verum factum in effect sunders history from nature as an object of possible human knowledge.

10. See, for example, the pathbreaking work of Bruno Latour: (with Steve Woolgar) *Labora-tory Life* (Princeton: Princeton University Press, 1986) and *Science in Action* (Cambridge. Harvard University Press, 1987).

11. *History and Class Consciousness*, op. cit., 352/168. The form of the theory (often schemat-ically designated as the theory of "radical chains") obviously originates in Marx himself: see "Critique of Hegel's *Philosophy of Right*. Introduction," in *Early Writings* (London: Penguin, 1975), esp. 256.

12. See, in the English-language editions of *History and Class Consciousness*, xvii–xviii.

13. See in particular Hartsock, op. cit., 231–261; Harding, op. cit., 141–162; and Jaggar, op. cit., 369–385. The privileged test-case for the relationship between women's "stand-point" and scientific discovery has become the achievement of the molecular biologist Barbara McClintock; see Evelyn Fox Keller's biography, *A Feeling for the Organism* (San Francisco: Freeman, 1983), as well as her collection *Reflections on Gender and Science* (New Haven: Yale, 1984), particularly Part III, Sections 8 and 9, 150–177.

14. W. E. B. DuBois, *The Souls of Black Folk* in *Writings W. E. B. DuBois* (New York: Library of America, 1986), 364. See also Harold Cruse, *The Crisis of the Negro Intellectual* (New York: Quill, 1984). The omission of this reference in the first version of the present essay is more than surprising and can only be explained: 1) by my anti-Americanism (according to Cornel West); 2) my racist blind spots; 3) sheer intellectual ignorance; and/or 4) by the protean and unclassifiable nature of DuBois's work and of his own status as an intellectual and a writer.

15. Gilles Deleuze, *Cinéma 2: L'Image-temps* (Paris: Minuit, 1985), 281: the entire section that follows contains a political lesson whose consequences we have yet to draw.

16. Hans Heinz Holz, Leo Kofler, and Wolfgang Abendroth, *Conversations with Lukács* (Cambridge: MIT, 1975), 62.

10
Choosing the Margin as a Space of Radical Openness

bell hooks

As a radical standpoint, perspective, position, "the politics of location" necessarily calls those of us who would participate in the formation of counterhegemonic cultural practice to identify the spaces where we begin the process
of re-vision. When asked, "What does it mean to enjoy reading *Beloved,* admire
Schooldaze, and have a theoretical interest in post-structuralist theory?" (one
of the "wild" questions posed by the Third World Cinema Focus Forum), I located my answer concretely in the realm of oppositional political struggle. Such
diverse pleasures can be experienced, enjoyed even, because one transgresses,
moves "out of one's place." For many of us, that movement requires pushing
against oppressive boundaries set by race, sex, and class domination. Initially,
then, it is a defiant political gesture. Moving, we confront the realities of choice
and location. Within complex and ever shifting realms of power relations, do
we position ourselves on the side of colonizing mentality? Or do we continue to
stand in political resistance with the oppressed, ready to offer our ways of seeing
and theorizing, of making culture, toward that revolutionary effort which seeks
to create space where there is unlimited access to the pleasure and power of
knowing, where transformation is possible? This choice is crucial. It shapes and
determines our response to existing cultural practice and our capacity to envision new, alternative, oppositional aesthetic acts. It informs the way we speak
about these issues, the language we choose. Language is also a place of struggle.

To me, the effort to speak about issues of "space and location" evoked
pain. The questions raised compelled difficult explorations of "silences"—
unaddressed places within my personal political and artistic evolution. Before
I could consider answers, I had to face ways these issues were intimately connected to intense personal emotional upheaval regarding place, identity, desire.
In an intense all-night-long conversation with Eddie George (member of Black
Audio Film Collective) talking about the struggle of oppressed people to come
to voice, he made the very "down" comment that "ours is a broken voice." My
response was simply that when you hear the broken voice you also hear the pain
contained within that brokenness—a speech of suffering; often it's that sound
nobody wants to hear. Stuart Hall talks about the need for a "politics of articulation." He and Eddie have engaged in dialogue with me in a deeply soulful

way, hearing my struggle for words. It is this dialogue between comrades that is a gesture of love; I am grateful.

I have been working to change the way I speak and write, to incorporate in the manner of telling a sense of place, of not just who I am in the present but where I am coming from, the multiple voices within me. I have confronted silence, inarticulateness. When I say, then, that these words emerge from suffering, I refer to that personal struggle to name that location from which I come to voice—that space of my theorizing.

Often when the radical voice speaks about domination we are speaking to those who dominate. Their presence changes the nature and direction of our words. Language is also a place of struggle. I was just a girl coming slowly into womanhood when I read Adrienne Rich's words, "This is the oppressor's language, yet I need it to talk to you." This language that enabled me to attend graduate school, to write a dissertation, to speak at job interviews, carries the scent of oppression. Language is also a place of struggle. The Australian aborigines say "that smell of the white man is killing us." I remember the smells of my childhood, hot water corn bread, turnip greens, fried pies. I remember the way we talked to one another, our words thickly accented black Southern speech. Language is also a place of struggle. We are wedded in language, have our being in words. Language is also a place of struggle. Dare I speak to oppressed and oppressor in the same voice? Dare I speak to you in a language that will move beyond the boundaries of domination—a language that will not bind you, fence you in, or hold you? Language is also a place of struggle. The oppressed struggle in language to recover ourselves, to reconcile, to reunite, to renew. Our words are not without meaning, they are an action, a resistance. Language is also a place of struggle.

It is no easy task to find ways to include our multiple voices within the various texts we create—in film, poetry, feminist theory. Those are sounds and images that mainstream consumers find difficult to understand. Sounds and scenes which cannot be appropriated are often that sign everyone questions, wants to erase, to "wipe out." I feel it even now, writing this piece when I gave it talking and reading, talking spontaneously, using familiar academic speech now and then, "talking the talk"—using black vernacular speech, the intimate sounds and gestures I normally save for family and loved ones. Private speech in public discourse, intimate intervention, making another text, a space that enables me to recover all that I am in language, I find so many gaps, absences in this written text. To cite them at least is to let the reader know something has been missed, or remains there hinted at by words—there in the deep structure.

Throughout *Freedom Charter,* a work which traces aspects of the movement against racial apartheid in South Africa, this statement is constantly repeated: *our struggle is also a struggle of memory against forgetting.* In much new, exciting cultural practice, cultural texts—in film, black literature, critical theory—there is an effort to remember that is expressive of the need to create spaces where one is able to redeem and reclaim the past, legacies of pain, suffering, and triumph in ways that transform present reality. Fragments of memory are not simply represented as flat documentary but constructed to give a "new take" on the old, constructed to move us into a different mode of articulation. We see this in films like *Dreaming Rivers and Illusions,* and in books like *Mama Day* by Gloria Naylor. Thinking again about space and location, I heard the statement "our struggle is also a struggle of memory against forgetting"; a politicization of memory that distinguishes nostalgia, that longing for something to be as once it was, a kind of useless act, from that remembering that serves to illuminate and transform the present.

I have needed to remember, as part of a self-critical process where one pauses to reconsider choices and location, tracing my journey from small town Southern black life, from folk traditions, and church experience to cities, to the university, to neighborhoods that are not racially segregated, to places where I see for the first time independent cinema, where I read critical theory, where I write theory. Along that trajectory, I vividly recall efforts to silence my coming to voice. In my public presentation I was able to tell stories, to share memories. Here again I only hint at them. The opening essay in my book, *Talking Back,* describes my effort to emerge as critical thinker, artist, and writer in a context of repression. I talk about punishment, about mama and daddy aggressively silencing me, about the censorship of black communities. I had no choice. I had to struggle and resist to emerge from that context and then from other locations with mind intact, with an open heart. I had to leave that space I called home to move beyond boundaries, yet I needed also to return there. We sing a song in the black church tradition that says, "I'm going up the rough side of the mountain on my way home." Indeed the very meaning of "home" changes with experience of decolonization, of radicalization. At times, home is nowhere. At times, one knows only extreme estrangement and alienation. Then home is no longer just one place. It is locations. Home is that place which enables and promotes varied and everchanging perspectives, a place where one discovers new ways of seeing reality, frontiers of difference. One confronts and accepts dispersal and fragmentation as part of the construction of a new world order that reveals more fully where we are, who we can become, an order that does not demand forgetting. "Our struggle is also a struggle of memory against forgetting."

This experience of space and location is not the same for black folks who have always been privileged, or for black folks who desire only to move from underclass status to points of privilege; not the same for those of us from poor backgrounds who have had to continually engage in actual political struggle both within and outside black communities to assert an aesthetic and critical presence. Black folks coming from poor, underclass communities, who enter universities or privileged cultural settings unwilling to surrender every vestige of who we were before we were there, all "sign" of our class and cultural "difference," who are unwilling to play the role of "exotic Other," must create spaces within that culture of domination if we are to survive whole, our souls intact. Our very presence is a disruption. We are often as much an "Other," a threat to black people from privileged class backgrounds who do not understand or share our perspectives, as we are to uninformed white folks. Everywhere we go there is pressure to silence our voices, to co-opt and undermine them. Mostly, of course, we are not there. We never "arrive" or "can't stay." Back in those spaces where we come from, we kill ourselves in despair, drowning in nihilism, caught in poverty, in addiction, in every postmodern mode of dying that can be named. Yet when we few remain in that "other" space, we are often too isolated, too alone. We die there, too. Those of us who live, who "make it," passionately holding on to aspects of that "downhome" life we do not intend to lose while simultaneously seeking new knowledge and experience, invent spaces of radical openness. Without such spaces we would not survive. Our living depends on our ability to conceptualize alternatives, often improvised. Theorizing about this experience aesthetically, critically is an agenda for radical cultural practice.

For me this space of radical openness is a margin—a profound edge. Locating oneself there is difficult yet necessary. It is not a "safe" place. One is always at risk. One needs a community of resistance.

In the preface to *Feminist Theory: From Margin to Center*, I expressed these thoughts on marginality:

> To be in the margin is to be part of the whole but outside the main body. As black Americans living in a small Kentucky town, the railroad tracks were a daily reminder of our marginality. Across those tracks were paved streets, stores we could not enter, restaurants we could not eat in, and people we could not look directly in the face. Across those tracks was a world we could work in as maids, as janitors, as prostitutes, as long as it was in a service capacity. We could enter that world but we could not live there. We had always to return to the margin, to cross the tracks to shacks and abandoned houses on the edge of town.
>
> There were laws to ensure our return. Not to return was to risk being punished. Living as we did—on the edge—we developed a particular way of seeing reality. We looked both from the outside in and from the inside out. We focused our attention on the center as well as on the margin. We understood both. This mode of seeing reminded us of the existence of a whole universe, a main body made up of both margin and center. Our survival depended on an ongoing public awareness of the separation between margin and center and an ongoing private acknowledgement that we were a necessary, vital part of that whole.
>
> This sense of wholeness, impressed upon our consciousness by the structure of our daily lives, provided us with an oppositional world-view—a mode of seeing unknown to most of our oppressors, that sustained us, aided us in our struggle to transcend poverty and despair, strengthened our sense of self and our solidarity.

Though incomplete, these statements identify marginality as much more than a site of deprivation; in fact I was saying just the opposite, that it is also the site of radical possibility, a space of resistance. It was this marginality that

I was naming as a central location for the production of a counter-hegemonic discourse that is not just found in words but in habits of being and the way one lives. As such, I was not speaking of a marginality one wishes to lose—to give up or surrender as part of moving into the center—but rather of a site one stays in, clings to even, because it nourishes one's capacity to resist. It offers to one the possibility of radical perspective from which to see and create, to imagine alternatives, new worlds.

This is not a mythic notion of marginality. It comes from lived experience. Yet I want to talk about what it means to struggle to maintain that marginality even as one works, produces, lives, if you will, at the center. I no longer live in that segregated world across the tracks. Central to life in that world was the ongoing awareness of the necessity of opposition. When Bob Marley sings, "We refuse to be what you want us to be, we are what we are, and that's the way it's going to be," that space of refusal, where one can say no to the colonizer, no to the downpressor, is located in the margins. And one can only say no, speak the voice of resistance, because there exists a counter-language. While it may resemble the colonizer's tongue, it has undergone a transformation, it has been irrevocably changed. When I left that concrete space in the margins, I kept alive in my heart ways of knowing reality which affirm continually not only the primacy of resistance but the necessity of a resistance that is sustained by remembrance of the past, which includes recollections of broken tongues giving us ways to speak that decolonize our minds, our very beings. Once mama said to me as I was about to go again to the predominantly white university, "You can take what the white people have to offer, but you do not have to love them." Now understanding her cultural codes, I know that she was not saying to me not to love people of other races. She was speaking about colonization and the reality of what it means to be taught in a culture of domination by those who dominate. She was insisting on my power to be able to separate useful knowledge that I might get from the dominating group from participation in ways of knowing that would lead to estrangement, alienation, and worse—assimilation and co-optation. She was saying that it is not necessary to give yourself over to them to learn. Not having been in those institutions, she knew that I might be faced again and again with situations where I would be "tried," made to feel as though a central requirement of my being accepted would mean participation in this system of exchange to ensure my success, my "making it." She was reminding me of the necessity of opposition and simultaneously encouraging me not to lose that radical perspective shaped and formed by marginality.

Understanding marginality as position and place of resistance is crucial for oppressed, exploited, colonized people. If we only view the margin as sign marking the despair, a deep nihilism penetrates in a destructive way the very ground of our being. It is there in that space of collective despair that one's creativity, one's imagination is at risk, there that one's mind is fully colonized, there that the freedom one longs for is lost. Truly the mind that resists colonization

struggles for freedom one longs for as lost. Truly the mind that resists colonization struggles for freedom of expression. The struggle may not even begin with
the colonizer; it may begin within one's segregated, colonized community and
family. So I want to note that I am not trying to romantically re-inscribe the
notion of that space of marginality where the oppressed live apart from their
oppressors as "pure." I want to say that these margins have been both sites of
repression and sites of resistance. And since we are well able to name the nature
of that repression we know better the margin as site of deprivation. We are more
silent when it comes to speaking of the margin as site of resistance. We are more
often silenced when it comes to speaking of the margin as site of resistance.

Silenced. During my graduate years I heard myself speaking often in the
voice of resistance. I cannot say that my speech was welcomed. I cannot say that
my speech was heard in such a way that it altered relations between colonizer
and colonized. Yet what I have noticed is that those scholars, most especially
those who name themselves radical critical thinkers, feminist thinkers, now
fully participate in the construction of a discourse about the "Other." I was
made "Other" there in that space with them. In that space in the margins, that
lived-in segregated world of my past and present. They did not meet me there
in that space. They met me at the center. They greeted me as colonizers. I am
waiting to learn from them the path of their resistance, of how it came to be that
they were able to surrender the power to act as colonizers. I am waiting for them
to bear witness, to give testimony. They say that the discourse on marginality,
on difference has moved beyond a discussion of "us and them." They do not
speak of how this movement has taken place. This is a response from the radical
space of my marginality. It is a space of resistance. It is a space I choose.

I am waiting for them to stop talking about the "Other," to stop even describing how important it is to be able to speak about difference. It is not just
important what we speak about, but how and why we speak. Often this speech
about the "Other" is also a mask, an oppressive talk hiding gaps, absences, that
space where our words would be if we were speaking, if there were silence, if we
were there. This "we" is that "us" in the margins, that "we" who inhabit marginal
space that is not a site of domination but a place of resistance. Enter that space.
Often this speech about the "Other" annihilates, erases: "No need to hear your
voice when I can talk about you better than you can speak about yourself. No
need to hear your voice. Only tell me about your pain. I want to know your
story. And then I will tell it back to you in a new way. Tell it back to you in such a
way that it has become mine, my own. Re-writing you, I write myself anew. I am
still author, authority. I am still the colonizer, the speaking subject, and you are
now at the center of my talk." Stop. We greet you as liberators. This "we" is that
"us" in the margins, that "we" who inhabit marginal space that is not a site of
domination but a place of resistance. Enter that space. This is an intervention.
I am writing to you. I am speaking from a place in the margins where I am
different, where I see things differently. I am talking about what I see.

Speaking from margins. Speaking in resistance. I open a book. There are words on the back cover, *Never in the Shadows Again.* A book which suggests the possibility of speaking as liberators. Only who is speaking and who is silent. Only who stands in the shadows—the shadow in a doorway, the space where images of black women are represented voiceless, the space where our words are invoked to serve and support, the space of our absence. Only small echoes of protest. We are re-written. We are "Other." We are the margin. Who is speaking and to whom. Where do we locate ourselves and comrades.

Silenced. We fear those who speak about us, who do not speak to us and with us. We know what it is like to be silenced. We know that the forces that silence us, because they never want us to speak, differ from the forces that say speak, tell me your story. Only do not speak in a voice of resistance. Only speak from that space in the margin that is a sign of deprivation, a wound, an unfulfilled longing. Only speak your pain.

This is an intervention. A message from that space in the margin that is a site of creativity and power, that inclusive space where we recover ourselves, where we move in solidarity to erase the category colonized/colonizer. Marginality as site of resistance. Enter that space. Let us meet there. Enter that space. We greet you as liberators.

Spaces can be real and imagined. Spaces can tell stories and unfold histories. Spaces can be interrupted, appropriated, and transformed through artistic and literary practice.

As Pratibha Parma notes, "The appropriation and use of space are political acts."

To speak about that location from which work emerges, I choose familiar politicized language, old codes, words like "struggle, marginality, resistance." I choose these words knowing that they are no longer popular or "cool"—hold onto them and the political legacies they evoke and affirm, even as I work to change what they say, to give them renewed and different meaning.

I am located in the margin. I make a definite distinction between that marginality which is imposed by oppressive structures and that marginality one chooses as site of resistance—as location of radical openness and possibility. This site of resistance is continually formed in that segregated culture of opposition that is our critical response to domination. We come to this space through suffering and pain, through struggle. We know struggle to be that which pleasures, delights, and fulfills desire. We are transformed, individually, collectively, as we make radical creative space which affirms and sustains our subjectivity, which gives us a new location from which to articulate our sense of the world.

11
Maternal Thinking as a Feminist Standpoint

SARA RUDDICK

I have written of maternal thinking as if it were only one discipline among others—no ax to grind, no particular story to impose upon the many stories people tell, no meta-message in the quilt that different artists make together. To be sure, women's and mothers' voices have been silenced, their thinking distorted and sentimentalized. Hence it will take sustained political and intellectual effort before maternal thinking is truly heard. Well-intentioned generosity and space and time to speak are not enough. Nonetheless, I have envisioned a future in which maternal thinkers are respected and self-respecting without making for them/us any claims of moral and political advantage.

Temperamentally I am a pluralist. From grade school, I welcomed the idea that there were many perspectives and hence many truths. In my childhood, it was Nazis, white supremacists, and later McCarthyites who claimed to speak from a privileged standpoint. Not surprisingly, when I studied philosophy I was drawn to traditions that rejected the ambition, pervasive among philosophers, of ordering ways of knowing from the least to the most adequate. I learned that to imagine a language—or a discipline—was to imagine what Wittgenstein called a "form of life."[1] If there was no God, then there was also no philosopher who stood outside or at the beginning, giving grounds, justifying evidence, making a place for epistemological and moral certainty. Reasons begin in and ultimately end in action. To quote Wittgenstein again:

> Giving grounds, however, justifying the evidence, comes to an end; but the end is not certain propositions striking us immediately as true, i.e., it is not a kind of seeing on our part; it is our *acting,* which lies at the bottom of the language game.[2]

If the statement "A child's life must be protected" strikes us as immediately true, this is because we daily act protectively and our true statement expresses as it reveals our commitment. What the sentence expresses and the commitment reveals is not only the truth that children are deserving of protection but also the form of life in which that truth is indubitable. Preservative love is a "form of life": "What has to be accepted, the given, is—so one could say—*Forms of Life.*"[3]

In feminism too I have applauded those who reject the large picture for multiple perspectives. Catharine MacKinnon, for example, expresses my epistemological stance:

> Feminism not only challenges masculine partiality but questions the universality imperative itself. Aperspectivity is revealed as a strategy of male hegemony. . . . Nor is feminism objective, abstract, or universal. . . . Feminism does not begin with the premise that it is unpremised. It does not desire to persuade an unpremised audience because there is no such audience.[4]

I continue to share the epistemological prejudices of the *Women's Ways of Knowing* collective, whose members celebrate women for recognizing "that all knowledge is constructed . . . that answers to all questions vary depending on the context in which they are asked and on the frame of reference of the person doing the asking."[5]

Nonetheless, only a few years after I began writing about maternal thinking, my pluralism began to give way to angry and insistent claims of superiority. My son was reaching draft age in a country whose government was prone to invade the islands, gulfs, and governments of peoples and resources it wished to control. If conscripted, my son would serve a "defense" establishment that deliberately "targets" millions of strangers with weapons no one could survive and devises war plans that no one could live long enough to execute. I became preoccupied with the immorality—and the madness—of organized, deliberate violence. I read the works of pacifists, just-war theorists, and military historians, began teaching seminars on the choice between violence and nonviolence, joined a women's peace group, and took part in a working conference of philosophers, defense department analysts, and defense sociologists who were charged with studying conscription but often spent their time planning and remembering war. Soon I had frightened myself thoroughly. For a time I felt as if I were pathologically obsessed and hopelessly sentimental.

> I didn't raise my son to be a soldier
> I brought him up to be my pride and joy
> Who dares to put a musket on his shoulder
> To kill some other mother's darling boy?[6]

It was in this mood that I received a copy of an article by Nancy Hartsock that both developed and transformed the Marxian notion of a privileged political and epistemological "standpoint."[7] A standpoint is an engaged vision of the world opposed and superior to dominant ways of thinking. As a proletarian standpoint is a superior vision produced by the experience and oppressive conditions of labor, a feminist standpoint is a superior vision produced by the political conditions and distinctive work of women. Although the epistemological and moral values of any standpoint are obscured by dominant ideals of reason and despised by dominant peoples, subordination can be overturned through political and intellectual struggle. Even now, the vision offered by a feminist standpoint reveals that dominant ways of knowing are, in Hartsock's words, "partial and perverse."

By "women's work"—the basis for a feminist standpoint—Hartsock has in mind "caring labor": birthing labor and lactation; production and preparation of food; mothering; kin work; housework; nursing; many kinds of teaching; and care of the frail elderly, work that is characteristically performed in exploitative and oppressive circumstances. I believe . . . that it is at least premature to assimilate these different kinds of work as maternal work. Nonetheless, it is certainly the case that maternal practices make up a central part of caring labor, and hence maternal thinking in its many variations could be considered a constituent element of the standpoint that Hartsock envisions. Or, to put the point romantically—adapting Foucault—maternal thinking is a "subjugated knowledge," "lost in an all-encompassing theoretical framework or erased in a triumphal history of ideas"—"regarded with disdain by intellectuals as being either primitive or woefully incomplete" yet likely to become "insurrectionary."[8]

This invigorating language is more than rhetoric. Hartsock not only proclaimed the worth of caring labor; she substantiated her claim by detailing characteristics of caring labor that were responsible for the standpoint's superiority. Caretakers are immersed in the materials of the physical world. The physical phenomena of human and other bodies must be interpreted in relation to the demands of caretaking. It is not useful to abstract to "air, earth, fire, and water," let alone to electrons. Whether care workers are cleaning toilet bowls, attending to the incontinence of dying patients, or toilet training children; whether they nurse a baby, invent a sauce, or mash potatoes thin enough to allow a toothless, elderly person to feed herself, care workers depend on a practical knowledge of the qualities of the material world, including the human bodily world, in which they deal.

This means that the material world, seen under the aspect of caring labor, is organized in terms of people's needs and pleasures and, by extension, of the needs and pleasures of any animal or plant that is instrumental in human caring or is tended for its own sake. The value of objects and accomplishments turns on their usefulness in satisfying needs and giving pleasures rather than on the money to be made by selling them or the prestige by owning them or the attention by displaying them. Finally, caretakers work with subjects; they give birth to and tend self-generating, autonomously willing lives. A defining task of their work is to maintain mutually helpful connections with another person—or animal—whose separateness they create and respect. Hence they are continuously involved with issues of connection, separation, development, change, and the limits of control.

If this characterization of caring labor sounds like the maternal practices and thinking I have described, this is not coincidental. Reading Hartsock from a perspective influenced by my own concerns, I felt as if "maternal thinking" were given both an epistemological and political base; moreover, from the time

I first read "The Feminist Standpoint," my understanding of maternal practice has been deepened by Hartsock's account of the characteristics of caring labor. Even more heartening, by looking and acting from a feminist standpoint, dominant ways of thinking—and I had in mind primarily militarist thinking—were revealed to be as abstract and destructive as I suspected. This gave maternal thinking, as part of the feminist standpoint, a critical power I had not imagined.

To diagnose and account for the destructiveness of dominant modes of thought that the standpoint reveals, Hartsock constructed an account of the "abstract masculinity" that characterizes dominant views, adapting a well-known story to her purposes.[9] ...

Feminist standpoint philosophers—among them philosophically minded and feminist maternal thinkers—directly oppose this "masculine" fantasy of transcendence. Their task is to redefine reason and restructure its priorities so that thoughtful people will be able to "generalize the potentiality made available by the activity of women"—i.e., caring labor—to society as a whole.[10] Since they actively participate in caring labor and therefore know first-hand the temptations, failures, and subtle intellectual challenges of their work, they will not idealize caretakers. What they have been taught by Hartsock, they will recognize daily: "[masculine] men's power to structure social relations in their own image means that women [and other caring laborers] too must participate in social relations which manifest and express abstract masculinity."[11] However alienated they are by the discrepancy between their experiences and the sentimental and abstract conceptual schemes that distort them, maternal thinkers know that they have learned to speak in the dominant languages, as do all members of a culture. To articulate maternal thinking they have had to cling to realities that they were in danger of forgetting and at the same time forge a way of thinking that is new. They will bring this heritage to the philosophical task of articulating standpoint theory, setting themselves to resist the lure of abstraction and the social rewards that "transcendence" brings. Together with other standpoint theorists, they work to articulate an engaged vision that must be "struggled for and represents an achievement."[12] ...

Despite their rejection of dualisms and their respect for difference, these standpoint philosophers seem very different from the Wittgensteinian pluralist who imagined maternal thinking as one discipline among others. Standpoint thinkers are ready, as the Wittgensteinian pluralist would never be, to declare that dominant values are destructive and perverse and that the feminist standpoint represents the "real" appropriately human order of life. One might say that standpoint theorists, including the maternal thinkers among them, have seen the Truth—and, indeed, many of the standpoint theorists whose invigorating work I have found indispensable seem to say just that.

Although I count myself among standpoint theorists, I do not take the final step that some appear to take of claiming for one standpoint a Truth that is exhaustive and absolute. Epistemologically, I continue to believe that all reasons are tested by the practices from which they arise; hence justifications end in the commitments with which they begin. Although I envision a world organized by the values of caring labor, I cannot identify the grounds, reason, or god that would legitimate that vision. There is, for example, nothing above or below preservative love, only the ongoing intellectual-practical acts of seeing children as vulnerable and responding to that vulnerability with a determination to protect rather than to abandon or assault.

I am also suspicious of any dualistic ordering of appearance and reality, perversion and utopia. The values of care do not stand to dominant values of abstract masculinity as the one reality stands to appearance; standpoint theorists know this, of course, but any dualistic formulations tend to reduce the richness and unpredictability both of the world and of the ways in which we think about it. I also fear that despite their stated convictions, standpoint theorists or their followers will lose sight of the failures and temptations of the caretakers they celebrate. It would then be easy to slip into a formulation of a feminine/feminist standpoint as an achievement rather than a place from which to create a sturdy, sane vision of the natural and social world. Perhaps most worrisome, being on the side of good can foster a repressive self-righteousness that legitimates killing or, alternatively, condemns violence without attending to the despair and abuse from which it arises. Directly to the point of my project, dualistic righteousness encourages a mythical division between women's peacefulness and men's wars that is belied by history and obscures the flawed, complex peacefulness that is latent in maternal practice and thinking.

In the last few years I have consciously assessed moral and political decisions in the light of the values of care and then in turn reassessed those values. I am confident that persistent efforts to see and act from the standpoint of care will reveal the greater safety, pleasure, and justice of a world where the values of care are dominant. But I realize that for those who are not already committed to the values of caring labor, a case must be made for the moral and epistemological superiority of the kind of thinking to which it gives rise. This requires specific oppositional comparisons between particular concepts and values of caring labor and their counterparts in dominant, abstractly masculine ways of knowing—for example, comparisons of maternal and military concepts of the body and of control. These specific comparisons will reveal incrementally the superiority of the rationality of care to the abstract masculine ways of knowing that dominate our lives.

. . . I bring maternal thinking to bear on military thinking. As part of a feminist standpoint, I take maternal thinking to be an engaged critical and visionary perspective that illuminates both the destructiveness of war and the requirements of peace. Yet one of my principal points is that maternal thinking itself is often militarist. Like the standpoint of which it is a part, an antimilitarist maternal perspective is an engaged vision that must be achieved through struggle and change.

I do not think maternal thinking, any more than the standpoint of which it is a part, represents a True or Total discourse. Nor are mothers, any more than other women, the quintessential revolutionary subjects. It is enough to say that there is a peacefulness latent in maternal practice and that a transformed maternal thinking could make a distinctive contribution to peace politics. Given the violence we live in and the disasters that threaten us, enough seems a feast. . . .

Notes

1. Ludwig Wittgenstein, *Philosophical Investigations,* no. 19.
2. Wittgenstein, *On Certainty,* no. 204.
3. Wittgenstein, *Philosophical Investigations,* Part II, p. 226.
4. Catharine A. MacKinnon, "Feminism, Marxism, Method, and the State: An Agenda for Theory," *Signs,* vol. 7, no. 3 (1982), p. 534.
5. Mary Belenky, Blythe Clichy, Nancy Goldberger, and Jill Tarule, *Women's Ways of Knowing* (New York: Basic Books, 1986), pp. 137–38.
6. Adela Pankhurst, "I Didn't Raise My Son to Be a Soldier," in *My Country Is the Whole World,* ed. Cambridge Women's Peace Collective (London: Pandora Press, 1984), p. 100.
7. The full title of the article is "The Feminist Standpoint: Developing the Ground for a Specifically Feminist Historical Materialism." It was first printed in Sandra Harding and Merrill Hintikka, eds., *Discovering Reality* (London: D. Reidel, 1983), pp. 283–310. All of my page references are to this version. A nearly equivalent version of this article appears in Hartsock's book *Money, Sex, and Power* (New York: Longman, 1983). The entire book is relevant to my discussion here. My reading of standpoint theory emphasizes caring labor and slights the complex but important strengths of any perspective derived from the experience of oppression. There is now a considerable literature on the feminist standpoint. I am particularly indebted to Hilary Rose, "Hand, Brain, and Heart," *Signs,* vol. 9, no. 11 (1983), and "Women's Work, Women's Knowledge," in *What Is Feminism?,* ed. Juliet Mitchell and Ann Oakley (New York: Pantheon, 1986). I am also indebted to Sandra Harding's discussion of the feminist standpoint in her book *The Science Question in Feminism* (Ithaca, NY: Cornell University Press, 1986), and to Alison Jaggar's discussion in *Feminist Politics and Human Nature* (Totowa, NJ: Roman and Allenheld, 1983), and to Terry Winant, "The Feminist Standpoint: A Matter of Language," *Hypatia,* vol. 2, no. 1 (Winter 1987). In addition I have had numerous and valuable conversations with Harding about our interpretations of Hartsock and more generally about standpoint theory that have revealed the considerable differences in our readings and the ways in which standpoint theory can be variously interpreted. In my view there can be several epistemological perspectives systematically derived from experiences of women other than caring labor and transformed by feminist consciousness and politics.
8. Michel Foucault, *Power/Knowledge* (New York: Pantheon, 1985), pp. 81–82. The phrase "lost in an all-encompassing knowledge" comes from Sharon Welch, *Communities of Resistance and Solidarity: A Feminist Theology of Liberation* (New York: Orbis, Maryknoll, 1985), p. 19. I am indebted to Welch for a distinct and potentially antimilitarist reading of Foucault. Although I am adapting Foucault's idea of subjugated knowledge to my purposes, other current notions—for example of "minority," "peripheral," or "marginal" "discourses"—are unsuitable to the points I am making. Although any variant of maternal thinking might be considered "minor"—as, for example, white middle-class, heterosexual, North American maternal thinking represents only a minority of thinkers—maternal thinking as a whole and the rationality of care of which it is a part derive from practices ubiquitous and central to the human enterprise. Hartsock has recently addressed these issues in "Rethinking Modernism: Minority vs. Majority Theories," *Cultural Critique* (Fall 1987), pp. 187–206, where she discusses and rejects the critiques of Rorty and Foucault. To adapt her current terms, maternal thinking is a "revolutionary discourse" that has been marginal and peripheral but that, as a central discourse, could transform dominant, so-called normal ways of thinking.

9.   I consider myself an agnostic in respect to psychoanalytic theory. In particular, object
      relations theory seems a primary case of what Cixous identified as "reproduc[ing]
      the masculine view of which it is one of the effects." Hélène Cixous, "Laugh of the
      Medusa," *New French Feminisms,* ed. Elaine Marks and Isabelle de Cortivron (New York:
      Schocken, 1981), p. 255. Nonetheless, I believe that psychoanalytic theory, in its many
      versions, is the only theory of subjectivity worth serious feminist consideration and I do
      believe some account of the development of subjectivity is required. Among the many
      psychoanalytic feminist theorists, the following have been of special use to me: Dorothy
      Dinnerstein, *The Mermaid and the Minotaur* (New York: Harper & Row, 1976); Evelyn
      Fox Keller, *Reflections on Gender and Science* (New Haven: Yale University Press, 1986),
      Part II; Nancy Chodorow, especially "Feminism and Difference: Gender, Relation and
      Difference in Scientific Perspective," *Socialist Review,* no. 46 (1979); Jessica Benjamin,
      The Bonds of Love (New York: Pantheon, 1988); Isaac Balbus, *Marxism and Domination*
      (Princeton: Princeton University Press, 1981); Susan Bordo, *The Flight to Objectivity:
      Essays on Cartesianism and Culture* (Albany: SUNY Press, 1987).
10.   Hartsock, "Feminist Standpoint," p. 304.
11.   Hartsock, "Feminist Standpoint," p. 302.
12.   Hartsock, "Feminist Standpoint," pp. 288, 302.

12

Feminism, Marxism, Method, and the State: Toward Feminist Jurisprudence

CATHARINE A. MacKINNON

Feminism has no theory of the state. It has a theory of power: sexuality is gendered as gender is sexualized.... A methodologically post-marxist feminism must confront, on our own terms, the issue of the relation between the state and society, within a theory of social determination adequate to the specificity of sex.... The question for feminism, for the first time on its own terms, is: what is this state, from women's point of view?

As a beginning, I propose that the state is male in the feminist sense.[1] The law sees and treats women the way men see and treat women. The liberal state coercively and authoritatively constitutes the social order in the interest of men as a gender, through its legitimizing norms, relation to society, and substantive policies. It achieves this through embodying and ensuring male control over women's sexuality at every level, occasionally cushioning, qualifying, or de jure prohibiting its excesses when necessary to its normalization. Substantively, the way the male point of view frames an experience is the way it is framed by state policy. To the extent possession is the point of sex, rape is sex with a woman who is not yours, unless the act is so as to make her yours. If part of the kick of pornography involves eroticizing the putatively prohibited, obscenity law will putatively prohibit pornography enough to maintain its desirability without ever making it unavailable or truly illegitimate. The same with prostitution. As male is the implicit reference for human, maleness will be the measure of equality in sex discrimination law. To the extent that the point of abortion is to control the reproductive sequelae of intercourse, so as to facilitate male sexual access to women, access to abortion will be controlled by "a man or The Man."[2] Gender, elaborated and sustained by behavioral patterns of application and administration, is maintained as a division of power.

Formally, the state is male in that objectivity is its norm. Objectivity is liberal legalism's conception of itself. It legitimizes itself by reflecting its view of existing society, a society it made and makes by so seeing it, and calling that view, and that relation, practical rationality. If rationality is measured by point-of-viewlessness, what counts as reason will be that which corresponds to the way things are.

Practical will mean that which can be done without changing anything. In this framework, the task of legal interpretation becomes "to perfect the state as mirror of the society."[3] Objectivist epistemology is the law of law. It ensures that the law will most reinforce existing distributions of power when it most closely adheres to its own highest ideal of fairness. Like the science it emulates, this epistemological stance cannot see the social specificity of reflection as method or its choice to embrace that which it reflects. Such law not only reflects a society in which men rule women; it rules in a male way: "The phallus means everything that sets itself up as a mirror."[4] The rule form, which unites scientific knowledge with state control in its conception of what law is, institutionalizes the objective stance as jurisprudence. A closer look at the substantive law of rape[5] in light of such an argument suggests that the relation between objectification (understood as the primary process of the subordination of women) and the power of the state is the relation between the personal and the political at the level of government. This is not because the state is presumptively the sphere of politics. It is because the state, in part through law, institutionalizes male power. If male power is systemic, it *is* the regime. . . .

Like heterosexuality, the crime of rape centers on penetration.[6] The law to protect women's sexuality from forcible violation/expropriation defines the protected in male genital terms. Women do resent forced penetration. But penile invasion of the vagina may be less pivotal to women's sexuality, pleasure or violation, than it is to male sexuality. This definitive element of rape centers upon a male-defined loss, not coincidentally also upon the way men define loss of exclusive access. In this light, rape, as legally defined, appears more a crime against female monogamy than against female sexuality. Property concepts fail fully to comprehend this,[7] however, not because women's sexuality is not, finally, a thing, but because it is never ours. The moment we "have" it—"have sex" in the dual sexuality/gender sense—it is lost as ours. This may explain the male incomprehension that, once a woman has had sex, she loses anything when raped. To them we *have nothing* to lose. Dignitary harms, because nonmaterial, are remote to the legal mind. But women's loss through rape is not only less tangible, it is less existent. It is difficult to avoid the conclusion that penetration itself is known to be a violation and that women's sexuality, our gender definition, is itself stigmatic. If this is so, the pressing question for explanation is not why some of us accept rape but why any of us resent it.

The law of rape divides the world of women into spheres of consent according to how much say we are legally presumed to have over sexual access to us by various categories of men. Little girls may not consent; wives must. If rape laws existed to enforce women's control over our own sexuality, as the consent defense implies, marital rape would not be a widespread exception,[8] nor would statutory rape proscribe all sexual intercourse with underage girls regardless of their wishes. The rest of us fall into parallel provinces: good girls, like children, are unconsenting, virginal, rapable; bad girls, like wives, are consenting; whores, unrapable. The age line under which girls are presumed disabled from withholding consent to sex rationalizes a condition of sexual coercion women never outgrow. As with protective labor laws for women only, dividing and protecting the most vulnerable becomes a device for not protecting everyone. Risking loss of even so little cannot be afforded. Yet the protection is denigrating and limiting (girls may not choose to be sexual) as well as perverse (girls are eroticized as untouchable; now reconsider the data on incest).

If the accused knows us, consent is inferred. The exemption for rape in marriage is consistent with the assumption underlying most adjudications of forcible rape: to the extent the parties relate, it was not really rape, it was personal.[9] As the marital exemptions erode, preclusions for cohabitants and voluntary social companions may expand. In this light, the partial erosion of the marital rape exemption looks less like a change in the equation between women's experience of sexual violation and men's experience of intimacy, and more like a legal adjustment to the social fact that acceptable heterosexual sex is increasingly not limited to the legal family. So although the rape law may not now always assume that the woman consented simply because the parties are legally one, indices of closeness, of relationship ranging from nodding acquaintance to living together, still contraindicate rape. Perhaps this reflects men's experience that women they know meaningfully consent to sex with them. That cannot be rape; rape must be by someone else someone unknown. But *women* experience rape most often by men we know.[10] Men believe that it is less awful to be raped by someone one is close to: "The emotional trauma suffered by a person victimized by an individual with whom sexual intimacy is shared as a normal part of an ongoing marital relationship is not nearly as severe as that suffered by a person who is victimized by one with whom that intimacy is not shared."[11] But women feel as much, if not more, traumatized by being raped by someone we have known or trusted, someone we have shared at least an illusion of mutuality with, than by some stranger. In whose interest is it to believe that it is not so bad to be raped by someone who has fucked you before as by someone who has not? Disallowing charges of rape in marriage may also "remove a substantial obstacle to the resumption of normal marital relations."[12] Depending upon your view of normal. Note that the obstacle to normalcy here is not the rape but the law against it. Apparently someone besides feminists finds sexual victimization and sexual intimacy not all that contradictory. Sometimes I think women and men live in different cultures.

Having defined rape in male sexual terms, the law's problem, which becomes the victim's problem, is distinguishing rape from sex in specific cases. The law does this by adjudicating the level of acceptable force starting just above the level set by what is seen as normal male sexual behavior, rather than at the victim's, or women's, point of violation. Rape cases finding insufficient force reveal that acceptable sex, in the legal perspective, can entail a lot of force. This is not only because of the way specific facts are perceived and interpreted, but because of the way the injury itself is defined as illegal. Rape is a sex crime that is not a crime when it looks like sex. To seek to define rape as violent, not sexual, is understandable in this context, and often seems strategic. But assault that is consented to is still assault; rape consented to is intercourse. The substantive reference point implicit in existing legal standards is the sexually normative level of force. Until this norm is confronted as such, no distinction between violence and sexuality will prohibit more instances of women's experienced violation than does the existing definition. The question is what is *seen as* force, hence as violence, in the sexual arena. Most rapes, as women live them, will not be seen to violate women until sex and violence are confronted as mutually definitive. It is not only men convicted of rape who believe that the only thing they did different from what men do all the time is get caught.

The line between rape and intercourse commonly centers on some measure of the woman's "will." But from what should the law know woman's will? Like much existing law, Brownmiller tends to treat will as a question of consent and consent as a factual issue of the presence of force.[13] Proof problems aside, force and desire are not mutually exclusive. So long as dominance is eroticized, they never will be. Women are socialized to passive receptivity; may have or perceive no alternative to acquiescence; may prefer it to the escalated risk of injury and the humiliation of a lost fight; submit to survive. Some eroticize dominance and submission; it beats feeling forced. Sexual intercourse may be deeply unwanted—the woman would never have initiated it—yet no force may be present. Too, force may be used, yet the woman may want the sex—to avoid more force or because she, too, eroticizes dominance. Women and men know this. Calling rape violence, not sex, thus evades, at the moment it most seems to confront, the issue of who controls women's sexuality and the dominance/submission dynamic that has defined it. When sex is violent, women may have lost control over what is done to us, but absence of force does not ensure the presence of that control. Nor, under conditions of male dominance, does the presence of force make an interaction nonsexual. If sex is normally something men do to women, the issue is less whether there was force and more whether consent is a meaningful concept.[14]

To explain women's gender status as a function of rape, Brownmiller argues that the threat of rape benefits all men.[15] She does not specify in what way. Perhaps it benefits them sexually, hence as a gender male initiatives toward women carry the fear of rape as support for persuading compliance, the resulting appearance of which has been called consent. Here the victims' perspective grasps what liberalism applied to women denies: that forced sex as sexuality is not exceptional in relations between the sexes but constitutes the social meaning of gender: "Rape is a man's act, whether it is male or a female man and whether it is a man relatively permanently or relatively temporarily; and being raped is a woman's experience, whether it is a female or a male woman and whether it is a woman relatively permanently or relatively temporarily."[16] To be rap*able*, a position which is social, not biological, defines what a woman *is*.

Most women get the message that the law against rape is virtually unenforceable as applied to them. Our own experience is more often delegitimized by this than the law is. Women radically distinguish between rape and experiences of sexual violation, concluding that we have not "really" been raped if we have ever seen or dated or slept with or been married to the man, if we were fashionably dressed or are not provably virgin, if we are prostitutes, if we put up with it or tried to get it over with, if we were force-fucked over a period of years. If we probably couldn't prove it in court, it wasn't rape. The distance between most sexual violations of women and the legally perfect rape measures the imposition of someone else's definition upon women's experiences. Rape, from women's point of view, is not prohibited; it is regulated. Even women who know we have been raped do not believe that the legal system will see it the way we do. We are often not wrong. Rather than deterring or avenging rape, the state, in many victims' experiences, perpetuates it. Women who charge rape say they were raped twice, the second time in court. If the state is male, this is more than a figure of speech.

The law distinguishes rape from intercourse by the woman's lack of consent coupled with a man's (usually) knowing disregard of it. A feminist distinction between rape and intercourse, to hazard a beginning approach, lies instead in the *meaning* of the act from women's point of view. What is wrong with rape is that it is an act of the subordination of women to men. Seen this way, the issue is not so much what rape "is" as the way its social conception is shaped to interpret particular encounters. Under conditions of sex inequality, with perspective bound up with situation, whether a contested interaction is rape comes down to whose meaning wins. If sexuality is relational, specifically if it is a power relation of gender, consent is a communication under conditions of inequality. It transpires somewhere between what the woman actually wanted and what the man comprehended she wanted. Instead of capturing this dynamic, the law gives us linear statics face to face. Nonconsent in law becomes a question of the man's force or the woman's resistance or both.[17] Rape, like many crimes and torts, requires that the accused possess a criminal mind (mens rea) for his acts to be criminal. The man's mental state refers to what he actually understood at the time or to what a reasonable man should have understood under the circumstances. The problem is this: the injury of rape lies in the meaning of the act to its victims, but the standard for its criminality lies in the meaning of the same act to the assailants. Rape is only an injury from women's point of view. It is only a crime from the male point of view, explicitly including that of the accused.

Thus is the crime of rape defined and adjudicated from the male standpoint, that is, presuming that (what feminists see as) forced sex is sex. Under male supremacy, of course, it is. What this means doctrinally is that the man's perceptions of the woman's desires often determine whether she is deemed violated. This might be like other crimes of subjective intent if rape were like other crimes. But with rape, because sexuality defines gender, the only difference between assault and (what is socially considered) noninjury is the meaning of the encounter to the woman. Interpreted this way, the legal problem has been to determine whose view of that meaning constitutes what really happened, as if what happened objectively exists to be objectively determined, thus as if this task of determination is separable from the gender of the participants and the gendered nature of their exchange. Thus, even though the rape law oscillates between subjective tests and more objective standards invoking social reasonableness, it uniformly presumes a single underlying reality, not a reality split by divergent meanings, such as those inequality produces. Many women are raped by men who know the meaning of their acts to women and proceed anyway.[18] But women are also violated every day by men who have no idea of the meaning of their acts to women. To them, it is sex. Therefore, to the law, it is sex. That is the single reality of what happened. When a rape prosecution is lost on a consent defense, the woman has not only failed to prove lack of consent, she is not considered to have been injured at all. Hermeneutically unpacked, read: because he did not perceive she did not want him, she was not violated. She had sex. Sex itself cannot be an injury. Women consent to sex every day. Sex makes a woman a woman. Sex is what women are *for*.

To a feminist analysis, men set sexual mores ideologically and behaviorally, define rape as they imagine the sexual violation of women through distinguishing it from their image of what they normally do, and sit in judgment in most accusations of sex crimes. So rape comes to mean a strange (read Black) man knowing a woman does not want sex and going ahead anyway. But men are systematically conditioned not even to notice what women want. They may have not a glimmer of women's indifference or revulsion. Rapists typically believe the woman loved it.[19] Women, as a survival strategy, must ignore or devalue or mute our desires (particularly lack of them) to convey the impression that the man will get what he wants regardless of what we want. In this context, consider measuring the genuineness of consent from the individual assailant's (or even the socially reasonable, i.e., objective, man's) point of view.

Men's pervasive belief that women fabricate rape charges after consenting to sex makes sense in this light. To them, the accusations *are* false because, to them, the facts describe sex. To interpret such events as rapes distorts their experience. Since they seldom consider that their experience of the real is anything other than reality, they can only explain the woman's version as maliciously invented. Similarly, the male anxiety that rape is easy to charge and difficult to disprove (also widely believed in the face of overwhelming evidence to the contrary) arises because rape accusations express one thing men cannot seem to control: the meaning to women of sexual encounters.

Thus do legal doctrines, incoherent or puzzling as syllogistic logic, become coherent as ideology. For example, when an accused wrongly but sincerely believes that a woman he sexually forced consented, he may have a defense of mistaken belief or fail to satisfy the mental requirement of knowingly proceeding against her will.[20] One commentator notes, discussing the conceptually similar issue of revocation of prior consent (i.e., on the issue of the conditions under which women are allowed to control access to their sexuality from one time to the next): "Even where a woman revokes prior consent, such is the male ego that, seized of an exaggerated assessment of his sexual prowess, a man might genuinely believe her still to be consenting; resistance may be misinterpreted as enthusiastic cooperation; protestations of pain or disinclination, a spur to more sophisticated or more ardent love-making; a clear statement to stop, taken as referring to a particular intimacy rather than the entire performance."[21] This equally vividly captures common male readings of women's indications of disinclination under all kinds of circumstances.[22] Now reconsider to what extent the man's perceptions should determine whether a rape occurred. From whose standpoint, and in whose interest, is a law that allows one person's conditioned unconsciousness to contraindicate another's experienced violation? This aspect of the rape law reflects the sex inequality of the society not only in conceiving a cognizable injury from the viewpoint of the reasonable rapist, but in affirmatively rewarding men with acquittals for not comprehending women's point of view on sexual encounters.

Whether the law calls this coerced consent or mistake of fact, the more the sexual violation of women is routine, the more beliefs equating sexuality with violation become reasonable, and the more honestly women can be defined in terms of our fuckability. It would be comparatively simple if the legal problem were limited to avoiding retroactive falsification of the accused's state of mind. Surely there are incentives to lie. But the deeper problem is the rape law's assumption that a single, objective state of affairs existed, one which merely needs to be determined by evidence, when many (maybe even most) rapes involve honest men and violated women. When the reality is split—a woman is raped but not by a rapist?—the law tends to conclude that a rape *did not happen*. To attempt to solve this by adopting the standard of reasonable belief without asking, on a substantive social basis, to whom the belief is reasonable and why—meaning, what conditions make it reasonable—is one-sided: male-sided. What is it reasonable for a man to believe concerning a woman's desire for sex when heterosexuality is compulsory? Whose subjectivity becomes the objectivity of "what happened" is a matter of social meaning, that is, it has been a matter of sexual politics. One-sidedly erasing women's violation or dissolving the presumptions into the subjectivity of either side are alternatives dictated by the terms of the object/subject split, respectively. These are alternatives that will only retrace that split until its terms are confronted as gendered to the ground.

Desirability to men is commonly supposed to be a woman's form of power. This echoes the view that consent is women's form of control over intercourse, different but equal to the custom of male initiative. Look at it: man initiates, woman chooses. Even the ideal is not mutual. Apart from the disparate consequences of refusal, or openness of original options, this model does not envision a situation the woman controls being placed in, or choices she frames, yet the consequences are attributed to her as if the sexes began at arm's length, on equal terrain, as in the contract fiction. Ambiguous cases of consent are often archetypically referred to as "half won arguments in parked cars."[23] Why not half lost? Why isn't half enough? Why is it an argument? Why do men still want "it," feel entitled to "it," when women don't want them? That sexual expression is even framed as a matter of woman's consent, without exposing these presuppositions, is integral to gender inequality. Woman's so-called power presupposes her more fundamental powerlessness.[24]

The state's formal norms recapitulate the male point of view on the level of design. In Anglo-American jurisprudence, morals (value judgments) are deemed separable and separated from politics (power contests), and both from adjudication (interpretation). Neutrality, including judicial decision making that is dispassionate, impersonal, disinterested, and precedential, is considered desirable and descriptive. Courts, forums without predisposition among parties and with no interest of their own, reflect society back to itself resolved. Government of laws, not men, limits partiality with written constraints and tempers force with reasonable rule following. This law aspires to science: to the immanent generalization subsuming the emergent particularity, to prediction and control of social regularities and regulations, preferably codified. The formulaic "tests" of "doctrine" aspire to mechanism, classification to taxonomy. Courts intervene only in properly "factualized" disputes,[25] cognizing social conflicts as if collecting empirical data. But the demarcations between morals and politics, the personality of the judge and the judicial role, bare coercion and the rule of law,[26] tend to merge in women's experience. Relatively seamlessly they promote the dominance of men as a social group through privileging the form of power—the perspective on social life—feminist consciousness reveals as socially male. The separation of form from substance, process from policy, role from theory and practice, echoes and reechoes at each level of the regime its basic norm: objectivity. . . .

Notes

For A. D. and D. K. H. In addition to all those whose help is acknowledged in the first part of this article, "Feminism, Marxism, Method, and the State: An Agenda for Theory," *Signs: Journal of Women in Culture and Society* 7, no. 3 (Spring 1982): 515–44 (hereafter cited as part 1), my students and colleagues at Yale, Harvard, and Stanford contributed profoundly to the larger project of which both articles are parts. Among them, Sonia E. Alvarez, Jeanne M. Barkey, Paul Brest, Ruth Colker, Karen E. Davis, Sharon Dyer, Tom Emerson, Daniel Gunther, Patricia Kliendienst Joplin, Mark Kelman, Duncan Kennedy, John Kaplan, Lyn Lemaire, Mira

Marshall, Rebecca Mark, Martha Minow, Helen M. A. Neally, Lisa Rofel, Sharon Silverstein, Dean Spencer, Laurence Tribe, and Mary Whisner stand out vividly in retrospect. None of it would have happened without Lu Ann Carter and David Rayson. And thank you, Meg Baldwin, Annie McCombs, and Janet Spector.

Marxism appears in lowercase, Black in uppercase, for reasons explained in part 1....

1. See Susan Rae Peterson, "Coercion and Rape: The State as a Male Protection Racket," in *Feminism and Philosophy*, ed. Mary Vetterling-Braggin, Frederick A. Elliston, and Jane English (Totowa, N.J.: Littlefield, Adams & Co., 1977), pp. 360–71; Janet Rifkin, "Toward a Theory of Law Patriarchy," *Harvard Women's Law Journal* 3 (Spring 1980): 83–92.

2. Johnnie Tillmon, "Welfare Is a Women's Issue," *Liberation News Service* (February 26, 1972), in *America's Working Women: A Documentary History, 1600 to the Present*, ed. Rosalyn Baxandall, Linda Gordon, and Susan Reverby (New York: Vintage Books, 1976), pp. 357–58.

3. Laurence Tribe, "Constitution as Point of View" (Harvard Law School, Cambridge, Mass., 1982, mimeographed), p. 13.

4. Madeleine Gagnon, "Body I," in *New French Feminisms*, ed. Elaine Marks and Isabelle de Courtivron (Amherst, Mass.: University of Massachusetts Press, 1980), p. 180. Turns on the mirroring trope, which I see as metaphoric analyses of the epistemological/political dimension of objectification, are ubiquitous in feminist writing: "Into the room of the dressing where the walls are covered with mirrors. Where mirrors are like eyes of men, and the women reflect the judgments of mirrors" (Susan Griffin, *Woman and Nature: The Roaring Inside Her* [New York: Harper & Row Publishers, 1979], p. 155). See also Mary Daly, *Beyond God the Father: Toward a Philosophy of Women's Liberation* (Boston: Beacon Press, 1975), pp. 195, 197; Sheila Rowbotham, *Women's Consciousness, Man's World* (Harmondsworth: Pelican Books, 1973), pp. 26–29. "She did suffer, the witch/trying to peer round the looking/glass, she forgot/someone was in the way" (Michelene, "Reflexion," quoted in Rowbotham, p. 2). Virginia Woolf wrote the figure around ("So I reflected . . ."), noticing "the necessity that women so often are to men" of serving as a looking glass in which a man can "see himself at breakfast and at dinner at least twice the size he really is." Notice the doubled sexual/gender meaning: "Whatever may be their use in civilized societies, mirrors are essential to all violent and heroic action. That is why Napoleon and Mussolini both insist so emphatically upon the inferiority of women, for if they were not inferior, they would cease to enlarge" (*A Room of One's Own* [New York: Harcourt, Brace & World, 1969], p. 36).

5. Space limitations made it necessary to eliminate sections on pornography, sex discrimination, and abortion. For the same reason, most supporting references, including those to case law, have been cut. The final section accordingly states the systemic implications of the analysis more tentatively than I think them, but as strongly as I felt I could, on the basis of the single substantive examination that appears here.

6. Sec. 213.0 of the *Model Penal Code* (Official Draft and Revised Comments 1980), like most states, defines rape as sexual intercourse with a female who is not the wife of the perpetrator "with some penetration however slight." Impotency is sometimes a defense. Michigan's gender-neutral sexual assault statute includes penetration by objects (sec. 520a[h]; 520[b]). See *Model Penal Code*, annotation to sec. 213.1(d) (Official Draft and Revised Comments 1980).

7. Although it is true that men possess women and that women's bodies are, socially, men's things, I have not analyzed rape as men treating women like property. In the manner of many socialist-feminist adaptations of marxian categories to women's situation, that analysis short-circuits analysis of rape as male sexuality and presumes rather than develops links between sex and class. We need to rethink sexual dimensions of property as well as property dimensions of sexuality.

8. For an excellent summary of the current state of the marital exemption, see Joanne Schulman, "State-by-State Information on Marital Rape Exemption Laws," in *Rape in Marriage*, Diana E. H. Russell ed. (New York: Macmillan Publishing Co., 1982), pp. 375–81.

9. On "social interaction as an element of consent," in a voluntary social companion context, see *Model Penal Code*, sec. 213.1. "The prior *social* interaction is an indicator of

consent in addition to actor's and victim's *behavioral* interaction during the commission of the offense" (Wallace Loh, "Q: What Has Reform of Rape Legislation Wrought? A Truth in Criminal Labeling," *Journal of Social Issues* 37, no. 4 [1981]: 28–52, 47). Perhaps consent should be an affirmative defense, pleaded and proven by the defendant.

10. Pauline Bart found that women were more likely to be raped—that is, less able to stop a rape in progress—when they knew their assailant, particularly when they had a prior or current sexual relationship ("A Study of Women Who Both Were Raped and Avoided Rape," *Journal of Social Issues* 37, no. 4 [1981]: 123–37, 132). See also Linda Belden, "Why Women Do Not Report Sexual Assault" (City of Portland Public Service Employment Program, Portland Women's Crisis Line, Portland, Ore., March 1979, mimeographed); Diana E. H. Russell and Nancy Howell, "The Prevalence of Rape in the United States Revisited," in this issue [of *Signs*]; and Menachem Amir, *Patterns in Forcible Rape* (Chicago: University of Chicago Press, 1971), pp. 229–52.

11. Answer Brief for Plaintiff-Appellee at 10, *People v. Brown*, 632 P.2d 1025 (Colo. 1981).

12. *Brown*, 632 P.2d at 1027 (citing Comment, "Rape and Battery between Husband and Wife," *Stanford Law Review* 6 [1954]: 719–28, 719, 725).

13. Brownmiller *Against Our Will: Men, Women and Rape* (New York: Simon & Schuster, 1976), pp. 8, 196, 400–407, 427–36.

14. See Carol Pateman, "Women and Consent," *Political Theory* 8, no. 2 (May 1980): 149–68.

15. Brownmiller (n.13 above), p. 5.

16. Carolyn M. Shafer and Marilyn Frye, "Rape and Respect," in Vetterling-Braggin, Elliston, and English, eds. [n.1 above], p. 334. . . .

17. Even when nonconsent is not a legal element of the offense (as in Michigan), juries tend to infer rape from evidence of force or resistance.

18. This is apparently true of undetected as well as convicted rapists. Samuel David Smithyman's sample, composed largely of the former, contained self-selected respondents to his ad, which read: "Are you a rapist? Researchers Interviewing Anonymously by Phone to Protect Your Identity. Call. . . ." Presumably those who chose to call defined their acts as rapes, at least at the time of responding ("The Undetected Rapist" [Ph.D. diss., Claremont Graduate School, 1978], pp. 54–60, 63–76, 80–90, 97–107).

19. "Probably the single most used cry of rapist to victim is 'You bitch . . . slut . . . you know you want it. You *all* want it' and afterward, 'there now, you really enjoyed it, didn't you?' " (Nancy Gager and Cathleen Schurr, *Sexual Assault: Confronting Rape in America* [New York: Grosset & Dunlap, 1976], p. 244).

20. See *Director of Public Prosecutions v. Morgan*, 2411 E.R.H.L. 347 (1975); *Pappajohn v. The Queen*, 11 D.L.R. 3d 1 (1980); *People v. Mayberry*, 15 Cal. 3d 143, 542 P.2d 1337 (1975).

21. Richard H.S. Tur, "Rape: Reasonableness and Time," *Oxford Journal of Legal Studies* 3 (Winter 1981): 432–41, 441. Tur, in the context of the Morgan and Pappajohn cases, says the "law ought not to be astute to equate wickedness and wishful, albeit mistaken, thinking" (p. 437). In feminist analysis, a rape is not an isolated or individual or moral transgression but a terrorist act within a systematic context of group subjection, like lynching.

22. See Silke Vogelmann-Sine et al., "Sex Differences in Feelings Attributed to Woman in Situations Involving Coercion and Sexual Advances," *Journal of Personality* 47, no. 3 (September 1979): 420–31, esp. 429–30.

23. Note, "Forcible and Statutory Rape: An Exploration of the Operation and Objectives of the Consent Standard," *Yale Law Journal* 62 (1952): 55–56.

24. A similar analysis of sexual harassment suggests that women have such "power" only so long as we behave according to male definitions of female desirability, that is, only so long as we accede the definition of our sexuality (hence, ourselves, as gender female) to male terms. We have this power only so long as we remain powerless.

25. Peter Gabel, "Reification in Legal Reasoning" (New College Law School, San Francisco, 1980, mimeographed), p. 3.

26. Rawls's "original position," for instance, is a version of my objective standpoint (John Rawls, *A Theory of Justice* [Cambridge, Mass.: Harvard University Press, 1971]). Not only apologists for the liberal state, but also some of its most trenchant critics, see a real distinction between the rule of law and absolute arbitrary force. E. P. Thompson, *Whigs and Hunters: The Origin of the Black Act* (New York: Pantheon Books, 1975), pp. 258–69.

Douglas Hay argues that making and enforcing certain acts as illegal reinforces a structure of subordination ("Property, Authority, and the Criminal Law," in *Albion's Fatal Tree: Crime and Society in Eighteenth Century England*, D. Hay et al., eds. [New York: Pantheon Books 1975], pp. 17–31). Michael D. A. Freeman ("Violence against Women: Does the Legal System Provide Solutions or Itself Constitute the Problem?" [Madison, Wis., 1980, mimeographed], p. 12, n. 161) applies this argument to domestic battery of women. Here I extend it to women's situation as a whole, without suggesting that the analysis can *end* there.

13
Labor, Standpoints, and Feminist Subjects

KATHI WEEKS

Beyond Modernism vs. Postmodernism

In the wake of the postmodern critiques of the 1980s, feminists have been struggling to develop theories of the subject that are adequate to a feminist politics. Many of us want to move beyond models of the subject organized with reference to a natural core, authentic humanity, or enduring metaphysical essence and to trade the older focus on the unified subject of feminism for a multiplicity of feminist subjects. At the same time, we want a theory of feminist subjectivity that can acknowledge feminism's antagonistic force and cultivate its subversive potential, one that does not simply attach to a theory of social determinacy a vague evocation of voluntarist refusal. For us, then, the puzzle has been to understand how it could be that subjects so systematically constructed and well prepared to submit to the existing order of things can also collectively defy it. In other words, we want to endorse the critiques of humanism, functionalism, determinism, and essentialism without denying the possibility of agency.

This project, however, has been hampered by certain stubborn remnants of the modernist-postmodernist paradigm debate, a debate that helped to set this agenda but that also placed certain limits on our ability to pursue it. Although many will argue that the modernist-postmodernist debate that animated political theory and feminist theory throughout most of the 1980s is finished, having exhausted its potential, it lingers on nonetheless in the way we recall arguments from the past and conceive alternatives for the future. Here I focus on one specific configuration of this debate, a form that should be familiar to those of us reading in political theory and feminist theory over the years, wherein modernism and postmodernism are conceived as mutually exclusive theoretical paradigms. According to this particular conception of the debate (and of course, it is not the only way that the debate was conceived), the modernist tradition (with its wealth of differences) was equated with a paradigm that perhaps most closely resembled certain themes within Enlightenment modernism, poststructuralism (in all its heterogeneity) was identified with something called postmodernism, and the rest of us were compelled by the relentlessly oppositional logic used to maintain this dualistic framework to choose either one side

181

or the other. By means of this formula, modernism was all too often effectively reduced to a caricature opposed to another caricature called postmodernism. This reactive dynamic left us with two equally unsatisfactory choices: a reaffirmation of the humanist subject in some form or the death of the subject *tout court,* a voluntaristic theory of political agency or a thoroughgoing social determinism. What now remains in the wake of this particular formulation of the debate (a formulation I refer to as the modernist-postmodernist *paradigm debate*) is a history of distortions and a continuing inability by many to recognize the potential of, and the nuances within, the rich traditions of thought that were subsumed into the category of modernism and the equally valuable theoretical frameworks confined by the category of postmodernism. The vestiges of this paradigm debate can also account for some of the defensiveness and dismissiveness that continues to characterize many of our exchanges. The modernist-postmodernist paradigm debate may be dead, but its legacy still haunts our analyses.

If we were to comply with the terms of this paradigm debate, the project of developing a nonessentialist theory of subjective agency would be a very difficult one indeed: too many potentially productive lines of inquiry would be closed to us. Thus my project is conceived in part as an effort to circumvent this propensity toward either/or formulas and to counter this inattention to the specificity of, and the potential affinities among, different theoretical undertakings. Here I present a nonessentialist theory of feminist subjectivity that draws upon a variety of resources, including "postmodernists" like Friedrich Nietzsche, Michel Foucault, and Judith Butler, as well as "modernists" from the Marxist and socialist feminist traditions. By staging their encounters on a different terrain, outside these paradigm categories, I believe that we can develop some potentially productive lines of dialogue among these diverse theoretical projects.

I cast this reconfiguration of a feminist subject in terms of a version of socialist feminism known as feminist standpoint theory. The tradition of standpoint theory includes the contributions of many theorists who propose very different arguments.[1] This account is based on a selective appropriation and extension of a specific set of arguments from a limited group of texts. I do not, then, offer a detailed summary of the literature, one that explains my support for or quarrels with each of the different versions. Since my goal is not to present a faithful account of standpoint theories in all their difference and specificity, I make no claim to remain true to the methods, contents, or aims of any one author.[2] Rather than present a critical overview of existing standpoint theories, an endeavor that has already been admirably completed elsewhere, I intend to concentrate my efforts on constructing an alternative feminist standpoint theory, one that builds selectively on some of the fundamental themes of these original theories in a way that can render the basic project as I conceive it more compatible with a contemporary theoretical agenda.[3]

But why would I want to begin with standpoint theory? According to its critics, feminist standpoint theory is a relic of a bygone era in Anglo-American feminism: a throwback to an outmoded 1970s agenda, an archaic mode of theorizing anchored in the second rather than the third wave, a humorless operation in contrast to a playful gesture, in short, an obsolete approach situated within a modernist as opposed to a postmodernist horizon. If we accept the characterization presented by many of these reviewers, standpoint theory is so thoroughly mired in the pitfalls and conundrums of an older, irreparably foundationalist and essentialist brand of feminism that it can no longer speak to our concerns. There is, of course, some truth to this indictment: like the larger body of socialist feminist theory of which it is an instance, standpoint theory grew out of a particular historical conjuncture with its own specific openings for, and obstacles to, theoretical reflection; some of these we cannot recreate, others we would not wish to. The problem with this assessment, however, is that while it may serve to help us identify some of standpoint theory's failings (although, in this form, the critique is indebted to the modernist-postmodernist paradigm debate and, therefore, too often based on a caricature to provide many accurate critiques), it is blind to its distinctive strengths and potential contributions. While remaining alert to standpoint theory's weaknesses, I want nonetheless to argue for and expand upon its continuing promise and vitality. There are three fundamental reasons why I choose to enroll standpoint theory in this project of reconstituting a feminist subject, three sources of its enduring power and relevance. These can be encapsulated within three of its key concepts: totality, labor, and standpoint.

The Project of Totality

The concept of totality was one of the most frequently discussed under the auspices of the modernist-postmodernist paradigm debate and, unfortunately, one of the most often confused by its specifications. As I develop it here, the term "totality" designates an important set of theoretical and practical commitments. A notion of *gendered* subjectivity necessarily presupposes some conception of the social formation within which it is constructed and maintained, just as a notion of *feminist* subjectivity necessarily presupposes some conception of the complex relationships among the social forces it seeks to challenge. In the absence of some sense of the whole, some conception of the complex social formations that constitute and constrain subjects, we end up with an impoverished model of the subject that overestimates its capacities for self-creation and self-transformation, as well as a very limited understanding of the forces we must subvert in order to make possible the construction of alternative subjects. The project of totality—which I will try to distinguish from totalizing theory, or theories that reduce subjectivity to some functional effect of an abstract, determinable, and monolithic system of structures—refers to an attempt to locate some of the specific connections between our everyday lives and practices and the larger framework of social structures within which they are organized. The project of totality thus involves a methodological mandate to relate and connect, to situate and contextualize, to conceive the social systematically as a complex process of relationships. For example, capitalism, patriarchy, and white supremacy are not isolated forces, but rather systems that traverse the entire social horizon and intersect at multiple points. Standpoint theory cuts into this system by trying to make specific connections between certain modes of gendered subjectivity, women's laboring practices, the gender and racial divisions of labor, and global capitalism. How, standpoint theorists ask, are our practices both constituted by and constitutive of the structures that organize our experience? This "aspiration to totality"[4] that one can find in standpoint theory recalls some of the earliest and, I believe, strongest impulses of socialist feminism. Under the sign of totality, socialist feminism linked its interest in systemic analysis with a dedication to social transformation. Socialist feminists fashioned theories to help map the connections among the different social forces implicated in the construction of gender hierarchies; a feminist politics was conceived as a revolutionary politics, one that ultimately sought to transform the forces that maintain these systematic and institutional hierarchies. With this term, then, I want to preserve and develop two central commitments of socialist feminist standpoint theory: a theoretical commitment to understand the relationships between social structures and subjectivities and a political commitment to social transformation.[5]

The Ontology of Labor

Labor, as one of many mutually constitutive links between social structures and subjectivities, is the second source of what I see as standpoint theory's continuing appeal. Here I build selectively on those versions of standpoint theory that draw on, among other resources, the Marxist tradition to ground a feminist standpoint in some account of women's laboring practices in late capitalist social formations.[6] I focus most frequently on the work of Hilary Rose, Nancy Hartsock, and Dorothy Smith. These accounts begin with the assumption that what we do can have consequences for who we are and what and how we think, and that what we do is determined in part by a gender division of labor.[7] Critical of Marxism's narrow conception of production which fails to recognize the possibility of a standpoint grounded in women's laboring activity, these theories begin with alternative analyses of "women's work." The accounts differ depending on which types of practices are featured and the potential consequences the author wants to highlight. Thus, for example, in some accounts the practices for which women are disproportionately responsible are described in terms of "caring labor" or emotional labor, a set of practices that involves personal service.[8] Here we could include "maternal labor," the work of raising children,[9] and "kin work," the work of maintaining relationships among friends and extended family.[10] Women's labor is similarly characterized as "reproductive labor," a term designed to include many of the most common modes of women's labor not only in the home but also in the wage labor market, since women are so frequently channeled into those paid jobs that resemble their unpaid work in the household.[11] Finally, aspects of women's work have been conceived as "labor in the concrete bodily mode" to highlight those practices that give form to and provide support services for those engaged in more abstract conceptual practices or mental labor.[12] Note that in all these accounts, labor is not just activity that directly produces capital, but activity that produces society itself, including the networks of sociality and the subjects they sustain. These are constitutive practices that, whether waged or not, are socially necessary. Yet despite its importance, this labor is often invisible and many of the skills developed in and through these practices are naturalized and undervalued (Rose 1986, 165)....

Labor is the basic building block of this version of feminist standpoint theory. But before describing what the role of labor is, I should clarify what it is not. First, the notion of women's labor proposed here is not a set of practices allocated to women by nature (that is, it does not entail a biological essentialism). The gender division of labor is the product of culturally and historically specific determinations, not the inevitable product of sex differences. The laboring practices that figure in these versions of feminist standpoint theory—caring labor, kin work, labor in the concrete bodily mode, etc.—have no necessary connection to women's specific biological capacities. Neither is women's labor tied to some conception of an essential humanity (that is, a metaphysical essentialism), as can be found in some versions of humanist Marxism that privilege the concept of alienation. Rather than an original, authentically human essence from which we are estranged and to which we should be restored, labor refers in this account to variable practices that are constitutive of ever-changing forms of existence and modes of subjectivity. In contrast to both of these approaches, labor is posited here as an immanent and creative force of social production and historical change.

We can locate an instructive formulation of this conception of labor in the work of Marx and Engels. They explain the premises from which they begin (in highly polemical terms) as "real individuals, their activity and the material conditions under which they live, both those which they find already existing and those produced by their activity" (1978, 149). These premises are then separated for analytical purposes into four specific claims. The first premise of history is that human beings—those who collectively "make history"—must meet their basic subsistence needs. If we can presume life as a fundamental fact, then we can also presume that life can be sustained. The second premise is that the satisfaction of these needs leads to the production of new needs; necessity, they suggest, is for the most part an historical construct. Third, they presume that humans reproduce one another and fourth, that social relations of cooperation develop in the process. According to Marx and Engels, this mode of cooperation is a "productive force":

> As individuals express their life, so they are. What they are, therefore, coincides with their production, both with *what* they produce and with *how* they produce. The nature of individuals thus depends on the material conditions determining their production (1978, 150).[13]

Along these lines, then, labor is conceived in our account as an immanent ontological dynamic. As Marx describes it, "[l]abour is the living, form-giving fire: it is the transitoriness of things, their temporality, as their formation by living time" (1973, 361).[14] In other words, labor serves as a causal force or principle of historical motion. Dorothy Smith describes the ontological assumptions of her standpoint theory in very similar terms:

> These practices, these objects, our world, are continually created again and again and are already social. Because they arise in actual activities, they are always coming into being as a local historical process, falling away behind us as we move forward into the future. They are being brought into being (1987, 135).

When deployed in the context of a Marxist analysis that rejects all notions of necessary developments and predetermined ends, the category of labor, as it is elaborated here, leads us to a field of constitutive practices, forces of assertion, or lines of movement that provides us with a particular angle of vision on and site of intervention into the social construction of subjectivities.

The category of labor is also intrinsically strategic; which is to say that its philosophical attributes—in this case, its immanence and creativity—cannot not be separated from its practical value. This strategic or practical dimension of the category is accentuated when we characterize labor as value-creating activity.[15] Obviously, the determination of what counts as a value-creating activity is never fixed; it is an unstable social judgment of enormous consequence which can be contested. Thus, when we claim that women's laboring practices create value, we frame a specific political problematic: Why and how are the practices in question recognized and rewarded? What is the social value of these activities and the subjectivities they engender? The point of focusing on women's labor is neither to glorify work nor to extol the realization or lament the loss of some genuine mode of being; the point is to create sites of contestation over the social construction of specific constitutive practices where we can raise questions about what we can do and who we can become. (Consider, for example, how feminists have contested the ways in which the labor of child care is organized and valued.) That is, what is at stake here is not the alienation from or restoration to our essence as humans, but rather, the economic, political, and cultural value ascribed to various practices. In this way we pull the category away from the more abstract problematic of a humanist Marxism and its discourse of interiority and attach it to a more practical problematic that focuses our attention instead on struggles over the institutionalization of our practices. Thus, rather than resting on philosophical claims about essential selves, the category of labor can be deployed to provoke political debate over questions of social value.

My contention is that by highlighting the immanent, creative, and strategic dimensions of this ontological principle we can move beyond both the metaphysical logic of voluntarism and the mechanistic logic of determinism. When we build our models of subjectivity around labor, we do not presume to identify the voluntary source of an only superficially determined identity, but rather attempt to isolate a mechanism of and a point of entry into the larger process of engendering which can double as a means to or a site of resistance to this procedure. By this reading, labor is a category that enables us to acknowledge our historical immanence and to recognize the determined dimensions of social life while simultaneously affirming the creative force of the subjective will. . . .

Regardless of whether particular women actually do this kind of work (and of course, many do not), women are generally (though differently) constructed to be the kinds of people who can perform these duties, and are usually (though variously) expected to be the ones who should (see Hartsock 1983a, 291). For this reason, theories of feminist subjectivities based on accounts of women's labor carry the potential to speak to broad audiences of women, and particularly to women outside the academy. However, it should be noted that this focus on labor is also what marks most clearly the specificity of this version of standpoint theory. Obviously one cannot claim that every object of feminist inquiry can be explained by reference to the gender division of labor. I do not, then, profess to offer a new feminist metanarrative or a General Feminist Theory of Everything that identifies labor as the fundamental source of women's oppression and the only site of feminist agitation. What I hope to present is a carefully delimited theoretical approach that aspires to help us think about and cultivate the possible consequences of a specific set of practices in a particular place and time.

Standpoint theories try to consider the ontological and epistemological consequences of these laboring practices. How might some of our laboring practices be suggestive of different ways of being in and knowing the world? How can they help us locate and develop alternatives to the existing configuration of social relations? What, in other words, is the subversive potential of women's laboring practices? I argue that—to the extent that these practices exceed the scope of current standards of cultural and socioeconomic valorization, to the extent that, for example, the labor of creating and sustaining socially necessary forms of sociality cannot be contained, cannot be accounted for, and cannot be valued adequately within the existing mode of production—they carry the potential to enable and to cultivate antagonistic subjects. Standpoint theories attempt to fashion from our everyday practices a chain of critical levers that can inspire our disloyalty and disobedience to the values of the larger social formation. By this interpretation, "women's work" is not just an instance of women's oppression and exploitation, it is also a site where alternatives can be constructed; women's laboring practices are not only constraining, but also potentially enabling. This potential power, these alternatives, are located not in some natural or metaphysical essence, but in our practices; more specifically, these possibilities of feminist subjectivity, of feminist political agency, are grounded in an ontology of laboring practices.

Feminist Standpoints

A standpoint, a collective project designed to affirm and pursue some of these possibilities, is the final element of this theoretical tradition that I want to highlight and affirm. Standpoints are constructed around the potential ontological and epistemological consequences of these laboring practices, around the subjectivities that emerge from these practices. A standpoint is constitutive of and constituted by a collective subject, in this case a feminist subject grounded in women's laboring practices and situated within the larger field of social relations that I call totality. In a time when some feminist theorists are reacting to the valuable critiques of essentialism by retreating from every theory of subjectivity, when some would seem to be translating the critique of humanism into the death of the subject, when some are responding to the oppressive and homogenizing focus on unity that has informed so many accounts and practices of feminist collectivities by committing themselves just as exclusively to the valorization of difference in a way that often simply recapitulates the logic of liberal individualism, standpoint theory points us in the direction of one possible alternative, toward models of collective subjectivity.

Once again, to locate the particular conception of a standpoint that is most in keeping with this project, we must be selective in our appropriation of standpoint theories. Here I focus on those accounts dedicated to the construction of *feminist* standpoints; that is, on those versions in which standpoints are conceived as political projects based on feminist reappropriations of women's practices. For this element I draw most frequently on the work of Hartsock and Rose, both of whom insist that the standpoint they propose is a feminist standpoint: it is a collective interpretation or reworking of a particular subject position rather than an immediate perspective automatically acquired by an individual; it is an ongoing achievement rather than a spontaneous attribute or consciousness of all women. For these theorists, a standpoint is neither self-evident nor obvious (Hartsock 1983a, 303); instead it must be derived from political practice (Rose 1986, 162). A feminist standpoint is, by this formulation, a collective project that is both a product and an instrument of feminist struggle.[16] When we put these last two dimensions together, the focus on labor and the feminist political project, we have the basic tenets of a political project based on the alternative ways of being, desiring, and knowing that can be developed from women's laboring practices.

Conceived as an achieved, constructed collectivity, I believe that a feminist standpoint can serve as an inspiring example of a collective subject, a subject that is neither modeled after the individual, and thus somehow unitary and homogeneous, nor conceived as spontaneous and natural community. Standpoint theory builds on an account of how women's subject positions are systematically constituted within a social field in order then to think about how antagonistic subjects—in this case, feminist collectivities—can be constructed on their basis; fashioned, as it were, from the same materials. Here I believe that we can find a productive account (though certainly not the only productive account) of the subjective bases of a feminist politics; here we can find the basic outlines not just of an ontology of practices, but of a political ontology of practices, an ontology that is inextricably bound to a politics.

Standpoint theorists have generally concentrated their attention on the potential *epistemological* consequences of the gender division of labor: these practices can suggest alternative methods or knowledges which, depending on the account, avoid the subject-object split, emphasize relational thinking, and revalue the concrete, everyday, and bodily dimensions of existence. Here I will focus instead on a relatively less accentuated dimension of these analyses—namely, the ontology that informs a standpoint and the constructions of subjectivity to which it gives rise. This is conceived, then, as an ontological rather than an epistemological project: whereas the primary goal of most of these original theories was to develop alternative epistemologies based on feminist cognitive practices, the primary focus of this account is the constitution of alternative subjects, feminist collectivities.[17] These projects are not incompatible; ontology and epistemology, being and knowing, are intimately related to one another and by no means do these theorists ignore this link. There are, nonetheless, some important differences between the two projects. For example, as a consequence of their focus on the epistemological possibilities of a standpoint in the original versions, the subject of standpoint theory tends to be cast as a knowing subject and, as a consequence, questions of subjectivity are often reduced to questions of consciousness. Here I will be less interested in what or how we know (and the controversies that attach to this epistemological question), than in what we are, or, better yet, in what we can be (and some of the issues of constitution that are involved in this question). To put it in different terms, it is not the possibilities of *becoming conscious* but rather—and here I anticipate a Nietzschean formula—the *being of becoming* that is my primary concern. The collective subjects of this account will be defined primarily not by the consciousness or knowledge they achieve but by the practices they enact and the desires and pleasures that they cultivate. This is where I find the most promising and timely contribution of standpoint theory: rather than an epistemological project, the political efficacy of which is linked to its claims about what or how feminists can know, claims that are supposed to legitimize the alternatives we seek, I believe that a feminist standpoint is more powerful as an ontological project dedicated to the construction of antagonistic subjects with dreams, passions, and interests at odds with the existing order of things, subjects with the will and the capacity to seek alternatives.

What I find valuable in the tradition of standpoint theory, then, is its commitment to make connections among what we are, what we do, and the larger framework of social relations we call totality; its interest in the subversive possibilities of women's laboring practices; and its efforts to assemble a collective feminist subject that is based on and dedicated to pursuing some of these possibilities. There are, however, several problems with these standpoint theories, problems that many different critiques informed by the discourse of postmodernism have helped identify. Among the most significant of these limitations is that the aspiration to totality, the ontology of labor, and the construction of a standpoint have, in some cases, been conceived in ways that betray a reliance on functionalist logics and humanist or otherwise essentialist formulations. First, the problem of functionalism turns up in those attempts to situate subjects in the context of a totality of social relations that deploy an insufficiently complex account of the multiplicity of social structures and subjects, and which limit their interaction to a closed and predictable logic. Second, the achieved and constructed character of a standpoint is not always rigorously attended to so that one can find residues of classic humanist formulations—gestures to some notion of a pre-existing, authentic humanity—in these accounts of a feminist subject. For example, labor, besides being frequently undertheorized, is often presented as the equivalent of a human essence, a universal creative potential from which we are estranged and to which we should be restored. Third, one can also find other forms of essentialist thinking (besides the classic humanist evocation of essence)[18] at work in the early conception of a single feminist standpoint, "the" feminist standpoint, rather than a multiplicity of feminist standpoints, a formula that reveals an inattention to differences among women. To help us move beyond these reductive and determinist conceptions of the social totality and falsely generalized and essentialist conceptions of subjectivity, I will draw on a variety of resources....

Notes

1. Feminist standpoint theory is, like any other label applied ex post facto to a group of theoretical projects, a rather dubious category. To characterize these heterogeneous texts as part of a coherent school of thought is to run roughshod over the substantial differences in their methods, contents, and goals. At least one of these standpoint theorists, Dorothy Smith, has expressed her aversion to being "caged" by this label, claiming that her work is now read through the filter of these interpretations—which, in Smith's estimation, often distort her arguments (1992, 91; see also 1997, 392–393). Of course, one should never confuse an ideal type constructed from a variety of texts with the specific arguments in the texts themselves. Categories are constructed to highlight certain similarities among particular phenomena at the expense of other elements that are different. The value of such a classificatory category lies in its ability to underscore important affinities among these texts that can suggest distinctive and productive lines of inquiry, and I continue to deploy the label of standpoint theory, problematic though it may be, for that reason.
2. Indeed, in some cases I may take the work of the authors on whose work I build in directions they did not wish to pursue. I am thinking here in particular of Dorothy Smith, whose project, while a source of inspiration and instruction in many respects, is ultimately quite different from mine (for example, see note 16).

3. Useful overviews of feminist standpoint theories can be found in Ferguson 1993; Harding 1986a, 1986b, 1991; and Jaggar 1983.
4. Here I anticipate a Lukácsian formulation developed by Fredric Jameson.
5. See Rosemary Hennessy 1993 for an excellent argument for systemic analyses of social totalities within feminism.
6. There are other attempts to rework standpoint theory that do not privilege these accounts of women's labor in the same way. Sandra Harding, for example, focuses on the epistemological dimensions of standpoint theories, grounding them in the more general conditions of women's lives (including but not confined to laboring practices) and the position of marginality (see 1991, 119–134). Similarly, Patricia Hill Collins (1991) grounds Black feminist thought in Black women's experience, of which labor is one determinant among many. Nancy Hirschmann (1992), to cite yet another important example, takes up and develops the psychological focus of those standpoint projects that draw on feminist theories of psychosexual development.
7. The category of women's labor (which is deployed here to examine the practices of women in Western capitalist social formations) is posed as an abstract, unmarked category of gender analysis that can be further specified. For example, the concept of the gender division of labor has been rendered more complex and nuanced by authors detailing how it is simultaneously organized along racial lines. See, for example, Amott and Matthaei 1996, Glenn 1992, and Malveaux 1990. Collins (1991) incorporates some of these insights into her analysis of a Black women's standpoint.
8. This account is drawn from Rose (see 1983, 83).
9. See Ruddick 1989. Ruddick identifies maternal labor, the focus of her study, as one of the specific forms of caring labor (1989, 46–47).
10. The term is from Micaela di Leonardo 1987.
11. See, for example, Hartsock's (1983a; 1983b) account of the sexual division of labor.
12. See Smith 1987. As Smith explains it, women "do those things that give concrete form to the conceptual activities. They do the clerical work, giving material form to the words or thoughts of the boss. They do the routine computer work, the interviewing for the survey, the nursing, the secretarial work. At almost every point women mediate for men the relation between the conceptual mode of action and the actual concrete forms on which it depends" (83).
13. Diane Elson reads this passage to claim that labor "is a fluidity, a potential, which in any society has to be socially 'fixed' or objectified in the production of particular goods, by particular people in particular ways" (1979, 128).
14. These are the terms that Deleuze (1983, 91) and Warren (1988, 111) used to describe the will to power.
15. This notion of labor as value-creating activity is developed by Michael Hardt and Antonio Negri (1994; 7–11).
16. It should be noted that this marks a clear departure from the work of Dorothy Smith, who conceives a standpoint in other terms and uses it for a different purpose. Smith proposes what she calls a women's standpoint as the centerpiece of a proposed method of social inquiry: the standpoint of women directs our research to the local and everyday worlds of our subjects. One could characterize my version of standpoint theory as an attempt to incorporate specific elements of Smith's sociological work combined with certain aspects of Hartsock's and Rose's political project. The category of standpoint is also conceived differently in the work of Patricia Hill Collins. Collins employs the term "standpoint" to refer to the immediate perspective of a group, in this case, of African American women. The term "Black feminist thought," on the other hand, is used to designate a conscious reworking of some of the themes located in this standpoint or immediate perspective (1991, 22). Again, I reserve the term "standpoint" for a mediated construction rather than a spontaneous development.
17. It is worth noting that this focus on epistemology in the original standpoint theories was consistent with a more general interest in questions of knowledge and method among feminist theorists at the time.
18. As I use the terms here, humanism is a type of essentialism. There are, however, other forms of essentialist thinking about subjectivity beyond the classic humanist variety. For example, theories that locate the essence of women in some biological core have been described as essentialist. For a useful discussion of some of the different meanings of essentialism in feminist theory, see Ferguson 1993, 81–83.

References

Amott, Teresa L., and Julie A. Matthaei. 1996. *Race, Gender, and Work: A Multicultural Economic History of Women in the United States*. Boston: South End Press.

Bordo, Susan. 1992. "Feminist Skepticism and the 'Maleness' of Philosophy." In *Women and Reason*, ed. Elizabeth Harvey and Kathleen Okruhlik, 143–162. Ann Arbor: University of Michigan Press.

Butler, Judith. 1990. *Gender Trouble: Feminism and the Subversion of Identity*. New York: Routledge.

———. 1991. "Imitation and Gender Insubordination." In *Inside/Out: Lesbian Theories, Gay Theories*, ed. Diana Fuss, 13–31. New York: Routledge.

———. 1992. "Contingent Foundations: Feminism and the Question of 'Postmodernism.'" In *Feminists Theorize the Political*, ed. Judith Butler and Joan W. Scott, 3–21. New York: Routledge.

———. 1993. *Bodies That Matter: On the Discursive Limits of Sex*. New York: Routledge.

Collins, Patricia Hill. 1991. *Black Feminist Thought: Knowledge, Consciousness, and the Politics of Empowerment*. New York: Routledge.

Deleuze, Gilles. 1983. *Nietzsche and Philosophy*. Trans. Hugh Tomlinson. New York: Columbia University Press.

Di Leonardo, Micaela. 1987. "The Female World of Cards and Holidays: Women, Families, and the Work of Kinship." *Signs* 12 (3): 440–453.

Di Stefano, Christine. 1991. "Am I That Performance? Vicissitudes of Gender." Paper presented to the American Political Science Association, Washington, D.C.

Elson, Diane. 1979. "The Value Theory of Labour." In *Value: The Representation of Labour in Capitalism*, ed. Diane Elson, 115–180. Atlantic Highlands, NJ: Humanities Press.

Ferguson, Ann, and Nancy Folbre. 1981. "The Unhappy Marriage of Patriarchy and Capitalism." In *Women and Revolution*, ed. Lydia Sargent, 313–338. Boston: South End Press.

Ferguson, Kathy. 1993. *The Man Question: Visions of Subjectivity in Feminist Theory*. Berkeley: University of California Press.

Glenn, Evelyn Nakano. 1992. "From Servitude to Service Work: Historical Continuities in the Racial Division of Paid Reproductive Labor." *Signs* 18 (1): 1–43.

Harding, Sandra. 1986a. *The Science Question in Feminism*. Ithaca: Cornell University Press.

———. 1986b. "The Instability of the Analytical Categories of Feminist Theory." *Signs* 11 (4): 645–664.

———. 1991. *Whose Science? Whose Knowledge? Thinking from Women's Lives*. Ithaca: Cornell University Press.

Hardt, Michael, and Antonio Negri. 1994. *Labor of Dionysus: A Critique of the State-Form*. Minneapolis: University of Minnesota Press.

Hartsock, Nancy. 1979. "Feminist Theory and the Development of Revolutionary Strategy." In *Capitalist Patriarchy and the Case for Socialist Feminism*, ed. Zillah Eisenstein, 56–77. New York: Monthly Review Press.

———. 1981. "Fundamental Feminism: Process and Perspective." In *Building Feminist Theory: Essays from Quest a Feminist Quarterly*, ed. Quest Staff. New York: Longman.

———. 1983a. "The Feminist Standpoint: Developing the Ground for a Specifically Feminist Historical Materialism." In *Discovering Reality: Feminist Perspectives on Epistemology, Metaphysics, Methodology, and Philosophy of Science*, ed. Sandra Harding and Merrill Hintikka, 283–310. Dordrecht: D. Reidel Publishing.

———. 1983b. *Money, Sex, and Power: Toward a Feminist Historical Materialism*. Boston: Northeastern University Press.

———. 1989–1990. "Postmodernism and Political Change: Issues for Feminist Theory." *Cultural Critique* 14: 15–33.

Hennessy, Rosemary. 1993. *Materialist Feminism and the Politics of Discourse*. New York: Routledge.

Hirschmann, Nancy J. 1992. *Rethinking Obligation: A Feminist Method for Political Theory*. Ithaca: Cornell University Press.

Jaggar, Alison M. 1983. *Feminist Politics and Human Nature*. Totowa, N.J.: Rowman and Allanheld.

Jameson, Fredric. 1981. *The Political Unconscious: Narrative as a Socially Symbolic Act*. Ithaca: Cornell University Press.

Malveaux, Julianne. 1990. "Gender Difference and Beyond: An Economic Perspective on Diversity and Commonality among Women." In *Theoretical Perspectives on Sexual Difference*, ed. Deborah L. Rhode, 226–238. New Haven: Yale University Press.

Marx, Karl. 1973. *Grundrisse.* Trans. Martin Nicolaus. New York: Vintage Books.

———. 1977. *Capital,* vol. 1. Trans. Ben Fowkes. New York: Vintage Books.

Rose, Hilary. 1983. "Hand, Brain, and Heart: A Feminist Epistemology for the Natural Sciences." *Signs* 9 (1): 73–90.

———. 1986. "Women's Work: Women's Knowledge." In *What Is Feminism?,* ed. Juliet Mitchell and Ann Oakley, 161–183. Oxford: Basil Blackwell.

Ruddick, Sara. 1989. *Maternal Thinking: Toward a Politics of Peace.* New York: Ballantine Books.

Smith, Dorothy E. 1987. *The Everyday World as Problematic: A Feminist Sociology.* Boston: Northeastern University Press.

———. 1990. *Texts, Facts, and Femininity: Exploring the Relations of Ruling.* New York: Routledge.

———. 1992. "Sociology from Women's Experience: A Reaffirmation." *Sociological Theory* 10 (1): 88–98.

———. 1997. "Comment on Hekman's 'Truth and Method: Feminist Standpoint Theory Revisited.'" *Signs* 22 (2): 392–398.

Warren, Mark. 1988. *Nietzsche and Political Thought.* Cambridge: MIT Press.

14

U.S. Third World Feminism: The Theory and Method of Differential Oppositional Consciousness[1]

CHELA SANDOVAL

The enigma that is U.S. third world feminism has yet to be fully confronted by theorists of social change. To these late twentieth-century analysts it has remained inconceivable that U.S. third world feminism might represent a form of historical consciousness whose very structure lies outside the conditions of possibility which regulate the oppositional expressions of dominant feminism. In enacting this new form of historical consciousness, U.S. third world feminism provides access to a different way of conceptualizing not only U.S. feminist consciousness but oppositional activity in general; it comprises a formulation capable of aligning such movements for social justice with what have been identified as world-wide movements of decolonization.

Both in spite of and yet because they represent varying internally colonized communities, U.S. third world feminists have generated a common speech, a theoretical structure which, however, remained just outside the purview of the dominant feminist theory emerging in the 1970s, functioning within it—but only as the unimaginable. Even though this unimaginable presence arose to reinvigorate and refocus the politics and priorities of dominant feminist theory during the 1980s, what remains is an uneasy alliance between what appears on the surface to be two different understandings of domination, subordination, and the nature of effective resistance—a shot-gun arrangement at best between what literary critic Gayatri Spivak characterizes as a "hegemonic feminist theory"[2] on the one side and what I have been naming "U.S. third world feminism" on the other.[3] I do not mean to suggest here, however, that the perplexing situation that exists between U.S. third world and hegemonic feminisms should be understood merely in binary terms. On the contrary, what this investigation reveals is the way in which the new theory of oppositional consciousness considered here and enacted by U.S. third world feminism is at least partially contained, though made deeply invisible by the manner of its appropriation, in the terms of what has become a hegemonic feminist theory.

U.S. third world feminism arose out of the matrix of the very discourses denying, permitting, and producing difference. Out of the imperatives born of necessity arose a mobility of identity that generated the activities of a new citizen-subject, and which reveals yet another model for the self-conscious production of political opposition. In this essay I will lay out U.S. third world feminism as the design for oppositional political activity and consciousness in the United States. In mapping this new design, a model is revealed by which social actors can chart the points through which differing oppositional ideologies can meet, in spite of their varying trajectories. This knowledge becomes important when one begins to wonder, along with late twentieth century cultural critics such as Fredric Jameson, how organized oppositional activity and consciousness can be made possible under the co-opting nature of the so-called "post-modern" cultural condition.[4]

The ideas put forth in this essay are my rearticulation of the theories embedded in the great oppositional practices of the latter half of this century especially in the United States—the Civil Rights movement, the women's movement, and ethnic, race, and gender liberation movements. During this period of great social activity, it became clear to many of us that oppositional social movements which were weakening from internal divisions over strategies, tactics, and aims would benefit by examining philosopher Louis Althusser's theory of "ideology and the ideological state apparatuses."[5] In this now fundamental essay, Althusser lays out the principles by which humans are called into being as citizen/subjects who act—even when in resistance—in order to sustain and reinforce the dominant social order. In this sense, for Althusser, all citizens endure ideological subjection. Althusser's postulations begin to suggest, however, that "means and occasions"[6] do become generated whereby individuals and groups in opposition are able to effectively challenge and transform the current hierarchical nature of the social order, but he does not specify how or on what terms such challenges are mounted.

In supplementing Althusser's propositions, I want to apply his general theory of ideology to the particular cultural concerns raised within North American liberation movements and develop a new theory of ideology which considers consciousness not only in its subordinated and resistant yet appropriated versions—the subject of Althusser's theory of ideology—but in its more effective and persistent oppositional manifestations. In practical terms, this theory focuses on identifying forms of consciousness in opposition, which can be generated and coordinated by those classes self-consciously seeking affective oppositional stances in relation to the dominant social order. The idea here, that the subject-citizen can learn to identify, develop, and control the means of ideology, that is, marshal the knowledge necessary to "break with ideology" while also speaking in and from within ideology, is an idea which lays the philosophical foundations enabling us to make the vital connections between the seemingly disparate social and political aims which drive yet ultimately divide liberation movements from within. From Althusser's point of view, then, the theory I am proposing would be considered a science of oppositional ideology."

This study identifies five principal categories by which "oppositional consciousness" is organized, and which are politically effective means for changing the dominant order of power. I characterize them as "equal rights," "revolutionary," "supremacist," "separatist," and "differential" ideological forms. All these forms of consciousness are kaleidoscoped into view when the fifth form is utilized as a theoretical model which retroactively clarifies and gives new meaning to the others. Differential consciousness represents the strategy of another form of oppositional ideology that functions on an altogether different register. Its power can be thought of as mobile—not nomadic but rather cinematographic: a kinetic motion that maneuvers, poetically transfigures, and orchestrates while demanding alienation, perversion, and reformation in both spectators and practitioners. Differential consciousness is the expression of the new subject position called for by Althusser—it permits functioning within yet beyond the demands of dominant ideology. This differential form of oppositional consciousness has been enacted in the practice of U.S. third world feminism since the 1960s.

This essay also investigates the forms of oppositional consciousness that were generated within one of the great oppositional movements of the late twentieth century, the second wave of the women's movement. What emerges in this discussion is an outline of the oppositional ideological forms which worked against one another to divide the movement from within. I trace these ideological forms as they are manifested in the critical writings of some of the prominent hegemonic feminist theorists of the 1980s. In their attempts to identify a feminist history of consciousness, many of these thinkers believe they detect four fundamentally distinct phases through which feminists have passed in their quest to end the subordination of women. But viewed in terms of another paradigm, "differential consciousness," here made available for study through the activity of U.S. third world feminism, these four historical phases are revealed as sublimated versions of the very forms of consciousness in opposition which were also conceived within post-1950s U.S. liberation movements.

These earlier movements were involved in seeking effective forms of resistance outside of those determined by the social order itself. My contention is that hegemonic feminist forms of resistance represent only other versions of the forms of oppositional consciousness expressed within all liberation movements active in the United States during the later half of the twentieth century. What I want to do here is systematize in theoretical form a theory of oppositional consciousness as it comes embedded but hidden within U.S. hegemonic feminist theoretical tracts. At the end of this essay, I present the outline of a corresponding theory which engages with these hegemonic feminist theoretical forms while at the same time going beyond them to produce a more general theory and method of oppositional consciousness.

The often discussed race and class conflict between white and third world feminists in the United States allows us a clear view of these forms of consciousness in action. The history of the relationship between first and third world feminists has been tense and rife with antagonisms. My thesis is that at the root of these conflicts is the refusal of U.S. third world feminism to buckle under, to submit to sublimation or assimilation within hegemonic feminist praxis. This refusal is based, in large part, upon loyalty to the differential mode of consciousness and activity outlined in this essay but which has remained largely unaccounted for within the structure of the hegemonic feminist theories of the 1980s....

A Brief History

From the beginning of what has been known as the second wave of the women's movement, U.S. third world feminists have claimed a feminism at odds with that being developed by U.S. white women. Already in 1970 with the publication of *Sisterhood Is Powerful,* black feminist Francis Beal was naming the second wave of U.S. feminism as a "white women's movement" because it insisted on organizing along the binary gender division male/female alone[7] U.S. third world feminists, however, have long understood that one's race, culture, or class often denies comfortable or easy access to either category, that the interactions between social categories produce other genders within the social hierarchy. As far back as the middle of the last century, Sojourner Truth found it necessary to remind a convention of white suffragettes of her female gender with the rhetorical question "ar'n't I a woman?"[8] American Indian Paula Gunn Allen has written of Native women that "the place we live now is an idea, because whiteman took all the rest."[9] In 1971, Toni Morrison went so far as to write of U.S. third world women that "there is something inside us that makes us different from other people. It is not like men and it is not like white women."[10] That same year Chicana Velia Hancock continued: "Unfortunately, many white women focus on the maleness of our present social system as though, by implication, a female dominated white America would have taken a more reasonable course" for people of color of either sex.[11]

These signs of a lived experience of difference from white female experience in the United States repeatedly appear throughout U.S. third world feminist writings. Such expressions imply the existence of at least one other category of gender which is reflected in the very titles of books written by U.S. feminists of color such as *All the Blacks Are Men, All the Women Are White, But Some of Us Are Brave*[12] or *This Bridge Called My Back,*[13] titles which imply that women of color somehow exist in the interstices between the legitimated categories of the social order. Moreover, in the title of bell hooks's 1981 book, the question "Ain't I a Woman" is transformed into a defiant statement,[14] while Amy Ling's feminist analysis of Asian American writings, *Between Worlds,*[15] or the title of the journal for U.S. third world feminist writings, *The Third Woman,*[16] also call for the recognition of a new category for social identity. This in-between space, this third gender category, is also explored in the writings of such well-known authors as Maxine Hong Kingston, Gloria Anzaldua, Audre Lorde, Alice Walker, and Cherrie Moraga, all of whom argue that U.S. third world feminists represent a different kind of human—new "mestizas,"[17] "Woman Warriors" who live and are gendered "between and among" the lines,[18] "Sister Outsiders"[19] who inhabit a new psychic terrain which Anzaldua calls "the Borderlands," "la nueva Frontera." In 1980, Audre Lorde summarized the U.S. white women's movement by saying that "today, there is a pretense to a homogeneity of experience covered by the word SISTERHOOD in the white women's movement. When white feminists call for 'unity,' they are mis-naming a deeper and real need for homogeneity." We began the 1980s, she says, with "white women" agreeing "to focus upon their oppression as women" while continuing "to ignore difference." Chicana sociologist Maxine Baca Zinn rearticulated this position in a 1986 essay in *Signs*, saying that "there now exists in women's studies an increased awareness of the variability of womanhood" yet for U.S. feminists of color "such work is often tacked on, its significance for feminist knowledge still unrecognized and unregarded."[20] . . .

U.S. third world feminism, however, functions just outside the rationality of the four-phase hegemonic structure we have just identified. Its recognition will require of hegemonic feminism a paradigm shift which is capable of rescuing its theoretical and practical expressions from their exclusionary and racist forms. I am going to introduce this shift in paradigm by proposing a new kind of taxonomy which I believe prepares the ground for a new theory and method of oppositional consciousness. The recognition of this new taxonomy should also bring into view a new set of alterities and another way of understanding "otherness" in general, for it demands that oppositional actors claim new grounds for generating identity, ethics, and political activity.

Meanwhile, U.S. third world feminism has been sublimated, both denied yet spoken about incessantly, or, as black literary critic Sheila Radford Hill put it in 1986, U.S. third world feminism is "used" within hegemonic feminism only as a "rhetorical platform" which allows white feminist scholars to "launch arguments for or against" the same four basic configurations of hegemonic feminism.[21] It is not surprising, therefore, that the writings of feminist third world theorists are laced through with bitterness. For, according to bell hooks in 1982, the sublimation of U.S. third world feminist writing is linked to racist "exclusionary practices" which have made it "practically impossible" for any new feminist paradigms to emerge. Two years before Jaggar's *Feminist Politics and Human Nature*, hooks wrote that although "feminist theory is the guiding set of beliefs and principles that become the basis for action," the development of feminist theory is a task permitted only within the "hegemonic dominance" and approval "of white academic women."[22] Four years later Gayatri Spivak stated that "the emergent perspective" of hegemonic "feminist criticism" tenaciously reproduces "the

axioms of imperialism." Clearly, the theoretical structure of hegemonic feminism has produced enlightening and new feminist intellectual spaces, but these
coalesce in what Spivak characterizes as a "high feminist norm" which culmi-
nates in reinforcing the "basically isolationist" and narcissistic "admiration" of
hegemonic feminist thinkers "for the literature of the female subject in Europe
and Anglo America."[23] . . .

Toward a Theory of Oppositional Consciousness

Let me suggest, then, another kind of typology, this one generated from the insights born of oppositional activity beyond the inclusive scope of the hegemonic
women's movement. . . .

Any social order that is hierarchically organized into relations of domination
and subordination creates particular subject positions within which the subordinated can legitimately function.[24] These subject positions, once self-consciously
recognized by their inhabitants, can become transformed into more effective
sites of resistance to the current ordering of power relations. From the perspective of a differential U.S. third world feminism, the histories of consciousness
produced by U.S. white feminists are, above all, only other examples of subordinated consciousness in opposition. In order to make U.S. third world feminism
visible within U.S. feminist theory, I suggest a topography of consciousness that
identifies nothing more and nothing less than the modes the subordinated of
the United States (of any gender, race, or class) claim as politicized and oppositional stances in resistance to domination. The topography that follows, unlike
its hegemonic feminist version, is not historically organized, no enactment is
privileged over any other, and the recognition that each site is as potentially effective in opposition as any other makes possible another mode of consciousness
which is particularly effective under late capitalist and postmodern cultural conditions in the United States. I call this mode of consciousness "differential"—it
is the ideological mode enacted by U.S. third world feminists over the last thirty
years.

The first four enactments of consciousness that I describe next reveal hegemonic feminist political strategies as the forms of oppositional consciousness
most often utilized in resistance under earlier (modern, if you will) modes of capitalist production. The following topography, however, does not simply replace
previous lists of feminist consciousness with a new set of categories, because
the fifth and differential method of oppositional consciousness has a mobile,
retroactive, and transformative effect on the previous four forms (the "equal
rights," "revolutionary," "supremacist," and "separatist" forms) setting them into
new processual relationships. Moreover, this topography compasses the perime-
ters for a new theory of consciousness in opposition as it gathers up the modes
of ideology-praxis represented within previous liberation movements into the
fifth, differential, and postmodern paradigm. This paradigm can, among other
things, make clear the vital connections that exist between feminist theory in

general and other theoretical modes concerned with issues of social hierarchy, race marginality, and resistance. U.S. third world feminism, considered as an enabling theory and method of differential consciousness, brings the following oppositional ideological forms into view:

1. Under an "equal rights" mode of consciousness in opposition, the subordinated group argue that their differences—for which they have been assigned inferior status—are only in appearance, not reality. Behind their exterior physical difference, they argue, is an essence the same as the essence of the human already in power. On the basis that all individuals are created equal, subscribers to this particular ideological tactic will demand that their own humanity be legitimated, recognized as the same under the law, and assimilated into the most favored form of the human in power. The expression of this mode of political behavior and identity politics can be traced throughout the writings generated from within U.S. liberation movements of the post–World War II era. Hegemonic feminist theorists have claimed this oppositional expression of resistance to social inequality as "liberal feminism."

2. Under the second ideological tactic generated in response to social hierarchy, which I call "revolutionary," the subordinated group claim their *differences* from those in power and call for a social transformation that will accommodate and legitimate those differences, by force if necessary. Unlike the previous tactic, which insists on the similarity between social, racial, and gender classes across their differences, there is no desire for assimilation within the present traditions and values of the social order. Rather, this tactic of revolutionary ideology seeks to affirm subordinated differences through a radical societal reformation. The hope is to produce a new culture beyond the domination/subordination power axis. This second revolutionary mode of consciousness was enacted within the white women's movement under the rubric of either "socialist" or "Marxist" feminisms.

3. In "supremacism," the third ideological tactic, not only do the oppressed claim their differences, but they also assert that those very differences have provided them access to a superior evolutionary level than those currently in power. Whether their differences are of biological or social origin is of little practical concern, of more importance is the result. The belief is that this group has evolved to a higher stage of social and psychological existence than those currently holding power, moreover, their differences now comprise the essence of what is good in human existence. Their mission is to provide the social order with a higher ethical and moral vision and consequently a more effective leadership. Within the hegemonic feminist schema "radical" and "cultural" feminisms are organized under these precepts.

202 • Chela Sandoval

4. "Separatism" is the final of the most commonly utilized tactics of opposition organized under previous modes of capitalist development. As in the previous three forms, practitioners of this form of resistance also recognize that their differences have been branded as inferior with respect to the category of the most human. Under this mode of thought and activity, however, the subordinated do not desire an "equal rights" type of integration with the dominant order, nor do they seek its leadership or revolutionary transformation. Instead, this form of political resistance is organized to protect and nurture the differences that define it through complete separation from the dominant social order. A utopian landscape beckons these practitioners . . . their hope has inspired the multiple visions of the other forms of consciousness as well.

In the post–WWII period in the United States, we have witnessed how the maturation of a resistance movement means not only that four such ideological positions emerge in response to dominating powers, but that these positions become more and more clearly articulated. Unfortunately, however, as we were able to witness in the late 1970s white women's movement, such ideological positions eventually divide the movement of resistance from within, for each of these sites tends to generate sets of tactics, strategies, and identities which historically have appeared to be mutually exclusive under modernist oppositional practices. What remains all the more profound, however, is that the differential practice of U.S. third world feminism undermines the appearance of the mutual exclusivity of oppositional strategies of consciousness; moreover, it is U.S. third world feminism which allows their reconceptualization on the new terms just proposed. U.S. feminists of color, insofar as they involved themselves with the 1970s white women's liberation movement, were also enacting one or more of the ideological positionings just outlined, but rarely for long, and rarely adopting the kind of fervid belief systems and identity politics that tend to accompany their construction under hegemonic understanding. This unusual affiliation with the movement was variously interpreted as disloyalty, betrayal, absence, or lack: "When they were there, they were rarely there for long" went the usual complaint, or "they seemed to shift from one type of women's group to another." They were the mobile (yet ever present in their "absence") members of this particular liberation movement. It is precisely the significance of this mobility which most inventories of oppositional ideology cannot register.

It is in the activity of weaving "between and among" oppositional ideologies as conceived in this new topological space where another and fifth mode of oppositional consciousness and activity can be found.[25] I have named this activity of consciousness "differential" insofar as it enables movement "between and among" the other equal rights, revolutionary, supremacist, and separatist modes of oppositional consciousness considered as variables, in order to disclose the distinctions among them. In this sense the differential mode of consciousness operates like the clutch of an automobile: the mechanism that permits the driver to select, engage, and disengage gears in a system for the transmission of power.[26] Differential consciousness represents the variant, emerging out of correlations, intensities, junctures, crises. What is differential functions through hierarchy, location, and value—enacting the recovery, revenge, or reparation; its processes produce justice. For analytic purposes I place this mode of differential consciousness in the fifth position, even though it functions as the medium through which the "equal rights," "revolutionary," "supremacist," and "separatist" modes of oppositional consciousness became effectively transformed out of their hegemonic versions. Each is now ideological and *tactical* weaponry for confronting the shifting currents of power.

The differences between this five-location and processual topography of consciousness in opposition, and the previous typology of hegemonic feminism, have been made available for analysis through the praxis of U.S. third world feminism understood as a differential method for understanding oppositional political consciousness and activity. U.S. third world feminism represents a central locus of possibility, an insurgent movement which shatters the construction of any one of the collective ideologies as the single most correct site where truth can be represented. Without making this move beyond each of the four modes of oppositional ideology outlined above, any liberation movement is destined to repeat the oppressive authoritarianism from which it is attempting to free itself and become trapped inside a drive for truth which can only end in producing its own brand of dominations. What U.S. third world feminism demands is a new subjectivity, a political revision that denies any one ideology as the final answer, while instead positing a *tactical subjectivity* with the capacity to recenter depending upon the kinds of oppression to be confronted. This is what the shift from hegemonic oppositional theory and practice to a U.S. third world theory and method of oppositional consciousness requires.

Chicana theorist Aida Hurtado explains the importance of differential consciousness to effective oppositional praxis this way: "by the time women of color reach adulthood, we have developed informal political skills to deal with State intervention. The political skills required by women of color are neither the political skills of the White power structure that White liberal feminists have adopted nor the free spirited experimentation followed by the radical feminists." Rather, "women of color are more like urban guerrillas trained through everyday battle with the state apparatus." As such, "women of color's fighting capabilities are often neither understood by white middle-class feminists" nor leftist activists in general, and up until now, these fighting capabilities have "not been codified anywhere for them to learn."[27] Cherríe Moraga defines U.S. third world feminist "guerrilla warfare" as a way of life: "Our strategy is how we cope" on an everyday basis, she says, "how we measure and weigh what is to be said and when, what is to be done and how, and to whom . . . daily deciding/risking who it is we can call an ally, call a friend (whatever that person's skin, sex, or sexuality)."

Feminists of color are "women without a line. We are women who contradict each other."[28]

In 1981, Anzaldua identified the growing coalition between U.S. feminists of color as one of women who do not have the same culture, language, race, or "ideology, nor do we derive similar solutions" to the problems of oppression. For U.S. third world feminism enacted as a differential mode of oppositional consciousness, however, these differences do not become "opposed to each other."[29] Instead, writes Lorde in 1979, ideological differences must be seen as "a fund of necessary polarities between which our creativities spark like a dialectic. Only within that interdependency," each ideological position "acknowledged and equal, can the power to seek new ways of being in the world generate, as well as the courage and sustenance to act where there are no charters."[30] This movement between ideologies along with the concurrent desire for ideological commitment are necessary for enacting differential consciousness. Differential consciousness makes the second topography of consciousness in opposition visible as a new theory and method for comprehending oppositional subjectivities and social movements in the United States.

The differential mode of oppositional consciousness depends upon the ability to read the current situation of power and of self-consciously choosing and adopting the ideological form best suited to push against its configurations, a survival skill well known to oppressed peoples.[31] Differential consciousness requires grace, flexibility, and strength: enough strength to confidently commit to a well-defined structure of identity for one hour, day, week, month, year; enough flexibility to self-consciously transform that identity according to the requisites of another oppositional ideological tactic if readings of power's formation require it; enough grace to recognize alliance with others committed to egalitarian social relations and race, gender, and class justice, when their readings of power call for alternative oppositional stands. Within the realm of differential consciousness, oppositional ideological positions, unlike their incarnations under hegemonic feminist comprehension, are tactics—not strategies. Self-conscious agents of differential consciousness recognize one another as allies, country-women and men of the same psychic terrain. As the clutch of a car provides the driver the ability to shift gears, differential consciousness permits the practitioner to choose tactical positions, that is, to self-consciously break and reform ties to ideology, activities which are imperative for the psychological and political practices that permit the achievement of coalition across differences. Differential consciousness occurs within the only possible space where, in the words of third world feminist philosopher Maria Lugones, "cross-cultural and cross-racial loving" can take place, through the ability of the self to shift its identities in an activity she calls "world traveling."[32]

Perhaps we can now better understand the overarching utopian content contained in definitions of U.S. third world feminism, as in this statement made by black literary critic Barbara Christian in 1985 who, writing to other U.S.

feminists of color, said: "The struggle is not won. Our vision is still seen, even by many progressives, as secondary, our words trivialized as minority issues," our oppositional stances "characterized by others as divisive. But there is a deep philosophical reordering that is occurring" among us "that is already having its effects on so many of us whose lives and expressions are an increasing revelation of the INTIMATE face of universal struggle."[33] This "philosophical reordering," referred to by Christian, the "different strategy, a different foundation" called for by hooks are, in the words of Audre Lorde, part of "a whole other structure of opposition that touches every aspect of our existence at the same time that we are resisting."[34] I contend that this structure is the recognition of a five-mode theory and method of oppositional consciousness, made visible through one mode in particular, differential consciousness, or U.S. third world feminism, what Gloria Anzaldua has recently named "la conciencia de la mestiza" and what Alice Walker calls "womanism."[35] For Barbara Smith, the recognition of this fundamentally different paradigm can "alter life as we know it" for oppositional actors. In 1981, Merle Woo insisted that U.S. third world feminism represents a "new framework which will not support repression, hatred, exploitation and isolation, but will be a human and beautiful framework, created in a community, bonded not by color, sex or class, but by love and the common goal for the liberation of mind, heart, and spirit."[36] It has been the praxis of a differential form of oppositional consciousness which has stubbornly called up utopian visions such as these. . . .

The praxis of U.S. third world feminism represented by the differential form of oppositional consciousness is threaded throughout the experience of social marginality. As such it is also being woven into the fabric of experiences belonging to more and more citizens who are caught in the crisis of late capitalist conditions and expressed in the cultural angst most often referred to as the postmodern dilemma. The juncture I am proposing, therefore, is extreme. It is a location wherein the praxis of U.S. third world feminism links with the aims of white feminism, studies of race, ethnicity, and marginality, and with postmodern theories of culture as they crosscut and join together in new relationships through a shared comprehension of an emerging theory and method of oppositional consciousness.

Notes

1. This is an early version of a chapter from my book on "Oppositional Consciousness in the Postmodern World." A debt of gratitude is owed the friends, teachers, and politically committed scholars who made the publication of this essay possible, especially Hayden White, Donna Haraway, James Clifford, Ronaldo Balderrama, Ruth Frankenberg, Lata Mani (who coerced me into publishing this now), Rosa Maria Villafane-Sisolak, A. Pearl Sandoval, Mary John, Vivian Sobchak, Helene Moglan, T. de Lauretis, Audre Lorde, Traci Chapman, and the Student of Color Coalition. Haraway's own commitments to social, gender, race, and class justice are embodied in the fact that she discusses and cites an earlier version of this essay in her own work. See especially her 1985 essay where she defines an oppositional postmodern consciousness grounded in multiple identities in her "A Manifesto for Cyborgs: Science, Technology, and Socialist Feminism in the 1980s," *Socialist Review*, no. 80 (March 1985). At a time when theoretical work by

women of color is so frequently dismissed, Haraway's recognition and discussion of my work on oppositional consciousness has allowed it to receive wide critical visibility, as reflected in references to the manuscript that appear in the works of authors such as Sandra Harding, Nancy Hartsock, Biddy Martin, and Katherine Hayles. I am happy that my work has also received attention from Caren Kaplan, Katie King, Gloria Anzaldua, Teresa de Lauretis, Chandra Mohanty, and Yvonne Yarboro-Bejarano. Thanks also are due Fredric Jameson, who in 1979 recognized a theory of "oppositional consciousness" in my work. It was he who encouraged its further development.

This manuscript was first presented publically at the 1981 National Women's Studies Association conference. In the ten years following, five other versions have been circulated. I could not resist the temptation to collapse sections from these earlier manuscripts here in the footnotes; any resulting awkwardness is not due to the vigilance of my editors. This essay is published now to honor the political, intellectual, and personal aspirations of Rosa Maria Villafane-Sisolak, "West Indian Princess," who died April 20, 1990. Ro's compassion, her sharp intellectual prowess and honesty, and her unwavering commitment to social justice continue to inspire, guide, and support many of us. To her, to those named here, and to all new generations of U.S. third world feminists this work is dedicated.

2.   Gayatri Spivak, "The Rani of Sirmur," in *Europe and Its Others*, ed. F. Barker, vol. 1 (Essex: University of Essex, 1985), 147.

3.   Here, U.S. third world feminism represents the political alliance made during the 1960s and 1970s between a generation of U.S. feminists of color who were separated by culture, race, class, or gender identifications but united through similar responses to the experience of race oppression. The theory and method of oppositional consciousness outlined in this essay is visible in the activities of the recent political unity variously named "U.S. third world feminist," "feminist women of color," and "womanist." This unity has coalesced across differences in race, class, language, ideology, culture, and color. These differences are painfully manifest: materially marked physiologically or in language, socially value laden, and shot through with power. They confront each feminist of color in any gathering where they serve as constant reminders of their undeniability. These constantly speaking differences stand at the crux of another, mutant unity, for this unity does not occur in the name of all "women," nor in the name of race, class, culture, or "humanity" in general. Instead, as many U.S. third world feminists have pointed out, it is unity mobilized in a location heretofore unrecognized. As Cherrie Moraga argues, this unity mobilizes "between the seemingly irreconcilable lines—class lines, politically correct lines, the daily lines we run to each other to keep difference and desire at a distance," it is *between* these lines "that the truth of our connection lies." This connection is a mobile unity, constantly weaving and reweaving an interaction of differences into coalition. In what follows I demonstrate how it is that inside this coalition, differences are viewed as varying survival tactics constructed in response to recognizable power dynamics. See Cherrie Moraga, "Between the Lines: On Culture, Class and Homophobia," in *This Bridge Called My Back, A Collection of Writings by Radical Women of Color*, ed. Cherrie Moraga and Gloria Anzaldua (Watertown, MA: Persephone Press, 1981), 106. During the national conference of the Women's Studies Association in 1981, three hundred feminists of color met to agree that "it is white men who have access to the greatest amount of freedom from necessity in this culture, with women as their 'helpmates' and chattels, and people of color as their women's servants. People of color form a striated social formation which allow men of color to call upon the circuits of power which charge the category of 'male' with its privileges, leaving women of color as the final chattel, the ultimate servant in a racist and sexist class hierarchy. U.S. third world feminists seek to undo this hierarchy by reconceptualizing the notion of 'freedom' and who may inhabit its realm." See Sandoval, "The Struggle Within: A Report on the 1981 NWSA Conference," published by the Center for Third World Organizing, 1982, reprinted by Gloria Anzaldua in *Making Faces Making Soul, Haciendo Caras* (San Francisco: Spinsters/Aunt Lute, 1990), 55–71. See also "Comment on Krieger's *The Mirror Dance*," a U.S. third world feminist perspective, in *Signs* 9, no. 4 (Summer 1984): 725.

4.   See Fredric Jameson's "Postmodernism, or the Cultural Logic of Late Capitalism," *New Left Review* 146 (July–August 1984).

5. Louis Althusser, "Ideology and Ideological State Apparatuses (Notes Towards an Investigation)," in *Lenin and Philosophy and Other Essays* (London: New Left Books, 1970), 123–73.
6. Althusser, "Ideology," 147.
7. Francis Beal, "Double Jeopardy: To Be Black and Female," in *Sisterhood Is Powerful: An Anthology of Writings from the Women's Liberation Movement*, ed. Robin Morgan (New York: Random House, 1970), 136.
8. Soujourner Truth, "Ain't I a Woman?" in *The Norton Anthology of Literature by Women* (New York: Norton, 1985), 252.
9. Paula Gunn Allen, "Some Like Indians Endure," in *Living the Spirit* (New York: St. Martin's Press, 1987), 9.
10. Toni Morrison, in Bettye J. Parker, "Complexity: Toni Morrison's Women—an Interview Essay," in *Sturdy Black Bridges: Visions of Black Women in Literature*, ed. Roseanne Bell, Bettye Parker, and Beverly Guy-Sheftall (New York: Anchor/Doubleday, 1979).
11. Velia Hancock, "La Chicana, Chicano Movement and Women's Liberation," *Chicano Studies Newsletter* (February–March 1971).
    The sense that people of color occupy an "in-between/outsider" status is a frequent theme among third world liberationists who write both in and outside of the United States. Rev. Desmond Mpilo Tutu, on receiving the Nobel prize, said he faces a "rough passage" as intermediary between ideological factions, for he has long considered himself "detribalized." Rosa Maria Villafane-Sisolak, a West Indian from the Island of St. Croix, has written: "I am from an island whose history is steeped in the abuses of Western imperialism, whose people still suffer the deformities caused by Euro-American colonialism, old and new. Unlike many third world liberationists, however, I cannot claim to be descendent of any particular strain, noble or ignoble. I am, however, 'purely bred,'—descendent of all the parties involved in that cataclysmic epoch. I . . . despair, for the various parts of me cry out for retribution at having been brutally uprooted and transplanted to fulfill the profit-cy of 'white' righteousness and dominance. My soul moans that part of me that was destroyed by that callous righteousness. My heart weeps for that part of me that was the instrument . . . the gun, the whip, the book. My mind echos with the screams of disruption, desecration, destruction." Alice Walker, in a controversial letter to an African-American friend, told him she believes that "we are the African and the trader. We are the Indian and the Settler. We are oppressor and oppressed . . . we are the mestizos of North America. We are black, yes, but we are 'white,' too, and we are red. To attempt to function as only one, when you are really two or three, leads, I believe, to psychic illness: 'white' people have shown us the madness of that." And Gloria Anzaldua, "You say my name is Ambivalence: Not so. Only your labels split me." Desmond Tutu, as reported by Richard N. Osting, "Searching for New Worlds," *Time Magazine*, Oct. 29, 1984. Rosa Maria Villafane-Sisolak, from a 1983 journal entry cited in *Haciendo Caras, Making Face Making Soul*, ed. Gloria Anzaldua; Alice Walker, "In the Closet of the Soul: A Letter to an African-American Friend," *Ms. Magazine* 15 (November 1986): 32–35; Gloria Anzaldua, "La Prieta," *This Bridge Called My Back: A Collection of Writings by Radical Women of Color* (Watertown, MA: Persephone Press, 1981), 198–209.
12. Gloria Hull, Patricia Bell Scott, and Barbara Smith, *All the Women Are White, All the Blacks Are Men, But Some of Us Are Brave: Black Women's Studies* (New York: Feminist Press, 1982).
13. Cherrie Moraga and Gloria Anzaldua, *This Bridge Called My Back: A Collection of Writings by Radical Women of Color* (Watertown, MA: Persephone Press, 1981).
14. bell hooks, *Ain't I a Woman: Black Women and Feminism* (Boston: South End Press, 1981).
15. Amy Ling, *Between Worlds* (New York: Pergamon Press, 1990).
16. Norma Alarcon, ed., *The Third Woman* (Bloomington, IN: Third Woman Press, 1981).
17. See Alice Walker, "Letter to an Afro-American Friend," *Ms. Magazine*, 1986. Also Gloria Anzaldua, *Borderlands, La Frontera: The New Mestiza* (San Francisco: Spinsters/Aunt Lute, 1987).
18. Maxine Hong Kingston, *The Woman Warrior* (New York: Vintage Books, 1977); Cherrie Moraga and Gloria Anzaldua, *The Bridge Called My Back: A Collection of Writings by Radical Women of Color*.

19. Audre Lorde, *Sister Outsider* (New York: The Crossing Press, 1984).

20. Maxine Baca Zinn, Lynn Weber Cannon, Elizabeth Higginbotham, and Bonnie Thornton Dill, "The Costs of Exclusionary Practices in Women's Studies," in *Signs: Journal of Women in Culture and Society* 11, no. 2 (Winter 1986): 296.

21. Sheila Radford-Hall, "Considering Feminism as a Model for Social Change," in *Feminist Studies/Critical Studies*, ed. Teresa de Lauretis (Bloomington: Indiana University Press, 1986), 160.

22. bell hooks, *Feminist Theory from Margin to Center* (Boston: South End Press, 1984), 9.

23. Gayatri Chakravorty Spivak, "Three Women's Texts and a Critique of Imperialism," *Critical Inquiry* 12 (Autumn 1985): 243–61.

24. In another essay I characterize such legitimated idioms of subordination as "human," "pet," "game," and "wild."

25. Gloria Anzaldua writes that she lives "between and among" cultures in "La Prieta," *This Bridge Called My Back,* 209.

26. Differential consciousness functioning like a "car clutch" is a metaphor suggested by Yves Labissiere in a personal conversation.

27. Aida Hurtado, "Reflections on White Feminism: A Perspective from a Woman of Color" (1985), 25, from an unpublished manuscript. Another version of this quotation appears in Hurtado's essay, "Relating to Privilege: Seduction and Rejection in the Subordination of White Women and Women of Color," in *Signs* 14, no. 4 (Summer 1989): 833–55.

28. Moraga and Anzaldua, *This Bridge Called My Back,* xix. Also see the beautiful passage from Margaret Walker's *Jubilee* which enacts this mobile mode of consciousness from the viewpoint of the female protagonist. See the Bantam Books edition (New York, 1985), 404–407.

29. Gloria Anzaldua, "La Prieta," *This Bridge Called My Back,* 209.

30. Audre Lorde, "Comments at 'The Personal and the Political Panel,' " Second Sex Conference, New York, September 1979. Published in *This Bridge Called My Back,* 98. Also see "The Uses of the Erotic" in *Sister Outsider,* 58–63, which calls for challenging and undoing authority in order to enter a utopian realm only accessible through a processual form of consciousness which she names the "erotic."

31. Anzaldua refers to this survival skill as "la facultad, the capacity to see in surface phenomena the meaning of deeper realities" in *Borderlands, La Frontera,* 38.

    The consciousness which typifies la facultad is not naive to the moves of power: it is constantly surveying and negotiating its moves. Often dismissed as "intuition," this kind of "perceptiveness," "sensitivity," consciousness if you will, is not determined by race, sex, or any other genetic status, neither does its activity belong solely to the "proletariat," the "feminist," nor to the oppressed, if the oppressed is considered a unitary category, but it is a learned emotional and intellectual skill which is developed amidst hegemonic powers. It is the recognition of "la facultad" which moves Lorde to say that it is marginality, "whatever its nature . . . which is also the source of our greatest strength," for the cultivation of la facultad creates the opportunity for a particularly effective form of opposition to the dominant culture within which it is formed. The skills required by la facultad are capable of disrupting the dominations and subordinations that scar U.S. culture. But it is not enough to utilize them on an individual and situational basis. Through an ethical and political commitment, U.S. third world feminism requires the development of la facultad to a methodological level capable of generating a political strategy and identity politics from which a new citizenry arises.

    Movements of resistance have always relied upon the ability to read below the surfaces—a way of mobilizing—to resee reality and call it by different names. This form of la facultad inspires new visions and strategies for action. But there is always the danger that even the most revolutionary of readings can become bankrupt as a form of resistance when it becomes reified, unchanging. The tendency of la facultad to end in frozen, privileged "readings" is the most divisive dynamic inside of any liberation movement. In order for this survival skill to provide the basis for a differential and unifying methodology, it must be remembered that la facultad is a process. Answers located may be only temporarily effective, so that wedded to the process of la facultad is a flexibility that continually woos change.

32. Maria Lugones, "Playfulness, World-Travelling, and Loving Perception," from *Hypatia: A Journal of Feminist Philosophy* 2, no. 2 (1987).

33. Barbara Christian, "Creating a Universal Literature: Afro-American Women Writers," *KPFA Folio. Special African History) (unth Edition, Februur y 1985, front page. Reissued in *Black Feminist Criticism: Perspectives on Black Women Writers* (New York: Pergamon Press, 1985), 163.

34. bell hooks, "Feminist Theory: From Margin to Center," 9; Audre Lorde, "An Interview: Audre Lorde and Adrienne Rich" held in August 1979, *Signs* 6, no. 4 (Summer 1981); and Barbara Smith, *Home Girls: A Black Feminist Anthology*, xxv.

35. Alice Walker coined the neologism "womanist" as one of many attempts by feminists of color to find a name which could signal their commitment to egalitarian social relations, a commitment which the name "feminism" had seemingly betrayed. See Walker, *In Search of Our Mother's Gardens: Womanist Prose* (New York: Harcourt Brace Jovanovich, 1983), xi–xiii. Anzaldua, *Borderlands, La Nueva Frontera*.

36. Merle Woo, "Letter to Ma," *This Bridge Called My Back*, 147.

Controversies, Limits, Revisionings

Introduction

Of course every section in this anthology is focused on controversies, the limits of usefulness of standpoint projects, and on revisioning both the logic of a standpoint and the kinds of social relations we should desire. Yet it will be useful to look together at some essays that reflect on the strengths and limits of standpoint theory in different disciplinary, global, and political contexts.

Philosopher Uma Narayan considers how very Western the conceptual framework and politics of standpoint epistemology can appear from a feminist perspective outside the West. Narayan is not arguing that standpoint epistemology is not valuable. Instead she is concerned that some of its preoccupations—revaluing women, their values and lives, criticizing positivism, and taking a stand that is somewhat outside one's culture—can appear less valuable, and have distinctive costs in the context of Indian feminists, including those living in the United States.

Political philosopher Susan Hekman is a defender of standpoint theory, though she argues that some of its original authors have taken it in unproductive directions. Hekman's essay appeared in the journal *Signs* along with comments on Hekman's argument by four of those standpoint theorists, and Hekman's response to these comments. Readers will want to ask themselves what is at issue in these exchanges. What are the authors' diverse stakes in the way Hekman understands standpoint theory? (See also discussions of this set of papers in the later essays here by Hirschmann and Wylie.) One issue that separates Hekman from her respondents is the usefulness of the Marxian tradition; how does Hekman leave it behind? A related issue on which all of the commentators focus is politics; how does Hekman's paper seem to refocus standpoint epistemology away from the various political concerns of the four commentators? From whose perspective is the conceptual framework of Hekman's paper constructed? Another issue is disciplinary commitments (as Dorothy E. Smith notes). How are political philosopher Hekman's concerns different from those of the two sociologists of knowledge and the philosopher of science? Additionally, readers can ask if Hekman shares with the respondents the same understanding of the role of group consciousness in standpoint production of knowledge.

Dutch philosopher Dick Pels similarly sets feminist standpoint analyses on a broad canvas of standpoint claims, beginning with those by Machiavelli and continuing on to examine the three recent class-, race-, and gender-based "epistemologies of marginality." Pels asks provocative questions about the social position of standpoint theorizing. For example, he points out that when tempted to promote epistemologies of marginality, we must consider not only the standpoints of the usually discussed progressive social movements, but also of such other kinds of marginalized groups as the Nazis and the radical right: not all marginality is potentially equally politically progressive.[1]

Moreover, Pels raises questions about the interests of the intellectuals who promote marginality as a uniquely progressive social position. To what extent do the standpoint theorists commit the "intellectualist fallacy" of speaking from their own marginalized positions more than from the positions of the oppressed for whom they claim to speak? Pels also identifies effective attempts to block such romanticizations of and false identifications with the oppressed in standpoint theory (e.g., by Haraway and Collins). Yet he doesn't take up the explicit commitments to robust forms of critical reflexivity articulated by a number of standpoint theorists and their commentators.[2] Would consideration of these concerns have changed his argument? Nevertheless, Pels sees standpoint theory as offering important resources for the oppressed in the social world's "chronic 'war of positions.'"

Two additional sites of controversy are the focus of essays in the last section.

Notes

1. Here Pels's account parallels in interesting ways analyses of the comparative prodemocratic potential of various new social movements by urban sociologist Manuel Castells in *The Power of Identity*, Vol. II of *The Information Age: Economy, Society and Culture* (Oxford: Blackwell, 1997). Castells, like Pels, also notes the use of standpoint type arguments (Castells does not so name them) by politically regressive social groups such as Nazis, neo-Nazis, American Patriot groups, and religious and land-based fundamentalists. This phenomenon confirms the perception of some standpoint theorists that there is no magic, epistemological mechanism to insure that scientific research can be firmly separated from undesirable ethical and political consequences.

2. See, for example, Harding's "Robust Reflexivity," chapter 11 in *Is Science Multicultural? Postcolonialisms, Feminisms, and Epistemologies* (Bloomington: Indiana University Press, 1998). Tim May has argued that it is feminist standpoint theory that makes the most important move in the long history of thinking about reflexivity in the social sciences. Tim May, "Reflexivity in the Age of Reconstructive Social Science," *Social Research Methodology*, vol. 1, no. 1 (1998), pp. 7–24.

15

The Project of Feminist Epistemology: Perspectives from a Nonwestern Feminist

UMA NARAYAN

A fundamental thesis of feminist epistemology is that our location in the world as women makes it possible for us to perceive and understand different aspects of both the world and human activities in ways that challenge the male bias of existing perspectives. Feminist epistemology is a particular manifestation of the general insight that the nature of women's experiences as individuals and as social beings, our contributions to work, culture, knowledge, and our history and political interests have been systematically ignored or misrepresented by mainstream discourses in different areas.

Women have been often excluded from prestigious areas of human activity (for example, politics or science) and this has often made these activities seem clearly "male." In areas where women were not excluded (for example, subsistence work), their contribution has been misrepresented as secondary and inferior to that of men. Feminist epistemology sees mainstream theories about various human enterprises, including mainstream theories about human knowledge, as one-dimensional and deeply flawed because of the exclusion and misrepresentation of women's contributions.

Feminist epistemology suggests that integrating women's contribution into the domain of science and knowledge will not constitute a mere adding of details; it will not merely widen the canvas but result in a shift of perspective enabling us to see a very different picture. The inclusion of women's perspective will not merely amount to women participating in greater numbers in the existing practice of science and knowledge, but it will change the very nature of these activities and their self-understanding.

It would be misleading to suggest that feminist epistemology is a homogenous and cohesive enterprise. Its practitioners differ both philosophically and politically in a number of significant ways (Harding 1986). But an important theme on its agenda has been to undermine the abstract, rationalistic, and universal image of the scientific enterprise by using several different strategies. It has studied, for instance, how contingent historical factors have colored both scientific theories and practices and provided the (often sexist) metaphors in which scientists

213

have conceptualized their activity (Bordo 1986; Keller 1985; Harding and O'Barr 1987). It has tried to reintegrate values and emotions into our account of our cognitive activities, arguing for both the inevitability of their presence and the importance of the contributions they are capable of making to our knowledge (Gilligan 1982; Jaggar and Tronto essays in this volume). It has also attacked various sets of dualisms characteristic of western philosophical thinking—reason versus emotion, culture versus nature, universal versus particular—in which the first of each set is identified with science, rationality, and the masculine and the second is relegated to the nonscientific, the nonrational, and the feminine (Harding and Hintikka 1983; Lloyd 1984; Wilshire 1989).

At the most general level, feminist epistemology resembles the efforts of many oppressed groups to reclaim for themselves the value of their own experience. The writing of novels that focused on working-class life in England or the lives of black people in the United States shares a motivation similar to that of feminist epistemology—to depict an experience different from the norm and to assert the value of this difference.

In a similar manner, feminist epistemology also resembles attempts by third-world writers and historians to document the wealth and complexity of local economic and social structures that existed prior to colonialism. These attempts are useful for their ability to restore to colonized peoples a sense of the richness of their own history and culture. These projects also mitigate the tendency of intellectuals in former colonies who are westernized through their education to think that anything western is necessarily better and more "progressive." In some cases, such studies help to preserve the knowledge of many local arts, crafts, lore, and techniques that were part of the former way of life before they are lost not only to practice but even to memory.

These enterprises are analogous to feminist epistemology's project of restoring to women a sense of the richness of their history, to mitigate our tendency to see the stereotypically "masculine" as better or more progressive, and to preserve for posterity the contents of "feminine" areas of knowledge and expertise—medical lore, knowledge associated with the practices of childbirth and child rearing, traditionally feminine crafts, and so on. Feminist epistemology, like these other enterprises, must attempt to balance the assertion of the value of a different culture or experience against the dangers of romanticizing it to the extent that the limitations and oppressions it confers on its subjects are ignored.

My essay will attempt to examine some dangers of approaching feminist theorizing and epistemological values in a noncontextual and nonpragmatic way, which could convert important feminist insights and theses into feminist epistemological dogmas. I will use my perspective as a nonwestern, Indian feminist to examine critically the predominantly Anglo-American project of feminist epistemology and to reflect on what such a project might signify for women in nonwestern cultures in general and for nonwestern feminists in particular. I will suggest that different cultural contexts and political agendas may cast a very different light on both the "idols" and the "enemies" of knowledge as they have characteristically been typed in western feminist epistemology.

In keeping with my respect for contexts, I would like to stress that I do not see nonwestern feminists as a homogenous group and that none of the concerns I express as a nonwestern feminist may be pertinent to or shared by *all* nonwestern feminists, although I do think they will make sense to many.

In the first section, I will show that the enterprise of feminist epistemology poses some political problems for nonwestern feminists that it does not pose, in the same way, for western feminists. In the second section, I will explore some problems that nonwestern feminists may have with feminist epistemology's critical focus on positivism. In the third section, I will examine some political implications of feminist epistemology's thesis of the "epistemic privilege" of oppressed groups for nonwestern feminists. And in the last section, I will discuss the claim that oppressed groups gain epistemic advantages by inhabiting a larger number of contexts, arguing that such situations may not always confer advantages and may sometimes create painful problems.

Nonwestern Feminist Politics and Feminist Epistemology

Some themes of feminist epistemology may be problematic for nonwestern feminists in ways that they are not problematic for western feminists. Feminism has a much narrower base in most nonwestern countries. It is primarily of significance to some urban, educated, middle-class, and hence relatively westernized women, like myself. Although feminist groups in these countries do try to extend the scope of feminist concerns to other groups (for example, by fighting for childcare, women's health issues, and equal wages issues through trade union structures), some major preoccupations of western feminism—its critique of marriage, the family, compulsory heterosexuality—presently engage the attention of mainly small groups of middle-class feminists.

These feminists must think and function within the context of a powerful tradition that, although it systematically oppresses women, also contains within itself a discourse that confers a high value on women's place in the general scheme of things. Not only are the roles of wife and mother highly praised, but women also are seen as the cornerstones of the spiritual well-being of their husbands and children, admired for their supposedly higher moral, religious, and spiritual qualities, and so on. In cultures that have a pervasive religious component, like the Hindu culture with which I am familiar, everything seems assigned a place and value as long as it keeps to its place. Confronted with a powerful traditional discourse that values woman's place as long as she keeps to the place prescribed, it may be politically counterproductive for nonwestern feminists to echo uncritically the themes of western feminist epistemology that seek to restore the value, cognitive and otherwise, of "women's experience."

The danger is that, even if the nonwestern feminist talks about the value of women's experience in terms totally different from those of the traditional discourse, the difference is likely to be drowned out by the louder and more powerful voice of the traditional discourse, which will then claim that "what those feminists say" vindicates its view that the roles and experiences it assigns to women have value and that women should stick to those roles.

I do not intend to suggest that this is not a danger for western feminism or to imply that there is no tension for western feminists between being critical of the experiences that their societies have provided for women and finding things to value in them nevertheless. But I am suggesting that perhaps there is less at risk for western feminists in trying to strike this balance. I am inclined to think that in nonwestern countries feminists must still stress the negative sides of the female experience within that culture and that the time for a more sympathetic evaluation is not quite ripe.

But the issue is not simple and seems even less so when another point is considered. The imperative we experience as feminists to be critical of how our culture and traditions oppress women conflicts with our desire as members of once colonized cultures to affirm the value of the same culture and traditions.

There are seldom any easy resolutions to these sorts of tensions. As an Indian feminist currently living in the United States, I often find myself torn between the desire to communicate with honesty the miseries and oppressions that I think my own culture confers on its women and the fear that this communication is going to reinforce, however unconsciously, western prejudices about the "superiority" of western culture. I have often felt compelled to interrupt my communication, say on the problems of the Indian system of arranged marriages, to remind my western friends that the experiences of women under their system of "romantic love" seem no more enviable. Perhaps we should all attempt to cultivate the methodological habit of trying to understand the complexities of the oppression involved in different historical and cultural settings while eschewing, at least for now, the temptation to make comparisions across such settings, given the dangers of attempting to compare what may well be incommensurable in any neat terms.

The Nonprimacy of Positivism as A Problematic Perspective

As a nonwestern feminist, I also have some reservations about the way in which feminist epistemology seems to have picked positivism as its main target of attack. The choice of positivism as the main target is reasonable because it has been a dominant and influential western position and it most clearly embodies some flaws that feminist epistemology seeks to remedy.

But this focus on positivism should not blind us to the facts that it is not our only enemy and that nonpositivist frameworks are not, by virtue of that bare qualification, any more worthy of our tolerance. Most traditional frameworks that nonwestern feminists regard as oppressive to women are not positivist, and it would be wrong to see feminist epistemology's critique of positivism given the same political importance for nonwestern feminists that it has for western feminists. Traditions like my own, where the influence of religion is pervasive are suffused through and through with values. We must fight not frameworks that assert the separation of fact and value but frameworks that are pervaded by values to which we, as feminists, find ourselves opposed. Positivism in epistemology flourished at the same time as liberalism in western political theory. Positivism's view of values as individual and subjective related to liberalism's political emphasis on individual rights that were supposed to protect an individual's freedom to live according to the values she espoused.

Nonwestern feminists may find themselves in a curious bind when confronting the interrelations between positivism and political liberalism. As colonized people, we are well aware of the facts that many political concepts of liberalism are both suspicious and confused and that the practice of liberalism in the colonies was marked by brutalities unaccounted for by its theory. However, as feminists, we often find some of its concepts, such as individual rights, very useful in our attempts to fight problems rooted in our traditional cultures.

Nonwestern feminists will no doubt be sensitive to the fact that positivism is not our only enemy. Western feminists too must learn not to uncritically claim any nonpositivist framework as an ally; despite commonalities, there are apt to be many differences. A temperate look at positions we espouse as allies is necessary since "the enemy of my enemy is my friend" is a principle likely to be as misleading in epistemology as it is in the domain of Realpolitik.

The critical theorists of the Frankfurt School will serve well to illustrate this point. Begun as a group of young intellectuals in the post–World War I Weimar Republic, the members were significantly influenced by Marxism, and their interests ranged from aesthetics to political theory to epistemology. Jürgen Habermas, the most eminent critical theorist today, has in his works attacked positivism and the claim of scientific theories to be value neutral or "disinterested." He has attempted to show the constitutive role played by human interests in different domains of human knowledge. He is interested, as are feminists, in the role that knowledge plays in the reproduction of social relations of domination. But, as feminist epistemology is critical of all perspectives that place a lopsided stress on reason, it must also necessarily be critical of the rationalist underpinnings of critical theory.

Such rationalist foundations are visible, for example, in Habermas's "rational reconstruction" of what he calls "an ideal speech situation," supposedly characterized by "pure intersubjectivity," that is, by the absence of any barriers to communication. That Habermas's "ideal speech situation" is a creature of reason is clear from its admitted character as a "rationally reconstructed ideal" and its symmetrical distribution of chances for all of its participants to choose and apply speech acts.

This seems to involve a stress on formal and procedural equality among speakers that ignores substantive differences imposed by class, race, or gender that may affect a speaker's knowledge of the facts or the capacity to assert herself or command the attention of others. Women in academia often can testify to the fact that, despite not being forcibly restrained from speaking in public forums, they have to overcome much conditioning in order to learn to assert themselves. They can also testify as to how, especially in male-dominated disciplines, their speech is often ignored or treated with condescension by male colleagues.

Habermas either ignores the existence of such substantive differences among speakers or else assumes they do not exist. In the latter case, if one assumes that the speakers in the ideal speech situation are not significantly different from each other, then there may not be much of significance for them to speak about. Often it is precisely our differences that make dialogue imperative. If the ideal speakers of the ideal speech situation are unmarked by differences, there may be nothing for them to surmount on their way to a "rational consensus." If there are such differences between the speakers, then Habermas provides nothing that will rule out the sorts of problems I have mentioned.

Another rationalist facet of critical theory is revealed in Habermas's assumption that justifiable agreement and genuine knowledge arise only out of "rational consensus." This seems to overlook the possibility of agreement and knowledge based on sympathy or solidarity. Sympathy or solidarity may very well promote the uncovering of truth, especially in situations when people who divulge information are rendering themselves vulnerable in the process. For instance, women are more likely to talk about experiences of sexual harassment to other women because they would expect similar experiences to have made them more sympathetic and understanding. Therefore, feminists should be cautious about assuming that they necessarily have much in common with a framework simply because it is nonpositivist. Nonwestern feminists may be more alert to this error because many problems they confront arise in nonpositivist contexts.

The Political Uses of "Epistemic Privilege"

Important strands in feminist epistemology hold the view that our concrete embodiments as members of a specific class, race, and gender as well as our concrete historical situations necessarily play significant roles in our perspective on the world; moreover, no point of view is "neutral" because no one exists unembedded in the world. Knowledge is seen as gained not by solitary individuals but by socially constituted members of groups that emerge and change through history.

Feminists have also argued that groups living under various forms of oppression are more likely to have a critical perspective on their situation and that this critical view is both generated and partly constituted by critical emotional responses that subjects experience vis-à-vis their life situations. This perspective in feminist epistemology rejects the "Dumb View" of emotions and favors an intentional conception that emphasizes the cognitive aspect of emotions. It is critical of the traditional view of the emotions as wholly and always impediments to knowledge and argues that many emotions often help rather than hinder our understanding of a person or situation (see Jaggar 1989).

Bringing together these views on the role of the emotions in knowledge, the possibility of critical insights being generated by oppression, and the contextual nature of knowledge may suggest some answers to serious and interesting political questions. I will consider what these epistemic positions entail regarding the possibility of understanding and political cooperation between oppressed groups and sympathetic members of a dominant group—say, between white people and people of color over issues of race or between men and women over issues of gender.

These considerations are also relevant to questions of understanding and cooperation between western and nonwestern feminists. Western feminists, despite their critical understanding of their own culture, often tend to be more a part of it than they realize. If they fail to see the contexts of their theories and assume that their perspective has universal validity for all feminists, they tend to participate in the dominance that western culture has exercised over nonwestern cultures.

Our position must explain and justify our dual need to criticize members of a dominant group (say men or white people or western feminists) for their lack of attention to or concern with problems that affect an oppressed group (say, women or people of color or nonwestern feminists, respectively), as well as for our frequent hostility toward those who express interest, even sympathetic interest, in issues that concern groups of which they are not a part.

Both attitudes are often warranted. On the one hand, one cannot but be angry at those who minimize, ignore, or dismiss the pain and conflict that racism and sexism inflict on their victims. On the other hand, living in a state of siege also necessarily makes us suspicious of expressions of concern and support from those who do not live these oppressions. We are suspicious of the motives of our sympathizers or the extent of their sincerity, and we worry, often with good reason, that they may claim that their interest provides a warrant for them to speak for us, as dominant groups throughout history have spoken for the dominated.

This is all the more threatening to groups aware of how recently they have acquired the power to articulate their own points of view. Nonwestern feminists are especially aware of this because they have a double struggle in trying to find their own voice: they have to learn to articulate their differences, not only from their own traditional contexts but also from western feminism.

Politically, we face interesting questions whose answers hinge on the nature and extent of the communication that we think possible between different groups. Should we try to share our perspectives and insights with those who have not lived our oppressions and accept that they may fully come to share them? Or should we seek only the affirmation of those like ourselves, who share common features of oppression, and rule out the possibility of those who have not lived these oppressions ever acquiring a genuine understanding of them?

I argue that it would be a mistake to move from the thesis that knowledge is constructed by human subjects who are socially constituted to the conclusion that those who are differently located socially can never attain *some* understanding of our experience or *some* sympathy with our cause. In that case, we would be committed to not just a perspectival view of knowledge but a relativistic one. Relativism, as I am using it, implies that a person could have knowledge of only the sorts of things she had experienced personally and that she would be totally unable to communicate any of the contents of her knowledge to someone who did not have the same sorts of experiences. Not only does this seem clearly false and perhaps even absurd, but it is probably a good idea not to have any a priori views that would imply either that all our knowledge is always capable of being communicated to every other person or that would imply that some of our knowledge is necessarily incapable of being communicated to some class of persons.

"Nonanalytic" and "nonrational" forms of discourse, like fiction or poetry, may be better able than other forms to convey the complex life experiences of one group to members of another. One can also hope that being part of one oppressed group may enable an individual to have a more sympathetic understanding of issues relating to another kind of oppression—that, for instance, being a woman may sensitize one to issues of race and class even if one is a woman privileged in those respects.

Again, this should not be reduced to some kind of metaphysical presumption. Historical circumstances have sometimes conspired, say, to making working-class men more chauvinistic in some of their attitudes than other men. Sometimes one sort of suffering may simply harden individuals to other sorts or leave them without energy to take any interest in the problems of other groups. But we can at least try to foster such sensitivity by focusing on parallels, not identities, between different sorts of oppressions.

Our commitment to the contextual nature of knowledge does not require us to claim that those who do not inhabit these contexts can never have any knowledge of them. But this commitment does permit us to argue that it is *easier* and *more likely* for the oppressed to have critical insights into the conditions of their own oppression than it is for those who live outside these structures. Those who actually *live* the oppressions of class, race, or gender have faced the issues that such oppressions generate in a variety of different situations. The insights and emotional responses engendered by these situations are a legacy with which they confront any new issue or situation.

Those who display sympathy as outsiders often fail both to understand fully the emotional complexities of living as a member of an oppressed group and to carry what they have learned and understood about one situation to the way they perceive another. It is a commonplace that even sympathetic men will often fail to perceive subtle instances of sexist behavior or discourse.

Sympathetic individuals who are not members of an oppressed group should keep in mind the possibility of this sort of failure regarding their understanding of issues relating to an oppression they do not share. They should realize that nothing they may do, from participating in demonstrations to changing their lifestyles, can make them one of the oppressed. For instance, men who share household and child-rearing responsibilities with women are mistaken if they think that this act of choice, often buttressed by the gratitude and admiration of others, is anything like the woman's experience of being forcibly socialized into these tasks and of having others perceive this as her natural function in the scheme of things.

The view that we can understand much about the perspectives of those whose oppression we do not share allows us the space to criticize dominant groups for their blindness to the facts of oppression. The view that such an understanding, despite great effort and interest, is likely to be incomplete or limited, provides us with the ground for denying total parity to members of a dominant group in their ability to understand our situation.

Sympathetic members of a dominant group need not necessarily defer to our views on any particular issue because that may reduce itself to another subtle form of condescension, but at least they must keep in mind the very real difficulties and possibility of failure to fully understand our concerns. This and the very important need for dominated groups to control the means of discourse about their own situations are important reasons for taking seriously the claim that oppressed groups have an "epistemic advantage."

The Dark Side of "Double Vision"

I think that one of the most interesting insights of feminist epistemology is the view that oppressed groups, whether women, the poor, or racial minorities, may derive an "epistemic advantage" from having knowledge of the practices of both their own contexts and those of their oppressors. The practices of the dominant groups (for instance, men) govern a society; the dominated group (for instance, women) must acquire some fluency with these practices in order to survive in that society.

There is no similar pressure on members of the dominant group to acquire knowledge of the practices of the dominated groups. For instance, colonized people had to learn the language and culture of their colonizers. The colonizers seldom found it necessary to have more than a sketchy acquaintance with the language and culture of the "natives." Thus, the oppressed are seen as having an "epistemic advantage" because they can operate with two sets of practices and in two different contexts. This advantage is thought to lead to critical insights because each framework provides a critical perspective on the other.

I would like to balance this account with a few comments about the "dark side," the disadvantages, of being able to or of having to inhabit two mutually incompatible frameworks that provide differing perspectives on social reality. I suspect that nonwestern feminists, given the often complex and troublesome interrelationships between the contexts they must inhabit, are less likely to express unqualified enthusiasm about the benefits of straddling a multiplicity of contexts. Mere access to two different and incompatible contexts is not a guarantee that a critical stance on the part of an individual will result. There are many ways in which she may deal with the situation.

First, the person may be tempted to dichotomize her life and reserve the framework of a different context for each part. The middle class of nonwestern countries supplies numerous examples of people who are very westernized in public life but who return to a very traditional lifestyle in the realm of the family. Women may choose to live their public lives in a "male" mode, displaying characteristics of aggressiveness, competition, and so on, while continuing to play dependent and compliant roles in their private lives. The pressures of jumping between two different lifestyles may be mitigated by justifications of how each pattern of behavior is appropriate to its particular context and of how it enables them to "get the best of both worlds."

Second, the individual may try to reject the practices of her own context and try to be as much as possible like members of the dominant group. Westernized intellectuals in the nonwestern world often may almost lose knowledge of their own cultures and practices and be ashamed of the little that they do still know. Women may try both to acquire stereotypically male characteristics, like aggressiveness, and to expunge stereotypically female characteristics, like emotionality. Or the individual could try to reject entirely the framework of the dominant group and assert the virtues of her own despite the risks of being marginalized from the power structures of the society; consider, for example, women who seek a certain sort of security in traditionally defined roles.

The choice to inhabit two contexts critically is an alternative to these choices and, I would argue, a more useful one. But the presence of alternative contexts does not by itself guarantee that one of the other choices will not be made. Moreover, the decision to inhabit two contexts critically, although it may lead to an "epistemic advantage," is likely to exact a certain price. It may lead to a sense of totally lacking roots or any space where one is at home in a relaxed manner.

This sense of alienation may be minimized if the critical straddling of two contexts is part of an ongoing critical politics, due to the support of others and a deeper understanding of what is going on. When it is not so rooted, it may generate ambivalence, uncertainty, despair, and even madness, rather than more positive critical emotions and attitudes. However such a person determines her locus, there may be a sense of being an outsider in both contexts and a sense of clumsiness or lack of fluency in both sets of practices. Consider this simple linguistic example: most people who learn two different languages that are associated with two very different cultures seldom acquire both with equal fluency; they may find themselves devoid of vocabulary in one language for certain contexts of life or be unable to match real objects with terms they have acquired in their vocabulary. For instance, people from my sort of background would know words in Indian languages for some spices, fruits, and vegetables that they do not know in English. Similarly, they might be unable to discuss "technical" subjects like economics or biology in their own languages because they learned about these subjects and acquired their technical vocabularies only in English.

The relation between the two contexts the individual inhabits may not be simple or straightforward. The individual subject is seldom in a position to carry out a perfect "dialectical synthesis" that preserves all the advantages of both contexts and transcends all their problems. There may be a number of different "syntheses," each of which avoids a different subset of the problems and preserves a different subset of the benefits.

No solution may be perfect or even palatable to the agent confronted with a choice. For example, some Indian feminists may find some western modes of dress (say trousers) either more comfortable or more their "style" than some local modes of dress. However, they may find that wearing the local mode of dress is less socially troublesome, alienates them less from more traditional people they want to work with, and so on. Either choice is bound to leave them partly frustrated in their desires.

Feminist theory must be temperate in the use it makes of this doctrine of "double vision"—the claim that oppressed groups have an epistemic advantage and access to greater critical conceptual space. Certain types and contexts of oppression certainly may bear out the truth of this claim. Others certainly do not seem to do so; and even if they do provide space for critical insights, they may also rule out the possibility of actions subversive of the oppressive state of affairs.

Certain kinds of oppressive contexts, such as the contexts in which women of my grandmother's background lived, rendered their subjects entirely devoid of skills required to function as independent entities in the culture. Girls were married off barely past puberty, trained for nothing beyond household tasks and the rearing of children, and passed from economic dependency on their fathers to economic dependency on their husbands to economic dependency on their sons in old age. Their criticisms of their lot were articulated, if at all, in terms that precluded a desire for any radical change. They saw themselves sometimes as personally unfortunate, but they did not locate the causes of their misery in larger social arrangements.

I conclude by stressing that the important insight incorporated in the doctrine of "double vision" should not be reified into a metaphysics that serves as a substitute for concrete social analysis. Furthermore, the alternative to "buying" into an oppressive social system need not be a celebration of exclusion and the mechanisms of marginalization. The thesis that oppression may bestow an epistemic advantage should not tempt us in the direction of idealizing or romanticizing oppression and blind us to its real material and psychic deprivations.

Note

I would like to acknowledge the enormous amount of help that Alison Jaggar and Susan Bordo have given me with this essay. Alison has been influential all the way from suggesting the nature of the project to suggesting changes that cleared up minor flaws in writing. Susan's careful reading has suggested valuable changes in the structure of the paper, and she has also been very helpful with references. I would like to thank them both for the insightful nature of their comments and the graciousness with which they made them. I would like to thank Dilys Page for her painstaking reading and comments on the first draft of this paper. I would also like to thank Radhika Balasubramanian, Sue Cataldi, Mary Geer, Mary Gibson, Rhoda Linton, Josie Rodriguez-Hewitt, and Joyce Tigner for sharing their work with me, for taking an interest in my work, and for providing me with a community of women who sustain me in many, many ways.

References

Bordo, S. 1986. "The Cartesian Masculinization of Thought." *Signs* 11:439–456.
Gilligan, C. 1982. *In a Different Voice: Psychological Theory and Women's Development.* Cambridge, Mass.: Harvard University Press.
Harding, S. 1986. *The Science Question in Feminism.* Ithaca, N.Y.: Cornell University Press.
Harding, S., and M. Hintikka, eds. 1983. *Discovering Reality: Feminist Perspectives on Epistemology, Metaphysics, Methodology, and Philosophy of Science.* Dordrecht: Reidel.
Harding, S., and J. O'Barr, eds. 1987. *Sex and Scientific Inquiry.* Chicago: University of Chicago Press.
Jaggar, Alison M. 1989. "Love and Knowledge: Emotion in Feminist Epistemology." In Alison M. Jaggar and Susan R. Bordo, eds. *Gender/Body/Knowledge.* New Brunswick, N.J.: Rutgers University Press.
Keller, E. F. 1985. *Reflections on Gender and Science.* New Haven, Conn.: Yale University Press.
Lloyd, G. 1984. *The Man of Reason.* Minneapolis: University of Minnesota Press.
Wilshire, Donna. 1989. "The Uses of Myth, Image, and the Female Body in Revisioning Knowledge." In Alison M. Jaggar and Susan Bordo, eds., *Gender/Body/Knowledge.* New Brunswick, N.J.: Rutgers University Press.

16
Truth and Method: Feminist Standpoint Theory Revisited

SUSAN HEKMAN

In 1983, the publication of Nancy Hartsock's *Money, Sex, and Power* changed the landscape of feminist theory. The scope of the book alone ensures it a prominent place in feminist thought. It includes a comprehensive critique of positivism, an indictment of masculinist theories of power, and even a textual analysis of Greek mythology. The central concern of the book, however, and the source of its lasting influence, is Hartsock's epistemological and methodological argument. Her goal is to define the nature of the truth claims that feminists advance and to provide a methodological grounding that will validate those claims. The method she defines is the feminist standpoint. Borrowing heavily from Marx, yet adapting her insights to her specifically feminist ends, Hartsock claims that it is women's unique standpoint in society that provides the justification for the truth claims of feminism while also providing it with a method with which to analyze reality.

In the succeeding decade, feminist standpoint theory has become a staple of feminist theory. Nancy Hartsock's essay in Sandra Harding and Merrill Hintikka's pathbreaking book, *Discovering Reality* (1983), brought the concept to a philosophical audience. In a number of influential publications, Dorothy Smith developed a sociological method from the "standpoint of women." Harding featured feminist standpoint theory in her two important books on science and feminism. Patricia Hill Collins articulated a specifically black feminist standpoint. But in the late 1980s and early 1990s criticisms of the position mounted, and fewer discussions of it were published. Today the concept occupies a much less prominent position. Particularly among younger feminist theorists, feminist standpoint theory is frequently regarded as a quaint relic of feminism's less sophisticated past. Several developments in the late 1980s have led to this declining influence. First, the inspiration for feminist standpoint theory, Marxism, has been discredited in both theory and practice. Second, feminist standpoint theory appears to be at odds with the issue that has dominated feminist debate in the past decade: difference. Third, feminist standpoint theory appears to be opposed to two of the most significant influences in recent feminist theory: postmodernism and poststructuralism. The Marxist roots of the theory seem to contradict what many define as the antimaterialism of postmodernism. For all of these reasons, the conclusion that feminist standpoint theory should be discarded seems obvious.

I think this conclusion is premature, that it is a mistake to write off feminist standpoint theory too quickly. Feminist standpoint theory raises a central and unavoidable question for feminist theory: How do we justify the truth of the feminist claim that women have been and are oppressed? Feminist standpoint theory was initially formulated in the context of Marxist politics. But from the outset, feminist standpoint theorists have recognized that feminist politics demand a justification for the truth claims of feminist theory, that is, that feminist politics are necessarily epistemological. Throughout the theory's development, feminist standpoint theorists' quest for truth and politics has been shaped by two central understandings: that knowledge is situated and perspectival and that there are multiple standpoints from which knowledge is produced. As the theory has developed, feminist standpoint theorists have explored, first, how knowledge can be situated yet "true," and, second, how we can acknowledge difference without obviating the possibility of critique and thus a viable feminist politics. Feminist standpoint theorists have answered these questions in a variety of ways; many of these answers have been unsatisfactory; the theory has been frequently reformulated. In the course of their arguments, however, these theorists have made an indispensable contribution to feminist theory.

It is my contention that feminist standpoint theory represents the beginning of a paradigm shift in the concept of knowledge, a shift that is transforming not only feminist theory but also epistemology itself. What Lorraine Code (1991) calls a "new mapping of the epistemic domain" that characterizes feminist theory owes much to the articulation and development of feminist standpoint theory. Finally, I assert that this theory remains central to contemporary feminism because the questions it raises are crucial to the future development of feminist theory and politics. Recently there has been much discussion among feminists of the parameters of a "politics of difference." I believe that feminist standpoint theory has laid the groundwork for such a politics by initiating the discussion of situated knowledges. . . .

Despite their significant differences, all of these accounts share the conviction that the feminist standpoint is rooted in a "reality" that is the opposite of the abstract conceptual world inhabited by men, particularly the men of the ruling class, and that in this reality lies the truth of the human condition. There are three problems with this formulation. First, it assumes that the dichotomy between concepts and reality can be resolved by embracing reality and rejecting concepts. This strategy is self-defeating. The two elements of the dichotomy are interdependent; to embrace one is to acknowledge the epistemological validity of both sides of the dichotomy, not to solve the problem it poses. Second, it denies that the lifeworld is, like every other human activity, discursively constituted. It is a discourse distinct from that of abstract science, but a discourse nonetheless.[1] Third, as both Schutz and Max Weber clearly realized, one can argue that sociological analysis *should* begin with the actors' concepts and that any other approach will miss the object of its study—the lifeworld—but that this requires a specific *argument*. Opposing concepts to reality is not an argument and, furthermore, entails an epistemological fallacy.

The Challenge of Difference: Redefining the Feminist Standpoint

The original formulations of feminist standpoint theory rest on two assumptions: that all knowledge is located and situated, and that one location, that of the standpoint of women, is privileged because it provides a vantage point that reveals the truth of social reality. It is my thesis that the deconstruction of this second assumption is implicit in the first and that as the theory developed the problematic nature of the second assumption came to the forefront. Another way of putting this is that a new paradigm of knowledge was implicit in the first formulations of feminist standpoint theory, a definition of knowledge as situated and perspectival, but that these first formulations retained elements of the paradigm it was replacing.

Epistemologists have devoted much attention to the concept of "reality" in the past decade, offering powerful arguments against the notion of a given, pre-conceptual reality that grounds knowledge. The "linguistic turn" of twentieth-century philosophy and the influence of hermeneutics, postmodernism, and poststructuralism have all contributed to the present skepticism about "reality." These speculations are directly relevant to the evolution of feminist standpoint theory, an approach initially grounded in just such a concept of reality. But it was another discussion, the discussion of difference within the feminist community, that stimulated a reassessment of feminist standpoint theory in the late 1980s and early 1990s. Originally, feminist standpoint theorists claimed that the standpoint of women offers a privileged vantage point for knowledge. But if the differences among women are taken seriously and we accept the conclusion that women occupy many different standpoints and thus inhabit many realities, this thesis must be reexamined. The current reevaluation of feminist standpoint theory is an attempt to reconstitute the theory from the perspective of difference. These discussions focus on two questions that are central not only to this approach but also to feminist theory itself. First, if, as we must, we acknowledge that there are many realities that women inhabit, how does this affect the status of the truth claims that feminists advance? Second, if we abandon a single axis of analysis, *the* standpoint of women, and instead try to accommodate the multiple, potentially infinite standpoints of diverse women, do we not also lose the analytic force of our argument? Or, in other words, how many axes can our arguments encompass before they slip into hopeless confusion?[2] The political implications of these questions, furthermore, inform both of these arguments. If we abandon the monolithic concept of "woman," what are the possibilities of a cohesive feminist politics?

The concern both to accommodate difference and preserve the analytic and political force of feminist theory, specifically feminist standpoint theory, is prominent in the recent work of Nancy Hartsock. It is obvious that Hartsock cares very deeply about these issues. She is painfully aware of the evils of racism, particularly within the women's movement. She is also passionately committed to feminist social criticism as a force for social change and is determined not to let forces such as postmodernism erode that potential. These concerns emerge forcefully in a 1987 article, "Rethinking Modernism." The point of departure for Hartsock's argument is the differences among women. She asserts that we need to develop an understanding of difference by creating a politics in which previously marginalized groups can name themselves and participate in defining the terms that structure their world (1987, 189). Central to Hartsock's argument is the claim that unless we provide a systematic understanding of the world, we will be unable to change it. The object of her polemic in this and several other recent articles is postmodernism. In the past decade the issues of difference and multiplicity have come to be closely identified with postmodernism. Hartsock wants to reject this identification. She wants to valorize difference, to claim that the differences among women are significant both theoretically and practically, while at the same time rejecting postmodernism on the grounds that it obviates the possibility of the systemic knowledge that is necessary for social change.

Hartsock's efforts both to valorize difference and to retain at least some notion of reality and truth, of the "way the world is," produce some odd results. In "Rethinking Modernism," she significantly alters the basic thesis of feminist standpoint theory by asserting that although women are not a unitary group, white, ruling-class, Eurocentric men are (1987, 192). The ruling class, now referred to as the "center," is defined as unitary, while those on the periphery, the "others," are defined as heterogeneous. Hartsock's argument is that we must create a politics that lets the "others" into the center, a center that, she claims, will "obviously" look different when occupied by women and men of color (201). Hartsock's solution raises some troubling questions. It posits a center that is heterogeneous rather than homogeneous, but this suggests that it may not be a "center" at all. We might also ask whether, if the "others" have moved into the center, this move effectively eliminates the periphery. We can, I think, assume that Hartsock would not endorse a politics in which any group was marginalized. But it is difficult to retain the concept of "center," as she does, without a corresponding concept of periphery.[3]

All of these questions could be quite easily eliminated by abandoning the center/periphery dichotomy. But Hartsock is adamantly opposed to this move. Those of us who have been constituted as "other," she states, must insist on a world in which we are at the center rather than the periphery. The postmoderns, she claims, who want to eliminate the center, thereby deny us our right of self-definition. She also claims that they deny us the right to speak the truth about our subjugation, obviating the very possibility of knowledge and truth. Informing all of Hartsock's recent work is a fundamental dichotomy: either we have systemic knowledge of the way the world is or we have no knowledge, no truth, and no politics. For Hartsock, postmodernism represents the second term of this dichotomy (1990). I could argue, against Hartsock, that truth, knowledge, and politics are possible without an absolute grounding and that some postmodern writers make this argument quite persuasively. But I would like to examine Hartsock's position from a different angle. Her fears for the future of feminist analysis are not unfounded. If, as she realizes we must, feminism abandons *the* feminist standpoint and, with it, *the* correct view of reality, then we are in danger of abandoning the whole point of feminist analysis and politics: revealing the oppression of "women" and arguing for a less repressive society. If there are multiple feminist standpoints, then there must be multiple truths and multiple realities. This is a difficult position for those who want to change the world according to a new image.

I would argue that Hartsock has defined the problem correctly but is pursuing a solution in the wrong direction. She wants to embrace the "situated knowledges" that Haraway and others have theorized, but she cannot accept the logical consequence of this position: that no perspective/standpoint is epistemologically privileged. She wants to retain a notion of privileged knowledge that can accommodate both diversity and locatedness. But her attempts to achieve this goal are not successful. "Situated knowledges," she claims, are "located in a particular time and place. They are therefore partial. They do not see everything from nowhere but they do see some things from somewhere." Borrowing postmodern terminology, she refers to the knowledges produced from the various subject positions of different women as "the epistemologies of these marked subjectivities." She then goes on to argue: "The struggles they represent and express, if made self-conscious, can go beyond efforts at survival to recognize the centrality of systemic power relations" (1989–90, 28–30). What this formulation requires is a sustained argument for how such systemic knowledge is possible. But such an argument is not forthcoming.

Other feminist standpoint theorists have also attempted to deal with the challenge of difference and its implications for the truth claims of the feminist standpoint. Dorothy Smith (1990a, 1990b) gets around the problem of difference by definitional fiat: she defines "women's actually lived experience" as a category that encompasses the diversity of women's lives and activities. She then opposes this category to the abstract concepts of sociological analysis, contrasting the "ideological" categories of the sociologist to "what actually happened"—the "primary narrative" (1990a, 157). But the method that she derives from this dichotomy is flawed and incomplete. First, despite the unmistakable influence of Schutz's work, Smith does not offer any argument for why the located knowledge of women is superior to the abstract knowledge of the sociologist; this is assumed to be obvious. Second, despite frequent references to Foucault and his theory of discourse, Smith refuses to identify the women's standpoint as a knowledge-producing discursive formation. She offers a detailed discussion of how the sociologist's discursive formations constitute the instruments of state power. At times she comes close to admitting that the discourse that women have developed about their lived reality, a discourse that includes concepts such as rape, sexual harassment, and battery, is also constituted. But ultimately she shies away from this conclusion. Like Hartsock, she continues to privilege the standpoint of women because she assumes that without such privileging the knowledge women claim loses its necessary grounding.

Patricia Hill Collins has a particular stake in theorizing difference: she wants to account for the unique standpoint of black women. She defines her problem in the context of the issue of difference: her goal, she states, is to articulate the unique aspects of black women's standpoint without denying the differences among black women. She tackles this problem by claiming, following Hartsock, that the black feminist standpoint she articulates, although rooted in everyday experiences, is constructed by the theorists who reflect on that experience. One of the goals of her own theory is to define the common experiences of black women that constitute their unique standpoint (1989; 1990, 208–21). Collins deals with the difficult issue of the truth status of the black feminist standpoint in an ambiguous way. In an early article she claims "objectivity" for the "outsider within" status of black women (1986, 15). In her more recent work, however, Collins retreats from this claim. In *Black Feminist Thought* she appeals to Donna Haraway's concept of standpoint as the most valid and concludes that "a Black women's standpoint is only one angle of vision," a "partial perspective" (1990, 234). But despite her endorsement of Haraway's position, Collins is unwilling to embrace the full implications of situated knowledge. She rejects the claim that the perspective of the oppressed yields "absolute truth," but she also rejects "relativism," which she defines as the claim that all visions are equal (1990, 235). Her final position holds out some hope for a redefined concept of objectivity. She asserts that black feminists who develop knowledge claims that can accommodate both black feminist epistemology and white masculinist epistemology "may have found a route to the elusive goal of generating so-called objective generalizations that can stand as universal truth." The ideas that are validated by different standpoints, she concludes, produce "the most objective truths" (1989, 773).

Other than Haraway herself, the only prominent feminist standpoint theorist to embrace fully what Collins labels the "relativist" position is Sara Ruddick. Citing Wittgenstein as her intellectual influence, Ruddick claims that feminism challenges the universality imperative of masculine thinking (1989, 128). In her discussion of "Maternal Thinking as a Feminist Standpoint," Ruddick appeals to both Hartsock and Foucault, apparently seeing no contradiction between Hartsock's definition of the feminist standpoint and Foucault's theory of subjugated knowledges (130). She concludes, "Although I count myself among standpoint theorists, I do not take the final step that some appear to take of claiming for one standpoint a truth that is exhaustive and absolute.... Although I envision a world organized by the values of caring labor, I cannot identify the grounds, reason, or god that would legitimate that vision" (135).[4]

Ruddick's solution to the problem of difference and privilege would not sat-isfy many feminist theorists. Like Collins and Hartsock, few feminist theorists are content to define the feminist standpoint as simply a "different voice" (or voices), one perspective among many. The difficulties of redefining feminist standpoint theory in light of the epistemological issues raised by difference and the challenges to "reality" are most fully explored in the work of Sandra Harding. In her influential *The Science Question in Feminism* (1986) Harding defines three feminist epistemologies: feminist empiricism, feminist standpoint theory, and feminist postmodernism. Although sympathetic to standpoint epis-temologies, Harding is persuaded that there cannot be *one* feminist standpoint; the situations of women are too diverse. Yet she also sees problems with the postmodern alternative. On her reading, postmodernism posits fractured iden-tities, an apolitical approach, and the rejection of any kind of knowledge that results in an absolute relativism. In this book, Harding avoids choosing one epistemology over another by arguing for the necessary instability of feminist theories. Coherent theories in an incoherent world, she concludes, are either silly, uninteresting, or oppressive (1986, 164).

In *Whose Science? Whose Knowledge?* (1991), Harding appears to reverse her position by fashioning a coherent theory for feminist science. The theory she offers, however, is a blend of diverse elements and thus continues the eclectic spirit of her earlier book. The aim of the book, she states, is not to resolve all tensions and contradictions between feminism and Western science but to "ad-vance more useful ways for us to think about and plan their future encounters" (xi). Harding defines her position as "a postmodernist standpoint approach that is nevertheless committed to rethinking and revising some important notions from conventional metatheories of science" (49). In the course of developing her approach, Harding offers both a critique and a redefinition of standpoint the-ory, developing "the logic of the standpoint theory in ways that more vigorously pull it away from its modernist origins and more clearly enable it to advance some postmodernist goals" (106). For Harding, standpoint theory is attractive because it offers an alternative to a crucial and seemingly irresolvable dichotomy facing feminist theory: essentialism versus relativism. Her rejection of *one* fem-inist standpoint avoids the danger of essentialism; relativism is defeated by her claim that we must insist on an objective location—women's lives—for the place where research should begin (134–42). But as her theory unfolds it be-comes clear that Harding does not so much deconstruct this dichotomy as locate her position along the continuum it creates.

The ubiquitous issue of relativism leads Harding to her most significant con-tribution to standpoint theory: "strong objectivity." She begins by noting that "although diversity, pluralism, relativism, and difference have their valuable and political uses, embracing them resolves the political-scientific-epistemological conflict to almost no one's satisfaction" (140). Standpoint epistemologists, she argues, embrace historical-cultural-sociological relativism while rejecting judgmental or epistemological relativism (142). The "strong objectivity" she advocates recognizes the social situatedness of all knowledge but also requires "a critical evaluation to determine which social situations tend to generate the most objective knowledge claims" (142). It is significant that Harding follows traditional standpoint epistemology in assuming that the higher the level of oppression, the more objective the account: "It should be clear that if it is beneficial to start research, scholarship and theory in white women's situations, then we should be able to learn even more about the social and natural orders if we start from the situations of women in devalued and oppressed races, classes and cultures" (179–80).

Harding argues for keeping the concept of objectivity despite its historical associations with masculinist science because of its "glorious intellectual history" (160). The concept of objectivity she advocates departs from the masculinist definition in that it does not lay claim to "true beliefs" or "transhistorical privilege." But it also retains one important aspect of that definition: "Starting research in women's lives leads to socially constructed claims that are less false—less partial and distorted—than are the (also socially constructed) claims that result if one starts from the lives of men in the dominant groups" (185). The "less false stories" Harding advocates mediate between transhistorical universals on the one hand and absolute relativism on the other, forming a kind of middle ground between the polarities of this dichotomy. Harding intends this middle ground to be a critique of postmodern and poststructuralist positions. The postmodernists, Harding declares, assume that giving up on the goal of telling one true story about reality entails giving up on telling less false stories (187), a position that is unlikely to satisfy feminists' desire to know "how the world is" (304).

Once more, I could argue that Harding, like Hartsock, misinterprets the postmodern definition of knowledge and that at least one "postmodern" writer, Foucault, is very interested in telling stories that will result in a less oppressive social order. But, again, I will take a different tack in my criticism. Harding's reassessment of standpoint theory contains two serious oversights. First, she argues that starting research from the reality of women's lives, preferably those of women who are also oppressed by race and class, will lead to a more objective account of social reality. Like Hartsock, Harding offers no argument as to why this is the case. Particularly from the vantage point of the 1990s, it is not enough simply to assume that Marx got it right on such a crucial point. And, like Smith, Harding does not acknowledge that "the reality of women's lives" is itself a socially constructed discursive formation. It is a discourse that has been constructed, at least in part, by feminist standpoint theorists who define it as the ground of their method. The fact that it is closely tied to the social actors' own concepts and provides a counter to the hegemonic discourse of masculinist science makes it no less a discourse. Feminist standpoint theory can and, I argue, should be defined as a counterhegemonic discourse that works to destabilize hegemonic discourse. But this can be achieved without denying that it is a discourse or according it epistemological privilege.

Second, all of Harding's talk of "less false stories," "less partial and perverse accounts," and more "objective" research necessarily presupposes a shared discourse—a metanarrative, even—that establishes standards by which these judgments can be validated. Yet the centerpiece of Harding's critique of masculinist science is the denial of the possibility of such a metanarrative. She seems to assume that when feminist scholars offer their "less false stories" they will be universally acknowledged as such. This assumption fails both practically and theoretically. It seems abundantly obvious that within the masculinist discourse of science the accounts of feminist standpoint theorists have not been judged "better" than conventional scientific accounts. On the contrary, the scientific establishment has devoted much effort to discrediting feminist claims. Comparative statements such as those Harding advances require shared standards of judgment; no such standards bridge the gap between feminist and masculinist science. It is ironic that Harding's polemic against the metanarrative of masculinist science ultimately relies on the reconstruction of a similar standard for its validity.

Truths and Methods: Toward a New Paradigm

When feminist standpoint theory emerged in the early 1980s, it appeared to be exactly what the feminist movement needed: a method for naming the oppression of women grounded in the truth of women's lives. Standpoint theory constituted a challenge to the masculinist definition of truth and method embodied in modern Western science and epistemology. It established an alternative vision of truth and, with it, hope for a less repressive society. But the theoretical tensions implicit in the theory soon came to the forefront. The contradiction between social constructionist and absolutist conceptions of truth that characterizes Marx's theory were translated into feminist standpoint theory. As the theory developed in the late 1980s and early 1990s questions of how feminists should theorize differences among women and the status of feminism's truth claims became impossible to ignore—and equally impossible to answer within the confines of the original theory.

I argue that although it was conceived as an alternative vision of truth and reality, this vision does not constitute the theoretical legacy of feminist standpoint theory. Throughout the second half of the twentieth century a paradigm shift has been under way in epistemology, a movement from an absolutist, subject-centered conception of truth to a conception of truth as situated, perspectival, and discursive. It is my contention, first, that feminism was and continues to be at the forefront of this paradigm shift and, second, that feminist standpoint theory has contributed an important dimension to that shift within feminist theory. Because of the dualistic conception of truth and reality that characterized its original formulation, feminist standpoint theory has had the effect of problematizing absolutes and universals, focusing attention instead on the situated, local, and communal constitution of knowledge.

Another way of putting this is that in attempting to interpret feminist standpoint theory, we should look to Kuhn, not Marx. Feminist standpoint theory is part of an emerging paradigm of knowledge and knowledge production that constitutes an epistemological break with modernism. Feminist standpoint theory defines knowledge as particular rather than universal; it jettisons the neutral observer of modernist epistemology; it defines subjects as constructed by relational forces rather than as transcendent. As feminist standpoint theory has developed, the original tension between social construction and universal truth has dissolved. But it is significant that this has been accomplished, not by privileging one side of the dichotomy, but by deconstructing the dichotomy itself. The new paradigm of knowledge of which feminist standpoint theory is a part involves rejecting the definition of knowledge and truth as either universal or relative in favor of a conception of all knowledge as situated and discursive.

This new paradigm of knowledge necessarily defines a new approach to politics. Modernist epistemology defines politics in terms of the dichotomies that inform it. Thus for the modernist, politics must be grounded in absolute, universal principles and enacted by political agents defined as universal subjects. Under the new paradigm, politics is defined as a local and situated activity undertaken by discursively constituted subjects. Political resistance, furthermore, is defined as challenging the hegemonic discourse that writes a particular script for a certain category of subjects. Resistance is effected by employing other discursive formations to oppose that script, not by appealing to universal subjectivity or absolute principles.

As a way of illustrating my thesis that a new paradigm is emerging, it is useful to look at the three epistemic positions that Harding defines in her 1986 book. In the course of a decade the distinctions between these categories have nearly collapsed. Feminist empiricism has been radically redefined by epistemologists such as Lynn Hankinson Nelson and Helen Longino. Nelson (1990) provides a redefinition of empiricism from a feminist perspective that conforms to what I call the new paradigm of knowledge. Relying on the work of W. V. Quine, Nelson defines an empiricism in which, as she puts it, the world matters, but scientific communities produce knowledge. Her principal thesis is that it is not individuals but communities who know. Nelson's empiricism involves evidence, but it is evidence defined and constrained by public standards, not data observed from an Archimedean point by a neutral observer.[5] Longino offers a similar argument in *Science as Social Knowledge* (1990). She defines her position as "contextual empiricism," a view of science in which scientific knowledge is socially created and objectivity is a function of community practices. It is significant that both Nelson and Longino reject what they call "relativism," but they do so by appealing to widely shared but communal—that is, constructed—standards of evidence.

Harding herself has been instrumental in blurring the distinction between feminist standpoint theory and feminist postmodernism with her advocacy of "a postmodernist standpoint approach." The principal theme of feminist standpoint theory, that knowledge is situated in the material lives of social actors, has become the definitive characteristic not only of feminists influenced by postmodernism but of feminist theory as a whole. The major distinction between postmodernism and standpoint theory, the claim of privileged knowledge and one true reality, has been almost entirely abandoned. Both Hartsock and Harding radically modify the claim to privileged knowledge. Ruddick abandons any claim to privileged knowledge at all. Flax, an early proponent of the feminist standpoint, has enthusiastically embraced postmodernism and the multiple truths it entails. The notion of a feminist standpoint that is truer than previous (male) ones, she now claims, rests on problematic and unexamined assumptions (1990, 56).[6] What these theorists are effecting is what Lorraine Code calls "remapping the epistemic terrain into numerous fluid conversations" (1991, 309). What is significant about this remapping, however, is that for all of these theorists, defining reality as socially constructed and multiple does not obviate but, rather, facilitates critical analysis.

The feminist theorist who has done the most to define what I am calling the new paradigm of truth and method is Donna Haraway. Her famous essay "A Manifesto for Cyborgs," even though it does not mention feminist standpoint theory, can be read as an attempt to refashion that theory in light of the challenge to privileged reality. Haraway asks, What would another political myth for socialist feminism look like? What kind of politics can embrace fractured selves and still be effective and socialist feminist? (1990, 199). Implicit in these questions is the assumption that the "myth" of socialist feminism— feminist standpoint theory—cannot be sustained and that feminists must look for another. What is also implicit is that, for Haraway, what we must look for is not "truth" and "reality" but, rather, another story. "Women's experience," she claims, "is a fiction and a fact of the most crucial, political kind. Liberation rests on the construction of consciousness, the imaginative apprehension, of oppression, and so of possibility" (191).

In an equally famous article, "Situated Knowledges," Haraway relates her position directly to feminist standpoint theory: "There is no single feminist standpoint because our maps require too many dimensions for that metaphor to ground our visions. But the feminist standpoint theorists' goal of an epistemology and politics of engaged, accountable positioning remains eminently potent. The goal is better accounts of the world, that is, 'science'" (1988, 590). In this passage Haraway defines what I see as the central problem facing feminist theory today: given multiple standpoints, the social construction of "reality," and the necessity of an engaged political position, how can we talk about "better accounts of the world," "less false stories"? And, indeed, how can we talk about accounts of the world at all if the multiplicity of standpoints is, quite literally, endless? . . .

In conclusion, I would like to suggest another answer to these questions. The problem of constructing a viable method for feminist analysis, a method that also provides the basis for a feminist politics, is twofold. First, if we take the multiplicity of feminist standpoints to its logical conclusion, coherent analysis becomes impossible because we have too many axes of analysis. Ultimately, every woman is unique; if we analyze each in her uniqueness, systemic analysis is obviated. So is feminist politics: we lose the ability even to speak for certain categories of women. Second, if we acknowledge multiple realities, multiple standpoints, how do we discriminate among them? How do we select the perspectives and standpoints that are useful to us, that will help us achieve our theoretical and practical goals, or are we necessarily condemned to the "absolute relativism" that some critics fear? . . .

I suggest that the methodological tool that meets these requirements, a tool that fits the methodological and epistemological needs of feminism at this juncture, can be found in a source rarely employed in feminist discussions: Weber's methodology and, specifically, his concept of the ideal type. Weber's methodology has many advantages for the current debate over feminist methodology. Most fundamental is that his approach presupposes that social analysis is always undertaken by situated, engaged agents who live in a discursively constituted world. Although a range of contemporary theorists—most notably Foucault—share this presumption, Weber's position supplies three elements that these contemporary approaches lack. First, Weber provides a detailed analysis of the conceptual tool that can effect this analysis: the ideal type. Second, he provides extensive examples of how this concept operates in empirical analysis. Third, he develops an elaborate justification for the partial and circumscribed approach he advocates.

At the root of Weber's concept of the ideal type is his claim that no aspect of social reality can be apprehended without presuppositions: "As soon as we attempt to reflect about the way in which life confronts us in immediate concrete situations, it presents an infinite multiplicity of successively and coexistently emerging and disappearing events" (1949, 72). Weber argues that we bring order to this multiplicity by relying on values and, specifically, cultural values: "Order is brought into this chaos only on the condition that in every case only a *part* of concrete reality is interesting and *significant* to us, because only it is related to the *cultural values* with which we approach reality" (78; emphasis in original). The cultural values of a society, thus, impose an initial ordering of the multiplicity of possible meanings that confront social actors. But Weber argues that values also structure the meaning apprehension of the social scientist. It is the investigator's individual value choice that guides the selection of a subject of analysis: "Without the investigator's evaluative ideas, there would be no principle of selection of subject-matter and no meaningful knowledge of the concrete reality" (82). The result of the investigator's choice is the conceptual tool that Weber calls the "ideal type": "An ideal type is formed by the one-sided *accentuation* of one or more points of view and by the synthesis of a great many diffuse, discrete, more or less present and occasionally absent *concrete individual phenomena,* which are arranged according to one-sidedly emphasized viewpoints into a unified *analytic* construct" (90; emphasis in original).[7]

For Weber, ideal types are neither hypotheses nor descriptions of reality but "yardsticks" to which reality can be compared; they are neither historical reality nor "true reality" but are purely limiting concepts or "utopias"; the purpose of ideal types is to provide a means of comparison with concrete reality in order to reveal the significance of that reality (90–93). This aspect of Weber's concept is crucial. We cannot justify ideal types by claiming that they accurately reproduce social reality. No concept can do that—all positions are partial and perspectival. But neither can we justify ideal types on the grounds that they uncover the universal truth of social reality, that they have the status of the universal laws of the natural sciences. Universal laws, Weber claims, can reveal nothing about what social scientists want to explain: the meaning and significance of social reality. Unlike universal laws, ideal types cannot be refuted by contradictory cases; the discovery of contradictory cases reveals the irrelevance of the concept to the problem at hand, not its "error" (1975, 190). The only justification we can appeal to, Weber concludes, is significance: an ideal type is valid if it helps us understand social reality.

Weber's concept of the ideal type can be useful in explaining the epistemological status of feminist research. First, it makes explicit that no perspective is total, all are partial; ideal types are, in his words, one-sided. Knowledge is always situated in a particular locality, the particular standpoint of these particular women. Second, it specifies that the subject of any analysis is dictated by the interest of the investigator. It is the values of feminist researchers and their political goals that have motivated them to investigate issues like wife battery, rape, incest, and even the origins of patriarchy itself. In Weber's terminology, what feminist social science has accomplished is to create a set of ideal types that allow us to "see" a different social world. Carole Pateman's "sexual contract" (1988), Arlie Hochschild's "second shift" (1989), and Karen Sacks's "center-woman" (1988) are but a few examples of this conceptual set. Third, the ideal type rests on the assumption that what the social researcher studies, the activities and concepts of social actors, is already constituted; it is, in postmodern jargon, a discursive formation that constitutes "reality" for those who participate in it. This is a crucial point for the critique of many versions of feminist standpoint theory. Hartsock, Smith, and even, occasionally, Harding make the mistake of assuming that women's daily lives constitute a given reality that provides the necessary grounding for feminist theory. Weber's concept emphasizes that, like all other aspects of social life, women's daily life is a reality constituted by shared concepts.

The epistemology of Weber's ideal type also provides an answer to the charge of "absolute relativism" that many feminist theorists have raised. The problem is this: How do we convince nonfeminists that the ideal types of feminist analysis, concepts informed by the values of feminist researchers, are useful and insightful? How do we construct an argument for *these* ideal types rather than for the infinite variety of concepts that is possible? Weber argues that there is no metanarrative to which we can appeal to justify our value choices. Thus he would argue that the values that lead feminists to investigate the workings of patriarchy cannot be shown to be "objectively" correct. But Weber does have an answer to this problem. Although he argues that values are necessarily irreconcilable, he maintains that the logic of analysis itself rests on universal grounds (1949, 58). His argument is that although we cannot agree that we should be studying a particular topic—this is a value choice—we can agree on whether the analysis is logical. I would not offer quite so optimistic an answer. Weber's neat separation between facts and values is unfeasible. But this need not be cause for despair. Wittgenstein (1958) offers an argument that can be useful here. He asserts that our society is held together by certain basic values and assumptions that constitute what he calls "a form of life"; one of these assumptions is a very broadly based and loosely defined concept of what constitutes a persuasive argument. Because of the long-standing domination of patriarchy, these assumptions are masculinist; rationality, as many feminists have argued, is gendered masculine. But it does not follow that feminists cannot use these masculinist assumptions for their own purposes and, in so doing, transform them. We may not be able to persuade nonfeminists that the institutions of patriarchy are evil and should be dismantled. But we may be, and indeed have been, able to persuade them, through the use of skillful arguments, that sexual harassment, marital rape, and wife battery should be defined as crimes.

I am not claiming that the ideal type solves all the epistemological and methodological problems of feminist theory. I am claiming that it is highly appropriate to some of the problems that feminist theory is currently confronting, problems raised in large part by the development and evolution of feminist standpoint theory. The ideal type emphasizes that there is no metanarrative, either normative or methodological, to which we can appeal. Nor is there a truth about social totality that is waiting to be discovered. But this does not mean that the systemic analysis of the institutions of patriarchy is necessarily precluded. Weber's ideal type makes it clear that social analysis is a necessarily political activity, undertaken by agents who live in a world constituted by language and, hence, values. We engage in specific analyses because we are committed to certain values. These values dictate that certain analyses are trivial and others are important; all are not equal.[8] It is our values, then, that save us from the "absolute relativism" that the defenders of modernism so feared. Feminists cannot prove their values to be the objectively correct ones. On this point the postmoderns are correct: we live in a world devoid of a normative metanarrative. But we can offer persuasive arguments in defense of our values and the politics they entail. Some of these arguments will be persuasive: in the past decades feminists have been successful in beginning to change the parameters of patriarchal economic and political institutions. Other arguments will not be persuasive.[9] But by advancing both persuasive and unpersuasive arguments, feminists are, in the process, changing the norms of what constitutes an argument.

I think that recasting feminist standpoint theory in terms of the epistemology of the ideal type can make a significant contribution to contemporary feminist theory. Such a recasting would involve defining the feminist standpoint as situated and engaged knowledge, as a place from which feminists can articulate a counterhegemonic discourse and argue for a less repressive society. Women speak from multiple standpoints, producing multiple knowledges. But this does not prevent women from coming together to work for specific political goals.[10] Feminists in the twentieth century have done precisely this and have, as a consequence, changed the language game of politics. And, ultimately, this is the point of feminist theory.

Notes

1. See Grant 1993 for a similar critique.
2. See Bordo 1990 for a cogent statement of this problem.
3. Bar On 1993 offers an excellent account of the epistemological problems entailed by the claim to epistemic privilege and that of the center/margin dichotomy.
4. For other recent accounts of standpoint theory, see Winant 1987; Aptheker 1989; Stanley and Wise 1990; and Campbell 1994.
5. See Tuana 1991 for a compatible analysis of Nelson.
6. See also Hirschmann 1992; and Bar On 1993.
7. See Hekman 1983, 1995.
8. Flax 1993 makes a similar argument.
9. MacKinnon's antipornography argument (1987) is a notable example.
10. In a similar argument, Judith Grant asserts that political similarities can be cultivated to help feminists speak across suppressed differences (1993, 123).

References

Aptheker, Bettina. 1989. *Tapestries of Life: Women's Work, Women's Consciousness and the Meaning of Daily Experience.* Amherst: University of Massachusetts Press.

Bar On, Bat-Ami. 1993. "Marginality and Epistemic Privilege." In *Feminist Epistemologies,* ed. Linda Alcoff and Elizabeth Potter, 83–100. New York: Routledge.

Bordo, Susan. 1990. "Feminism, Postmodernism, and Gender-Skepticism." In *Feminism/Postmodernism,* ed. Linda Nicholson, 133–76. New York: Routledge.

Campbell, Richmond. 1994. "The Virtues of Feminist Empiricism." *Hypatia* 9(1):90–115.

Code, Lorraine. 1991. *What Can She Know? Feminist Theory and the Construction of Knowledge.* Ithaca, N.Y.: Cornell University Press.

Collins, Patricia Hill. 1986. "Learning from the Outsider Within: The Sociological Significance of Black Feminist Thought." *Social Problems* 33(6):14–32.

———. 1989. "The Social Construction of Black Feminist Thought." *Signs: Journal of Women in Culture and Society* 14(4):745–73.

———. 1990. *Black Feminist Thought.* Boston: Unwin Hyman.

Coward, Rosalind, and John Ellis. 1977. *Language and Materialism: Developments in Semiology and the Theory of the Subject.* London: Routledge & Kegan Paul.

Flax, Jane. 1983. "Political Philosophy and the Patriarchal Unconscious: A Psychoanalytic Perspective on Epistemology and Metaphysics." In Harding and Hintikka 1983, 245–81.

—————. 1990. "Postmodernism and Gender Relations in Feminist Theory." In *Feminism/Postmodernism,* ed. Linda Nicholson, 39–61. New York: Routledge.

—————. 1993. *Disputed Subjects: Essays on Psychoanalysis, Politics and Philosophy.* New York: Routledge.

Foucault, Michel. 1980. *Power/Knowledge.* New York: Pantheon.

Grant, Judith. 1993. *Fundamental Feminism: Contesting the Core Concepts of Feminist Theory.* New York: Routledge.

Haraway, Donna. 1988. "Situated Knowledges: The Science Question in Feminism and the Priviledge of Partial Perspective." *Feminist Studies* 14:575–99.

—————. 1990. "A Manifesto for Cyborgs: Science, Technology and Socialist Feminism in the 1980s." In *Feminism/Postmodernism,* ed. Linda Nicholson, 190–233. New York: Routledge.

Harding, Sandra. 1986. *The Science Question in Feminism.* Ithaca, N.Y.: Cornell University Press.

—————. 1991. *Whose Science? Whose Knowledge? Thinking from Women's Lives.* Ithaca, N.Y.: Cornell University Press.

Harding, Sandra, and Merrill Hintikka, eds. 1983. *Discovering Reality: Feminist Perspectives on Epistemology, Metaphysics, Methodology, and the Philosophy of Science.* Dordrecht: Reidel.

Hartsock, Nancy. 1981. "Fundamental Feminism: Prospect and Perspective." In *Building Feminist Theory,* ed. Charlotte Bunch, 32–43. New York: Longman.

—————. 1983a. "Difference and Domination in the Women's Movement: The Dialectic of Theory and Practice." In *Class, Race and Sex,* ed. Amy Swerdlow and Hanna Lessinger, 157–72. Boston: Hall.

—————. 1983b. "The Feminist Standpoint: Developing the Ground for a Specifically Feminist Historical Materialism." In Harding and Hintikka 1983, 283–310.

—————. 1983c. *Money, Sex, and Power.* New York: Longman.

—————. 1987. "Rethinking Modernism: Minority vs. Majority Theories." *Cultural Critique* 7:187–206.

—————. 1989–90. "Postmodernism and Political Change: Issues for Feminist Theory." *Cultural Critique* 14:15–33.

—————. 1990. "Foucault on Power: A Theory for Women?" In *Feminism/Postmodernism,* ed. Linda Nicholson, 157–75. New York: Routledge.

Hekman, Susan. 1983. *Weber, the Ideal Type and Contemporary Social Theory.* Notre Dame, Ind.: University of Notre Dame Press.

—————. 1995. "A Method for Difference: Feminist Methodology and the Challenge of Difference." Paper presented at the annual meeting of the American Political Science Association, Chicago.

Hirschmann, Nancy. 1992. *Rethinking Obligation: A Feminist Method for Political Inquiry.* Ithaca, N.Y.: Cornell University Press.

Hochschild, Arlie, with Anne Machung. 1989. *The Second Shift.* New York: Viking.

Jaggar, Alison. 1983. *Feminist Politics and Human Nature.* Totowa, N.J.: Rowman & Allanheld.

Kay, Judith. 1994. "Politics without Human Nature? Reconstructing a Common Humanity." *Hypatia* 9(1):21–52.

Longino, Helen. 1990. *Science as Social Knowledge.* Princeton, N.J.: Princeton University Press.

MacKinnon, Catharine. 1987. *Feminism Unmodified: Discourses on Life and Law.* Cambridge, Mass.: Harvard University Press.

Nelson, Lynn Hankinson. 1990. *Who Knows: From Quine to a Feminist Empiricism.* Philadelphia: Temple University Press.

Nussbaum, Martha. 1992. "Human Functioning and Social Justice: In Defense of Aristotelian Essentialism." *Political Theory* 20(2):202–46.

O'Brien, Mary. 1981. *The Politics of Reproduction.* New York: Routledge & Kegan Paul.

Okin, Susan Moller. 1994. "Gender Inequality and Cultural Differences." *Political Theory* 22(1):5–24.

Pateman, Carole. 1988. *The Sexual Contract.* Stanford, Calif.: Stanford University Press.

Rose, Hilary. 1983. "Hand, Brain and Heart: A Feminist Epistemology for the Natural Sciences." *Signs* 9:73–90.

—————. 1986. "Women's Work: Women's Knowledge." In *What Is Feminism? A Reexamination,* ed. Juliet Mitchell and Ann Oakley, 616–83. New York: Pantheon.

Ruddick, Sara. 1989. *Maternal Thinking. Toward a Politics of Peace.* Boston: Beacon.
Sacks, Karen. 1988. *Caring by the Hour: Women, Work and Organizing at the Duke Medical Center.* Urbana and Chicago: University of Illinois Press.
Schutz, Alfred. 1967. *The Phenomenology of the Social World,* trans. George Walsch and Frederick Lehnert. Evanston, Ill.: Northwestern University Press.
Smith, Dorothy. 1979. "A Sociology of Women." In *The Prism of Sex,* ed. Julia Sherman and Evelyn Beck, 135–87. Madison: University of Wisconsin Press.
———. 1987a. *The Everyday World as Problematic: A Feminist Sociology.* Boston: Northeastern University Press.
———. 1987b. "Women's Perspective as a Radical Critique of Sociology." In *Feminism and Methodology,* ed. Sandra Harding, 84–96. Bloomington: Indiana University Press.
———. 1990a. *The Conceptual Practices of Power: A Feminist Sociology of Knowledge.* Boston: Northeastern University Press.
———. 1990b. *Texts, Facts, and Femininity: Exploring Relations of Ruling.* London: Routledge.
Stanley, Liz, and Sue Wise. 1990. "Method, Methodology and Epistemology in Feminist Research Processes." In *Feminist Praxis: Research, Theory and Epistemology,* ed. Liz Stanley, 20–60. London: Routledge.
Tuana, Nancy. 1991. "The Radical Future of Feminist Empiricism." *Hypatia* 7(1):100–14.
Weber, Max. 1949. *The Methodology of the Social Sciences,* trans. and ed. Edward Shils and Henry Finch. New York: Free Press.
———. 1975. *Roscher and Knies,* trans. Guy Oakes. New York: Free Press.
Winant, Terry. 1987. "The Feminist Standpoint: A Matter of Language." *Hypatia* 2(1):123–48.
Wittgenstein, Ludwig. 1958. *Philosophical Investigations.* New York: Macmillan.
Young, Iris. 1980. "Socialist Feminism and the Limits of Dual System Theory." *Socialist Review* 10(2/3):169–88.

17

Comment on Hekman's "Truth and Method: Feminist Standpoint Theory Revisited": Truth or Justice?

NANCY C. M. HARTSOCK

Susan Hekman's article begins with a good summary of the current situation of feminist standpoint theories. She makes several important points that are often unrecognized in discussions of standpoint theories. First, she notes that standpoint theories come in a variety of forms. Second, she argues that these theories must be understood as a counterhegemonic discourse, that is, as centrally concerned with politics. And third, she reminds us that at least my version of standpoint theory operates with a social constructivist theory of the subject. There is much that is useful in her article, but here I want to address three areas where I think she reads standpoint theories through a kind of American pluralism that prefers to speak not about power or justice but, rather, about knowledge and epistemology. She is not alone in this.[1]

First, there is the question of the nature of the subject—If not pregiven but, rather, socially constructed, how is the subject exactly constructed, and what is the nature of this subject (subjected/collective/historically specific, etc.)? Second, What is the nature of the knowledge produced by this subject? Here I want to take up the question of whether truth, as usually understood, is the relevant category for the knowledge that is a social production. What is meant by truth, and how can it be achieved or justified? And third, What kind of privilege can one claim (or is one justified in claiming) for knowledge that arises from any particular social location, with the understanding that social locations are fundamentally structured by power relations?

As I read Hekman's article, and other critiques of standpoint theories as well, I am struck by the extent to which the Marxist roots of standpoint theories have gone unrecognized. This leads to the criticism that standpoint theories are by nature essentialist, that they assume a fixed human nature for individuals with pregiven selves and pregiven needs and wants. . . . I see Marx as an anti-Enlightenment figure on balance, although it must be recognized that his relationship to the Enlightenment and whole tradition of Western political thought is that of both the inheriting son and the rebellious son (see, e.g., Benhabib 1990, 11).... As I read Marx, he argues that the worker encounters himself in a world he has himself created, albeit in a very negative form.

Feminism, too, exists in an ambivalent relation to the Enlightenment. On the one hand, feminist theorists sometimes argue for a "me too" position in order to work for women's inclusion in a number of societal institutions.[2] On the other hand, women as women have never been the "subjects" of Enlightenment/liberal theory, and so women's insistence on speaking at all troubles those theories (see, e.g., Eisenstein 1981; and Kipnis 1988)....

But let me now turn to the several questions I want to address. First, [is].... the search for truth is not at all the way to understand Marx's project. The point, most fundamentally, is to understand power relations—in this case, power relations centered on the development of capitalism and the commodification of increasingly greater areas of human existence. But the point of understanding power relations is to change them....

To turn to the second issue—the nature of the subject—I found in Marx the kinds of social constructivist theories of the subject that others have encountered in poststructuralism. But in contrast to the American tendency (certainly with the help of some European poststructuralists themselves) to interpret these theories in liberal pluralist, and in some cases libertarian, terms, terms that rely on accounts of the microprocesses of power, I found in the Marxian tradition an insistence on what some have called a "global" as opposed to a "totalizing" theory (see Hennessy 1993). The focus is on the macroprocesses of power, those that, although they may be played out in individual lives, can be fully understood only at the level of society as a whole. To claim that we can understand the totality of social relations from a single perspective is as futile an effort as to claim that we can see everything from nowhere.

A focus on large-scale social forces highlights different aspects of the subject. Thus, Marx can be read as providing a theory of the subject as subjected, as does Foucault.... The subjects who matter are not individual subjects but collective subjects, or groups. These groups must not be seen as formed unproblematically by existing in a particular social location and therefore seeing the world in a particular way. My effort to develop the idea of a feminist standpoint, in contrast to "women's viewpoint," was an effort to move in this direction. Chela Sandoval's notion of the importance of strategic identity for women of color represents an important advance in understanding this process, as does her development of the notion of oppositional consciousness.[3]

Sandoval argues that U.S. Third World feminism can function as a model for oppositional political activity. She proposes that we view the world as a kind of "topography" that defines the points around which "individuals and groups seeking to transform oppressive powers *constitute themselves* as resistant and oppositional subjects" (1991, 11; emphasis mine). She holds that once the "subject positions" of the dominated are "self-consciously recognized by their inhabitants," they can be "transformed into more effective sites of resistance" (11). She discusses a "differential consciousness," which she states operates like the clutch of an automobile, allowing the driver to engage gears in a "system for the transmission of power" (14).

Here, Sandoval's views parallel those of Gramsci, who suggests that we re-think the nature of identity: "Our capacity to think and act on the world is dependent on other people who are themselves also both subjects and objects of history" (Gramsci 1971, 346). In addition, one must reform the concept of individual to see it as a "series of active relationships, a process in which individuality, though perhaps most important, is not the only element to be taken into account." Individuality, then, is to be understood as the "ensemble of these relations. . . . To create one's personality means to acquire consciousness of them and to modify one's own personality means to modify the ensemble of these relations" (352). Moreover, Gramsci holds that each individual is the synthesis of these relations and also of the history of these relations, a "précis of the past" (353). The constitution of the subject, then, is the result of a complex interplay of "individuals" and larger-scale social forces. Groups are not to be understood, as Hekman seems to do, as aggregates of individuals. Moreover, the constitution of the "collective subject" posited by standpoint theories re-quires an always contingent and fragile (re)construction/transformation of these complex subject positions. As Kathi Weeks has put it, "This project of trans-forming subject-positions into standpoints involves an active intervention, a conscious and concerted effort to reinterpret and restructure our lives. . . . A standpoint is a project, not an inheritance; it is achieved, not given" (1996, 101).

I turn now to my third point, the issue of privileged knowledge. Fundamen-tally, I argue that the criteria for privileging some knowledges over others are ethical and political rather than purely "epistemological." The quotation marks here are to indicate that I see ethical and political concepts such as power as involving epistemological claims on the one hand and ideas of what is to count as knowledge involving profoundly important political and ethical stakes on the other. Hekman is right that I want to privilege some knowledges over others because they seem to me to offer possibilities for envisioning more just social relations. I believe there is a second aspect to the idea that some knowledges are "better" than others, and here I think Sandoval has stated the most im-portant point: the self-conscious transformation of individuals into resistant, oppositional, and collective subjects.

The most important issue for me is the question of how we can use theoretical tools and insights to create theories of justice and social change that address the concerns of the present. Marx, for all of the difficulties with both his theoretical work and the state of actually (non)existing socialism, calls our attention to certain macrolevel issues to be addressed. In addition, one can find in the work of theorists such as Gramsci a much more useful and complex theorization of relations between "individuals" and society as a whole, one that opens up possibilities for both new knowledges and new collectivities.

Notes

I would like to thank Judy Aks and Karen Stuhldreher for comments on an earlier draft of this comment. I also want to thank Nancy Hirschman for organizing a panel on standpoint theory at the 1994 American Political Science Association meetings, where a number of these ideas were discussed.

1. See also Brown 1995 for an account that not only treats my work as putting forward a model of subjects as pregiven but also argues that my work should be put in the same category as that of Allan Bloom!
2. See Ferguson 1993 for a discussion of this issue.
3. Sandoval (1990) makes an excellent point in her article on the development of the category of "women of color" out of the consciousness-raising sessions at the 1981 National Women's Studies Association meeting. Much of what follows comes from Sandoval's (1991) article on U.S. Third World feminism.

References

Benhabib, Seyla. 1990. "Epistemologies of Postmodernism." In *Feminism/Postmodernism*, ed. Linda Nicholson, 107–30. New York: Routledge.

Brown, Wendy. 1995. *States of Injury: Power and Freedom in Late Modernity*. Princeton, N.J.: Princeton University Press.

Derrida, Jacques. 1994. *Spectres of Marx*, trans. Peggy Kamuf. New York: Routledge.

Ebert, Teresa. 1996. *Ludic Feminism and After: Postmodernism, Desire and Labor in Late Capitalism*. Ann Arbor: University of Michigan Press.

Eisenstein, Zillah. 1981. *The Radical Future of Liberal Feminism*. New York: Longman.

Ferguson, Kathy. 1993. *The Man Question: Visions of Subjectivity in Feminist Theory*. Berkeley and Los Angeles: University of California Press.

Foucault, Michel. 1980. *Language, Counter-Memory, Practice: Selected Essays and Interviews*. Ithaca, N.Y.: Cornell University Press.

Gramsci, Antonio. 1971. *Selections from the Prison Notebooks*, ed. and trans. Quintin Hoare and Geoffrey Nowell Smith. New York: International.

Hartsock, Nancy. 1983. "The Feminist Standpoint: Developing the Ground for a Specifically Feminist Historical Materialism." In *Discovering Reality: Feminist Perspectives on Epistemology, Metaphysics, Methodology and Philosophy of Science*, ed. Sandra Harding and Merrill Hintikka, 283–310. Dordrecht: Reidel/Kluwer.

———. 1991. "Louis Althusser's Structural Marxism." *Rethinking Marxism* 4(4):10–40.

Hennessy, Rosemary. 1993. *Materialist Feminism and the Politics of Discourse*. New York: Routledge.

hooks, bell. 1990. *Yearning: Race, Gender, and Cultural Politics*. Toronto: Between-the-Lines.

Jameson, Fredric. 1996. "Actually Existing Marxism." In *Marxism beyond Marxism*, ed. Saree Makdisis, Cesare Casarino, and Rebecca E. Karl, 14–54. New York: Routledge.

Kipnis, Laura. 1988. "Feminism: The Political Conscience of Postmodernism." In *Universal Abandon? The Politics of Postmodernism*, ed. Andrew Ross, 149–66. Minneapolis: University of Minnesota Press.

Lukacs, George. 1971. "Reification and the Standpoint of the Proletariat." In his *History and Class Consciousness*. Boston: Beacon.

Marx, Karl. 1967. *Capital*, vol. 1. New York: International.

Marx, Karl, and Friedrich Engels. 1975. *Collected Works*, vol. 5, 3d ed. New York: International.

———. 1978. *The Marx-Engels Reader*, ed. Robert Tucker, 2d ed. New York: Norton.

Sandoval, Chela. 1990. "Feminism and Racism: A Report on the 1981 National Women's Studies Association Conference." In *Making Face, Making Soul/Haciendo Caras*, ed. Gloria Anzaldúa, 55–71. San Francisco: Aunt Lute.

———. 1991. "U.S. Third World Feminism: The Theory and Method of Oppositional Consciousness in the Postmodern World." *Genders* 10 (Spring): 1–24.

Weeks, Kathi. 1996. "Subject for a Feminist Standpoint." In *Marxism beyond Marxism*, ed. Saree Makdisis, Cesare Casarino, and Rebecca E. Karl, 89–118. New York: Routledge.

18

Comment on Hekman's "Truth and Method: Feminist Standpoint Theory Revisited": Where's the Power?

PATRICIA HILL COLLINS

My reading of standpoint theory sees it as an interpretive framework dedicated to explicating how knowledge remains central to maintaining and changing unjust systems of power. While the main arguments in Susan Hekman's article contain surface validity, because standpoint theory never was designed to be argued as a theory of truth or method, Hekman's article simply misses the point of standpoint theory overall. By decontextualizing standpoint theory from its initial moorings in a knowledge/power framework while simultaneously recontextualizing it in an apolitical discussion of feminist truth and method, Hekman essentially depoliticizes the potentially radical content of standpoint theory.

First, the notion of a standpoint refers to historically shared, *group*-based experiences. Groups have a degree of permanence over time such that group realities transcend individual experiences. For example, African Americans as a stigmatized racial group existed long before I was born and will probably continue long after I die. While my individual experiences with institutionalized racism will be unique, the types of opportunities and constraints that I encounter on a daily basis will resemble those confronting African Americans as a group. Arguing that Blacks as a group come into being or disappear on the basis of my participation seems narcissistic, egocentric, and archetypally postmodern. In contrast, standpoint theory places less emphasis on individual experiences within socially constructed groups than on the social conditions that construct such groups.

I stress this difference between the individual and the group as units of analysis because using these two constructs as if they were interchangeable clouds understanding of a host of topics, in this case, the very notion of a group-based standpoint. Individualism continues as a taproot in Western theorizing, including feminist versions. Whether bourgeois liberalism positing notions of individual

247

rights or postmodern social theory's celebration of human differences, market-based choice models grounded in individualism argue that freedom exists via the absence of constraints of all sorts, including those of mandatory group membership. Freedom occurs when individuals have rights of mobility in and out of groups, much as we join clubs and other voluntary associations.

But the individual as proxy for the group becomes particularly problematic because standpoint theory's treatment of the group is not synonymous with a "family resemblance" of individual choice expanded to the level of voluntary group association. The notion of standpoint refers to groups having shared histories based on their shared location in relations of power—standpoints arise neither from crowds of individuals nor from groups analytically created by scholars or bureaucrats. Take, for example, the commonality of experiences that emerges from long-standing patterns of racial segregation in the United States. The degree of racial segregation between Blacks and Whites as *groups* is routinely underestimated. Blacks and Whites live in racially segregated neighborhoods, and this basic feature generates distinctive experiences in schools, recreational facilities, shopping areas, health-care systems, and occupational opportunities. Moreover, middle-class Blacks have not been exempt from the effects of diminished opportunities that accompany racial segregation and group discrimination. It is common location within hierarchical power relations that creates groups, not the results of collective decision making of the individuals within the groups. Race, gender, social class, ethnicity, age, and sexuality are not descriptive categories of identity applied to individuals. Instead, these elements of social structure emerge as fundamental devices that foster inequality resulting in groups.

To ignore power relations is simply to misread standpoint theory—its raison d'être, its continuing salience, and its ability to explain social inequality. Hekman's treatment of groups as an accumulation of individuals and not as entities with their own reality allows her to do just this. Note the slippage between individual and group standpoint in the following passage: "If we take the multiplicity of feminist standpoints to its logical conclusion, coherent analysis becomes impossible because we have too many axes of analysis. Ultimately, every woman is unique; if we analyze each in her uniqueness, systemic analysis is obviated. So is feminist politics: we lose the ability even to speak for certain categories of women" (359). Hekman clearly identifies the very construct of standpoint with the idea of individual perspective or point of view. This assumption allows her to collapse the individual and group as units of analysis and proceed to reason that *individuals* and *collectivities* undergo similar processes. But because she remains focused on the individual as proxy for the group, it becomes difficult to construct the group from such "unique" individuals. Arriving at the dead end of the impossibility of systemic analysis that leads to systemic change appears as the result. By omitting a discussion of group-based realities grounded in an equally central notion of group-based oppression, we move into the sterile ground of a discussion of how effectively standpoint theory serves as an epistemology of truth.

In contrast to Hekman's view that attention to multiplicity fosters incoherence, current attention to the theme of intersectionality situated within assumptions of group-based power relations reveals a growing understanding of the complexity of the processes both of generating groups and accompanying standpoints. Initially examining only one dimension of power relations, namely, that of social class, Marx posited that, however unarticulated and inchoate, oppressed groups possessed a particular standpoint on inequality. In more contemporary versions, inequality has been revised to reflect a greater degree of complexity, especially that of race and gender. What we now have is increasing sophistication about how to discuss group location, not in the singular social class framework proposed by Marx, nor in the early feminist frameworks arguing the primacy of gender, but within constructs of multiplicity residing in social structures themselves and not in individual women. Fluidity does not mean that groups themselves disappear, to be replaced by an accumulation of decontexualized, unique women whose complexity erases politics. Instead, the fluidity of boundaries operates as a new lens that potentially deepens understanding of how the actual mechanisms of institutional power can change dramatically while continuing to reproduce longstanding inequalities of race, gender, and class that result in group stability. In this sense, group history and location can be seen as points of convergence within hierarchical, multiple, and changing structural power relations.

A second feature of standpoint theory concerns the commonality of experiences and perspectives that emerge for groups differentially arrayed within hierarchical power relations. Keep in mind that if the group has been theorized away, there can be no common experiences or perspectives. Standpoint theory argues that groups who share common placement in hierarchical power relations also share common experiences in such power relations. Such shared angles of vision lead those in similar social locations to be predisposed to interpret these experiences in a comparable fashion. The existence of the group as the unit of analysis neither means that all individuals within the group have the same experiences nor that they interpret them in the same way. Using the group as the focal point provides space for individual agency. While these themes remain meritorious, they simply do not lie at the center of standpoint theory as a theory of group power and the knowledges that group location and power generate.

Unfortunately, the much-deserved attention to issues of individual agency and diversity often overshadows investigating the continued salience of group-based experiences. But group-based experience, especially that of race and/or social class, continues to matter. For example, African-American male rates of incarceration in American jails and prisons remain the highest in the world, exceeding even those of South Africa. Transcending social class, region of residence, command of English, ethnic background, or other markers of difference, all Black men must in some way grapple with the actual or potential treatment by the criminal justice system. Moreover, as mothers, daughters, wives, and lovers of Black men, Black women also participate in this common experience. Similarly, children from poor communities and homeless families are unlikely to attend college, not because they lack talent, but because they lack opportunity. Whatever their racial/ethnic classification, poor people as a group confront similar barriers for issues of basic survival. In this sense, standpoint theory seems especially suited to explaining relations of race and/or social class because these systems of power share similar institutional structures. Given the high degree of residential and occupational segregation separating Black and/or working-class groups from White middle-class realities, it becomes plausible to generate arguments about working-class and/or Black culture that emerge from long-standing shared experiences. For both class and race, a much clearer case of a group standpoint can be constructed. Whether individuals from or associated with these groups accept or reject these histories, they recognize the saliency of the notion of group standpoint.

But gender raises different issues, for women are distributed across these other groups. In contrast to standpoints that must learn to accommodate differences within, feminist standpoints must be constructed across differences such as these. Thus, gender represents a distinctly different intellectual and political project within standpoint theory. How effectively can a standpoint theory that was originally developed to explicate the wage exploitation and subsequent impoverishment of European, working-class populations be applied to the extremely heterogeneous population of women in the contemporary United States, let alone globally? For example, Black women and White women do not live in racially integrated women's communities, separated from men and children by processes such as gender steering into such communities, experience bank redlining that results in refusal to lend money to women's communities, attend inferior schools as a result of men moving to all-male suburban areas, and the like. Instead, Black and White women live in racially segregated communities, and the experiences they garner in such communities reflect the racial politics operating overall. Moreover, proximity in physical space is not necessarily the same as occupying a common location in the space of hierarchical power relations. For example, Black women and women of color routinely share academic office space with middle-class and/or White women academics. It is quite common for women of color to clean the office of the feminist academic writing the latest treatise on standpoint theory. While these women occupy the same physical space—this is why proximity should not be confused with group solidarity—they occupy fundamentally different locations in hierarchical power relations. These women did not just enter this space in a random fashion. An entire arsenal of social institutions collectively created paths in which the individuals assigned to one group received better housing, health care, education, and recreational facilities, while those relegated to the other group did with worse or did without. The accumulation of these different experiences led the two groups of women to that same academic space. The actual individuals matter less than the accumulation of social structures that lead to these outcomes. In this sense, developing a political theory for women involves confronting a different and more complex set of issues than that facing race theories or class-based theories because women's inequality is structured differently.

There is a third theme of standpoint theory in which power is erased, namely, the significance of group consciousness, group self-definition, and "voice" within this entire structure of power and experience. Collapsing individual and group identity emerges here as significant because applying standpoint theory to the individual as proxy for the group becomes particularly problematic in comparing individual voice with group voice or standpoint. Typically, this process operates via imagining how *individuals* negotiate self-definitions and then claiming a "family resemblance" positing that *collectivities* undergo a similar process. Because collectivities certainly do construct stories in framing their identity, this approach appears plausible. But can the individual stand as proxy for the group and the group for the individual? Moreover, can this particular version of the individual serve as the exemplar for collective group identity?

If an individual reasons from his or her own personal experiences by imagining that since "*we* are all the same under the skin, therefore, what *I* experience must be the same as what everybody else experiences," then a certain perception of group narrative structure emerges. If an individual believes that his or her personal experiences in coming to voice, especially the inner voices within his or her own individual consciousness hidden from hierarchal power relations, not only reflect a common human experience but, more to the point, also serve as an exemplar for how *group* consciousness and decision making operate, then individual experience becomes the model for comprehending group processes. This approach minimizes the significance of conflict within groups in generating group narratives. In the model in which an individual conducts inner dialogues among various parts of his or her "self," the process of mediating conflicting identities occurs within each individual. The individual always holds complete power or agency over the consciousness that he or she constructs in his or her own mind and the voice that she or he uses to express that consciousness.

Shifting this mode of coming to voice to the level of the small group provides space to think of groups as collections of individuals engaged in dialogue with one another. As equal and different, the concern lies in finding rules to decide whose voice has most validity. By asking, "If we acknowledge multiple realities, multiple standpoints, how do we discriminate among them?" (359), Hekman continues the search for rules that everyone can follow in order to come to a collective "voice." Within the scope of individuals engaged in face-to-face interaction, this seems reasonable. But does this work with the understanding of *group* that underlies standpoint theory?

Hekman quite rightly recognizes that multiple realities yield multiple perspectives on reality. But again, her concern with the question of who has the best, "truest," or privileged standpoint remains grounded in ambiguous notions of group that omit group-based conflicts and how hierarchical power relations generate differences in group voice or standpoint. Bracketing the question of power and restricting argument solely to the question of truth certainly reveals the limitations of using epistemological criteria in defense of privileged standpoints. But within the reality of hierarchical power relations, the standpoints of some groups are most certainly privileged over others. The amount of privilege granted to a particular standpoint lies less in its internal criteria in being truthful, the terrain in which Hekman situates her discussion, and more in the power of a group in making its standpoint prevail over other equally plausible perspectives. Within hierarchical power relations, it seems reasonable that groups disadvantaged by systems of power might see their strength in solidarity and collective responses to their common location and subjugation. In contrast, it seems equally plausible that those privileged by these types of group placements might want to do away with notions of the group altogether, in effect obscuring the privileges they gain from group membership.

Again, gender raises some particular challenges in using standpoint theory to represent the standpoint of women. One fundamental contribution of feminist movement grounded in standpoint theory was that it aimed to bring women's group consciousness into being. Early emphasis on women's coming to voice via the process of consciousness-raising and claiming individual "voice" inadvertently laid the foundation for the type of conceptual ambiguity between individual and group as categories of analysis. Contemporary feminist theorizing, especially the emergence of postmodern social theory's theme of deconstructing the subject, aggravates this long-standing commitment to bringing individual women to voice as emblematic of the collective struggle of women for "voice." Collapsing the processes of individual and group voice and using the process of individual women coming to voice as emblematic of women's collective coming to voice reinforces this notion that individual and collective voice or standpoint are the same. For many contemporary feminists, voicing their discontent with oppression is sufficient—actually changing institutional power relations seems less important. Gaining voice only to lose it again to a standpoint theory that replaces the freedom of individually negotiated friendships or sisterhood with the obligations of race, class, and gender "families" seems unacceptable to those with the means to escape.

Standpoint theory argues that ideas matter in systems of power. In this sense, standpoints may be judged not only by their epistemological contributions but also by the terms of their participation in hierarchical power relations. Do they inherently explain and condone injustice, or do they challenge it? Do they participate in relations of rule via creating knowledge, or do they reject such rule by generating cultures of resistance? Extracting any claims about knowledge from the power relations in which they are embedded violates the basic premise of standpoint theory because such theory exists primarily to explicate these power relations. Thus, attempts to take the knowledge while leaving the power behind inadvertently operate within the terrain of privileged knowledge. While I respect postmodern contributions in deconstructing languages of power, standpoint theory encompasses much more than changing the "language game of politics" (363). Oppression is not a game, nor is it solely about language—for many of us, it still remains profoundly real.

19

Comment on Hekman's "Truth and Method: Feminist Standpoint Theory Revisited": Whose Standpoint Needs the Regimes of Truth and Reality?

SANDRA HARDING

I agree with several of Susan Hekman's central arguments. Feminist standpoint theory has indeed made a major contribution to feminist theory and, as she indicates at the end, to late twentieth-century efforts to develop more useful ways of thinking about the production of knowledge in local and global political economies. We can note that feminists are not the only contemporary social theorists to struggle with projects of extricating ourselves from some of the constraints of those philosophies of modernity that began to emerge in Europe three or more centuries ago. Moreover, Hekman is certainly right that current reevaluations of Marxian projects, of the "difference" issues, and of poststructuralism are three sites of both resources and challenges to the further development of standpoint theories, as they must be also for other contemporary social theorizing. . . .

However, it seems to me that Hekman distorts the central project of standpoint theorists when she characterizes it as one of figuring out how to justify the truth of feminist claims to more accurate accounts of reality. Rather, it is relations between power and knowledge that concern these thinkers. They have wanted to identify ways that male supremacy and the production of knowledge have coconstituted each other in the past and to explore what heretofore unrecognized powers might be found in women's lives that could lead to knowledge that is more useful for enabling women to improve the conditions of our lives. This language about truth and reality certainly is one that can be found in early and some continuing standpoint accounts—including the title of the very book in which Nancy Hartsock's essay first appeared (1983), for which I am half responsible! Marxian and other older modernist discourses provided the framework for the feminist standpoint project initially, including the language about truth and reality. However, at least this standpoint theorist thinks that feminist standpoint projects and the modernist discourses they used turned out to be on a collision course. We can talk usefully about "less false beliefs"—ones apparently, as far as we can tell, less false than all *and only those* against which they have so far been tested—without invoking the notions of truth or reality in the conventional senses of these terms. That way we can avoid the truth claimant's position that "the one true story" has, now and forever, already been identified and that as far as the truth claimant is concerned, the matter is closed, *fini*, ended. And we can talk about such less false accounts of "nature and social relations," or however we want to refer to the object of our thoughts and research, without invoking the idea of a static, eternally fixed state of affairs "out there" that our representations have managed uniquely to capture. As N. Katharine Hayles puts the point, many highly useful but conflicting representations can be consistent with "how the world is," although none can be uniquely congruent with it (Hayles, 1993; see also Dupre 1993; Van Fraassen and Sigman 1993).

Relatedly, Hekman's account loses the point that standpoint epistemologies and methodologies were constructed in opposition to the all-powerful dictates of rationalist/empiricist epistemologies and methodologies ("positivism") in the natural and social sciences and in public institutions such as the law, medicine, state economic policy, and so forth. They were also constructed in opposition to the "interpretationist" oppositions to them imagined by most philosophers and social theorists to be the only possible such alternatives. Moreover, for such positivist and antipositivist theorists in philosophy and the social sciences, at least in the United States, Marxian approaches lay beyond the pale of reasonable discussion.

For the standpoint theorists, however, the Marxian epistemology/sociology of knowledge provided the only resources powerful enough to counter the prevailing conceptual frameworks for the kinds of natural and social science projects of feminism in the 1970s and early 1980s. At that time, poststructuralism did not yet seem to offer the resources for feminist science and social science studies that, at least for me, have now been identified in it. Discussions of ideology appeared to be able to handle the cultural configurations that are more richly and accurately, in my view, understood through poststructuralist analyses of socially constituted discourses.[1]

In the brief space remaining to me, I want to try to make vivid the (or, rather, a) "logic" of standpoint theory as it emerged in such a context. I shall try to show how the issues about truth and reality on which Hekman and others have focused need not arise if we reflect on this logic through the resources provided by the past three decades of work in the social studies of science and technology, on the one hand, and multicultural and global science studies and feminisms, on the other hand. This account will also help to clarify some aspects of my work that Hekman finds puzzling.

"Natural Experiments" as a Clue to Standpoint Logic

Standpoint theories argue that the social world in effect provides a kind of laboratory for "experiments" that can enable one to observe and explain patterns in the relations between social power and the production of knowledge claims. Recollect that ancient lesson from elementary school science classes: "Is that stick in the pond that appears to be bent really bent? Walk around to a different location and see that now it appears straight—as it really is." Then, theories of optics were invoked to explain the causes of the initially distorted appearances. In an analogous way, standpoint theorists use the "naturally occurring" relations of class, gender, race, or imperialism in the world around us to observe how different "locations" in such relations tend to generate distinctive accounts of nature and social relations. (They do not *determine* them, but only "tend to generate" accounts different from the dominant ones in distinctive ways.) Thus, the kinds of daily life activities socially assigned to different genders or classes or races within local social systems can provide illuminating possibilities for observing and explaining systemic relations between "what one does" and "what one can know." Observing these differing relations is like walking around the pond. Distinctive gender, class, race, or cultural positions in social orders provide different opportunities and limitations for "seeing" how the social order works. Societies provide a kind of "natural experiment" enabling accounts of how knowledge claims are always "socially situated."

Like the stick-bent-in-water example, although all knowledge claims are determinately situated, not all such social situations are equally good ones from which to be able to see how the social order works. Dominant groups have more interests than do those they dominate in not formulating and in excluding questions about how social relations and nature "really work." From the perspective of women's lives (as articulated by different and sometimes conflicting feminist accounts), such questions emerge as these: Are women "really" capable of only a lesser rationality than men's? Is the double day of work "really" a matter of nature's, not culture's, design? In social relations organized by domination, exploitation, and oppression, the "conceptual practices of power" (Smith's phrase [1990]) will construct institutions that make seem natural and normal those relations of domination, exploitation, and oppression.

This kind of structural political "difference" was exactly the point of standpoint theory projects, although which "system of domination" was centered depended on whether Marxist men or northern feminists or male antiracists and postcolonialists were doing the thinking. However, it took feminists of color, and multicultural and global feminisms, to develop the powerful resources of "intersectionality" necessary to analyze social relations from the standpoint of their daily lives, which were shaped by the mutually supportive or sometimes competitive relations between androcentrism, Eurocentrism, and bourgeois projects (e.g., hooks, 1981; Anzaldúa, 1987; Collins, 1991). Moreover, also not initially centered in standpoint logics and epistemologies was "mere difference"—the cultural differences that would shape different knowledge projects even where there were no oppressive social relations between different cultures (although the persistent attention to women's daily lives clearly required accounting for cultural differences in "what women do").

The "intersectionality" approaches use resources provided by thinking from both of these kinds of differences among women to shape what is often referred to as multicultural and global feminisms. If one starts asking questions about standard accounts of the growth of modern science, for example, from the lives of peoples who suffered from that growth and from the associated European expansion that made it possible and benefited from it (lives articulated through diverse "constructed" discourses), one—anyone—learns more than if such questions were not asked. Postcolonial science studies and the critiques of development, including feminist work in these fields, have asked such questions. They provide resources that northern, and northern feminist, science studies cannot provide. The reason for this is not because poor, Third World women are "more oppressed," as Hekman misstates my point, but, rather, because thought that begins from conceptual frameworks developed to answer questions arising in *their* lives starts from outside the Eurocentric conceptual frameworks within which northern and northern feminist science studies have been largely organized. Hekman's comment about more oppressed women (354), contrary to what I am sure were her intentions, functions to reinstate the Eurocentrism of dominant conceptual frameworks of northern discourses, including feminist ones, by encouraging hostile competitive relations between northern and southern women ("Who's most oppressed?").

One way to characterize what it is about different cultural locations (including those in relations of domination) that invariably will generate both enabling and limiting knowledge claims is the following. Cultures have different locations in the heterogeneous natural world (exposure to the demands of babies or factories, cancer-producing sunlight or too little sun, deserts or rain forests). They bring different interests even to the "same" natural or social environment (e.g., interests to fish, travel, mine, harvest seaweed from, desalinize, etc., the Atlantic Ocean). They draw on, and are positioned in different ways with respect to, culturally distinctive discursive resources—metaphors, models, narratives, conceptual frameworks—with which to think about themselves and the worlds around them. Moreover, they have culturally distinctive ways of organizing the production of knowledge, usually highly related to how they produce everything else—to work (see Harding, 1996, 1997).

This kind of framework can be used to explain differences in knowledge possibilities of the kinds of cultures conventionally of interest to anthropologists and historians. In fact, I draw it from the post-Kuhnian social studies of science and technology and the postcolonial cross-cultural studies of modern sciences as much like other local knowledge systems (see e.g., Watson-Verran and Turnbull 1995). It could have been drawn as easily from analyses of northern American societies, as were most of the original standpoint writings.

Hekman's Administrator Perspective

From this perspective, Hekman's questions about truth and reality can be avoided. Other questions that do much of the same work do arise—for example, about evidence, Eurocentric conceptual frameworks in every discipline, the culturally diverse purposes of science, and the relations between the expansion of European power and hegemonic conceptual apparatuses. But Hekman's preoccupations with truth and reality arise, I suggest, only from the standpoint of a Eurocentric reaction to these postcolonial accounts. Let us ask what social location one could infer for the author of the following (purportedly value neutral?) passage in which Hekman reacts to a statement by Haraway with what Hekman sees as "the central problem facing feminist theory today."[2] My question is: Who is the "we" in these passages? "Given multiple standpoints, the social construction of 'reality,' and the necessity of an engaged political position, how can we talk about 'better accounts of the world,' 'less false stories'? And, indeed, how can we talk about accounts of the world at all if the multiplicity of standpoints is, quite literally, endless?" (358). In the next paragraph she repeats her statement of this problem:

> First, if we take the multiplicity of feminist standpoints to its logical conclusion, coherent analysis becomes impossible because we have too many axes of analysis. Ultimately, every woman is unique; if we analyze each in her uniqueness, systemic analysis is obviated. So is feminist politics: we lose the ability even to speak for certain categories of women. Second, if we acknowledge multiple realities, multiple standpoints, how do we discriminate among them? How do we select the perspectives and standpoints that are useful to us, that will help us achieve our theoretical and practical goals, or are we necessarily condemned to the "absolute relativism" that some critics fear? (359).

Who is the repeated "we" of these paragraphs, with "too many axes of analysis," trying to "speak for certain [other?] categories of women," forced to acknowledge multiple realities with no guides to discriminating among them, no justifiable guides for selecting "the perspectives and standpoints that are useful to us," and so forth? Not women in their everyday lives, who must and do make reasoned, evidence-dependent judgments about such matters. In centering these questions, Hekman's standpoint remains that of the administrator faced with managing all those culturally local people, with their conflicting perspectives, claims, and demands. If "our" one true story of a world that is out there and available for the telling is not *the* true story, then the modernist paranoia begins: "We" are going to have to admit the legitimacy of everyone's story and world—some of which will probably conflict with our favored ones. Lost is the analysis of how knowledge projects are designed for local situations, including diverse interests in gaining and exercising power. This is not, of course, where Hekman wants to be positioned, but it seems to me that it is where the conceptual framework of her article is positioned.

Clarifications

This brings me to some clarifications. "Less false accounts." Science never gets us truth; it always promised something much better than truth claims. Truth claims were supposed to be thought of as expressing a relation to the world claimed only by religious or other dogmatic beliefs. Scientific procedures are supposed to get us claims that are less false than those—and only those— against which they have been tested. Further evidence can be collected, and conceptual shifts cast old claims into new frameworks. Thus, scientific claims are supposed to be held not as true but, only provisionally, as "least false" until counterevidence or a new conceptual framework no longer provides them with the status of "less false" than those against which they have been tested. Thus, my discussions of "strong objectivity" and of "less false" claims were intended to distance standpoint thinking from remnants of popular modernist ideology that did not even match modernist science theory. Another way to put this point is that claims to truth are harmless as long as they promise no more than the evidence that can be produced in support of such a claim. Of course the standards for what counts as "less false" can be at issue or change over time. The standards for knowledge claims, too, are provisional and tend to change over time. We need not avoid the useful notion of "less false" claims just because we turn away from the absolutist standards of modernism.

Hekman says I "offer no argument" as to why it is that "starting research from the reality of women's lives . . . will lead to a more objective account of social reality" (355). Yet chapter 5 of *Whose Science? Whose Knowledge?* did precisely that, pointing to diverse such arguments already "out there" in older history and social science research (Harding, 1991). I had already pointed to some of these in my earlier analysis of the differences between several feminist standpoint theory arguments (Harding, 1986). Hekman is right, in my view, about the necessity to understand "women's lives" or, in her terms, "the reality of women's lives," as socially constructed discursive formations. But, that some such discursive accounts provide richer resources than others for understanding natural and social worlds—that they are epistemically privileged in this sense—I did argue for, as has every other standpoint theorist. It is odd that nowhere in her article does she take up just what it is that Hartsock, Smith, Collins, myself, and others have identified in the women's lives that seemed to us to justify claims of epistemic preference. She seems to be interested not in the substantive claims of standpoint theories but only in their troubled participation in a truth/reality discourse.

Finally, something must be said about the misleading chronology for the development of feminist standpoint theory that Hekman gives in the first few paragraphs. Smith's first standpoint essay, the one Hekman references to my 1987 anthology, originally appeared in 1974 (Smith, 1974). Three more essays were published by 1981 (Smith, 1977, 1979, 1981). By 1979, four years before Hartsock's publications, Marcia Westkott could already include a review of the wide influence on sociologists of several of Smith's standpoint essays in her *Harvard Educational Review* essay (1979). It was Smith, not Hartsock, to whom Collins stated her indebtedness—which makes sense since Smith and Collins are both sociologists. Hartsock's two versions of her important essay appeared in the same year, 1983, as did published standpoint essays by Alison Jaggar, Hilary Rose (as Hekman indicates later on p. 348), and Harding. Moreover, there were a number of colloquia on Smith's and Harding's work in the late 1980s and early 1990s and discussions of feminist standpoint epistemologies in diverse journal articles, feminist philosophy collections, and disciplinary association meetings (evidently excluding political science discourses) during this period.

More than factual errors are at issue here. Hartsock's essay has indeed been immensely and justifiably influential. It does not devalue the brilliance of her work to recognize, however, that in retrospect one can see that feminist standpoint epistemology was evidently an idea whose time had come, since most of these authors worked independently and unaware of each other's work. (Standpoint theory would itself call for such a social history of ideas, would it not?) It was a project "straining at the bit" to emerge from feminist social theorists who were familiar with the Marxian epistemology. If one was familiar with Marx's, Engels's, and Lukacs's writings on epistemology, the potential parallels Hartsock so incisively delineates between the situations of "proletarians" and of "women" in thinking about relations between power and knowledge began to leap off the page. Moreover, standpoint theory's subsequent development tended to be constrained by the familiar disciplinary borders that evidently still limit Hekman's grasp of this history. These disciplinary development routes also created distinctively different standpoint theor*ies*, in the plural, each drawing on different disciplinary and other research interests, resources, and methodologies. Different political projects have also shaped how standpoint epistemologies have been developed....

Whose locations, interests, discourses, and ways of organizing the production of knowledge are silenced and suppressed by taking the administrative standpoint on standpoint theory that Hekman centers?

Notes

1. It should also be noted that while for Europeans, poststructuralism is a kind of post-marxism, for many U.S. poststructuralists, it is a *premarxism*. Like Hekman, they attach it to diverse liberal social science discourses—in her case, those of Thomas Kuhn and Max Weber.
2. Hekman says here that it is Haraway who defines the problem Hekman formulates below; however, this is not Haraway's formulation of it—it is Hekman's.

References

Anzaldúa, Gloria. 1987. *Borderlands/La Frontera*. San Francisco: Spinsters/Aunt Lute.

Collins, Patricia Hill. 1991. *Black Feminist Thought: Knowledge, Consciousness, and the Politics of Empowerment*. New York: Routledge.

Dupre, John. 1993. *The Disorder of Things: Metaphysical Foundations for the Disunity of Science*. Cambridge, Mass.: Harvard University Press.

Haraway, Donna. 1988. "Situated Knowledges: *The Science Question in Feminism* and the Privilege of Partial Perspective." *Feminist Studies* 14(3):575–99. Reprinted in her *Simians, Cyborgs and Women: The Reinvention of Nature*. New York: Routledge, 1991.

Harding, Sandra. 1983. "Why Has the Sex-Gender System Become Visible Only Now?" In *Discovering Reality: Feminist Perspectives on Epistemology, Metaphysics, Methodology, and Philosophy of Science*, ed. Sandra Harding and Merrill Hintikka, 311–24. Dordrecht: Reidel/Kluwer.

———. 1986. *The Science Question in Feminism*. Ithaca, N.Y.: Cornell University Press.

———. 1991. *Whose Science? Whose Knowledge? Thinking from Women's Lives*. Ithaca, N.Y.: Cornell University Press.

———. 1996. "Multicultural and Global Feminist Philosophies of Science: Resources and Challenges." In *Feminism, Philosophy and the Philosophy of Science*, ed. Lynn Hankinson Nelson and Jack Nelson. Dordrecht: Reidel, pp. 263–87

———. 1997. "Women's Standpoints on Nature: What Makes Them Possible?" *Osiris*. 12, pp. 1–15.

Hartsock, Nancy. 1983a. "The Feminist Standpoint: Developing the Ground for a Specifically Feminist Historical Materialism." In *Discovering Reality: Feminist Perspectives on Epistemology, Metaphysics, Methodology, and Philosophy of Science*, ed. Sandra Harding and Merrill Hintikka, 283–310. Dordrecht: Reidel/Kluwer.

———. 1983b. "The Feminist Standpoint: Toward a Specifically Feminist Historical Materialism." In her *Money, Sex, and Power*, 231–51. New York: Longman.

Hayles, N. Katherine. 1993. "Constrained Constructivism: Locating Scientific Inquiry in the Theater of Representation." In *Realism and Representation*, ed. George Levine, 27–43. Madison: University of Wisconsin Press.

hooks, bell. 1981. *Ain't I a Woman? Black Women and Feminism*. Boston: South End Press.

Jaggar, Alison. 1983. "Feminist Politics and Epistemology: Justifying Feminist Theory." In her *Feminist Politics and Human Nature*, 353–89. Totowa, N.J.: Rowman & Allenheld.

Rose, Hilary. 1983. "Hand, Brain and Heart: A Feminist Epistemology for the Natural Sciences." *Signs: Journal of Women in Culture and Society* 9(1):73–90. Reprinted in Sandra Harding and Jean O'Barr, eds., *Sex and Scientific Inquiry*. Chicago: University of Chicago Press, 1987.

Smith, Dorothy. 1974. "Women's Perspective as a Radical Critique of Sociology." *Sociological Inquiry* 44:7–14. Reprinted in Sandra Harding, ed., *Feminism and Methodology: Social Science Issues*. Bloomington: Indiana University Press, 1987.

———. 1977. "Some Implications of a Sociology for Women." In *Woman in a Man-Made World: A Socioeconomic Handbook*, ed. Nona Y. Glazer and Helen Waehrer, 15–29. Chicago: Rand-McNally.

———. 1979. "A Sociology for Women." In *The Prism of Sex: Essays in the Sociology of Knowledge*, ed. Julia Sherman and Evelyn T. Beck, 135–87. Madison: University of Wisconsin Press.

———. 1981. "The Experienced World as Problematic: A Feminist Method." Sorokin Lecture no. 12, University of Saskatchewan, Saskatoon.

———. 1990. *The Conceptual Practices of Power: A Feminist Sociology of Knowledge*. Boston: Northeastern University Press.

Van Fraassen, Bas, and Jill Sigman. 1993. "Interpretation in Science and in the Arts." In *Realism and Representation*, ed. George Levine, 77–99. Madison: University of Wisconsin Press.

Watson-Verran, Helen, and David Turnbull. 1995. "Science and Other Indigenous Knowledge Systems." In *Handbook of Science and Technology Studies*, ed. Sheila Jasanoff et al., 115–39. Thousand Oaks, Calif.: Sage.

Westkott, Marcia. 1979. "Feminist Criticism of the Social Sciences." *Harvard Educational Review* 49:422–30.

20
Comment on Hekman's "Truth and Method: Feminist Standpoint Theory Revisited"

DOROTHY E. SMITH

I have written this grudgingly. Susan Hekman's interpretation of my work is so systematically out to lunch that it is difficult to write a response that does not involve a replication of what I have already said, at length and in various versions, elsewhere. But that would interest neither me nor readers. So I have asked myself: Apart from lack of care and thought, what is she doing that leads to her systematic misreading? And what might be systematic about other mistakes such as the chronology of "standpoint theory['s]" development (a work published in 1979 is attributed to the decade following, 1983), or that its roots were in Marxism (Where's the women's movement?), or that it is less used and interesting currently (speak for your own discipline, Susan; in sociology it flourishes), or that feminist standpoint theory has become identified with "object-relations" theory (news to me).

A major problem is the reification of "feminist standpoint theory." Feminist standpoint theory, as a general class of theory in feminism, was brought into being by Sandra Harding (1986), not to create a new theoretical enclave but to analyze the merits and problems of feminist theoretical work that sought a radical break with existing disciplines through locating knowledge or inquiry in women's standpoint or in women's experience. Those she identified had been working independently of one another and have continued to do so. In a sense, Harding created us. I do not think there was much interchange among us. As standpoint theorists, we became identifiable as a group through Harding's study. And as a construct of Harding's text, we appeared as isolated from the intellectual and political discourses with which our work was in active dialogue. I cannot speak here for Nancy Hartsock, Patricia Hill Collins, or others mentioned in Hekman's article, but, for myself, I am very much aware of being engaged with the debates and innovations of the many feminist experiments in sociology that, like mine, were exploring experience as a method of discovering the social from the standpoint of women's experience.

263

But Hekman goes beyond Harding to constitute us as a common theoretical position, indeed as a foundationalist theory justifying feminist theory as knowledge. A coherence is invented for us: "Despite their significant differences, all of these accounts share the conviction that the feminist standpoint is rooted in a 'reality' that is the opposite of the abstract conceptual world inhabited by men, particularly the men of the ruling class, and that in this reality lies the truth of the human condition" (Hekman, 348). Given the realities of our nonexistence as a group except on paper, she *must* distort in order to bring off this representation. The quotation comes on page 348, after Hartsock and Smith have been thoroughly worked over, and Smith at least (Hartsock is speaking for herself) has been tortured into the shape that fits this conclusion. What's wrong with this account so far as I am concerned?

First, I am not proposing a *feminist standpoint* at all; taking up women's standpoint as I have developed it is not at all the same thing and has nothing to do with justifying feminist knowledge. Second, I am not arguing that women's standpoint is rooted in a reality of any kind. Rather, I am arguing that women's standpoint returns us to the actualities of our lives as we live them in the local particularities of the everyday/everynight worlds in which our bodily being anchors us. As I use the term, *actuality* is not defined. The notion of "actual" in my writing is like the arrow on the map of the mall saying "You are here," that points in the text to a beyond-the-text in which the text, its reading, its reader, and its concepts also *are*. It is, so to speak, where we live and where discourse happens and does its constituting of "reality." Third, I do not embrace reality and reject concepts (Hekman, 348). It is precisely the force of women's standpoint (at least as I have developed it) that it folds concepts, theory, discourse, *into actuality* as people's actual practices or activities (a fully reflexive notion applying to the concepts of such a sociology). The contrast I draw between the abstract conceptual modes of ruling and a location of consciousness in the particularizing work that women do in relation to children does not constitute two equivalent regions, and the move I propose is not from concepts to reality. Rather, it is to recognize that concepts are also in actuality and that the objectifications of what I early on described as the relations of ruling are themselves people's socially organized practices in the actual locations of their lives. I and others working with this approach have developed a body of systematic study in which concepts and theories are examined for how they are activated in organizing social relations (Smith 1987; Walker 1990; Campbell and Manicom 1995). I realize that this is a bit tricky to grasp, but Hekman's (prince-pleasing) glass slipper will not fit the feet of this ugly sister.

In the end, the oddest thing is to find Hekman restoring us to the law of the father: Alfred Schutz, Michel Foucault, and, finally, Max Weber. Sandra Harding remarks, in her comments on Hekman, that she (Hekman) "loses the point that standpoint epistemologies and methodologies were constructed" oppositionally (383). Somehow Hekman misses altogether that such epistemologies and methods came out of and were dialogically implicated in a women's movement that offered a profound challenge to established discourses in almost every region of the political, artistic, and intellectual discourses. In various ways, those who have been identified with "feminist" standpoint theory became active in working with other women in our fields to undermine social science's embedding of the standpoint of white men as hidden agent and subject. Its distinctively experiential methodology was only a systematization of a political methodology that had been foundational to the women's movement.

Beginning in women's experiences told in women's words was and is a vital political moment in the women's movement. Experience is a method of speaking that is not preappropriated by the discourses of the relations of ruling. This is where women began to speak from as the women's movement of our time came into being. When we assembled *as* "women" and spoke together *as* "women," constituting "women" as a category of political mobilization, we discovered dimensions of "our" experience that had no prior discursive definition. In this political context, the category "women" is peculiarly nonexclusive since it was then and has remained open-ended, such that boundaries established at any one point are subject to the disruption of women who enter speaking from a different experience as well as an experience of difference. It is this commitment to the privileges of women to speak *from* experience that opens the women's movement to the critique of white and/or heterosexist hegemony from those it marginalizes and silences. The authority of experience is foundational to the women's movement (which is not to say that experience is foundational to knowledge) and has been and is at once explosive and fruitful.

Experience is a method of talk, a language game, in which what is not yet spoken struggles dialogically to appropriate language sedimented with meaning before the moment in which she speaks. It is through and through saturated with the social relations, including the social relations of discourse, in which what is being spoken of is embedded as well as those of which the moment of speaking is part. Experience gives direct access to the necessarily social character of people's worlds; it is in *how* people talk, the categories they use, the relations implicitly posited among them, and so forth, and in what is taken for granted in their talk, as well as in what they can talk about. It is the saturation of experience as a language game with social relations that makes nonsense of Hekman's notion that standpoint ultimately dissolves into the endless idiosyncratic consciousnesses of unique individuals.

The knowledge people have by virtue of their experience is a knowledge of the local practices of our everyday/everynight worlds. It is for the most part what Michael Polanyi (1967) called "tacit knowledge"—a knowing that is the very texture of our daily/nightly living in what we know how to do, how we go about things, and what we can get done. We know how and where to go shopping; we know how to read a book in the less-than-aware dimensions of turning pages from left to right; we know washing dishes, sweeping floors, cleaning;

we know putting on makeup and washing our hair; we know how to recognize the boundary between street and sidewalk; we may not know what it is to be battered by a man, but we would know if we had been; some of us know what it is to suckle children; some of us know menstruation; some of us know getting on a bus and going to work; we know how to do our work and who works with us; we know . . . ; we know . . . ; we know as a matter of doing. This is a knowing that is of the socially organized ground of our participation in living with others, some of it, indeed, altogether beyond consciousness, but no less what we know how to do.[1]

Such tacit knowing, of course, becomes a knowledge only at that point when it is entered into the language game of experience, that is, in the course of telling. For the most part, it remains the secret underpinning of everything we do. We discover it vividly as we learn from small children that they truly do not know the same world that we do or when we travel among a people whose everyday/everynight living is radically different from ours. A sociology built on such a social ontology differs from Hekman's interpretation of Weber (and I have some reservations about the accuracy of her interpretation) as resting "on the assumption that what the social researcher studies, the activities and concepts of social actors, is already constituted" (361). Rather, I take the view that the social is always *being brought into being* in the concerting of people's local activities. It is never already there.

The women's movement and its methodology of working from experience began to unearth the tacit underpinnings of gender. But at the very moment when experience is summoned by what women can find they have in common, it is being translated into the universalizing discourse of a movement making political claims across a variety of fronts. It has seemed to me that in the women's movement, some women have wanted to be able to go directly from what we know by virtue of how we participate in social relations to claims to knowledge at the level of a universalizing discourse. The critique of "essentialism" aims at this move. Standpoint theory is often understood, as I think Hekman understands it, as foundational to knowledge claims of this kind according to which women's experience is privileged. I do not make this claim. Rather, taking women's standpoint and beginning in experience gives access to a knowledge of what is tacit, known in the doing, and often not yet discursively appropriated (and often seen as uninteresting, unimportant, and routine). Here is where I have held we might begin, as sociologists committed to discovering society from where people are as participants in it.

I do not, therefore, argue, as Hekman says I do, that the "knowledge of women is superior to the abstract knowledge of the sociologist" (352), in part, of course, because my interest is in a sociology that does not displace what people know as the local practices of our everyday/everynight living but, rather, seeks to build on and enlarge it beyond the horizon of any one person's daily experience. I call this taking for sociology the problematic of the everyday/everynight world

(Smith 1987). To take up Sandra Harding's metaphor in her comment in this exchange, I want a sociology that would seek to discover the shape of the pond that positions the people and their perspectives vis-à-vis one another.

People's tacit knowledge of what they know as a matter of daily/nightly practices surfaces as people speak and as what they speak of is taken seriously, undistilled, untranslated. Speaking for themselves and from their experience has been a fundamental commitment of the women's movement, and it remains foundational to the method of inquiry I have been trying to develop for sociology. I stress "method of inquiry" since what I do as theory is not really an epistemology, although it must wrestle with epistemological problems; it is surely not a theory foundational to feminist theory, nor yet a theory of history, society, the laws of social systems, or anything of that kind. As a theory it is a systematic formulation of a method of developing investigations of the social that are anchored in, although not confined by, people's everyday working knowledge of the doing of their lives.

Since I want to take people's experience as a place to start, Weber's notions of "ideal types" leaves me cold. What could this be but an assertion of the right of the social scientist to impose her framework on the world and to resume the effectivity of the relations of ruling in subordinating voices speaking from people's experience in and of their lived actualities. "Ideal type" methodology brokers differences among intellectual colleagues but is wholly unreflexive with respect to observer-observed relations. Different idealizations could be constructed of the same historical events. They could coexist without being either exhaustive with respect to those events or necessarily in contradiction with one another.[2] But ideal type methodology creates no commitments to how things are experienced by those who live them. It creates no openness toward those it studies. The sociologist working with this method is not committed to hearing and honoring what the other has to say. Despite Weber's commitment to an interpretive sociology, his specification of *Verstehen* as a method in social science clearly privileges the standpoint of the external observer. For example, in his specification of "direct observational understanding" he discusses in terms of alternative motivational accounts the problem of explaining why a woodcutter is cutting wood in the forest:[3] Is he cutting wood to sell it? for his own use? because he is angry? But shift the standpoint to that of people's actual experience. The question of why he is cutting wood does not arise for the woodcutter who is *in the course of* cutting wood to sell, because he is angry, for his own use. From the Archimedean perch of social scientific discourse, the reality that comes into being only in relation to it (constituted by it, if you will) appears puzzling and confusing.[4] So it was for Weber, who struggled to comprehend the complexities of historical change and found in his "ideal type" a method of wresting order from what he conceded was beyond ordering. But from the standpoint of experience in and of the everyday/everynight actualities of our lives, it is the oppressively, routine organization, the persistence, the repetition, of capitalist forms of exploitation, of patriarchy, of racial subordination, of the forms of dominance Foucault (1980) has characterized as "power/knowledge," as the local contouring of people's lives that constitute a sociological problematic. The system of sociological principles that Weber developed and on which his "ideal type" methodology is based is incompatible with a sociology *for* women, or *for* people.

Notes

1. Ethnomethodology is that sociology that seeks to uncover the taken-for-granted that is prenormative and prior to discursive positing (Garfinkel 1967).
2. Note that much more needs to be done to show that Carole Pateman, Arlie Hochschild, or Karen Sacks makes use of ideal-type analyses. Hekman seems to conflate ideal types with concepts and typifications; the latter is in general use in the analysis of ethnographic types of materials in social science, and neither is the same as Weber's systematic exploration of the logic, say, of rational legal forms of authority.
3. This instance is extensively analyzed and discussed along with others in a chapter of my *The Everyday World as Problematic: A Feminist Sociology* (Smith 1987, n.1). In that chapter, I examine how the relations between observer and observed enter into (and can be found in) the accounts that are produced from the encounter.
4. The problem is endemic to a sociology that begins from a standpoint in its own self-sustaining theoretically constructed world and constitutes an Archimedean point for its discursive subject. "The disorganized flow of empirical social reality is the only thing that creates problems difficult enough to make it worthwhile to have a discipline trying to tame the flow into theoretically and methodologically unimpeachable sociology," writes Arthur Stinchcombe (1983, 10).

References

Campbell, Marie, and Ann Manicom, eds. 1995. *Experience, Knowledge, and Ruling Relations.* Toronto: University of Toronto Press.

Foucault, Michel. 1980. *Power/Knowledge: Selected Interviews and Other Writings, 1972–1977.* New York: Pantheon.

Garfinkel, Harold. 1967. *Studies in Ethnomethodology.* Englewood Cliffs, N.J.: Prentice Hall.

Harding, Sandra. 1986. *The Science Question in Feminism.* Ithaca, N.Y.: Cornell University Press.

Polanyi, Michael. 1967. *The Tacit Dimension.* Garden City, N.Y.: Doubleday.

Smith, Dorothy E. 1987. *The Everyday World as Problematic: A Feminist Sociology.* Boston: Northeastern University Press.

Stinchcombe, Arthur. 1983. "Origins of Sociology as a Discipline." *Ars Sociologica* 27(1):11.

Walker, Gillian. 1990. *Family Violence: The Politics of Conceptualization in the Women's Movement.* Toronto: University of Toronto Press.

21
Reply to Hartsock, Collins, Harding, and Smith

SUSAN HEKMAN

My purpose in writing "Truth and Method: Feminist Standpoint Theory Revisited" was to reopen the debate over feminist standpoint theory and to refocus the discussion of the central issues raised by the theory. The comments by Patricia Hill Collins, Sandra Harding, Dorothy Smith, and Nancy Hartsock on my article indicate that I have been at least partially successful in that purpose. I welcome the opportunity to further extend this discussion.

Patricia Hill Collins, Sandra Harding, and Nancy Hartsock all raise an objection that goes to the heart of the approach that I develop in the article. They argue, although in different ways, that I, as Collins puts it, "depoliticize" feminist standpoint theory. Claiming that standpoint theory was not designed to be argued as a theory of truth and method, Collins asserts that my "apolitical discussion of feminist truth and method" (375) denies the potentially radical content of standpoint theory. Similarly, Harding argues that I "distort" the central project of standpoint theorists by characterizing the approach as an attempt to justify the truth of feminist claims to more accurate accounts of reality. Against this she claims that it is "relations between power and knowledge that concern these thinkers" (382). Finally, Hartsock argues that I read feminist standpoint theory through "a kind of American pluralism that prefers to speak not about power or justice but, rather, about knowledge and epistemology" (367).

It is precisely the relation between power and knowledge that concerns me in the article. I begin my analysis of feminist standpoint theory with an assumption that is also the centerpiece of Hartsock's approach: politics and epistemology are inseparable. I argue that the central question of feminist standpoint theory has been how we justify the truth of the feminist claim that women have been and are oppressed. My claim is that women cannot resist oppression and gain political power unless they can legitimate this claim. I further argue that the shift in the theory that occurred in the 1980s had a political origin: the demand for recognition of differences among women. Finally, I turn to Weber's ideal type because it is an approach that explains and justifies the necessarily engaged (political) role of the social analyst. I do not think that this approach either distorts or depoliticizes feminist standpoint theory. On the contrary, I think it continues the tradition established by that theory: the necessary connection between knowledge and power.

Collins continues her criticism of the alleged depoliticization of my approach in her discussion of group-based experience. She claims that because I "remain focused on the individual as proxy for the group, it becomes difficult to construct the group from such 'unique' individuals" (376). Hartsock advances a similar criticism with her claim that I erroneously define groups as aggregates of individuals. Although I do argue that multiplicity fosters incoherence, the intent of this argument is to criticize an approach that denies the use of any general concepts. Far from advocating a feminism based in individual experiences, I see the move toward a highly individualistic feminist social theory as a danger to be avoided, a move that would paralyze feminist social analysis. The intent of my exploration of feminist ideal types is to explain and justify the use of general concepts, including those describing group experience, that can foster useful feminist social analysis and provide for the possibility of collective political action.

Sandra Harding approaches the relationship between knowledge and power in feminist standpoint theory from a different perspective than the one that I present in my article. In her discussion of what she calls "the logic of standpoint theory" Harding appeals to work in the social studies of science and technology, multicultural global science studies, and feminism to make her argument for "less false accounts" of the social and natural worlds. She uses these resources to argue that some social situations are good ones from which to see how the social order works and that some discursive accounts provide richer resources for understanding the natural and social world. Despite my criticism of aspects of her work, I agree with these claims. Our difference lies in the means by which we justify them. Relying on the perspectives provided by Weber and Wittgenstein, I argue that, ultimately, all we can do is to present what we hope will be persuasive arguments for the analytic/political perspective we adopt. In the absence of a universal metanarrative we can only argue that the feminist position we advocate will alleviate the oppression of women and that this is a good worth striving for. And, finally, as Wittgenstein wrote, at the end of reasons comes persuasion.

Harding's reference to my alleged "administrative standpoint" is a more disturbing criticism. Who, Harding asks, is the "we" that I refer to in my article? Not, she claims, women in their everyday lives, but an "administrator" faced with managing "all those culturally local people" (387). I would like to offer a different answer: the "we" is feminist social analysts who want to understand the world with the aim of changing it. No, this "we" is not "everyday women." It is women who are engaged in an activity that is worthwhile and has the potential for radically changing social reality: feminist social analysis. The perspective of the feminist social analyst is partial because all perspectives are partial. But it is a perspective that, I would argue, has the potential to change the world for the better. Part of my purpose in appealing to Weber's ideal type was to make explicit the necessarily partial nature of all analytic concepts while at the same time justifying their use.

My differences with Dorothy Smith are the most fundamental. Our disagreement hinges on my claim that she roots women's standpoint in the reality of women's experience and that this results in the (in my view, futile) attempt to replace concepts with brute reality/experience. Smith denies this charge. In her refutation she claims, rather, that "women's standpoint returns us to the actualities of our lives as we live them in the local particularities of the everyday/everynight worlds in which our bodily being anchors us." She concedes that this distinction is "a bit tricky to grasp" (393). I agree. I still don't grasp it.

Far from denying the validity of women's experience, I am trying to explain and justify the conceptual status of the appeal to "women's experience" so that it does not fall prey to the epistemological confusions that this appeal has generated. I turn to Weber's theory because he makes it explicit that, as social analysts, we are using concepts that are different from, although related to, those of social actors. This is the case because our goal is different. Unlike actors operating in the social world, our goal is to understand and clarify that world. To deny this seems to me to lead to yet more epistemological confusion. Ideal-type methodology, contrary to Smith's claim, is useful precisely because it *is* reflexive about the epistemological complexities of the observer/observed relationship.

In her comments on my article, Nancy Hartsock raises the vexed issue of the relationship of both feminism and Marxism to Enlightenment thinking. Her argument that Marx is an anti-Enlightenment thinker is a controversial one, but one that I will not take issue with here. Her claim that feminism has an "ambiguous" relationship to the Enlightenment, however, is germane to my central thesis regarding feminist standpoint theory. Hartsock claims that "women's insistence on speaking at all troubles those theories" (369). Although the context of this remark is different than that of my article, our arguments have important parallels. My purpose in writing the article was to trace the way in which feminist standpoint theory, a theory that emerged out of the Enlightenment tradition, deconstructed (if you will) that tradition. Women speaking their truth had the effect of transforming truth, knowledge, and power as the Enlightenment defined them. I identify this transformation as the emergence of a new paradigm. Although Hartsock and I differ in the ways we define this transformation, we are in agreement that the Enlightenment certainties have been exploded and that it is the speech of women that has accomplished this. And, ultimately, this is what the feminist standpoint is all about.

22
Strange Standpoints, or How to Define the Situation for Situated Knowledge

DICK PELS

The Point of Standpoint Theory

Standpoint epistemologies have long counted among the most powerful challenges to the conventional view that true knowledge is value-free, disinterested, and situationally transcendent. Severing the traditional epistemological linkage between objectivity and neutrality, and measuring truth claims in terms of particular social locations and experiences, standpoint theories typically assert that (scientific) knowledge is inescapably position-bound, and hence both partial and partisan in character. Accordingly, they plead a conscious and reflexive politicization of knowledge, and a novel assessment of the balance of opportunities and risks that positionally determined knowledges might entail. The search for truth "for its own sake" in the sense of acceding to a universally valid and context-transcending "view from nowhere" is abandoned in favor of a new social-epistemological question: "which social standpoint offers the best chance for reaching an optimum of truth?" (Mannheim, 1968: 71). Given the fact that all human beliefs, including our best scientific propositions, are socially situated, we require "a critical evaluation to determine which social situations tend to generate the most objective knowledge claims" (Harding, 1991: 142).

Standpoint epistemologies come in a great variety of historical forms.[1] Perhaps it is Machiavelli, in the famous dedication that prefaces *The Prince,* who offers the first powerful intuition. Excusing himself for his apparent presumption, as a man of humble condition, in venturing to discuss and lay down rules about princely government, he goes on to say:

> For those who paint landscapes place themselves on low ground, in order to understand the character of the mountains and other high points, and climb higher in order to understand the character of the plains. Likewise, one needs to be a ruler to understand properly the character of the people, and to be a man of the people to understand properly the character of rulers. (Machiavelli, 1988: 4)

But of course, it is especially the Hegelian dialectic of master and slave and classical Marxism's adoption of the class standpoint of the proletariat (as refined and updated in the writings of Lukács and Althusser), which have set the generative

273

matrix for all subsequent versions (see Pels, 2000: 27ff.). An additional and so far unjustifiably neglected source is found in radical nationalist or ethnicist (in German: *völkische*) affirmations of the "standpoint of the nation" or of "the people" as expressing a culturally or racially homogeneous essence. An early example was provided by the outcry of nationalist and racist "anti-intellectuals" such as Barrès and Maurras against *les intellectuels* during the Dreyfus Affair in turn-of-the-century France. Truth and justice, Barrès argued, were predicated upon finding a standpoint and adopting a perspective from which "all things arranged themselves according to the measure of a Frenchman" (Barrès, 1902: 12–13). This epistemological nationalism was even more articulate in conservative revolutionary intellectuals of Weimar Germany such as Freyer, Heidegger, and Schmitt. Standpoint theories of knowledge hence emerge in strength simultaneously from the radical left and the radical right, in order to pressurize the liberal idea(l) of autonomous and value-neutral knowledge and science from both ends of the political spectrum. Socialism and nationalism, the great ideological contenders of the nineteenth and twentieth centuries, mirror each other in intriguing fashion in advancing their alternative identity politics of the working class and the nation.

In past decades the left-wing Marxian inspiration, as generalized in Mannheim's sociology of knowledge, has been rekindled especially by feminist theorists, although similar arguments have recently been deployed by lesbian and gay theory, by postcolonial cultural criticism, and by the interesting hybrid constituted by Black feminist thought. If we add some representative arguments favoured by religious fundamentalists and neo-nationalist radicals from the New Right, one might even say that standpoint arguments, for good or for ill, presently offer the most persistently popular rationale for a politics of knowledge framed by particularist identities and the reclamation of cultural difference. While Mannheim extrapolated but also defused proletarian standpoint theory by privileging the mediating position of the "free-floating" intelligentsia, recent conceptualizations preserve the more radical particularist impulses of both left-wing and right-wing identity politics, while shopping for new historical agents of emancipation such as women, lesbians, people of color, or people of Third World descent (cf. Gouldner, 1985: 22–25; Harding, 1991: 268ff.).

The common point of departure inherited from classical standpoint thinking is the baseline conviction, already clearly supported by Machiavelli, that in a hierarchically structured and conflict-ridden society "you cannot see everything from everywhere." In such a society, there exist objectively opposed locations that generate disparate social experiences, which in turn define divergent, partial points of view with variable chances of faithfully representing social reality. As Hall declares,

> we all write and speak from a particular place and time, from a history and a culture which is specific. What we say is always 'in context', *positioned*. . . . Representation is possible only because enunciation is always

produced within codes which have a history, a position within the discursive formations of a particular space and time. The displacement of the 'centred' discourses of the West entails putting in question its universalist character and its transcendental claims to speak for everyone, while being itself everywhere and nowhere. (Hall, 1990: 222; 1996: 446)

Following this axiom about inevitable situatedness and perspectivity, standpoint theories characteristically introduce a second principle, equally adumbrated by Machiavelli, the self-styled "man of the people": that the dominated or marginal not only see differently but also see better and more.[2] Althusser has appropriately updated Machiavelli for advanced capitalist class society: in a class-divided society "one must be proletariat in order to know capital" (1993: 229). Harding outlines a more generalized vision, which is also inclusive of hierarchies structured by gender inequality and/or racial apartheid:

> In societies where power is organized hierarchically—for example by class or race or gender—there is no possibility of an Archimedean perspective, one that is disinterested, impartial, value-free, or detached from the particular, historical social relations in which everyone participates. Instead, each person can achieve only a partial view of reality from the perspective of his or her own position in the social hierarchy. And such a view is not only partial but also distorted by the way the relations of domination are organized. Further, the view from the perspective of the powerful is far more partial and distorted than that available from the perspective of the dominated; this is so for a variety of reasons. To name just one, the powerful have far more interests in obscuring the unjust conditions that produce their unearned privileges and authority than do the dominated groups in hiding the conditions that produce their situation. (Harding, 1991: 59)

In order to gain a critically objective view of society as whole, the best method is therefore "to start thought from marginal lives" (cf. also Harding, 1992: 581; 1993: 50). Haraway thinks that "there is good reason to believe vision is better from below the brilliant space platforms of the powerful.... There is a premium on establishing the capacity to see from the peripheries and the depths" (1991: 190–91). Hartsock similarly believes that in systems of domination, the vision available to the rulers will be "both partial and perverse," in contradistinction to the vision from below, such as represented by women in patriarchy: "women's lives make available a particular and privileged vantage point on male supremacy, a vantage point which can ground a powerful critique of the phallocratic institutions and ideology which constitute the capitalist form of patriarchy" (1983: 284). This epistemic asymmetry between the standpoints of the dominant and the subaltern, in its feminist version, implies that "starting off research from women's lives will generate less partial and distorted accounts not only of women's lives but also of men's lives and of the whole social order" (Harding, 1993: 56; cf. 1991: 48; 1995: 344).

Drifting Toward the Stranger

In the following, I will loosely though not exclusively focus upon the feminist critique and elucidate the promises and limits of standpoint theory's basic epistemological claims primarily in terms of gender inequality rather than in terms of class or race. In doing so, I trust that the formal structure of the argument does not dramatically vary between the three versions, even though both feminist and antiracist cultural studies have critically modified and fine-tuned important elements of the original class-based Marxian framework. Recent feminist theory, in its historic encounter with postmodernist philosophy and the cross-cutting issue of race (e.g., Black feminism), has taken the lead in recognizing both the precariously constructed, performed, and performative nature of all social identities, but also the sheer difficulty of abstracting the various social signifiers (or markers of oppression) from the complex web of their multiple interactions. The idea of an "interlocking system of oppression" and of domination as a "multiple system," which has not accidentally emerged from *Black* feminist thought (cf. Collins, 1986, 1991), reflects a parallel movement in postcolonial criticism, which is likewise engaged in distancing itself from a reductionist and missionary identity politics, in order to approach visions of hybridization, cultural syncretism, and multiple identity (Appiah and Gates Jr., 1995; Hall, 1990, 1996; Gilroy, 1993). Perhaps paradigmatic is Stuart Hall's identification of the shift from an essentialist notion of "the" Black experience as a singular and unifying framework toward what he calls a positive conception of "the ethnicity of the margins, of the periphery." Hall charts a transformation from a "mimetic" or expressive towards a constitutive or "formative" notion of the representation of Black culture, which puts an end to innocent accounts of an essential Black subject, and registers blackness as principally a constructed category that lacks transcendental or transcultural fixity (1996: 442–43).[3] This also implies that issues of race always appear historically in articulation with other categories and divisions and are constantly crossed by categories of class and gender. We are all ethnically located; but this insight calls precisely for a politics of ethnicity that is predicated on difference and diversity (Hall, 1996: 447, 465ff.).

In analyzing and evaluating recent standpoint analytics, I presently focus upon its recapitulation of a theme which is directly inherited from its classical left-wing and right-wing predecessors: that of *marginality, outsidership,* or *strangerhood.* Indeed, the trope of marginality, and of the redemptive and promissory character of the condition of alienation, has been equally intrinsic to the Marxian analysis of alienated labor and the missionary role of the class "with radical chains," as it has informed right-radical spokespersonship for the oppressed and humiliated people or race—namely the descriptions of France or Italy as a "proletarian nation" by the national syndicalists in the decade before World War I, or the similarly missionary alienation that was attributed to the German *Volk* after the war in its "darkest hour" of military defeat and economic depression. This recurrent topos of alienation, and of the redemptive privilege of outsidership and marginality, remains a persistent and magnetic theme across the entire history of standpoint theory and only gains in visibility and pertinence in its present-day elaborations. This is evident in the ubiquitous feminist references to woman's position and life experiences as those of a generic "stranger," "outsider within," or "resident alien," which supposedly generate a "bifurcated consciousness" or "double vision" that offers a privileged view of male-dominated society (cf. Smith, 1988; Harding, 1991; Collins, 1991; Bar On, 1993; Wolff, 1995). Hall's earlier-cited conception of an "ethnicity of the margins" indicates that postcolonial theory is similarly attracted to metaphors of "dislocation" and "in-betweenness," and to the epistemological virtues of "double consciousness" in a "third" or "hybrid" location (cf. Hall, 1990, 1992; Said, 1990; Bhabha, 1993; Gilroy, 1993).

Departing from their primary anchorages in class, gender, or race, and shedding all residues of "last instance" thinking, recent standpoint theories thus tend to converge upon a generalized discourse of marginality—which to some extent is defined *against* the standpoints with which they originally began. This is already a marked feature of neo-Marxist standpoint theorizing, which has in various (revisionist) ways said "farewell to the proletariat," and in the process, has gradually eclipsed the materialist criterion of nonpropertied, *alienated labour* in favor of a more flexible accentuatic n of *alienation as such*—a move that is variously illustrated by Fanon's idea of the "wretched of the earth," Sweezy's notion of the "substitute proletariat," Marcuse's high expectations about various "fringe groups," and Gorz's view of the postindustrial "non-class of non-workers" (see Pels, 2000: 27ff.). This decentering movement is equally discernible in modern feminist and postcolonial conceptions. Harding's writings, for example, have increasingly shifted between the idea to "start thinking from *women's* lives" and the more general admonition "to start thinking from *marginal* lives" (e.g., 1991: 125, 150; 1992: 581). The marginality of the "outsider within" has become a powerful topic in the Black feminism of, for example, Lorde (1984), hooks (1984), and Collins (1986, 1991). Haraway's ironic myth of the cyborg, a hybrid creature that transgresses all conventional boundaries and fractures all traditional identities, perhaps offers the most radical expression of this epistemological trend (Haraway, 1991).

Black cultural studies exemplify a similarly generalized metaphorics of displacement and alienation. Gilroy, for example, stylizes the Black experience in terms of a Black Atlantic diaspora, in which Black particularity is situated and constituted simultaneously inside and outside of Western culture. The concept of diaspora (which is modelled after Jewish experiences of dispersal) and its satellite metaphors of hybridity, homelessness, and exile are offered against the continuing obsession with absolutist conceptions of a timeless and totalized ethnic subjectivity, which disregard internal divisions in terms of class, gender, sexuality, age, or political consciousness. Against such roots- and rootedness-oriented conceptions, Gilroy associates the Black experience of modernity with "the standpoint of dislocation," and prefers to view identity as a process of movement and mediation, as a "changing same" (Gilroy, 1993).

This convergent theme of the "outsider within" who enjoys "double vision" establishes a powerful epistemological point, which might even be taken as the enduringly relevant "summary" of standpoint theory in its various historical manifestations. What standpoint theories ultimately seem to offer is a more general or abstract *social epistemology of the stranger* rather than a more concrete and particularized epistemology of class, gender, or race; an epistemology of diversity or multiplicity rather than of singular identity; of the double consciousness of "crossover" identities, rather than the single and stable consciousness of "taking responsibility for one's roots." In this sense, the theme of the stranger handsomely resonates with classical sociological conceptions about the advantages of a "third" position, as for example found in Simmel's remarks on the objectivity of the stranger's versus the native's gaze, or in Mannheim's argument about the visionary capacities of a free-floating intelligentsia that finds itself sociologically remote from *both* the dominant *and* the dominated classes in contemporary capitalism. Innovatory, rule-breaking knowledge is perceived as a function of marginality, of the location of the "outsider within," in all domains of social and professional life; an insight that can profitably be generalized beyond the more particular identifications espoused by Marxism, feminism, and antiracism.

An intriguing point about this generalized epistemology of strangerhood, as already intimated, is that this secondary identity must be partly secured *against* the primary affiliations of class, gender, or race with which it is initially defined as continuous; in all three cases, it tends to break up their supposed homogeneity and closure and kills residual claims about ontological priority. The "class trouble" that infected classical Marxism has presently spread to feminist "gender trouble" and postcolonial "ethnicity trouble," proliferating an excess of difference that creates a more generalized "difference trouble" (Seidman, 1995). Marxism's historic farewell to the working class is now vigorously copied in analogous farewells to Womanhood and Negritude. This threefold suspension or even dissolution of previously substantial figurations of identity has also triggered a systematic dilution of the determinative significance (the imputed sociological weight) of such primary situations for any credible conception of situated knowledges. Indeed, the epistemological salience of the primary determinations of class, gender, and race can only be rescued by way of recasting the various bearers of social identity (proletarians, women, or Blacks) as generically estranged from the dominant social and political order. But in principle, the stranger's condition focuses a more abstract and remote social situation—not so much a location but a *dis*location—since (s)he suffers and benefits from the cross-fertilization of views that arise in (and between) disparate experiential contexts. The stranger, by being partially estranged from his or her primary

identity, occupies a "standpoint against standpoints" (or an identity "in between" identities) that exceeds any preferential combination of elements from
the classical trinity of identity/difference.

A social epistemology of strangerhood, by focusing this second-order standpoint and its epistemological effects, hence also (strangely?) returns us to an
element of the traditional transcendental view of knowledge that standpoint theories have historically risen against. Indeed, while holding on to the principle
that knowledge is positionally determined and contextually relative, it simultaneously helps to recover the fruitful core suggestion of the rationalist ideal:
that knowledge, in order to be interesting or creatively new, must be relatively
context-*free*, must be able to rise above and transgress its primary situatedness.[4]
The pregnant suggestion of an epistemology of strangerhood is to delineate
a specific social situation that mediates between the "view from nowhere" of
the celebrated unitary and universal subject, and the politicized and particularized "view from somewhere" that is canvassed by traditional standpoint
epistemologies of the primary kind. It is the stranger who somehow embodies
and preserves the ancient philosophical promise of transcendence and distanciation; but (s)he simultaneously remains intensely place-bound, committed,
interested, and partisan. The stranger moves across contexts and encompasses
them in double vision; but this location is never a universal one that commands
a totalizing view. (S)he does not float above interests, but embodies a different
interest. There is no universal mediation, no shifting in and out of all conceiv-
able situations, in order to become once again the "nowhere (wo)man," but
a spatially and temporally bounded migration or switch between *two or three*
contexts or lifeworlds, in a third space that stretches somewhere in between the
local and the global.[5]

The Metonymic Fallacy of the Intellectuals

At this point, I like to introduce a second theme, which intriguingly spins around
and resonates with the theme of marginality and suggests a more critical balance of what standpoint epistemologies have to offer. Like the first theme, it
highlights a secondary location of the situated knowledge subject that to some
extent remains ensconced behind primary proletarian, female, or Black identifications. Also like the first, it focuses an identity and a "difference trouble" that
is embarassingly *common* to various standpoint theories, although it normally
remains silenced and suppressed. This secondary social persona is that of the
spokesperson or the ("organic") *intellectual*. All major variants of standpoint
epistemology confront a "spokesperson problem" that arises from the fact that
standpoints do not simply exist in the real world in order to be "recognized
for what they are" or "taken responsibility for" (cf. Rich, 1986: 219); all standpoints need to be *spoken for* in order to become constituted as standpoints in
the first place. Identities cannot simply be adopted as deep structures or natural
kinds, but must be attributed, constructed, and performed; they need to be

intellectually filtered and processed. This intellectual work of performance and construction is usually not taken into full reflexive account by the constructors themselves, who are easily seduced to "take on" a substantialized identity aligned with a larger emancipatory cause and that enables them to hide their secondary will to empowerment behind the supposedly primary one of a particular class, gender, or race. This *pars pro toto* identity play might be described as the "metonymic fallacy of the intellectuals."

Feminist standpoint theory, in consciously borrowing the architecture of Marxist epistemology, also tends to recapitulate some of its basic cognitive dilemmas. Proletarian theory was in a revealing sense a standpoint theory of its intellectual spokesmen, who hid behind the broad back of the proletariat in order to receive its historical grace for their own sense of revolutionary mission. More concretely, it was an expression of the standpoint of *marginal* intellectuals, revolutionary critics out of place with and resentful against the established bourgeois order, who tended to appropriate and construct a primary ontological identity by adding some salient characteristics, which in fact more readily reflected their own secondary one. As a result, the "really existing" historical proletariat was embellished (or burdened) with properties of intellectuality (a superior view) and marginality (a class with radical chains, a revolutionary class) that virtually guaranteed its self-transformation from a class "in itself" into a fully conscious class "for itself," which was firmly motivated to pull off its preordained historical mission. But of course, this historical mission was ordained first of all by the revolutionary intellectuals themselves; the "standpoint of the proletariat" was first of all their own; even while the proletariat was acclaimed as the primary agent of the socialist revolution, it was *theory* (and *theorists*) that operated as such by inventing, constructing, and representing its historically "necessary" standpoint. From its inception, therefore, proletarian standpoint theory was caught in a vicious circularity and a self-abnegating intellectualism.[6]

Feminist standpoint theory, insofar as it has extrapolated the Marxian epistemological structure, appears caught in a similarly circular conflict between primary and secondary identities, offering similar opportunities for an identity swap and for the resultant "absent presence" of intellectual spokespersons. The Marxist slippage between proletarians and intellectuals is repeated in terms of a similar metonymic transcription from the broad category of "women" to the more restricted one of feminists—who are usually intellectuals (and more often than not, also marginal ones). As in classical Marxism, this secondary identity is tendentially repressed, even though it is feminist critical theory that exclusively claims to define the situational interests and strivings of women in the first place.[7] Like the proletariat, which Marxists picture as the collective stranger in capitalist society, women are perceived by feminists to be collectively estranged from patriarchal or male-dominated society. But once again, such characteristics appear more readily ascribable to a small political elite or intellectual vanguard than to the represented constituency as a whole. Indeed, if feminist standpoint arguments are investigated more closely, it turns out that it is not so much the contradictory or marginal location of women as such, but precisely that of the female feminist *thinker* that is deemed to offer epistemological advantages. It is her peculiar intermediate condition of an outsider within, her distinct position of marginality *in the center* and the double consciousness induced by it, which is taken metonymically to reflect the standpoint of the "class" of women as a whole.

As in other critical projects of emancipation (nationalism not excepted), one identity is emphasized as primary while another one is held back. The frontstage identity (womanhood, whiteness or blackness, class or national affiliation) is invariably mediated by and processed through the backstage identity of intellectual spokespersonship. Usually also a self-consciously *marginal* identity, it dictates and projects a number of characteristics (of intellectuality and marginality), which structure the larger categories of class, nation, gender, and race that it undertakes to speak for and represent. In this fashion, marginal intellectuals create a false shadow of themselves, an ontological double that enables them to align their critical claims with a broader historical force and a more compelling sociological reality than their own.

Perhaps the rules of this mistaken identity play may be further spelled out by drawing a formal distinction between three epistemological positions. The *first* and *second* positions together define the dualistic field of contest identified by the various critical theories: bourgeois versus proletariat, male versus female, white versus Black (in generalized form: dominant versus dominated, or established versus outsiders). The critical theories invariably assume that it is advisable to depart from the standpoint of the latter in order to attain a more reliable view of the structure as a whole: to the view from below is attributed better epistemological vision than the view from the center. However, by emphasizing the contest between the first and second positions, the critical theories tend to silence a *third* position, which is the position from which they themselves speak (cf. Pels, 2000: 214–18). This third position is not only marginal vis-à-vis the powerful center, but also marginal (although to a lesser extent) vis-à-vis the situation of the powerless or dominated themselves. This is why Bourdieu identifies intellectuals as "dominated dominants," and insists that their positions are perhaps homologous but not identical with those of the dominated (Bourdieu, 1991: 243–45; 1993a: 43–45; 1993b: 44–45). Critical intellectuals indeed find themselves in a contradictory social location, because they identify with the oppressed but simultaneously take their distance from their unmediated experiences of oppression. Marginal standpoints by themselves do not suffice; they must be intellectualized, pass through theory, which evidently requires the guiding presence of the professionals of theory themselves.

Among feminist cultural theorists, it is perhaps Haraway who is most acutely aware of the intellectualist tendencies that engender such metonymic idealizations. Her work on cyborg feminism also marks the most prolific shift from the idea of primal, innocently centered identities towards metaphors of estrangement, heterogeneity, and hybridity (see Prins, 1995). Although she sets a premium on establishing the capacity to see "from the peripheries and the depths," Haraway also cautions that there is "a serious danger of romanticizing and/or appropriating the vision of the less powerful while claiming to see from their positions." To see from below "is neither easily learned nor unproblematic, even if we 'naturally' inhabit the great underground terrain of subjugated knowledges." While such standpoints seemingly promise more adequate accounts of the world, "*how* to see from below is a problem requiring at least as much skill with bodies and language, with the mediations of vision, as the 'highest' techno-scientific visualizations" (1991: 191). The standpoints of the subjugated are never innocent; they do not provide immediate vision. Subjugation is not sufficient grounds for an ontology; it might at most be a "visual clue." . . . "Identity, including self-identity, does not produce science; critical positioning does, that is, objectivity" (1991: 192–93). This requires one to seek points of view that are mobile and perspectives that are unexpected and extraordinary, which do not express fixed identities but require split and contradictory selves who can critically interrogate such positions. The promise of critical objectivity is not found in the subject position of identity, but in "partial connection," in the joining together of partial views (1991: 195).[8]

Whose Science? Whose Knowledge?

Sandra Harding's work arguably represents the most comprehensive and lucid expression of modern feminist standpoint theory and may hence be most informative about its generic strengths and difficulties. As in previously cited examples, Harding's writings feature an ubiquitous and inclusive "we" that permits a systematic elision between the broader category of "woman" and the narrower one of "feminist," that is, the feminist scientist or intellectual; her self-identification as an "outsider within" is also transcribed into a larger ontological marginality of women as such. The gap between the two identities and positions is characteristically bridged by means of critical theory and political struggle: women's experiences, although they provide an initial standpoint that promises a less partial and distorted perspective on male-dominated society, must be informed and corrected by feminist theorizing and feminist political engagement in order to create truly critical perspectives. Women's experiences, or the things women say, do not in themselves provide reliable grounds for knowledge claims. They may be good places to *begin* research, but cannot adjudicate which knowledge claims are preferable. Experiences may lie to us, and must therefore pass through the lenses of feminist theory; overcoming this spontaneous experiential consciousness is often a painful process of "second birth." In this sense, standpoint theory differs from an "ethnoscience" or an "identity science" project (Harding, 1991: passim; 1992: 582–83; 1995: 343–44).

The feminist standpoint hence projectively recasts the ontological condition of women as an experience of marginality that critically invalidates traditional categories of (scientific) knowing. Whereas "androcentric" epistemologies conventionally define the scientific habitus as one of dispassionate, disinterested impartiality, or as a concern with abstract principles and rules, what it means to be a woman is to be emotional, to be interested in the welfare of family and friends, and to be concerned with concrete practices and contextual relations. Because women are assigned the care of bodies (including men's) and of the localities where bodies exist (houses, offices, etc.), because they take up the care of young children and are more generally occupied with emotional work, they natively resist theories that tear knowledge from its social, sentimental, and partial contexts and describe it as transcendental and disinterested (Harding, 1991: 47). Women are, as such, "valuable strangers" to the social order, while men remain natives whose life patterns and ways of thinking "fit all too closely the dominant institutions and conceptual schemes." This alienation offers unique epistemological advantages, although once again it is feminist *theory* that must intervene in order to *teach* and *adjudicate* what is strange:

> Because women are treated as strangers, as aliens—some more so than others—by the dominant social institutions and conceptual schemes, their exclusion alone provides an edge, an advantage, for the generation of causal explanation of our social order from the perspectives of their lives. Additionally, however, feminism teaches women (and men) how to see the social order from the perspective of an outsider. . . . Feminism teaches women (and men) to see male supremacy and the dominant forms of gender expectations and social relations as the bizarre beliefs and practices of a social order that is "other" to us. (Harding, 1991: 125)

The corrolary of this strategic interposition of theory (and theorists) is that the constitutive principle of standpoint theory about the causal link between being and consciousness or objective position and subjective positioning is effectively reversed.[9] There remains a critical (and fully exploitable) ambiguity about the notion of the standpoint as a category of lived experience and of "being positioned," or as a wilfully achieved category of identi-*fication* and position-*taking*. Indeed, it is in all respects (feminist) theory that constructs and validates experience and effectively dictates how "to see strange." As in the Marxist parable of the proletariat, one assists at a curious reversal of terms: while the (class, gender, racial) standpoint is taken as point of departure of objectivity claims, it is to all effect the claim itself, the correct (proletarian, feminist, antiracist) consciousness, which defines and validates the standpoint. Standpoints need spokespersons in order to be constituted as such; it is their representational work that ultimately defines the situation for situated knowledges.

In a distinct sense, therefore, theory also *liberates* from standpoints: the correct consciousness opens up the correct standpoint, even if one "naturally" occupies an incorrect one. Theory provides an alienative methodology, a procedural code of distanciation, which is in principle accessible for all subjects of rational or emancipatory goodwill. Once again we are returning full circle to the methodological voluntarism that standpoint theory started out to combat. According to Harding, "thinking from the perspective of women's lives" makes strange what appears familiar, which is "the beginning of any scientific inquiry." Actually, however, such thinking must start in the lives not just of outsiders but of outsiders *within* (or feminist intellectuals), who are better placed to detect the relationship between outside and inside or margin and center (1991: 131–32, 150, 289; 1993: 65–66). It is they who actually occupy epistemically resourceful contradictory positions ("a woman thinker is a contradiction in terms") and may therefore exploit the frictions and dissonances that arise between their disparate experiences. The "monster problem," which is usually phrased in terms of the supposedly incongruous identities of male feminists or white antiracists (cf. Jardine and Smith, 1987; Harding, 1991: 274–75), is perhaps more internal and "visceral" because it marks a variably suppressed identity conflict of female or coloured intellectuals themselves. Indeed, whose science, whose knowledge is at stake here?

Like Marxist intellectuals such as Althusser, who claim the ability to *become* "proletariat" by adopting *theoretical* proletarian standpoints (1993: 229–30), feminist thinkers effectively suggest that one may turn into a stranger by thinking differently (Harding, 1991: 289). In principle, therefore, it is not necessary to have lived the experience of oppression in order to understand other oppressed identities or to generate what Harding calls "traitorous" analyses. Rather than marking out existentially given positions, the "traitorous" or "disloyal" social locations that Harding wishes (us) to occupy, are largely a matter of conscious engagement and self-education. Traitorous *locations,* one might say, are actually traitorous *agendas* (cf. Harding, 1991: 292), which can be methodically adopted, learned, and generalized beyond the scope of any specific primary social identity. Consciousness is decisive, not situation or place. Knowledge, or critical thought, may in principle emancipate itself from all situational determination. It is this vicious circularity and voluntarism that ultimately turns standpoint theory inside out and closely approximates the conventional transcendental view that it originally set out to criticize. If marginality is so much a matter of theoretical and political choice, the radical epistemological impulse of standpoint thinking is effectively eradicated.

The Reflexive Spokesperson

All three markings in the holy trinity of social identification (class, gender, race) invite gestures of idealization resembling Machiavelli's own somewhat deceptive claim as a "man of the people" (more nearly, of course, as a representative of the intellectual bourgeoisie and of the "popular" party) to be able "to understand properly the character of rulers." The three standpoint theories tended to maintain this intellectualist posture in their converging drift toward a more abstract epistemology of strangerhood. In attributing epistemic privilege to a

generalized condition of outsidership, they pictured it as ontologically continuous with the primary subject positions of workers, women, and people of
color, while surreptitiously identifying the more ambiguous situation of the
"outsider within" (i.e., of proletarian, female, or ethnic intellectuals) as the
proximate embodiment of such privileged estrangement. A first-order identity
swap is thus overhauled by a second-order one: the intellectual, while no longer
exclusively posing as authentically (organically) proletarian, female, or Black,
now also acts as a generalized stranger, pooling the hermeneutic advantages of
all three marginal identities in a new dream of "being everywhere" (cf. Bordo,
1990: 135–36).

Theories about situated knowledge, in sum, are likely to suffer from a vicious circularity resulting from their efforts to derive objectivity claims from
ontological situations that must first be defined as real before such claims can
be contextually situated. The presumed "last instance" determination of proletarian, female, or Black life experiences simultaneously conceals and justifies
the "first instance" domination of theorists who *intellectualize* the worker, the
woman, or the Black person and in a secondary movement, also intellectualize
the condition of marginality collectively attributed to them. In this fashion, the
social determination of knowledge claims ultimately dissolves into a certain free-
floating voluntarism of marginal intellectuals who are unwilling to calculate the
interests and advantages that define their specific *inter-esse* or "in betweenness."
The "outsider within" perspective, toward which the various standpoint theories interestingly gravitate, hence still underestimates the "monster problem" of
critical, emancipatory intellectuals who prioritize their class, gender, or racial
identities above their identities as marginal intellectuals and, in doing so, erase
the inequalities that separate them from the groups with which they politically
and emotionally identify. Arguably, this secondary identity is less welcome because it is partly shared with the enemy (i.e., with his organic intellectuals) and
as such inevitably transsects and dilutes the stark Manichean polarizations of
male and female, Black and white, or bourgeois and proletarian, which nourish
political correctness and a defiant psychology of war.

If our purpose, then, is to preserve standpoint theory's kernel suggestion
about the structural connection between marginality and creativity, we need to
incorporate the performative logic of spokespersonship and the second-order
marginality of intellectuals more intensely and reflexively into standpoint theory
itself. Instead of denying the specific "treason" that inevitably accompanies their
"translation" of social identities, marginal intellectuals need more definitely to
acknowledge the force fields that structure their specific role as strategic inter-
mediaries between social movements and the academy. This requires a more
precise demarcation between the condition of *alienation,* which situates the
intellectual outsiders as "dominated dominants" in the social field, and that
of *oppression* or *exploitation,* which describes the situation of the dominated
tout court, which many variants of standpoint theory easily tend to conflate.

Subjugation, Haraway rightly presumes, is not sufficient grounds for a critical ontology; instead, oppression and exploitation normally invite the quite contrary reactions of particularism, closure, and apathy. This requires a novel recognition of intellectual elites as special groups, whose distinctive ambitions engage them in productive, "consciousness-raising" tension with their primary constituencies in a form of reflexive elitism that counts on their *interested interaction* rather than *disinterested identification* with the "masses" they claim to represent.

What, finally, does this reflexive radicalization of positional thinking imply for the celebrated connection between marginality and conceptual innovation, which I have identified as the enduring "proceeds" of standpoint theory in its various historical manifestations? In answering this question, we may recollect a distinct ambiguity in the original Machiavellian metaphor of the landscape painter who, unlike peoples and princes, may freely move between low and high places in order to collect a comprehensive picture of the natural landscape. The first part of the metaphor expresses the conventional idea (which is also encountered in Mannheim) that positional objectivity is enhanced through the complementarity and synthetic reworking of various partial perspectives. The second part, however, implies that such free exchanges are unlikely to occur between high and low places in the *social* pyramid and that the spectral logic of the standpoint must acknowledge a principled dispersion of perspectives and the impossibility of their full totalization. It is unclear, moreover, to what extent Machiavelli presumes symmetry of epistemic resources between the people and the Prince, or rather anticipates an asymmetric claim such as the Marxist one, which, while dismissing as absurd any idea of free circulation among the class positions of bourgeoisie and proletariat, would nervously resists any suggestion that, if one needs to become "proletariat" in order to know "capital," perhaps one also needs to be "capital" in order to know the "proletariat." Machiavelli's balance between the epistemic powers of people and Prince may well express the ambition of the self-styled "man of the people," if not to *become* a prince himself, then at least to become *closer to* the prince as an advisor to the throne who commands a more comprehensive view of the political landscape than his sovereign master.

Sen has argued that, notwithstanding the parametric dependence of observation and inference on the position of the observer, objectivity may still be enhanced because different persons can occupy the same position and confirm the same observation, while the same person can occupy different positions and make dissimilar observations: observational claims can be both position-dependent and person-invariant (Sen, 1993: 126, 129). More radical standpoint theories, however, rightly object that such person-invariance and positional transcendence are socially unlikely and that, in a hierarchically structured society, you cannot see everything from everywhere, and that class-, gender-, or racially defined social experiences yield partial perspectives on the social world that cannot easily be totalized from any one of these perspectives. Positional parameters or markings of social difference differ dramatically to the extent that they operate closures and install boundaries that prevent individuals from crossing over to other places in the social universe. While Machiavelli's landscape artist may travel from low to high, the people and the Prince do not change seats so willingly or easily. The only "changeling" in the social world, who is forced into transcendence of place and is able to view trans-positionally, is the marginal person or "outsider within," who, like Machiavelli, undertakes to mediate between low and high or between margin and center. Not a "nowhere (wo)man" or universal subject, but not a firmly rooted and particularized subject either, the "outsider within" holds a place between places and embodies an interest that mediates other interests. This enables him/her to operate local transcendences, take third positions, and forge partial connections, which together delineate the small measure of synthesis and objectivity still available in the chronic "war of positions" waged in the social world.

Notes

1. I shall not dwell here on the exquisite parable of Tiresias, the blind seer, who lived seven years as a woman and seven years as a man—which triggers a welter of suggestive thoughts about the logic and limits of standpoint theory.

2. Some of the arbitrariness of this claim is suggested by Nietzsche's view (representing a broader elitist tradition) that there is better vision from the top (from the dominant *Herrenmoral*) and an urge to falsify from the standpoint of deferent and reactive "slave morality." Nietzsche also unearths and criticizes the false identity play of "ascetic" intellectuals posing as "the people" (Nietzsche, 1996).

3. Compare the parallel expressions in Butler, whose performative theory of gender familiarly focuses upon the politics of representation, arguing that gender attributions are not expressive but performative, and that political signifiers such as "woman" operate as performative rather than representational terms (1990: 141; 1993: 208–10). See also Seidman on homosexuality and queer theory, who registers that among the consequences of the constructionist questioning of essentialist (sexual) identities has been "the loss of innocence within the gay community" (1995: 139). Cf. also Mohanty (1995) and other contributions to Nicholson and Seidman (1995).

4. In choosing the path of the stranger, we may also escape the constraints of an overly *collectivist* sociology of knowledge (cf. Mannheim, 1968: 3–4, 25–29; Harding, 1991: 59; Collins, 1998: 3–7), which insufficiently acknowledges that innovative knowledge is often created *in estrangement from or opposition to* group beliefs and group values. Once again, this is a strong point of traditional individualist epistemology; it also calls for a more serious consideration of the *psychology of knowledge* (in the venerable tradition of Stirner, Nietzsche, and Freud) to complement and complete one-sided sociological approaches. This is effected not so much by reinstating the cognitive over against the social, but by theorizing the standpoints of marginal individuals.

5. At first sight, this may seem close to Bauman's view that universality arises out of estrangement and that "the standpoint of the exile is the only cognitive determinant of universally binding truth" (1991: 84). In my conception, however, the stranger cannot be universalized in this manner, since (s)he precisely escapes the traditional opposition between the "immaculate conception" of the transcendental subject and the immediate transposition of particularity into universality which is undertaken by traditional standpoint theories.

6. On this intrinsic circularity of standpoint theory, see more extensively Grant (1993) and Prins (1997).

7. This slippage between "woman" and "feminist intellectual" is also evident in Smith (1988: 52, 58, 86). See also Kristeva's somewhat hysterical intellectualization of

experiences such as pregnancy and maternity and her depiction of woman as generically dissident and "exiled," in a text that explicitly treats of the emergence of a new
type of *intellectual* (1986: 296–98). Compare Lukács's view that "historical materialism grows out of the 'immediate, natural' life principle of the proletariat; it means the
acquisition of total knowledge of reality from this one point of view. But it does not
follow from this that this knowledge or this methodological attitude is the inherent or
natural possession of the proletariat as a class (let alone of proletarian individuals). On
the contrary..." (1983: 21).

8.   Other criticisms of the "intellectualist fallacy" from within feminism itself include
De Lauretis (1990: 121–22), Alcoff and Potter (193: 14), and Mohanty (1995: 71, 74).
Mohanty targets what she calls the "feminist osmosis thesis," which declares that "females are feminists by association and identification with the experiences which constitutes us as female," so that feminism is a mere effect of being female rather than a
highly contested political terrain where "we cannot avoid the challenge of *theorizing*
experience." Grant points to the same gap and tension: "if 'woman' and 'feminist' were
the same thing... women could speak for themselves and would not have to be spoken
for in elaborate academic discussions" (1993: 115).

9.   In more recent work, Harding has explicated that, although each of us occupies a
determinate location in the matrix of social relations and oppressions, that location
does not determine one's consciousness (e.g., 1995: 345).

References

Alcoff, Linda and Elizabeth Potter. (1993). "Introduction: When Feminisms Intersect Epistemology." In idem (eds.), *Feminist Epistemologies*. New York and London: Routledge.

Althusser, Louis. (1970). *For Marx*. New York: Vintage Books.

———. (1993). *Écrits sur la psychanalyse: Freud et Lacan*. Paris: Editions Stock/IMEC.

Appiah, Kwame Anthony and Henry Louis Gates Jr. (1995). "Editor's Introduction: Multi-
plying Identities." In idem (eds.), *Identities*. Chicago and London: The University of
Chicago Press.

Bar On, Bat-Ami. (1993). "Marginality and Epistemic Privilege," pp. 83–100. In Alcoff and
Potter (eds.).

Barrès, Maurice. (1902). *Scènes et doctrines du nationalisme*. Paris: Émile-Paul.

Bauman, Zygmunt. (1991). *Modernity and Ambivalence*. Cambridge: Polity Press.

Bhabha, Homi K. (1993). *The Location of Culture*. New York and London: Routledge.

Bordo, Susan. (1990). "Feminism, Postmodernism, and Gender Skepticism," pp. 133–56. In
Linda Nicholson (ed.), *Feminism/Postmodernism*. New York and London: Routledge.

Bourdieu, Pierre. (1991). *Language and Symbolic Power*. Cambridge: Polity Press.

———. (1993a). *Sociology in Question*. London: Sage.

———. (1993b). *The Field of Cultural Production*. Cambridge: Polity Press.

Butler, Judith. (1990). *Gender Trouble: Feminism and the Subversion of Identity*. New York and
London: Routledge.

———. (1993). *Bodies That Matter: On the Discursive Limits of "Sex."* New York and London:
Routledge.

Collins, Patricia Hill. (1986). "Learning from the Outsider Within: The Sociological Significance of Black Feminist Thought." *Social Problems* 33,6: S14–S32.

———. (1991). *Black Feminist Thought*. New York and London: Routledge.

Collins, Randall. (1998). *The Sociology of Philosophies: A Global Theory of Intellectual Change*.
Cambridge, MA: Harvard University Press.

De Lauretis, Teresa. (1990). "Eccentric Subjects: Feminist Theory and Historical Consciousness." *Feminist Studies* 16,1: 115–50.

Gilroy, Paul. (1993). *The Black Atlantic: Modernity and Double Consciousness*. London: Verso.

Gouldner, Alvin. (1985). *Against Fragmentation: The Origins of Marxism and the Sociology of
Intellectuals*. New York: Oxford University Press.

Grant, Judith. (1993). *Fundamental Feminism*. New York and London: Routledge.

Hall, Stuart. (1990). "Cultural Identity and Diaspora," pp. 222–37. In Jonathan Rutherford
(ed.), *Identity: Community, Culture, Difference*. London: Lawrence & Wishart.

———. (1992). "The Question of Cultural Identity," pp. 273–316. In Stuart Hall, David Held,
and Tony McGrew (eds.), *Modernity and Its Futures*. Cambridge: Polity Press.

————. (1996). *Critical Dialogues in Cultural Studies.* Ed. David Morley and Kuan-Hsing Chen. London: Routledge.

Haraway, Donna. (1991). *Simians, Cyborgs, and Women.* London: Free Association Books.

Harding, Sandra. (1991). *Whose Science? Whose Knowledge?* Milton Keynes: Open University Press.

————. (1992). "After the Neutrality Ideal: Science, Politics, and 'Strong Objectivity.'" *Social Research* 59,3: 567–87.

————. (1993). "Rethinking Standpoint Epistemology: What is 'Strong Objectivity?'" pp. 49–82. In Alcoff and Potter (eds.).

————. (1995). "'Strong Objectivity': A Response to the New Objectivity Question." *Synthese* 104,3: 331–49.

Hartsock, Nancy. (1983). "The Feminist Standpoint," pp. 283–310. In Sandra Harding and Merrill B. Hintikka (eds.), *Discovering Reality.* Dordrecht: Reidel.

hooks, bell. (1984). *Feminist Theory: From Margin to Center.* Boston: South End Press.

Jardine, Alice and Paul Smith. (1987). *Men in Feminism.* New York and London: Routledge.

Kristeva, Julia. (1986). "A New Type of Intellectual: The Dissident," pp. 292–300. In Toril Moi (ed.), *The Kristeva Reader.* New York: Columbia University Press.

Lorde, Audre. (1984). *Sister Outsider.* Freedom, CA: The Crossing Press.

Lukács, Georg. (1983). *History and Class Consciousness.* London: Merlin Press.

Machiavelli, N. (1988 [1513/32]). *The Prince.* Ed. Q. Skinner and R. Price. Cambridge: Cambridge University Press.

Mannheim, Karl. (1968). *Ideology and Utopia.* London: Routledge and Kegan Paul.

Mohanty, Chandra Talpade. (1995). "Feminist Encounters: Locating the Politics of Experience," pp. 68–86. In Nicholson and Seidman (eds.).

Nicholson, Linda and Steven Seidman (eds.). (1995). *Social Postmodernism: Beyond Identity Politics.* Cambridge: Cambridge University Press.

Nietzsche, Friedrich. (1996 [1887]). *On the Genealogy of Morals.* Oxford: Oxford University Press.

O'Meara, Dan. (1983). *Volkskapitalisme: Class, Capital, and Ideology in the Development of Afrikaner Nationalism 1934-1948.* Cambridge: Cambridge University Press.

Pels, Dick. (2000). *The Intellectual as Stranger: Studies in Spokespersonship.* London and New York: Routledge.

Prins, Baukje. (1997). "The Ethics of Hybrid Subjects: Feminist Constructivism According to Donna Haraway." *Science, Technology, and Human Values* 20,3: 352–67.

————. (1997). "The Standpoint in Question: Situated Knowledges and the Dutch Minorities Discourse." Ph.D. Thesis, University of Utrecht.

Rattansi, Ali. (1995). "Just Framing: Ethnicities and Racisms in a 'Postmodern' Framework," pp. 250–86. In Nicholson and Seidman (eds.).

Rich, Adrienne. (1986). "Notes towards a Politics of Location," pp. 210–31. In *Blood, Bread, and Poetry: Selected Prose 1979–1985.* New York and London: W.W. Norton & Cie.

Said, Edward. (1990). "Reflections on Exile," pp. 357–66. In Russell Ferguson et al. (eds.), *Out There: Marginalization and Contemporary Culture.* Cambridge, MA: The MIT Press.

Schmitt, Carl. (1935). *Staat, Bewegung, Volk.* Hamburg: Hanseatische Verlagsanstalt.

Seidman, Steven. (1995). "Deconstructing Queer Theory, or the Under-theorization of the Social and the Ethical," pp. 116–41 in Nicholson and Seidman (eds.).

Sen, Amartya. (1993). "Positional Objectivity." *Philosophy & Public Affairs* 22,2: 126–45.

Smith, Dorothy. (1988). *The Everyday World as Problematic.* Milton Keynes: Open University Press.

Wolff, Janet. (1995). *Resident Alien: Feminist Cultural Criticism.* Cambridge: Polity Press.

Wright, Richard. (1965). *The Outsider.* New York: Harper & Row.

IV

Modern or Postmodern? Natural or Only Social Sciences?

Introduction

Are standpoint projects constructivist, rejecting the realism that both modern sciences and effective political movements are said to require? Or are they realist, rejecting a postmodern constructivism that some take to be so damaging to both founding assumptions of empirical research and to progressive political action? Do standpoint projects enable oppressed groups to "author" their own consciousnesses and political agendas, as their defenders claim? Or do they leave these embedded in cultural discourses outside of agents' control? Do they center new kinds of subjects of knowledge and history, or do they decenter them in a kind of standpoint pluralism, or perhaps even chaotic fragmentation? Do they invest in a totalizing, unitary history and rationality, or do they abandon such investments to a debilitating epistemological and ethical/political relativism? Are standpoint approaches suitable, at best, for only the social sciences, or can they also provide empirically, theoretically, and politically valuable approaches to natural science research? What is the relation of standpoint theory to post-positivist philosophy and social studies of the natural sciences?

Readers may reasonably think it rather late in the plan of this reader to be raising such questions; almost every one of the essays here from the late 1980s on finds such issues irresistible. Donna Haraway, Kathi Weeks, and Susan Hekman, to mention just three, have taken up explicitly the modernism/postmodernism issues in their essays here, and Rose, Haraway, and Harding have directly addressed the value of standpoint projects for the natural sciences. Virtually every author has explicitly or implicitly engaged critically with the still prevalent Enlightenment philosophy of science and its methodological directives. Yet it seemed worthwhile to draw attention to this feature of standpoint controversies by focusing one section on standpoint theory's relation to the modernism/postmodernism debates and to the natural sciences. These two sets of issues are strongly linked, whether or not those who address them overtly acknowledge such connections.

Some commentators have seen some standpoint theorists—such as Haraway and Harding—as simply confused insofar as they appear to weave together what are regarded as modern and postmodern elements in their writings. Other commentators, and some of the standpoint theorists themselves, insist that

291

standpoint theory is clearly a reformation, a strengthening of modernist tendencies. Another group is equally firm that it is clearly postmodern. Several of the essays here and earlier insist on refusing the choices posed so starkly in the questions above and instead note the way standpoint projects can effect a negotiation (which is different from a compromise!) both between and beyond modernist and postmodernist projects (see, e.g., the essays by Sarah Bracke and María Puig de la Bellacasa [chapter 24] and by Kathi Weeks [Chapter 13]). García Selgas (chapter 23) sees it, and especially Haraway's arguments for situated knowledge, as providing a solution to challenges postmodernism has raised for the field of Critical Social Theory. Political theorist Nancy Hirschmann shows how it provides a valuable postmodern strategy.

Indian physicist and environmental activist Vandana Shiva and German sociologist Maria Mies point to the "subsistence perspective," or what they elsewhere refer to as the "survival perspective." This can be produced if one starts out thinking from the standpoint of women, the environment, and peasants about the effects of the conceptual framework of Third World development policies on these three. The subsistence perspective substitutes interests in learning to live within nature's capacities for the familiar preoccupations with dominating nature. Mies's and Shiva's critical target is not only the first world political agendas that shape Third World development policies, but also the complicity of Western sciences and technologies with the de-development and maldevelopment that are the widespread result of such policies. Western philosophy of science is grounded in false assumptions about nature and social relations.

Meanwhile, philosophers Alison Wylie and Joseph Rouse locate feminist standpoint theory (and, in Rouse's case, elements that this theory shares with other strands of feminist epistemology) in the context of contemporary postpositivist philosophies and social studies of science. Feminist standpoint theory advances those fields in ways that the latter have failed to recognize. In part these advances are to be found in the way it negotiates through and past the modernist/postmodernist debates.[1]

Thus standpoint theory has seemed to provide an important terrain on which to locate reflections about leaving and/or reclaiming the Enlightenment, the strengths and limitations of realism and constructivism in the natural and social sciences, what could provide a satisfying substitute for the universal rationality that has earned so much contemporary skepticism, and other challenges postmodernism has raised to familiar Western assumptions.

Note

1.   See also Mark Elam and Oskar Juhlin, "When Harry Met Sandra: An Alternative Engagement After the Science Wars," in *Science as Culture*, vol. 7, no. 1 (1998), pp. 95–109, and Donna Haraway, *Modest_Witness@Second_Millennium:.FemaleMan_Meets_OncoMouse*™. (New York: Routledge, 1997), pp. 36–37.

23

Feminist Epistemologies for Critical Social Theory: From Standpoint Theory to Situated Knowledge

FERNANDO J. GARCÍA SELGAS

> If sociology cannot avoid being situated then sociology should
> take that as its beginnings and build it into its methodological
> and theoretical strategies.
>
> —D. Smith (1987:91)

Part of a broader research project on the conditions of possibility of Critical Social Theory in postmodernity, this paper will argue that some feminist epistemologies are one of the main sources to solve the crucial problems that we see nowadays in any kind of Critical Theory. Let me introduce three preliminary clarifications that frame this paper.[1]

1. Instead of Critical Theory, I will discuss Critical Social Theory (CST from now on) for two main reasons. First, remember that not only the Frankfurt School, but also other forms of Western Marxism are behind us. Authors such as Th. Veblen, C. Wright Mills, or many followers of F. Nietzsche and M. Foucault are also part of our past. As a consequence, I will appeal to a wider notion of critical theorizing, but not just any notion will do. A qualified attempt must try, first, to know and transform social structures or dynamics of domination, according to certain norms or values. Second, it must underline that we want to retain the idea of a scientific social theory: we look for a Social Theory that is critical. Our problems here are in fact the implications for critical thinking of some more general scientific problems.

2. In order to explore the possibilities of CST, we should examine current social and cognitive conditions. The former might be given by the connection to a social movement, and feminism could be one of the candidates. The latter might require an available epistemology. Only the latter, the epistemological or metatheoretical problems, will be our concern here. For this reason we have to step back from daily political

293

urgencies in order to further explore the very conditions of possibility of a scientific, critical, social theory. For example, we have to put aside well-known controversies about the difficult relations among feminism, Critical Theory, ethics, and postmodernity (Benhabib et al., 1987, 1995). To move within an epistemological level of inquiry, however, does not mean to forget that epistemology is a social and political issue.

3. Feminist epistemology (FE from now on) will be my candidate for solving these problems and, in this sense, a new source for CST. However, I do not consider any kind of FE, only those strands able to address the general postempiricist questions informing the social sciences. And my choice does not exclude other important candidates for the same job, such as certain developments of science studies (e.g., actor-network-theory) or cultural studies (the works of F. Jameson).

Facing Problems, Envisioning Solutions for Critical Social Theory

Traditional CST has been constructed around a historical development (supposedly) leading towards emancipation. This historical development, in turn, required several elements such as a general narrative, an image or idea of normative reference (utopia), the possibility of a rational ordering of the world, and the actions of a certain chosen subject. All these requirements or assumptions can be summed up into the three main assumptions of modern social science, that is, the assumed existence of the centered subject (creative, responsible, active), the universal reason (cosmic order, eventually captured by rational scientific work), and general history (as an ordered chain of events).

1.1   The crucial problem is that, one by one, these basic modern assumptions were subject to a process of breakdown, which we do not have space to recall here. The epistemologies and cognitive strategies they feed are no longer useful beyond their own reproduction. As a consequence, CST is facing not only the general withering away of its main assumptions, but also some more specific problems. For example, when considering the decentering of the subject, we could easily think of the construction of new and different subjectivities, a process in which feminism has played a key role. Instead, however, we should focus here on how the subject (consciousness) loses its capacity for impartial knowledge or evaluation and how we could establish a kind of "distance."

Let's remember just two facts at this stage. Ethnomethodological and poststructuralist studies have shown the textual nature of social reality. With this insight the scientific subject moves from the center of discourse production to the side of its byproducts. Feminist and postcolonial critics make it impossible to equate objective knowledge to analytical distance and heroic asceticism, as a liberal perspective proposes. Without any distance between subject and object, modern scientific knowledge looks deeply damaged. But things can get even worse in the case of critical tasks. While most critical traditions assume the so-called *"critical distance"* as a necessary condition for critique, the confusion between object and subject roles erases such a distance. The modern, that is, Kantian, foundation of critique on the subject-object opposition does not work anymore.

When we still shared an idea of a general historical development we had a way of ordering and differentiating things, roles, and natures. But now we are dealing with an intensified process in the opposite direction. F. Jameson, as early as 1984, claimed that the new space of consumer postmodernity was bringing together vanguard and popular esthetics and subsuming the economical under the cultural—from exchange value to sign value, as Baudrillard put it. The *implosion of dichotomies* and categories is a problematic, epistemological consequence of this narrative disorder.

We have been discussing different realms of reason, even different reasons, such as practical, pure (or theoretical), and esthetical reasons. In any case, the loss of universality produces the absence of a common frame of reference (of values, truth criteria, or esthetic cannon), which is the essence of *relativism*. The very same practice of distinguishing values from facts, private from public, was another way of feeding a kind of relativism. The center of our worries, however, will be cognitive relativism, understood as the partiality of any kind of knowledge, reason or perspective and the absence of privileged perspectives.

1.2   Any attempt to develop a CST needs some way of dealing with the three basic and specific problems mentioned above, while the old modern assumptions of subject, reason, and history are no longer useful as such. My take in the debate is that certain FE developments, facing the lack of a clear position/distance for CST, as well as the relativism in the air, have made their way through those bad times. By following some of the paths they have opened, we will be able to articulate epistemic conditions for CST.

I do not want to forget feminist critiques of scientific androcentrism, like studies proving the sexist use of science or the sexist selection and definition of problematics (Harding, 1986: 20–24). However, we start from the moment when FE moves from an internal correction of the scientific (universal) method to a postempiricist epistemology, in which there are no neutral or innocent methods, values, or beliefs. Because all of these are directly connected to social experiences and interests, it does matter who the subject of knowledge is and where s/he stands.

In this context, certain strands of FE have built criteria for claiming the best possible connection with social experience, the best possible knowledge and critical position/distance. This is the starting point of the movement that lies at the center of this paper: the plea for a privileged feminist standpoint. Our work will consist of following feminist standpoint theory from its arguments to empower specific epistemic positions, over the articulation of and the mobility between those positions, to the final transformation of that epistemic theory in a kind of a postmodern epistemic condition of possibility for CST. I do not intend to present a critical examination of FE in general nor feminist standpoint theory in particular. Rather, I will show that if we follow this theory, as an epistemology of transition to a postempiricist and postmodern vision of situated knowledge, we will be able to deal with crucial contemporary problems of CST such as relativism or lack of critical distance.

The Primacy of Some Standpoints

A range of different arguments exists for the primacy of a feminist standpoint. I will start from D. Smith's argument, rather than N. Hartsock's or any other possible candidate.

2.1 D. Smith assumes a phenomenological approach to sociology—a mode of discovering society from within in order to offer everybody knowledge of the social organization and determination of her/his direct experience—and a radical break between men's and women's worlds (1987: 85, 92). We can summarize her ideas in four complementary statements. Not only that women are "alienated from their experience," but also that sociology, as an administrative tool and a perspective from the top, "is part of the practice by which we are all governed," she claims (1987: 86). Second, "the institutions which lock sociology into the structures occupied by men are the same institutions which lock women into the situations in which they find themselves oppressed. To unlock the latter leads logically to an unlocking of the former" (ibid.). In the third instance, she points out that the same institutional procedures and processes that take everyday life out of sociology also omit women's experiences and sociology's own relation to its material conditions. Therefore women sociologists suffer "double estrangement" and a bifurcated consciousness (1987: 89–91). In a fourth step, however, Smith affirms that women's conditions render their position into a privileged one for the recovering of sociology: "making her direct experience of the everyday world the primary ground of her knowledge" she can relocate sociology where it already stands but denies. She can thus return to sociology's real aims of emancipation. Smith privileges women's standpoint because this reorganization of sociology "does begin from the analysis and critique originating in their [women's] situation" (95).

The main advantage of Smith's argument is that she considers women's experience as a starting, but not an ending or exclusive point (1987: 95). This important and cautious claim resulted from a couple of epistemological facts that should be remembered because, with them, we leave unnecessary inheritances behind and we begin to collect elements to feed our critical endeavor. One central element of Smith's argument lies in the (first) fact that women sociologists were, at the same time, (women) alien characters in the abstract works of scientific discourse and also (scientists) people who work at the center of those discourses and assume one universal position, which is not theirs. These contradictory locations and identities were a source of problems and suffering, mainly for feminist scientists, but were also the source of their privileged position. Using the powerful language of P. Hill Collins we can say: "the marginality that accompanies [that] outsider-within status can be the source of both frustration and creativity" (1991: 233). The *"outsider-within"* privileged status seems to be a result of both the claims by feminist movements for a voice and the radicalization of feminist science critiques. While the former began as a kind of identity politics of knowledge, it ended with the contradictory identity of scientific women and their outsider status (Harding, 1991: 272–75). The latter was the refusal of the idea that, by using pure scientific methods like, for example, the random repetition of experiments, knowledge could lose all its social fingerprints. As in the case of unquestioned suppositions, their dominant culture-wide assumptions could not be identified, unless we examine them from an outsider's point of view.

When an outside and contradictory experience is the clue for the privileged critical position, one has to double-check the location and materiality of that experience. Such a movement, however, also questions the unity of women's experiences and deals with the difficulty of articulating experiences that, besides being contradictory, could also be distorted by the dominant order. This is our second epistemic fact: women's experience could not be accepted without critical considerations; we need political struggles and theoretical feminist developments to articulate a common feminist standpoint. There are different women's standpoints, and some are feminist but some are not. The critical construction of a feminist standpoint would soon come to imply the articulation of different experiences and social positions. It would have to take into account, first, different women's lives and positions, and, subsequently, different feminisms and the question of whether all of them were a good location in which to start research. In sum, when FE remains attached to the idea that the outsider's perspective helps to bring objectivity in and to the consideration of the social preconditions of dominant conceptual schemes, it concludes that marginalized lives help to look into those preconditions and to take responsibility for one's own position (Harding, 1991: 283; 1998: 154).

2.2   Marginal standpoints enable FE to deal with internal differences. Their epistemic utility goes beyond the expansion of our knowledge by way of complementing scientific method and being aware of the cultural nature of the science that is expanding our knowledge. Crucial in this respect is that the cognitive privilege of marginalized lives turns "institutionalized power imbalances" into a lever to get "stronger objectivity" and to make "institutionalized power and its effects" visible (Harding, 1998: 141, 159).

In our search for a critical position or distance, this is a very important movement. It takes us from the differences within women's lives and feminisms—already a break with monotheistic foundations of knowledge or critique—to a kind of multicultural source of that power/knowledge inversion in "strong objectivity"[2] which is a way out of ethnocentric privilege of a single (here women's) culture.

The movement out of (feminist) ethnocentrism could be a definitive departure from epistemologies internal not only to bourgeois culture, but also to the modern West. The outside locations and differences that provide privileged positions for (critical) scientific knowledge, says Harding (1998: 149), are not only "*politically* assigned locations in social hierarchies, such as those created by class, racism, imperialism, or sexism," but also "*culturally* created locations, such as Chinese versus Puerto Rican, or Confucian versus Catholic." She argues that "different cultures' knowledge systems have different resources and limitations" and only from other cultures' perspectives can the shared cultural assumptions be made visible and an object of critique, which in turn would be an argument to state that cultures' knowledge systems "are not equal, but there is no single possible perfect one, either" (ibid.). As a result, we have a kind of polyphony of different cultural, social, and political privileged positions.

2.3   If visions from below, or from outside, appear to be better starting positions for CST, what happens with the question of relativism? Let's face three inconvenient facts. First, the vision from below is not simple but problematic, even for those that inhabit it. The subaltern's standpoint is not innocent; it has to be criticized and reexamined. That is why Harding claims that the ground of standpoint does not support "identity science projects" (1993: 63). Furthermore, it has been, and it is, possible for some people of dominant positions (like Marx) to think from other positions. The advantage of marginalized lives is that they provide a fresh and more critical starting point. They provide the problems and the agendas, but not the solutions. The danger lies in the double temptation of romanticizing those lives or becoming external spokespersons for them.

Second, we need to establish that not every position, even every marginalized position, has the same cognitive value. We have already dealt with facts like the partiality of those vantage views: they are grounded in specific social interests—therefore they cannot be impartial—and they see from somewhere—thus they cannot be total nor universal, even though they are claimed as the best. This partiality entailed a kind of cognitive relativism. Against both this relativism and the opposite universalistic positions, Harding asks: "equally or universally good for what? for getting to the moon? for sustaining fragile environments, or democratic social relations?" (1998: 162). Her final answer is that the workers' position is the best in critical research on class relations, while the position of slaves is the best in ethnic studies, and women's position in gender studies (ibid.). But where are the shared standards for comparing different views? asks S. Heckman (1997: 353–55). And how can we claim epistemic privilege for a marginal group that is not, at the same time, at the center of some social system (like proletarian within capitalist production), wonders Bat Ami (1993: 86–89).

Third, we can ask where visions from below get their critical character or will? Is it from their location on the losing side in a relationship of domination, like gender domination? But why should the transformations sought by the dominated be more progressive or better than the changes the dominant might implement! If the answer is because "we are in favor of the dominated," we slide into (moral) relativism, where the will of the dominant has the same value and well-intended power/knowledge positions might develop into the dangerous situation of "talking for others."

Mobile Positioning

FE takes a great step out of relativism and the dangers of ventriloquism when it allows for (men's) mobility into different (feminist) standpoints. That is the reason why Harding made an early acknowledgment of men's contributions to feminist thought (1987). To prevent men's misuse of feminism, however, Harding took a strong precaution: Women should, like any other oppressed group, have the *last word*. They will use their own experience "as the test of adequacy of the problems, concepts, hypotheses, research design, collection, and interpretation of data"; and they will check that "the researcher or theorist places himself in the same class, race, culture, and gender-sensitive critical plane as his subjects of study" (1987: 11).

To what extent can we move from one's own standpoint to another one is the question here. Let's recall three more developed ways of supporting men's feminism—first, a moralist one, in two steps. If feminists do not learn how to think out of the lives of marginalized locations other than gender—such as women of color, working class, etc.—they will develop kind of a "self-interest of dominant-group women" for white women, not much different from dominant men. If white academic women can and should learn to think from all those others standpoints, then why cannot men learn to think from a feminist standpoint? (Harding, 1991: 284–85).

The second argument runs like this: feminist standpoint is not a natural or unique perspective, it does not flow spontaneously from women's experience, and it has to be fought for and theoretically constructed. With the same basic fights (against androcentrism and patriarchy) and learnings (from feminist accounts and insights) men can begin their thought in/from women's lives (Harding, 1997b: 184–85).

The third argument is based on the fact that social (unequal) relations and arrangements became naturalized in such a way that the experience of the dominant groups becomes the "common sense." In this sense, we can argue that our experience lies to us, even more in the case of members of the dominant groups, and that there is not one particular form of human experience to become a feminist. One needs, says Harding, "to learn to overcome—to get critical, objective perspective on—the spontaneous consciousness" (1991: 287). From different locations, and through a more or less "painful process," everybody can walk in this direction.[3]

Behind these three arguments lies a strong tension between the hard and traditional arguments for a privileged standpoint (i.e., having the last word, being the one to judge) and the need for mobility out of one's own standpoint.

This tension shows that the mobility between different standpoints entails a softer concept of a standpoint—from the "last word" to a kind of a "native speaker"—and a "painful" displacement of one's own position.

3.1   The idea of women's experience as the native reality can be found in early arguments for feminist standpoint primacy.[4] The question is whether this "native clause" means a strong frame of reference ("last word") or just the initial but not final reference for CST.

P. H. Collins's influential book (*Black Feminist Thought*, 1991) argues that any thought starting from a Black woman's standpoint needs to have Black women's experiences and consciousness *"at the center."* Other groups cannot produce Black feminist thought without African American women. In other words, they will always require a *collaborative enterprise* with Black women. Harding also agrees with this spirit when she claims that the project of members of the dominant groups starting from, and collaborating with, marginal people "requires learning to listen attentively to marginalized people; it requires putting one's body on the front line for 'their' causes until they feel like 'our' causes. . . ." (1993: 68).

In a sense, it is like a collaboration of a foreign linguist and a native speaker, where in the end some agreement must be achieved. In another sense, it is more than that, because at stake is not just a code, a way of communication, but an entire world-view, a form of life, and social/power relations. While we can leave the existence of "one last word" behind, the metaphor of the "native speaker" is not enough either.

3.2   Arguments for standpoint mobility have brought under consideration not only that privileged standpoints are neither static nor essential, but also the painful consequences for the agents involved. Once more, Harding points out some of these consequences or conditions for the mobile agent of feminist (or "other liberatory movements") standpoints: i) They "must be multiple and contradictory" (1991: 284), because different and even conflicting women's cultural forms, thoughts, or knowledges exist, each of them with their own multiple and contradictory commitments; ii) they "must also be the subject of every other liberatory knowledge project . . . if feminism is to be emancipatory for marginalized women but also if it is to be maximally scientific for dominant-group women about their own situation" (1991: 285), in other words, they must search for affinities; and iii) they "cannot be the unique generators of feminist knowledge" (1991: 286) because the generation of knowledge by men about themselves and the world from the perspective of women's lives creates (like a "distant present") a broader context and a contrasting perspective.

The emerging figure is one of a conflicting, collective, fragmented, mobile, and different agent of knowledge. It confirms that, in order to rebuild conditions of possibility for CST, we must redefine its more basic elements. But it also strongly confirms that we are in the middle of a hard, difficult, and painful process.

Harding (1991) uses the image of "traitorous identities" to summarize those consequences/conditions. With "traitorous identities" she means those who were trying to relocate themselves in their own situation, but with a redefined experience that in some aspects goes against what should be their experience. They can neither become what they are not, (e.g., women for men) nor can they just see or think as others do (191: 289), precisely because knowledge is situated. Nor can they go on constructing their experience in the same old way that obscures their own privileges. They try to know, as first-hand as possible, what their (racist, sexist) world is and "how one sees it through a critically reflective, but still white [or men's], consciousness" (289). A "traitorous identity" is a deep logical, epistemological, and psychological tension, if not contradiction. It alienates the CST agent from her-himself, from her/his theoretical home, or from her/his "natural" perspective. Like a stranger at home, s/he will wander like a nomad, not only in the (Nietzschean) desert of values and frameworks of fixed reference, but also in the hallways of her/his own thought.

The agent of mobility between standpoints is not a strong self, a free-willing liberal intellectual (Mannheim), but a kind of new "subject" of knowledge that we should define or find. In this sense, if we connect the implications of "traitorous identities" with the already explained critical appraisal of women's experiences and facts indicated by the existence of feminist men who nonetheless remain within dominant positions,[5] then not only neutrality but also innocence and uniformity disappear from privileged standpoints. And this is another departure from the modern foundations of CST.

Standpoint Theory, an Epistemology of Transition

In her most recent work,[6] Harding questions what we consider as "natural" epistemic questions. For example, the incommensurability among cultures, paradigms, or standpoints is confronted with the facts that scientists do move from one paradigm to another and that there are translations and conversations between different cultures. The search for universal standards to determine better or privileged standpoints is confronted with the fact that we do not need them and that they perhaps have never existed except in the minds of some Western thinkers. The very idea of epistemic foundation itself is given up by an interconnected support between main epistemic concepts: antirelativism depends on the existence of privileged standpoints; standpoint privilege on the idea of "strong objectivity" and mobility; mobility on antirelativism; "strong objectivity" on a play of outside-inside; etc. (Harding, 1998: 141, 157–61).

Harding aims at studying how some (feminist) scientific research actually succeeded. She proposes to double-check any question that "naturally" rises in our discourse; probably because our "natural" discourse is temporally (modern) and spatially (Western) situated, and we are entering another "situation."

Our intuition becomes stronger when we study what we could call standpoint theory's second wave, presented to a general public in a well-known 1997 *Signs* issue. We do not need to go back to the two new major influences in this second wave, for example, poststructuralism and postcolonial studies, with their emphasis on the constructed nature of a standpoint and a social agent, and on the responsibility implied in our choices. Instead, we will just look at how this second wave links the fight against relativism to political (critical) engagement. When standpoint theory turns the differences between standpoints into a tool for greater objectivity, it claims a kind of knowledge that is neither essentialist (standpoints are constructed and mobility among them is necessary) nor relativist (it privileges marginalized standpoints). Subsequently, such a notion of knowledge becomes difficult to reconcile with the will to place the critique of dominant relations at the center of a privileged standpoint (and of any scientific project accordingly developed), without giving in to the strong temptation of intellectualism or to the perplexities of "self-transformation."

Some critics of standpoint theory point out that there is a contradiction between classical standpoint theory and the thesis of mobility between different standpoints: we should choose between the "materialism" of the former and the "idealism" of the latter. Choosing mobility, however, would imply falling into the idealist or intellectualism temptation. Other critics understand concepts such as "outsider-within," "mobility," or "dual vision" as strategic movements by feminist intellectuals in order to get constituted as the real privileged group instead of women or other marginalized groups (Pels, 1996: 73–79).

Such readings, however, forget that we have already been in motion. They do not see that the modern dichotomies they are based on are no longer justified. Mobility is not about "free-floating intelligentsia" but about the bodily, discursive, and material transformations of agents. There is no third position between external and internal (native) observers: there is no innocent or unpolluted gaze, all is constructed and changing. The consequences of feminist standpoint theory are neither privileged identities nor spokespersons for marginalized standpoints, but privileged and problematic knowledge situations for CST.[7]

Thus self-transformation is not only relevant for our general argument, but also for theoretical practices. Every standpoint is a "critically and theoretically constructed discursive position" (Harding, 1998: 17). Moving to a different standpoint than the one we are socialized in requires changing our own standpoint—linked to our own identity (1998: 67–68)—which both hurts (1998: 293) and entails a critical attitude. This painful self-transformation is much easier to see and study when we move to situated knowledge epistemology, where there is no "natural standpoint." This is true, for instance, concerning standpoint epistemology's pleas for a reflexive knowledge taking into account not only the consequences but also the current social situation of scientist and research projects, and what others, mostly the subaltern, think and say about all this (Harding, 93: 70–71). This "robust reflexivity" goes against the andro-centric and Eurocentric construction of the self (Harding, 1998: 193), which is very deeply located inside Western (especially male) thinkers. In the case of most northern scientists, the self-transformation standpoint epistemology is asking for is a kind of "clinical change" that is closer to situated knowledge epistemology.

If we recall, for instance, the initial standpoint theory's positions and the issues and changes we have being witnessing in the concept of experience or in the idea of subject-position,[8] we can summarize this journey by saying that standpoint is an epistemology of transition through the swamps of modern epistemology breakdown. Its port of call is situated knowledge epistemology, which has already provided important arguments and ideas for a nonmodern epistemology for CST, namely ideas about experience (De Lauretis, Haraway), the subject (Butler, Flax), the power/knowledge process and articulations (Haraway, Fox Keller), etc.

From Standpoint Theory to Situated Knowledge Epistemology

Political in nature and postmodern at birth, situated knowledge epistemology is neither innocent nor modest. [It has basic or general agreements with standpoint theory, such as an extended belief in the cultural, for example, local and historical; embeddedness of any scientific project, the fight against both universalism and relativism, the will to retain some modern scientific ideas and practices as a powerful instrument of control over our lives, and an important political arena.]

Beyond basic agreements, we find clear continuities, especially since standpoint theorists have come to share some critiques and issues put forward by postmodern thinkers.[9] With the end of innocence—an expressive title of J. Flax's work in 1992—and the acknowledgment of diversity within women's experiences, they only need to embark on the interrogation of the search for the last foundation of knowledge, as Harding already has done, finally to assume most postmodern challenges, such as the relationship between a fragile and transforming agent of knowledge and a much needed reflexivity. Jumping into situated knowledge epistemology is easier than ever, with the help of D. Haraway, who wrote the founding manifesto: "Situated Knowledge" (1988, now in 1991), originated as a commentary on Harding's *The Science Question in Feminism.* With her, we can incorporate and improve standpoint epistemic tools into situated knowledge epistemology.

Feminist standpoint theory today uses, more than its initial Hegelian view of history, varied research concepts and strategies, such as "the outsider inside" or "strong objectivity," to assure epistemic privilege for a critical, feminist standpoint. However, these concepts and strategies entail several problems that can only be worked out if we see these concepts as transitions to a new or different epistemic horizon. For example, Harding speaks of "strong objectivity" as the central device to use the dominant power/knowledge relations not only for social critique, but also as a program for better or more objective knowledge (98: 18–19, chap. 8). However, we find that "strong objectivity," perhaps because of its partial connection to the modern notion of objectivity, has several problems in achieving those aims. It retains a negative vision of objectivity, because, beyond the identification and recommendation of certain knowledge sites, objectivity seems a way of identifying and erasing inconvenient constraints to our vision. Moreover, it testifies to a kind of "oversocialization" of the notion of objectivity, because the only producers of objectivity would be subjects, and more specifically the researchers' community. The whole idea could even be read as a mere extension of the Popperian view of objectivity as the intersubjective implementation of the "scientific method."

We can get rid of the negativity and "oversocialization" in "strong objectivity" if we place its (social-formal) logic in the (material-discursive) logic of "embodied objectivity" (Haraway). We cannot continue to search for some kind of quality (objectivity) that will assure better knowledge claims (no relativism) and better knowledge positions (critical distance), because we always need some place to hang that quality—a place like a centered subject or a homogeneous collectivity (like women). In the end, without any steady hanger, the solution is worse than the initial problems.[10] Hence, it is better to look for a social, material, and fictional entity like situated knowledge, where we can see and experience how meaning and body join together in the so-called human nature and how vision can be considered as social and carnal embodiment. Of course, these transformations in the concept of objectivity, now filled with flesh and blood, entail different qualifications for our idea of knowledge: it is neither universal nor relative; it will always be partial and responsible. That means the end of "innocent politics of identity" and strong transformations in our idea of the subject of knowledge.

Rather than subjects, we will talk of agents of knowledge, who are embodied, social and meaning positions, nonisomorphic and moving among diverse narrative territories. When knowledge agents are fragmented and multidimensional, mobility is assured and connectivity is needed more than ever. Here we find a new reason for the possible privilege of subalterns' standpoints: they need connections and the coming together of different standpoints, and they will fulfil this condition better than the dominant (but also fragmented and multidimensional) standpoint. Identities are thus not only constructed and performative, but also impossible to reduce to a single social marker of oppression (gender, race, or class) because these markers are variously interlocked.

Important changes in our concept of the object of knowledge are inevitable. Situated knowledge, as a postmodern epistemology, has to deal with a dangerous drive to make of everything a code, a language, a narrative, a system of meanings, etc. Therefore Haraway claims a "real" or not totally discursive object ("body," "world") with power to intervene as an "actant" (a semiotic-material actor) in the production of knowledge (1991: 250, n.11). For her sciences or "accounts of a 'real' world do not, then, depend on a logic of 'discovery,' but on a power-charged social relation of 'conversation'" (1991: 198). It is easy to see how this noninvasive epistemology can give us a better pool of epistemic devices for CST than discovery logics or apostolic wills.

All these three basic transformations—a diverse and fragmented subject, a partial and responsible knowledge process, and an active and even ironic object—are a radical departure from modern epistemic tradition. While the latter has been built on the Enlightenment aim of bringing light to the hidden nature of objects, instead we are talking about a conversation with nature where there are no primary and secondary qualities (Latour versus Locke).[11]

Something similar happens with the idea of responsibility. Such an agent shows that responsibility—already a necessary implication of the partial and limited nature of embodied objectivity—is basic in a conversational knowledge production. Moreover, it is intertwined with the pragmatic hermeneutics inherent to every negotiation or translation between different positions.[12]

Responsibility is not only an important and basic feature of situated knowledge epistemology against the scientific tradition of uninterested practice, but it is also a space and a style of confluence with most of today's practices of political resistance, deployed by heterogeneous social movements. While these have nothing external and fixed to ensure their emancipatory character, as Laclau and Mouffe argue (1985), they do have to be responsible for everything they do. In both cases we can find privileged positions or standpoints but none of them will ever be innocent or beyond critique.

Critical Social Theory Epistemic Problems and Feminist (Dis)solutions: The Journey Continues

Some feminist thinkers, in their search for a "successor science project"—inheriting the modern science will to offer the best possible account of the world—have found their work historically situated in a complex and fragmented (postmodern) world. Their hard, sometimes contradictory, and ongoing journey has been opening doors and paths to (dis)solutions for some of the main epistemic problems of current critical, social theories.

It has not been a bed of roses. While it started by claiming a privileged position over all, which was perfect against relativism, it came to realize that "all" meant just (white) men's standpoint. In their second wave, these feminist thinkers learned to live with difference and multiplicity inside the assumed unique standpoint. This was, however, not enough. In the final instance, an epistemology of radical situatedness and of multiple and decentered subjects was needed—an epistemology without innocence.

From the beginning, however, the journey from modern feminist standpoint to postmodern situated knowledge epistemology has been very fruitful. It was, for example, useful to act on the basis of a kind of internal realism for a while, as if relativism were an outside (of feminism) problem. This was like taking a breath. And I hope standpoint theory's best contribution will stay with us for a long time in the way it uses the power/knowledge imbalance as a critical and scientific device to improve our "objectivity."

Throughout this journey we have been following some theoretical movements that, rather than accumulating elements and devices making it easier to deal with the CST problems we pointed to at the beginning, have taken us to a different and even opposite view of those problems. The implosion of dichotomies is finally assumed, deployed, and put to work, because the real problem was not in the dissolution of the dichotomies but in the unjustified will of keeping alive a radical opposition between subject and object, nature and culture, etc. Relativism, as the equal value of any position remains questioned, but now, redefined as partiality, it becomes an epistemic device. Distance—critical or whatever—is not wanted but questioned as false innocence, unreal, and a source of domination. Instead of distance, positioning is claimed as a way of bringing in clarity, responsibility, and the search for affinities.

While we could be a little more precise, this is only a start toward a situated knowledge epistemology for CST. And the journey goes on and on.

Notes

1. This paper has been inspired by a series of conversations with Sandra Harding (UCLA, 1999), made possible by her unique generosity and kindness. I also received financial support from the Del Amo Foundation (University Complutense of Madrid). I am grateful as well for the comments received at the Social Theory Research Committee's conference (Cambridge, UK, summer 2000) and for the editing work of Sarah Bracke and María Puig de la Bellacasa.

2. "Strong Objectivity" is presented as "a program for stronger standards for objectivity [that] draws attention to the sociological or historical relativism of all assumptions and knowledge claims ... [but] rejects the epistemological or judgmental relativism that assumes that because all such assumptions and claims have local, historical components, there is no rational, defensible way to evaluate them" (Harding, 1998: 18–19).

3. Smith, for example, stated that re-organizing sociology "begins from the analysis and critique originating in women's situation" (1987: 95). But not in exclusiveness, she said, because women are in the same position as native speakers for a linguist; they can be asked.

4. The latter seems to be the case when Harding states that feminist research starts from women's experiences in order to define what is important, what is a scientific problem: "it is *women* who should be expected to be able to reveal *for the first time* what women's experiences are" (1987: 7). But the former is the case when the same author claims that priority of women's voice makes men the least likely group to be able to detect whether their own beliefs or actions are feminist (1997b: 173, 180).

5. Feminist men, says Harding "can work to eliminate male supremacy, but no matter what they do, they will still be treated with the privilege (or suspicion!) accorded to men by students, sales people, coworkers, family members, and others" (1998: 161).

6. S. Harding's *Is Science Multicultural?* (1998), and in several discussions at UCLA (spring–summer 1999).

7. We should not forget that changes in feminist standpoint theory go hand in hand with deep general transformations in the role of intellectuals. Postmodernity, says Z. Bauman (1994), means a general crisis of intellectuals.

8. Remember how Smith's and Hartsock's arguments for the advantage of women's knowledge position are grounded in women's closer situation to material and everyday life, not on women's capability of making universal or abstract claims. Or remember that, according to Harding the subject becomes visible, heterogeneous, communitarian, and so on (1993: 63–65).

9.   Second wave standpoint theorists are now closer to accomplish what Ashende sees (1997: 54–58) as the main current tasks of any reborn or postmodern sociology. I mean, standpoint theory has begun questioning its own innocence, working on the contested constitution of identities, and assuming differences and power/knowledge relations in its own constitution.

10.   In addition, we cannot ignore important arguments and studies, such as the actor network theory, that propose a return to an old notion of objectivity as the manifestation or intervention of the object itself (Latour, 2000: 115–16).

11.   Instead of conversation Harding speaks of "co-constructivism" as the interaction between subject and object in the production of knowledge (1998: 11) and the relationship between cultures and their knowledge systems (1998: 20).

12.   "So," says Haraway, "science becomes the paradigmatic model not of closure, but of that which is contestable and contested. Science becomes the myth not of what escapes human agency and responsibility in a realm above the fray, but rather of accountability and responsibility for translations and solidarities linking the cacophonous visions and visionary voices that characterize the knowledges of the subjugated" (1991: 196).

References

Ashenden, S. (1997). "Feminism, Postmodernism and the Sociology of Gender." In D. Owen (ed.), *Sociology after Postmodernism.* London: Sage.

Bar On, Bat-Ami. (1993). "Marginality and Epistemic Privilege." In L. Alcoff & E. Potter (eds.), *Feminist Epistemologies.* London: Routledge.

Benhabib, S. & D. Cornell (eds.). (1987). *Feminism as Critique.* Cambridge: Polity Press.

Benhabib, S., J. Butler, D. Cornell & N. Fraser. (1995). *Feminist Contentions.* London: Routledge.

Bauman, Z. (1994). "Is There a Postmodern Sociology?" In S. Seidman (ed.), *The Postmodern Turn: New Perspectives in Social Theory.* Cambridge: Polity Press.

Chodorow, N. (1978). *The Reproduction of Mothering: Psychoanalysis and the Sociology of Gender.* Berkeley: University of California Press.

Collins, P. H. (1991). *Black Feminist Thought: Knowledge, Consciousness, and the Politics of Empowerment.* New York: Routledge.

Flax, J. (1992). "The End of Innocence." In J. Butler & J. Scott (eds.), *Feminists Theorize the Political.* London: Routledge.

Haraway, D. (1991). *Simians, Cyborgs, and Women.* London: Routledge.

Harding, S. (1986). *The Science Question in Feminism.* Ithaca: Cornell University Press.

Harding, S. (1991). *Whose Science? Whose Knowledge?* Ithaca: Cornell University Press.

Harding, S. (1993). "Rethinking Standpoint Epistemology: What Is 'Strong Objectivity?'" In L. Alcoff & E. Potter (eds.), *Feminist Epistemologies.* London: Routledge.

Harding, S. (1997a). "Comment on Hekman's 'Truth and Method: Feminist Standpoint Theory Revisited'." *Signs,* vol. 22, no. 2.

Harding, S. (1997b). "Can Men Be Subjects of Feminist Thought?" In T. Digby (ed.), *Men Doing Feminism,* New York: Routledge.

Harding, S. (1998). *Is Science Multicultural? Postcolonialisms, Feminisms, and Epistemologies.* Bloomington: Indiana University Press.

Harding, S. (ed.). (1987). *Feminism and Methodology: Social Science Issues.* Bloomington: Indiana University Press.

Harding, S. & M. Hintikka (eds.). (1983). *Discovering Reality: Feminist Perspectives on Epistemology, Metaphysics, Methodology, and Philosophy of Science.* Dordrecht: Reidel.

Hartsock, N. (1983). "The Feminist Standpoint: Developing the Ground for a Specifically Feminist Historical Materialism." In S. Harding & M. Hintikka (eds.), *Discovering Reality.* Dordrecht: Reidel.

Hekman, S. (1997). "Truth and Method: Feminist Standpoint Theory Revisited." *Signs,* vol. 22, no. 2.

Jameson, F. (1984). "Postmodernism—the Cultural Logic of Late Capitalism." *New Left Review* 146.

Laclau, E. & C. Mouffe. (1985). *Hegemony and Socialist Strategy: Towards a Radical Demoratic Politics.* London: Verso.

Latour, B. (1992). "Post scriptum: un giro más después del giro social." In *Ciencia en Acción*. Barcelona: Labor.

Latour, B. (2000). "When Things Strike Back: A Possible Contribution of 'Sciences Studies' to the Social Sciences." *British Journal of Sociology*, vol. 51, no. 1.

Pels, D. (1996). "Strange Standpoints." *Telos* 108.

Rose, H. (1986). "Women's Work: Women's Knowledge." In J. Mitchell & A. Oakley (eds.), *What is Feminism? A Re-Examination*. New York: Pantheon.

Smith, D. (1987). "Women's Perspective as a Radical Critique of Sociology." In S. Harding (ed.), *Feminism and Methodology*. Bloomington: Indiana University Press. (Originally published in 1973.)

24
Building Standpoints[1]

SARAH BRACKE

MARÍA PUIG DE LA BELLACASA

A Ground of Tensions

... We hope to show that the feminist discussions around the conceptualizations of standpoint theory, and its constant reformulation by those involved in the debates, express a liveliness, cultivated through feminist practices of theory, that perpetually challenges theoretical dichotomies, in particular modern/postmodern oppositions. Indeed, we see feminist knowledge politics as a collective endeavor and feel that the theoretical efforts to express its singularity are often ill-treated by our modern academic attitudes, "polemic" by tradition. As academics, we have been raised as "modernists" because we are supposed to *show that we know better* than those who came before us.[2] As *feminist* academics we feel we ought to resist this modernist attitude because we are aware that we do not know "better than" but "better with/because of" those who came before us. ... Probably from our own *generational*[3] situatedness in political and disciplinary terms, the main critique on standpoint we are confronted with is, roughly stated: standpoint feminism is *modern* and essentialist and left little space to other parameters of analysis, such as "race," ethnicity, class, and sexuality, facilitated by *postmodernism*. In this essay, we want to engage critically with the equation of standpoint with an "essentialized" or "universalized" vision of women, and/or the suggested incompatibility of standpoint theorizations with more "postmodern" visions of knowledge production.[4]

Relating Standpoint Theory and Postmodernism

> A feminist standpoint is a practical technology rooted in yearning, not an abstract philosophical foundation.
>
> —Haraway (1997: 198)

Arguments centered on standpoint theory have been opposed to postmodernism, and critiques of standpoint theory have been made on postmodernist and antiessentialist grounds. An example of these theoretical oppositions can be found in the work of Susan Hekman.[5] In her book *Gender and Knowledge* (1990) Hekman points out contradictions in Harding's position. She argues that Harding rejects postmodernism while adopting a number of postmodern issues, such as the refusal of dualistic thought and a commitment for feminist categories to remain unstable. For Hekman, however, these postmodern sensibilities are not compatible with Harding's use of Marxist and radical epistemologies that are "enlightenment epistemologies." In order to be able to reject dualisms, Hekman argues, feminism needs the "radical edge" of postmodern subjects (as processes) that "confront the masculinist heart of modernism": the Cartesian subject as "rational and autonomous" (135–36). According to Hekman, Harding "condemns the feminist standpoint theorists for attempting to express a single woman perspective" (134) and therefore failing to reflect the diversity of women's standpoints. For Hekman, Harding's "critique of standpoint is consistent with postmodernism"—especially some of her arguments dealing with dualisms such as relativism versus absolutism—yet Harding's concern with the difficulty of giving up a "one true story" for feminism is in contradiction with this postmodern perspective (151). Following these arguments, Harding's eclectic epistemology appears inconsistent.

Hekman writes: "a postmodern approach suggests that it is impossible to posit *either* a single women's perspective *or* a single, true feminist story of reality. Yet Harding wants to reject the former and espouse the latter." From our point of view, not only do we disagree with this interpretation, but also find it strange, taking into account Hekman's attachment to processual subjectivities and so-called postmodern sensibilities in this same text, to see her submitting Harding's work to the scholastic acidities of "non-contradiction" principles.

Hekman's critique in 1990 is addressed to Harding's earliest formulation of standpoint feminism in 1986; the discussion meanwhile has continued. Indeed, in a constant attempt to reformulate her propositions in dialogue with her critics, Harding too will say, in her 1991 reformulation of a standpoint, that she seeks a "postmodern standpoint"....

Harding's work is significant of the difficulty that many feminist theorists acknowledge in building new concepts out of the old ones. Harding herself recognizes her attempts to recraft old notions instead of renouncing to them: objectivity, epistemology, and methodology. This problem is present throughout feminist practices, which are since the very beginning confronted with the contradiction of building a struggle on a notion of "woman" simultaneously de-re-constructed.... Probably, the framework of classical normative concepts as "epistemology" and "method" do not facilitate the subtle task of accounting for "the difference" made by feminist theories in theoretical abstract discussions. In addition, our unease with Hekman's critique highlights the fact that most positions in Harding's work are not easily classifiable into modern or postmodern boxes. Indeed, the academic machine is a classificatory one; it appeals to "clarity": is standpoint postmodernist, modern—or both?

Hekman's early critique may serve here as an example of the way in which the field of feminist epistemology sometimes gets framed through a "standpoint-versus-postmodernism" lens. Against this way of framing, we want to juxtapose some reflections on Haraway's celebrated notion of "situated knowledges."

Often considered an example of postmodern scholarship (see, e.g., Prins, 1997), this notion can equally be considered—and is done so by the author herself—as yet another direction in which the ideas of feminist standpoint theories are further explored. Haraway (1997: 198–99) relates her work to standpoint theory in the following way: "A standpoint is not an empiricist appeal to or by 'the oppressed' but a cognitive, psychological, and political tool for more adequate knowledge judged by the non-essentialist, historical contingent, situated standards of strong objectivity. Such a standpoint is the always fraught but necessary fruit of the practices of oppositional and differential consciousness." Haraway continues to emphasize the importance of measuring our political and scientific practices against the positions of oppressed groups—among whom she includes oppressed nonhumans—and of learning to think from those "analytical and imaginative standpoints.... A feminist standpoint is a practical technology rooted in yearning, not an abstract philosophical foundation," writes Haraway (1997: 198).[6] Haraway's strategy reminds us here of how she, in a similar co-constructive move, deals with the subject of feminist knowledge, stepping out of the "modern versus postmodern" debates, including abstract statements of the "death of the modern subject."[7]

Moreover, in a footnote to the quote above, Haraway, mentioning the authors upon which she draws, sharply comments: "That Hartsock, Harding, Collins, Star, Bhavnani, Tsing, Haraway, Sandoval, hooks, and Butler are not supposed to agree about postmodernism, standpoints, science studies, or feminist theory is neither my problem nor theirs. The problem is the needless yet common cost of taxonomising everyone's positions without regard to the contexts of their development, or of refusing rereading and overlayering in order to make new patterns from previous disputes" (Haraway, 1997: 304–5). Indeed, the toughest effort linked to situatedness may indeed be a resistance to the abstractions we use to think with so often.

Our (re-)reading of feminist standpoint thinking is inspired by a vision of feminist standpoints as the collective achievements of both *analysis* and *political struggle* occuring in a particular historical space. Many authors have pointed out that "experience" and "women's voices" in themselves are unstable grounds for the project of a standpoint; in Paula Moya's words (1997: 136): "The simple fact of having been born as person of color or having suffered the effect of heterosexism or of economic deprivation does not, in and of itself, give someone a better understanding of knowledge of our society." Distinguishing a notion of epistemic privilege of oppressed groups from the unreliable idea that social locations would have an epistemic or political meaning in a self-evident way, Moya draws our attention to the *achieved* character of a standpoint. Jacqui Alexander and Chandra Mohanty (1997: xl) continue the argument: "[T]he experience of repression can be, but is not necessarily, a catalyst for organising. It is, in fact, the *interpretation* of that experience within a *collective* context that marks the moment of transformation from perceived contradictions and material disenfranchisement to participation in women's movements." Taking the interpretation of women's experiences in a collective context as a point of departure for standpoint thinking, we understand a standpoint as being produced in the practice of political struggle and in the articulation of a collective subject emerging in this struggle, requiring an "always contingent and fragile (re)construction/transformation of these complex subject positions" (Hartsock, 1998: 82). Such formulations reminds us of the critique of foundationalism developed by Ernesto Laclau and Chantal Mouffe (1985). While this is not the place to position our argument in detail vis-à-vis theirs, we note that our reading of standpoint theory runs parallel with their refusal to see the political process as the gathering or mobilizing of already existent actors, considering it instead in terms of the formation of new political subjects. As Judith Butler (1992: 4) pointedly argued in "Contingent Foundations," the refusal to assume a notion of the subject from the start is not the same as negating or dispensing with such a notion; rather it is to ask after the process of its construction. We consider feminist standpoint theory precisely in the light of such contextualized and historicized practices of the construction of political subjectivities—articulated collectively around the notion of women, including the very contestation of that notion—involving continuous inquiries into the process of construction itself.

. . . The path we propose is compatible with Tanesini's argument that critiques of "universalism" (of "a" woman), and of relying on "unmediated" experience, do not so much undermine the early formulations of standpoint theory as they have helped to develop them further (Tanesini, 2000: 149). We do not want to forget that the examples of the confrontations with universalistic taxonomies are, before being theoretical discussions, embodied conflicts. It is not postmodern theory, we believe, that provides the needed subject for feminism (as it is not the abstraction of Cartesian philosophy that enabled liberal revolutions). Rather, *situated* feminist practices have rendered it possible for women to embody new knowledge subjects that feminist epistemologies try to theorize. And even this formulation would be too poor to try to account for the "difference" that feminist theories often make: the very dichotomy of theory and practice is too sterile to provide the subtle descriptions needed to account for these creative differences. The liveliness of the debates around the notion of standpoint is for us an example of this difficult search for subtlety that is a precious ingredient of self-reflective feminist theories and debates. Paraphrasing Harding, we indeed see feminist theory as an inventive endeavor toward creating other kinds of theorizing (1986: 249).

Some (Un)conclusive Remarks

> We would not know to value that location so highly if women had not insisted on the importance of their experiences and voices

(Harding, 1991: 123–24)

Concepts of the feminist alliance of "politics of location"—such as standpoint, strong objectivity, and situated knowledges—are referred to by their crafters as made possible through practices and political achievements of the women's movement.[8] However, the success of a concept—when it succeeds as a useful and interesting tool, a fold of meanings that gathers collective meanings into a springboard term—has its particular consequences in academic contexts; as Stanley and Wise (2000) have argued, it may become a sort of *voie royale*, while her crafter may become a *star*. The same authors point out that we are not to dismiss the way a conceptual success is built, through an academic network where power relations are at stake that may silence other theoretical directions and the collective building of concepts. Critiques on the "becoming-a-brand" of feminist conceptualizations (including Harding's picture of feminist epistemological strands) go in this direction and show how, to some extent, the current success of popular notions as "situated knowledges" may mask the history of their construction—embedded within "the house of difference" (Lorde, 1982/1993) at the heart of feminist theory and politics as we see it—and therefore appear as, for instance, postmodern theoretical achievements. Liz Stanley (1997: 209) criticizes the tendencies to see Harding's particular vision of feminist epistemological strands as an actual description instead of "a" possible model. From our position, we would rather see it as a situated proposition, a version to be used and reflected upon. The success of Harding's work has probably suffered the effects of those academic manners in which we are still learned and trained: *penser classer.*

The liveliness of the concepts we have discussed—and generally of feminist theory—does not exclusively belong to the academy, we believe, and their empowering potential is not due to academic recognition or theoretical debates. It is therefore important to situate conceptual constructions not only in time and space but also in a "project" and an intellectual evolution, which is always situated and embodied, never neutral. We do not mean to dismiss the importance of theoretical achievements, academic constructs, and feminist contributions to those; the bibliography of this article could serve as an illustration of the kinds of feminist theorizing that has been crucial for our own thinking. The situated position we take in this article is no doubt marked by the (late) moment of our entrance into these debates, *and* by the practices of "the collective," articulated through alliances and web-like figurations, that we are familiar with. We find ourselves with vested interests in imagining theoretical and political practices that enable transformation. It is from these positions that we have appropriated feminist standpoint thinking to our own political and theoretical practices.

That is why, in spite of the academicization of these feminist debates, inevitably transforming concepts into "brands," we do not forget that Harding's concepts, such as her formulations of standpoint and strong objectivity, are also trying to *put into theory* feminist practices developed through struggle, positioning, and controversial debates that incessantly put into question new configurations of power relations. "It does not matter much," writes Haraway (1997: 191), "to the figure of the still gestating, feminist, antiracist, mutated modest witness whether freedom, justice and knowledge are branded as modernist or not; that is not our issue. We have never been modern (Latour, 1994). Rather, freedom, justice, and knowledge are—in bell hooks's terms—about 'yearning' not about putative Enlightenment foundations." As we wrote in our introduction, we are constantly trying to find words more attuned to our experiences of feminist knowledge politics than the progressist discourses of the overcoming of "modernism" towards "post-modernist" quarrels. When translating feminist struggles and their achievements into theories, we would rather be *better with/because of*—than *better than* those who came before us.

Notes

1. A version of this essay, entitled "Who's afraid of standpoint feminism?," was published in Dutch in the *Tijdschrift voor Genderstudies* (vol. 5, no. 2) 2002. We want to thank two anonymous readers and in particular Anne-Claire Mulder for their comments and suggestions. Sarah Bracke wants to thank the *Autonoom Feministisch Onderzoeks Kollektief* (AFOK), Rutvica Andrijasevic, and Elena Casado Aparicio for the joy of theoretical and other affinities. María Puig wants to thank Isabelle Stengers and Didier Demorcy for constant personal, political, and intellectual daring. We both want to thank Rosi Braidotti and the Women's Studies department in Utrecht and Sandra Harding.

2. We are inspired here by Bruno Latour's definition of the modern: "The adjective 'modern' points to a new regime, an acceleration, a break, a revolution of time. When words such as 'modern', 'modernisation', 'modernity' appear, by contrast an archaic and stable past is defined.... Moreover, the word is always brought up in a polemical context, in a quarrel where there are 'winners' and 'losers', Ancients and Moderns." (Latour, 1994: 20, our translation.)

3. The notion of *"genderation"* was brought up by the NextGENDERation network, a European network of young academic feminists (http://nextgenderation.let.uu.nl). Far from designing a political closure or a kind of *youngism*, "genderation" is taken as a starting point for reflecting on and engendering collective meanings of the ways we are situated by the times we live in and by intergenerational perceptions. Related examples of such a starting point are the Italian '30something' network and the discussions during the NOISE European Women's Studies Summer School in 2000 (in Pisa) about feminist politics in the academy.

4. Accounts taking another line of critique, arguing that standpoint theory implies the renunciation of scientific universal advancement and condemns political and cultural positions to incommensurability (as e.g., very recently Sylvia Walby [2000 and 2001] does, using "back to universal reason" arguments) are therefore not addressed in this article. However, we do hope that our present discussion will contribute to address critically the simplistic notions of standpoint theory that are constructed through such critiques, for example, standpoint as a postmodern renunciation of common (knowledge) politics.

5. Hekman deserves some special attention here because of the discussion her critiques generated in a special dossier in *Signs*, with responses by Nancy Hartsock, Dorothy E. Smith, Patricia Hill Collins, and Sandra Harding. In the scope of this article, however, we concentrate on Hekman's critique of 1990.

6. The notion of "yearning" builds on the work of bell hooks; "oppositional consciousness" refers to the work of Chela Sandoval.

7. "The boys in the human sciences have called this doubt about self-presence the 'death of the subject,' that single ordering point of will and consciousness. That judgement seems bizarre to me. I prefer to call this generative doubt, the opening of nonisomorphic

subjects, agents and territories, of stories unimaginable from the vantage point of the master's subject" (Haraway, 1991: 192).

8. To affirm such an alliance is not to deny the differences between the approaches. See Axeli Knapp (2000), for an interesting account of theoretical filiations of different visions of situatedness/locatedness.

References

Alexander, Jacqui and Chandra Mohanty (eds.). (1997). *Feminist Genealogies, Colonial Legacies, Democratic Futures*. New York: Routledge.

Butler, Judith. (1992). "Contingent Foundations: Feminism and the Question of 'Postmodernism,'" pp. 3–21. In Judith Butler and Joan W. Scott (eds.), *Feminists Theorize the Political*. New York: Routledge.

Collins, Patricia Hill. (1989). "The Social Construction of Black Feminist Thought: An Essay in the Sociology of Knowledge." *Signs* 14 (4): 745–773.

Collins, Patricia Hill. (1990). *Black Feminist Thought: Knowledge, Consciousness and the Politics of Empowerment*. London: HarperCollins.

Collins, Patricia Hill. (1997). "Comments on Hekman's 'Truth and Method: Feminist Standpoint Theory Revisited': Where's the Power?" *Signs* 22 (2): 375–381.

Flax, Jane. (1990). *Thinking Fragments*. Berkeley: University of California Press.

Haraway, Donna. (1991). "Situated Knowledges. The Privilege of Partial Perspective," pp. 183–201. In Donna Haraway, *Simians, Cyborgs and Women: The Reinvention of Nature*. New York: Routledge.

Haraway, Donna. (1997). *Modest_Witness@Second_Millennium:.FemaleMan_Meets_OncoMouse*™: *Feminism and Technoscience*. New York: Routledge.

Harding, Sandra. (1986). *The Science Question in Feminism*. Ithaca: Cornell University Press.

Harding, Sandra. (1990). "Feminism, Science and the Enlightenment Critiques," pp. 83–106. In L. J. Nicholson (ed.), *Feminism/ Postmodernism*. New York: Routledge.

Harding, Sandra. (1991). *Whose Science? Whose Knowledge? Thinking from Women's Lives*. Milton Keynes: Open University Press.

Harding, Sandra. (1993). "Rethinking Standpoint Epistemology: What is 'Strong Objectivity'?" pp. 49–82. In Linda Alcoff and Elizabeth Potter (eds.), *Feminist Epistemologies*. New York: London.

Harding, Sandra. (1998). *Is Science Multicultural? Postcolonialisms, Feminisms and Epistemologies*. Bloomington: Indiana University Press.

Hartsock, Nancy. (1983). "The Feminist Standpoint: Developing the Ground for a Specifically Feminist Historical Materialism," pp. 283–310. In Sandra Harding & Merrill B. Hintikka (eds.), *Discovering Reality*. Dordrecht: Reidel.

Hartsock, Nancy. (1998). *The Feminist Standpoint Revisited and Other Essays*. Boulder: Westview Press.

Hekman, Susan. (1990). *Gender and Knowledge Elements of a Postmodern Feminism*. Boston: Northeastern University Press.

Hekman, Susan. (1997). "Truth and Method: Feminist Standpoint Theory Revisited." *Signs* 22 (2): 341–365.

Hekman, Susan. (1999). *The Future of Differences, Truth and Method in Feminist Theory*. Cambridge: Polity Press.

Hekman, Susan. (2000). "Beyond Identity: Feminism, Identity and Identity Politics." *Feminist Theory* 1 (3): 289–308.

Hirsch, Gesa. (1999). *Ethical Dilemmas in Feminist Research*. New York: SUNY Press.

hooks, bell. (1984). *Feminist Theory: From Margin to Center*. Boston: South End Press.

hooks, bell. (1990). "Postmodern Blackness." *Postmodern Culture* 1(1). <http://muse.jhu.edu/journals/posmodern_culture/v001/1.1hooks.htm>.

Knapp, Axeli. (2000). "More Power to Argument." *Feminist Theory* 1 (2): 207–223.

Laclau, Ernesto and Chantal Mouffe. (1985). *Hegemony and Socialist Strategy: Towards a Radical Democratic Politics*. London: Verso.

Latour, Bruno. (1994). *Nous n'avons jamais été modernes: Essai d'anthropologie symétrique*. Paris: La découverte.

Lennon, Kathleen and Margaret Whitford (eds.). (1994). *Knowing the Difference: Feminist Perspectives in Epistemology*. London: Routledge.

Lorde, Audre. (1993). *Zami: A New Spelling of My Name*. 1982; reprint New York: Quality Paper Book Club.

Meguill, Alan (ed.). (1994). *Rethinking Objectivity*. Durham, N.C.: Duke University Press.

Moya, Paula. (1997). "Postmodernism, 'Realism', and the Politics of Identity: Cherríe Moraga and Chicana Feminism," pp. 125–150. In Jacqui Alexander and Chandra Mohanty (eds.), *Feminist Genealogies, Colonial Legacies, Democratic Futures*. New York: Routledge.

Prins, Baukje. (1997). "The Standpoint in Question: Situated Knowledges and the Dutch Minorities Discourse." Ph.D. dissertation. Utrecht University.

Puig de la Bellacasa, María. (2000). "Feminist Knowledge Politics: A Different Hi/story of Knowledge Construction." Draft paper for the 4th Feminist European Research Conference, Bologna, <http://www.women.it/quarta/workshops/epistemological4/mariapuig.htm>.

Rose, Hilary. (1983). "Hand Brain and Heart: A Feminist Epistemology for the Natural Sciences." *Signs* 9 (1): 72–90.

Rose, Hilary. (1994). *Love, Power and Knowledge*. Cambridge: Polity Press.

Rose, Hilary. (2000). "Building a New Team with Gaia?" *Signs* 25 (4): 1125–1128.

Scott, Joan W. (1992). "Experience," pp. 22–40. In Judith Butler and Joan W. Scott (eds.), *Feminists Theorize the Political*. New York: Routledge.

Smith, Dorothy E. (1988). *The Everyday World as Problematic: A Feminist Sociology*. Milton Keynes: Open University Press.

Smith, Dorothy E. (1997). "Comment on Hekman's 'Truth and Method: Feminist Standpoint Theory Revisited.'" *Signs* 22 (2): 392–398.

Stanley, Liz. (1997). "Methodology Matters!," pp. 198–219. In Victoria Robinson and Diane Richardson (eds.), *Introducing Women's Studies*, 2nd ed. London: Macmillan.

Stanley, Liz and Sue Wise. (2000). "But the Empress Has No Clothes! Some Awkward Questions about the 'Missing Revolution' in Feminist Theory." *Feminist Theory* 1 (3): 261–288.

Subramaniam, Banu and Lisa H. Weasel (eds.). (2001). *Feminist Science Studies: A New Generation*. New York: Routledge.

Tanesini, Alessandra. (1998). *An Introduction to Feminist Epistemologies*. Oxford: Blackwell.

Truth, Sojourner. (1851). *Ain't I a Woman*. Transcription: <http://www.feminist.com/sojour.htm>.

Walby, Sylvia. (2000). "Beyond the Politics of Location: The Power of Argument in a Global Era." *Feminist Theory* 1 (2): 189–206.

Walby, Sylvia. (2001). "Against Epistemological Chasms: The Science Question in Feminism Revisited." *Signs* 26 (2): 486–509.

Wesselius, Janet. (2001). "Objective Ambivalence: Feminist Negotiations in Epistemology." Ph.D. dissertation. Amsterdam University.

Winterson, Jeanette. (1997). *Gut Symmetries*. London: Granta Books.

25

Feminist Standpoint as Postmodern Strategy

NANCY J. HIRSCHMANN

In the approximately 15 years since Nancy Hartsock published "The Feminist Standpoint" (1983),[1] this epistemological methodology has had a profound affect on feminist theorizing and scholarship in a variety of fields ranging from philosophy (Ruddick 1989, Alcoff and Potter 1993), social work (Swigonski 1994), sociology (McLennon 1995, Ramazanoglu 1989, Smith 1990, Collins 1990), psychology (Henwood and Pidgeon 1995), and history (Offen 1990), to geography (McDowell 1992), and the biological and physical sciences (Harding 1986, 1991, Keller 1985). Within political science, it has had a significant impact not only on Hartsock's own field of political theory (Flax 1983, Hirschmann 1989, 1992, Jaggar 1983, Weeks 1995) but on public policy (Rixecker 1994) and international relations as well (Keohane 1989, Sylvester 1994).

At the same time, indeed perhaps because of this powerful influence, feminist standpoint theory has been subject to considerable criticism and contentious debate within feminism. The postmodern critique of standpoint theory has been particularly strong and fairly consistent. But I believe it is often mistaken. In this essay, I will briefly review the most common criticisms and show how Hartsock's formulation not only addresses many of them but shares important features with postmodernism as well. Though several feminists, including myself, have argued for a postmodern potential in the notion of multiple feminist standpoints, I carry this further to argue for a new way of conceptualizing the materialist dimensions of experience that may be more compatible with postmodern notions of discursivity without losing Hartsock's methodological foundation.

Essentially Universal?

Essentialism and universalism are the charges most commonly leveled against feminist standpoint theory, though not exclusively by postmodernists by any means. It is often held that Hartsock claimed to articulate "the" feminist standpoint, as if there were only one, and that it was the same for all women. Such universalist "truth-claims," the criticism goes, are based on ahistorical, crosscultural effects that link "women" to each other regardless of other identity aspects of culture, ethnicity, race, sexuality, or class (hooks 1984, Spelman 1988) and

simply replace one set of universal claims for another, thus replicating and rein-
scribing the hegemony it seeks to displace (Flax 1990, Hekman 1990). At the
same time, anti-essentialist critics have accused Hartsock of basing the standpoint on biology, reproduction, or "nature" (Fraser and Nicholson 1990, Grant
1993).

Such criticisms have fostered lively debates within feminism concerning the
"meaning of woman" and the "subject" of feminism that go well beyond the
immediate methodological and political concerns of Hartsock's argument. They
have highlighted the ways in which largely white-dominated academic feminism
has often worked to exclude the experiences and views of U.S. women of color,
poor women, Third World women, and lesbians (Narayan 1989, Collins 1990).
These debates have forced feminism to examine itself, to be more self-conscious,
self-aware, and self-critical in developing its analyses and theories, and to attend
more consistently to its avowed goals of equality and inclusion.

At the same time, however, such criticisms are often unfair to Hartsock. The
charge of essentialism, for instance, ignores the fact that Hartsock locates her
conception of a feminist standpoint in the culturally constructed social relations
of household production and reproduction in late capitalism (Hartsock 1984,
234–40). It may be true that the practices Hartsock bases her feminist standpoint
on are grounded in biology in a certain sense: for instance, the human need to
eat means that we have to provide food for ourselves; and the development
of human personality, psyche, emotions, and intellect requires some kind of
adult caretaking of human infants. But this hardly precludes historical analysis:
indeed, a feminist standpoint allows us to answer why it is that *women* have
been responsible for providing for these needs in most cultures and historical
periods. The social construction of experience, and particularly labor (Hartsock
1983, 283), is a critical aspect of Hartsock's approach (see also Ferguson 1993).

To this end, in contrast to some other theorists such as Dorothy Smith (1990)
and Nel Noddings (1990), who have written in terms of "women's" standpoints,
Hartsock explicitly distinguishes between "female" and "feminist" standpoints
(Hartsock 1984, 232). This distinction is due partly to an overt political commitment to the notion that there can be, must be, and indeed currently are male
feminists in the world; but it is also due to her central contention that a standpoint does not come "naturally" or spontaneously to anyone. Rather, it must be
achieved through "struggle," wherein lies its "liberatory" potential (Hartsock
1983, 235). As Sandra Harding (1991) has asserted in defense of standpoint
theory, its goal is not to "act out" women's experiences but to theorize them
critically and to learn about women's responses to oppression as much as about
oppression itself.

Of course, as Kathy Ferguson (1993) has noted, many anti-essentialist critiques are really criticisms of univeralism, not "essentialism per se" (81–82),
and this distinction is important. Charges of "universalism" often misrepresent

Hartsock's position as well. Indeed, in one of her early formulations of a feminist standpoint approach, Hartsock (1981) states explicitly that

> Women who call themselves feminists disagree on many things.... One would be hard pressed to find a set of beliefs or principles, or even a list of demands, that could safely be applied to all feminists. Still... there is a *methodology* common among feminists that differs from the practice of most social movements, particularly from those in advanced capitalist countries. At bottom, *feminism is a mode of analysis, a method of approaching life and politics, rather than a set of political conclusions about the oppression of women.* (35–6, emphasis added).

The notion of standpoint as a methodology is crucial. Universalist criticisms confuse Hartsock's particular time- and context-bound contingent account of what "a" (as in "one") feminist standpoint might look like for the *conception* of "feminist standpoint theory" that she develops as a *method* for feminism. The central notion of a standpoint approach, as Hartsock develops it, is that material experience shapes epistemology. Hence, to the degree that people share a particular set of experiences, for instance, if large numbers of women have exclusive responsibility for raising children or perform uncompensated household labor for men, then they may share a standpoint. But by the same token, to the degree that experience differs, as childbearing practices do from culture to culture, then standpoints will differ as well. The particulars of experience may be historically contingent, but their methodological similarities cross over these contingencies. The methodological similarity provides the means for women within various groups to resist their oppression by drawing on the epistemological power their particular shared experiences afford to rename those experiences. That each group may realize its own substantively distinct standpoint, in response to the particular differences in the forms oppression takes for women of different races, classes, or sexualities, does not undermine this methodological commonality.

Missing this methodological point leads to misunderstanding. For instance, Vicky Spelman (1988) criticizes standpoint theory for its supposed "plethorophobia" of differences among women evidenced by its "hegemonic" tendency to seek commonality among women, which she asserts is impossible. "Is there some*thing* all women have in common.... *An* underlying identity as women.... *A* shared viewpoint?" (160, my emphasis). Similarly, Judith Grant (1993) faults feminist standpoint epistemology because it does not "tell us *which* aspects of the lives of women count as epistemologically important... which parts of our lives and experiences are endemic to our being female. Therefore the epistemological question is precisely the one avoided" (100).

But Grant sets up the very problem for which she most excoriates standpoint theory: confusing a feminist standpoint with the essential experience of "being female" while simultaneously ignoring that Hartsock does in fact point to specific aspects of women's experience, namely unpaid household labor and reproduction in the broad sense of caregiving and nurturance. Spelman seems to lock Hartsock into a circle of her own creation: in order to be valid, feminist standpoint must be the same for all women; in order to be the same, experience must also be the same either through biological mandate or a universal construction; but experience is not the same; therefore, standpoint is wrong.[2]

But if we see instead that the *process* of developing a standpoint is similar, though the substance of particular standpoints will differ according to experience, then we see that the feminist standpoint approach readily accommodates difference, specificity, and history. The epistemological point is the methodological one: it refers to the general process of how knowledge is to be developed and understood. Epistemology is not a theory of *what* we know, but of *how* we know it. While standpoint feminism has been instrumental in highlighting the interactions of "what" and "how," the two are not identical. That is, if knowledge is developed through experience rather than in the abstract world of "Truth," then different experiences will yield different *bodies of knowledge*. However, the process of *developing knowledge out of* these different experiences will be similar for all. By focusing on standpoint as a methodological and epistemological strategy rather than a particular political positioning, Hartsock's formulation allows for a multiplicity of feminist *standpoints*.

Several theorists (e.g., Haraway 1991, Harding 1991, Hirschmann 1992) have argued precisely this point. Pluralizing the term to feminist *standpoints* allows the recognition of difference, particularity, and context while also putting certain parameters on what can count as a *feminist* standpoint. These parameters do not entail some universal and timeless conception of feminism or femaleness; rather, "feminism" is the product of ongoing political negotiation within and among various groups of women who theorize from the standpoint of their experiences of gender, race, class, and other oppressions. The materialist basis of feminist standpoint theory leads logically to the conclusion that differences in experience produce differences in standpoints; the pluralization of feminist standpoints recognizes differences among material experiences of women across history, race, class, and culture.

Feminism/Postmodernism

Even so, anti-universalist criticisms seem more persistent than anti-essentialist ones because they are based on the "logic" of standpoint arguments rather than a simple misreading: standpoint feminism does require shared group experiences. Although some theorists such as Collins (1990) have written of a "self-actualized standpoint," it is a central aspect of Hartsock's formulation that a feminist standpoint can only arise within circumstances of *shared oppression*. In keeping with its Marxist and Lukacian heritage, a standpoint is not simply a "perspective" or "point of view," which can vary from person to person, but is rather an epistemology, which must be shared between at least some numbers of people and which is a function of political struggle with other people who are similarly placed vis-à-vis oppressive power relations (Hartsock 1997). This may allow difference *among groups*, but it requires similarity *within* "epistemological communities" (Seller 1994).

Thus, an unmodified "feminist" standpoint logically presupposes an unmodified group of "women" who share similar experiences. This is not an exclusively postmodern criticism. Feminists-of-color are particularly critical of the way that standpoint's universalist potential has been unwittingly promoted by many white feminists through such usage of the term "feminist standpoint" rather than more specified terms such as "Black feminist standpoint" or "white feminist standpoint" (Mohanty 1992). Such criticisms are valid. When Hartsock tables the question of race to talk about "commonalities" in *Money, Sex and Power* (1984, 233), she ignores that race and class affect the gendered constructions of the very labor activities on which she wants to base her particular instance of a feminist standpoint.

While such substantive exclusions seriously undermine feminism, they do not mean that standpoint as a method is fundamentally irreconcilable with the lives of women of color or with the notion of "difference" more generally. Indeed, Collins (1990) and Narayan (1989) have argued that standpoint feminism provides an important method for developing feminist-of-color standpoints. This may be one place where feminism-of-color and postmodernism part company. Although feminist postmodernism has helped open up white academic feminism to questions of racism, classism, and other exclusions that are not only harmful to many women but also contradict and undermine feminism, it nevertheless maintains that it is logically impossible to reconcile standpoint theory with "difference." Postmodernists note that every modifier has its own universalistic potential; thus even a "Black feminist standpoint" does not sufficiently attend to differences among Black women's experiences in terms of class or sexuality (Spelman 1988). While a standpoint approach may be consistent with multiplicity, particularizing can get us only so far before difference runs up against the standpoint requirement of sharedness.

By emphasizing the ways in which language and "discourse" construct categories of meaning to create the "realities" of "who we are," feminist postmodernists point out the dangers in using terms like "women" such that feminists unintentionally silence or erase women of color or poor women who do not make up the majority of feminist theorists. At the same time, however, many feminists believe that postmodernism's continual contestation of identity as a contingent and fleeting construction of language threatens the central project of standpoint feminism (if not "feminism" in general) which is to secure the acknowledgement that various groups of "women" are oppressed in concrete ways.

The particulars of the often bitter and passionate debate over feminist postmodernism will not be rehearsed here (see Alcoff 1988, Hawksworth 1989), but this debate has created a strong ambivalence among many feminist scholars who seek a methodological strategy for studying "women." As Caroline Ramazanoglu (1989) notes, "reducing feminism to a post-modern philosophy excises feminist politics" and leads to "the political fragmentation of feminist strategies for change." Yet at the same time, she worries that a standpoint approach requires an epistemological and political unity among all women (432, 438). The apparent conflict between embracing and addressing "difference" among women and yet being able to hold onto a concept of "woman" which retains some conception of commonality across various differences leaves many feminists who are attracted to standpoint theory on the horns of a seemingly irresolvable dilemma.

While some might celebrate such irresolvability, including some standpoint sympathizers (e.g., Harding 1991, Haraway 1991), I believe that the notion of multiple feminist standpoints holds an answer to this dilemma in what it reveals about the methodological significance of standpoint as *epistemological*. As a way of seeing the world, redefining knowledge, reconceptualizing social relations, and renaming experience, standpoint theory provides a powerful methodology for understanding "reality" as an ongoing process. That is, the adoption of a particular feminist standpoint allows us to gain a "less partial and perverse" understanding of the world; but that does not mean we have achieved "truth." To begin with, the confluence of a variety of feminist standpoints reveals different *aspects* of "truth," different angles on achieving clarity, different pieces of a larger picture (Haraway 1991). But in turn each of these standpoints, separately and working together, allows a reconfiguration of the world as a whole which, presumably, should lend itself to other subsequent standpoints that are even *less* "partial and perverse." Standpoint is, true to its Marxian roots, an ongoing, dialectical process (contra Grant 1993, 115).

A focus on multiple standpoints reveals standpoint and postmodernism as more closely related than many want to admit; it suggests that standpoint indeed is "always already" a postmodern strategy. Admittedly, this claim might seem counterintuitive, given views such as those expressed by Ramazanoglu, and particularly given Hartsock's own steady and repeated criticisms of such leading and diverse postmodern theorists as Foucault and Rorty (Hartsock 1987, 1990). Furthermore, standpoint theory's Marxist legacy would seem to locate it squarely within modernism.

But it is a view that a number of feminists have put forth, some implicitly, others explicitly. Donna Haraway argues that we need to see a standpoint as offering only a "partial perspective" that is compatible with both multiplicity and "successor science projects" without sliding into either relativism or totalization (1991, 191). Christine Sylvester's defense of standpoint theory for international relations points out that feminist standpoint's giving voice to "so many different experiences of so many different types of people called women," resonates with postmodernists' concern to reveal "the power and politics laden in local acts of resistance to universalising narratives" (1994, 324). Sandra Harding (1991) argues that standpoint theory's location in "women's lives" can help feminists theorize the "permanent partiality" of knowledge. Following Harding and

Edward Said, Kathleen Lennon (1995) has argued for a "contrapuntal" approach to standpoint that both "highlights specificity and allows for the recognition of communalities" (141). I have elsewhere argued for seeing standpoint as a kind of "postmodern feminism," to be distinguished from "feminist postmodernism" (Hirschmann 1992).

Certainly, standpoint theory shares many features and goals with postmodernism. Postmodernism challenges the notion, central to modern political theory, that there is such a thing as "human nature." By emphasizing the notions of difference, particularity, and context, postmodernism seeks to shake us loose from modernist tendencies to make broad-sweeping generalizations that reflect particular historico-cultural locations, but which we try to pass off as "truth." Instead of having "natures," postmodern theory recognizes that we are "socially constructed." The idea of social construction central to postmodern theory suggests that we are who we are not because of "nature" but because of the social relations, institutions, and practices that shape our world. Our selfhood, subjectivity, identity, and way of seeing are all "constructed" by the contexts in which we live.

By challenging the naturalness of practices, social arrangements, and institutions, both standpoint theory and postmodernism see identity as socially constructed by particular historical and cultural contexts. As indicated earlier, the logic of materialism on which the feminist standpoint is based demands recognition that the structures of these activities have changed over time and differ across cultures, reflecting that they are in part the result of and responses to different forms of patriarchy in different cultures and different historical periods (Hartsock 1984, 150). Additionally, feminist standpoint theory explicitly acknowledges the ways in which the activities that women engage in have been for the most part assigned to them by men rather than "monopolized" by women (Hartsock 1984, 245).

Moreover, by providing a different approach to *epistemology*, feminist standpoint theory, like postmodernism, enables us to get beyond the superficial idea of "social construction" contained in such ideas as role learning or socialization. Humans are constructed not merely through quasi-conscious processes of learning sexist definitions of what a "woman" or "man" is within neutral conceptual vocabularies, linguistic forms, and frameworks for knowledge; rather, these latter profoundly affect, shape, and even determine the kinds of ideas, concepts, and visions of the self that are possible to conceive (Butler 1990). For instance, a feminist standpoint enables women to identify the activities they perform in the home as "work" and "labor," productive of "value," rather than simply the necessary and essential byproducts of "nature" or the function of biology which women "passively" experience (Hartsock 1984, 146–48). Such recognition involves a reconfiguring of meaning and discourse and not "just" a challenge to existing social relations of (re)production.

Feminist Standpoint and the Materialist Moment

Thus standpoint theory and feminist postmodernism share important features. However, this does not circumvent a deeper division between them, namely the *meaning* of "material reality" on which standpoint feminism is based and "discourse," central to postmodernism. Feminist postmodernists argue that we must give up any idea of a "material reality" that exists beyond discourse, that has an independent or objective status, otherwise we simply get caught by the very same essentialist and reductive assumptions that feminism was supposed to unmask in the first place. Feminist standpoint theorists want to assert that women's oppression is "real" and that it has an immediate, even tangible quality that pre-exists its naming in language. Indeed, the power of a standpoint is precisely its ability *to* name experiences that previously were defined in masculinist terms which made women's harm invisible.

But because such experiences *are* socially constructed, and because women are also located in other identity networks such as race and class, feminism also needs to engage discursivity as a way to appreciate how this invisibility operates and to understand the relationship of gender oppression to other forms of domination. In an essay otherwise critical of postmodernism, Mary Hawksworth (1989) faults standpoint theory because it "fails to grasp the manifold ways in which all human experiences...are mediated by theoretical presuppositions embedded in language and culture" (544). "Discourse" is not simply words, but a social force that sets the terms for the construction of material "reality." If "experience itself reflects and is partially constructed out of the self-understandings yielded by the imaginary and symbolic dimensions of our conceptual apparatus" (Lennon 1995, 135), then standpoint theory must recognize the discursive construction of the material experiences on which feminist standpoints are partially based.

This might suggest an insurmountable impasse: many would argue that once one concedes the importance of discourse, the notion of "prediscursivity" becomes unintelligible. But the word "partially" in the previous quote is crucial to avoiding a vicious circle. If feminists can understand women's experiences *solely* through discourses premised not only on women's oppression but on making that oppression invisible by naturalizing it, then it might seem that the basis for feminist standpoints evaporates. Standpoint feminism needs to hang onto at least some notion of "material reality" that is not entirely captured by discourse, as a way to hold onto the very concrete, immediate, and daily ways in which women suffer from the use and abuse of power specifically by men. However, this is precisely where the link between standpoint and postmodernism breaks down; even positing multiple standpoints is not enough to bring these two theoretical frameworks together. For postmodernists, it begs the question of whether *any* kind of standpoint simply reinscribes the old oppressions of truth and identity because the notion of an unmediated "experience" is by definition impossible. At the same time, the denial of such immediacy prompts standpoint theorists to fear a relativist erosion of the ability to make useful claims about women's oppression.

Rosemary Hennessy (1993) argues that the solution to this apparent impasse is for feminism to link the discursive to the nondiscursive (36), but so far, this link has only been one way, viz. acknowledging the ways in which discourse constructs the material conditions of women's lives, as even postmodernists like Judith Butler acknowledge. Butler (1993) claims that she does not dispute "the materiality of the body" but insists on the need to explore "the normative conditions under which the materiality of the body is framed and formed" (17). Her argument that "regulatory norms" are what "materialize" sex coheres with feminist standpoint's social constructivist arguments that the dominant ideology of patriarchy establishes and creates the reality of women's experience (e.g., Hartsock 1983, 288). Discourse makes "real," or "materializes," the concrete conditions of women's lives.

At the same time, however, the postmodern reiteration that "materiality is a function of discourse" begs the question for standpoint feminism, which wants to say that materiality can *challenge* discourse: that women's experience simultaneously sits *in contradiction to* discourse with a partially independent reality. This is a notion that postmodernists like Butler overtly reject; and yet Butler's use of the term "queer" as an empowering political positioning depends on precisely such notions (1993, 223). Gay and lesbian adoption of the term "queer" involves an ironic parodying of the dominant discourse, and its power lies in the fundamental belief that heteropatriarchy misunderstands and misdescribes gays and lesbians. The notion of "misdescription" presupposes a further notion of what they really are and that the dominant discourse "gets it wrong."

This suggests that we must not only see how discourse "materializes" experience but also acknowledge how material conditions construct and shape discourse. The problem, then, is how to make such a notion of a "prediscursive reality" intelligible within postmodern discursivity. To this end, I propose what I call a "materialist moment" that can serve as an interface between the possibility of a prediscursive "concrete reality" on which standpoint feminism logically depends and the postmodern emphasis on the constantly shifting discursive character of such "reality." The notion of a "moment" comes out of postmodern theory to indicate a disjunction between discourses, a figurative "moment" in time where individuals see that the existing dominant discourse is not "true." This moment need not be literally "momentary"; that is, moments do not necessarily last for just a few seconds but can mark historical epochs of transformation or shifting between dominant and resisting discourses. It is a "moment" of, and in the development of, consciousness, both individual and collective, which must change continually in response to historical events, even when it appears stable or static. Within the human mind, it may more literally be momentary, an almost instantaneous recognition that must immediately slide away into discourse and representation.[3]

For instance, Drucilla Cornell (1993, 102–10) writes about a "utopian mo-ment" where (following the French feminists) women's sexual *jouissance* can express itself outside of the patriarchal context and language that defines women's sexuality only as "that which is fucked." It is "utopian" because Cornell recognizes the impossibility of this *jouissance* ever having meaning outside of language; but it is a "moment" to affirm the fleeting recognition of women's experiencing of their own bodily sexuality in a way not wholly contained by discourse, evaporating even as it comes into being.

The materialist moment works off of a similar notion. In her early writings, Hartsock (1983) seems to acknowledge the paradoxical relationship between discourse and materiality when she admits to "grasping [bodily experience] over-firmly ... to keep it from evaporating altogether" (289). It may be this "over-firmness" that leads to the essentialist and universalist criticisms earlier cited, but it stems from her recognition of the fact that women's "experience" already exists within patriarchal discourse (Hartsock 1984, 245). Indeed, this is why a feminist standpoint yields "less partial and perverse" knowledge rather than "truth." Hartsock's point, however, is that this discursive construction is not and cannot be the sum total of women's experience. "Sensuous human activity" (Hartsock 1983, 235), materiality, underlies such construction and awaits its articulation in a new discourse to give it different meanings.

Putting material experience in terms of a "moment" allows standpoint the-ory to loosen its overfirm grasp without sacrificing its fundamental assertions about the concreteness, the "reality," of women's experiences. The idea of a materialist moment posits experience as having some prediscursive immediacy while simultaneously acknowledging the impossibility of ever capturing expe-rience outside of discourse. It allows feminists to acknowledge the concreteness of experience within languages that have the denial of those experiences at their core while at the same time acknowledging that there is no way to share expe-rience with others, or even to understand our own experiences, without those often hostile languages. It simultaneously recognizes that these experiences are in part functions of and created by language and that language can never, by its nature, contain the whole of such experiences. In the process, it also facilitates the transformation of language to reflect "nondiscursive" concrete experience more accurately, but it does so nonessentially because this transformation pos-tulates neither timelessness, naturalness, nor universality. The fact that we treat it as a "moment" locates its specificity and temporality in the social processes of language without allowing language to supercede its "realness."

Perhaps most significant to standpoint feminism, a "materialist moment" provides feminists with a place to "stand." As Ferguson (1993) notes, "all feminist analyses ... have to stand at least temporarily on some stable territory in order to bring other phenomena under scrutiny" (85). In order to critique discourse, in order to say "no" to the dominant picture of "reality," I have to stand some-where else, in a different reality. Yet where can that reality lie if not in the always already patriarchal world? In a sense, I must be not "in" the world/discourse but, nevertheless, "of" it. It is this moment of possibility that a feminist standpoint struggles for. It is the dual positioning of experience as both discursive and nondiscursive that makes feminist critique and resistance possible. A "materialist moment" suggests that while experience exists in discourse, discourse is not the totality of experience: since experience may always be reinterpreted and redescribed, there must be something in experience that escapes, or is even prior to, language.[4] This "something" does not have an essential and timeless meaning; that is the point of viewing it as a "moment," something that gives way to and cannot maintain a sustained meaningful existence outside of discourse. And yet its independent existence, its "materiality," provides women with a "place to stand," even if only "momentarily," which allows us to see how we participate in our own social construction in ways that are both destructive (e.g., women's mothering supports and reinforces patriarchy) and productive (it also yields an ethics of care).

Perhaps even more importantly, it also points the way to more active theoretical and political construction (for instance, developing a new vision of politics *out of* care [Ruddick 1989]). At the same time, it allows us to be wary of this last step, to see that any construction can go off in different unforeseen directions with unintended consequences (e.g., white feminism's definition of a care ethics may perpetuate the erasure of women of color [see Collins 1990]). So it can help feminists be more self-critical and intellectually cautious even as we challenge, destabilize, and deconstruct patriarchy by creating new pictures of "reality."

These pictures involve, of course, new discourses. Treating materialism in terms of a *moment* reminds us of that and prevents the universalizing and essentializing potential of standpoint approaches. But it is important to recognize that these discourses come from material experiences. Naming this moment *materialist* emphasizes that new discourses do not just come out of other discourses but out of something more immediate and concrete. To say that experience is material, that it provides meaning that exists in part prior to discourse, does not mean the meaning is "natural," nor does it deny that it has to exist in discourse before political change can be effected. But it reminds us of a basic standpoint tenet that discourses are, at least in part, the result of "sensuous human activity, practice" (Hartsock 1983, 235, quoting Marx 1970, 121). Discourse and materiality are in close relationship, but they are, nevertheless, distinct. I do not simply "reinterpret" my experiences through a new discourse; experience also *enables* reinterpretation. Women's experiences are discursive, but they come, at least in part, from somewhere else, not "just" from discourse in an endless devolution. That such experience can be shared only *through* language is important to recognize. Indeed, it may be a crucial dimension of the standpoint notion of *shared* experience that we communicate about it through language, but discourse cannot exhaust the "reality" of experience.

Conclusion: Toward Postmodern Feminist Standpoints

I believe this recasting of Hartsock's formulation not only is a better representation of the implications of her argument, thus addressing some key postmodern objections, but it can also help bring together postmodern and standpoint feminisms. In particular, by holding onto a nonessentializing notion of prediscursive experience, the "materialist moment" strengthens the methodological power of multiple standpoints by helping feminists develop a more meaningful understanding of "difference." The danger of postmodern approaches to feminism is that by focusing on difference and particularity at the *exclusion* of commonality and sharing, the concept of difference becomes increasingly abstract, ill-defined, even unreal. At the same time, insistence on the discursivity of difference makes oppression difficult to identify, since power is "always and everywhere" in discourse, we are all constructors and constructed (Foucault 1990). Indeed, the possibility of language that can even articulate the character of particular differences must be called into question (Alcoff 1988). Without such articulation, however, relations of domination and oppression become invisible, or at least those who would name them are struck mute.

By working through "materialist moments," the notion of "difference" does not lose sight of oppression. As Bat-Ami Bar On (1993) observes, it is not enough for feminists to theorize difference, or even "marginality," for many differences are marginalized; rather we must understand how what is marginal is also central to patriarchal power relations. On my reading, standpoint feminism allows us to understand degrees of power and privilege that cohere to particular "differences" by holding onto the material reality of oppression. For instance, it allows the recognition that a Black feminist standpoint as a starting point for theory can reveal things about white women's experiences which a white feminist standpoint cannot reveal, precisely because of the privilege that adheres to being white (Harding 1991). A Black feminist standpoint is "less partial and perverse" because it sits at the fulcrum of intersecting vectors of oppression (Collins 1990).

At the same time, since many white women (of various other positionalities) do experience oppression and marginality, it makes no sense to ignore their experiences just because Black women are "more" oppressed or marginal. By that logic, we could simply find the most oppressed person and use her standpoint as the basis for a new true theory that tells the whole story. Even putting aside the incommensurability of certain oppressions—are Chicanas more oppressed in the United States than Blacks? Jews more than Muslims?—such a caricature of standpoint ignores the interdependence of different kinds of oppression and, hence, the need to articulate a variety of feminist standpoints (Hirschmann 1992).

Pursuing multiplicity within a feminist-standpoints' approach *and* locating such standpoints in materialist moments acknowledges a more complicated notion of oppression than the often simplistic Marxist-feminist formula where "men" oppress "women." At the same time, it prevents the slide into relativism so often typical of the postmodern emphasis on "difference" (McDowell 1992), for it provides a collective means of evaluating and discriminating between various claims to a standpoint. In order to count as a standpoint rather than a relativist "perspective" or an oppressive "ideology," it would have to establish itself as stemming from shared experiences of oppression. In order to count as "feminist," it would have to demonstrate that it led to the promotion of gender equality, a concept which must include racial, economic, and other kinds of equality since gendered subjects occupy multiple intersections of identity categories, without eliminating difference. It also must include an understanding of (some group of) *women's* lived experience. Thus contemporary white male claims of "reverse discrimination" caused by affirmative action, for instance, fail these criteria because they attend only to white men's experiences and interests.

The "materialist moment" also addresses a paradox that many theorists have noted: if a standpoint is based in experience, must one have that experience to have the standpoint? If so, then all that multiple standpoints would seem to do is multiply the various camps of epistemologically separated groups who, by definition, cannot communicate with one another. If not, however, then what is to stop those with privilege from defining the standpoints of less powerful people in ways that simply perpetuate, rather than challenge, existing power inequalities? (Lennon 1995, 141–42). The "materialist moment" takes a both/and approach to this problem: it allows for the adoption of standpoints not immediately out of one's own experience, but it requires that the discursive understanding come *from* the experience. As Uma Narayan (1989) argues:

> Our commitment to the contextual nature of knowledge does not require us to claim that those who do not inhabit these contexts can never have any knowledge of them. But this commitment does permit us to argue that it is *easier* and *more likely* for the oppressed to have critical insights into the conditions of their own oppression than it is for those who live outside those structures. Those who actually *live* the oppressions of class, race, or gender have faced the issues that such oppressions generate in a variety of different situations. (264).

Such criteria allow the distinction between a standpoint and "ideology" which can be racist, misogynist, homophobic, classist, and so forth. A feminist-standpoints' approach acknowledges that men have insights to contribute to feminists, as do whites to African-Americans, heterosexuals to lesbians and gays. This is different from saying that "masculinism" has something to offer feminism, or "racism" has something to offer African-Americans, or "heterosexism" has something to offer lesbians and gays. The likelihood of masking ideology as standpoint is greater from the perspective of the more powerful in each of these pairs because such ideologies reinforce their preexisting claims to power. In keeping with Narayan's argument, the methodological advantage of standpoint epistemology for feminism lies in its notion that, at least at this point in history, women of various positionalities will be likely to have more to say to men of most positionalities about sexism. African-Americans would have more to say to whites about racism; and lesbians and homosexuals, more to say to heterosexuals about heterosexism because it considers the experiences of those oppressed by these ideologies and practices "less partial and perverse" than those of the more privileged position. The exchange of insights that follows from this is not exclusively from "the bottom up," but the burden of proof lies with the privileged, not the oppressed, to defend their vision of reality.

However, does all this make feminist standpoint a postmodern strategy? Or does it simply illustrate standpoint's (or perhaps my own) modernist blinders to the point that postmodernism is trying to make? It is a bit of both. We cannot get away from the fact that feminism is and must be in part a modernist discourse. Without the subject "woman," regardless of how we define it, feminism cannot exist; this subject, however, is at odds with postmodernism because it seems to freeze a notion of identity in time. *Standpoints'* feminism suggests that the definition of "who we are" will shift and change, in postmodern fashion, in response to different material conditions as well as to the fact that each individual occupies more than one experiential and identity location. This shifting within and between discourses and "materialist moments" does not mean that we cannot develop theories based on experience within particular and even contingent historical contexts. Indeed, we must. Hartsock's feminist standpoint theory allows us to occupy both theoretical positions at once and, thereby, provides a powerful and versatile strategy for addressing feminist theory's most contentious debates.

Notes

1. The fact that this special volume (in which the essay originally appeared-Ed.) is about "feminist standpoint theory" through the particular lens of Hartsock's work highlights the fact that Hartsock alone among the early standpoint theorists, such as Dorothy Smith and Sandra Harding, is a political scientist. Indeed, the fact that Hartsock's work has had such interdisciplinary impact from within political science is what led me to organize the 1994 APSA roundtable "The Feminist Standpoint: Ten Years Later," which in turn stimulated this *Women & Politics* special volume. The present paper is an expansion of my remarks on that panel. Thanks to panel participants, Sandra Harding, Susan Hekman, Sally Ruddick, Peregrine Schwartz-Shea, and most of all Nancy Hartsock, for whose personal and professional mentoring over the past fifteen years, I am truly grateful. Thanks also to the anonymous reviewers of *Women & Politics* as well as the guest editors of this volume for their helpful suggestions.

2. Similar errors are made by Susan Hekman (1990), who claims that Hartsock "has argued consistently that feminists must reject all epistemologies that are formulated by male theorists and adopt an epistemology that privileges the female standpoint" in direct contradiction to Hartsock's own statements; and by Jane Flax (1990), who, in apparent repudiation of her earlier reliance on standpoint theory (Flax 1983), claims that it presupposes "that people will act rationally on their 'interests' " again in direct contradiction to Hartsock's scathing critique of "market man's" psychology (Hartsock 1984, Chap. 7). Flax also maintains that the standpoint approach "assumes that the oppressed are not in some fundamental ways damaged by their social experience" (Flax 1990, 141), which ignores Hartsock's explicit acknowledgement of this paradoxical problem for standpoint theory (Hartsock 1984, 245).

3. If it lasted too long, of course, then the movement toward transformation would be lost; and once the moment is "frozen," it is no longer a moment but its own totalizing discourse. Hence, the temporal imagery suggested by the term "moment" indicates that

It is part of a moving and shifting process; it cannot be static or stationary, for stasis lies outside of time.

4. I say "even" to note that "escaping" language is quite different from being "prior to" it. Even theorists like Butler (1993) suggest the possibility of that which "escapes" discourse, though she is extremely uncertain about how and even whether one could go about identifying it. Standpoint theory's materialist moment posits something more concrete than Butler would allow.

References

Alcoff, Linda. 1988. "Cultural Feminism versus Poststructuralism: The Identity Crisis in Feminist Theory." *Signs: Journal of Women in Culture and Society* 13(3):405–36.

Alcoff, Linda and Elizabeth Potter, eds. 1993. *Feminist Epistemologies.* New York: Routledge.

Bar On, Bat-Ami. 1993. "Marginality and Epistemic Privilege." In *Feminist Epistemologies*, ed. Linda Alcoff and Elizabeth Potter. New York: Routledge.

Butler, Judith. 1990. *Gender Trouble: Feminism and the Subversion of Identity.* New York: Routledge.

Butler, Judith. 1993. *Bodies that Matter: On the Discursive Limits of "Sex."* New York: Routledge.

Collins, Patricia Hill. 1990. *Black Feminist Thought: Knowledge, Power, and the Politics of Empowerment.* New York: Unwin Hyman.

Cornell, Drucilla. 1993. *Transformations: Recollective Imagination and Sexual Difference.* New York: Routledge.

Ferguson, Kathy. 1993. *The Man Question: Visions of Subjectivity in Feminist Theory.* Berkeley: University of California Press.

Flax, Jane. 1983. "Political Philosophy and the Patriarchal Unconscious." In *Discovering Reality: Feminist Perspectives on Epistemology, Methodology, Metaphysics and Philosophy of Science*, ed. Sandra Harding and Merrill B. Hintikka. Boston: D. Reidel Publishing Co.

Flax, Jane. 1990. *Thinking Fragments: Feminism, Postmodernism, and Psychoanalysis.* Berkeley: University of California Press.

Foucault, Michel. 1990. *The History of Sexuality: Volume I, An Introduction.* New York: Vintage Books.

Fraser, Nancy and Linda Nicholson. 1990. "Social Criticism Without Philosophy: An Encounter Between Feminism and Postmodernism." *Feminism/Postmodernism*, ed. Linda Nicholson. New York: Routledge.

Grant, Judith. 1993. *Fundamental Feminism: Contesting the Core Concepts of Feminist Theory.* New York: Routledge.

Haraway, Donna J. 1991. *Simians, Cyborgs, and Women: The Reinvention of Nature.* New York: Routledge.

Harding, Sandra. 1986. *The Science Question in Feminism.* Ithaca: Cornell University Press.

Harding, Sandra. 1991. *Whose Science? Whose Knowledge? Thinking from Women's Lives.* Ithaca: Cornell University Press.

Hartsock, Nancy. 1981. "Political Change: Two Perspectives on Power." In *Building Feminist Theory: Essays from Quest, A Feminist Quarterly*, ed. Charlote Bunch. New York: Longman.

Hartsock, Nancy. 1983. "The Feminist Standpoint: Developing the Ground for a Specifically Feminist Historical Materialism." In *Discovering Reality: Feminist Perspectives on Epistemology, Methodology, Metaphysics and Philosophy of Science*, ed. Sandra Harding and Merrill B. Hintikka. Boston: D. Reidel Publishing Co.

Hartsock, Nancy. 1984. *Money, Sex, and Power: Toward a Feminist Historical Materialism.* Boston: Northeastern University Press.

Hartsock, Nancy. 1987. "Rethinking Modernism: Majority vs. Minority Theories." *Cultural Critique* 7:187–206.

Hartsock, Nancy. 1990. "Foucault on Power: A Theory for Women?" In *Feminism/Postmodernism*, ed. Linda Nicholson. New York: Routledge.

Hawksworth, Mary. 1989. "Knowers, Knowing, Known: Feminist Theory and Claims of Truth." *Signs: Journal of Culture and Society* 14(3):533–57.

Hekman, Susan. 1990. *Gender and Knowledge.* Boston: Northeastern University Press.

Hennessy, Rosemary. 1993. *Materialist Feminism and the Politics of Discourse.* New York: Routledge.

Henwood, Karen L. and Nick F. Pidgeon. 1995. "Remarking the Link: Qualitive Research and Feminist Standpoint Theory." *Feminism & Psychology* 5(1):7–30.

Hirschmann, Nancy J. 1989. "Freedom, Recognition and Obligation: A Feminist Approach to Political Theory." *American Political Science Review* 83(4):1227–44.

Hirschmann, Nancy J. 1992. *Rethinking Obligation: A Feminist Method for Political Theory.* Ithaca: Cornell University Press.

hooks, bell. 1984. *Feminist Theory: From Margin to Center.* Boston: South End Press.

Jaggar, Alison M. 1983. *Feminist Politics and Human Nature.* Totowa: Rowman and Allenheld.

Keller, Evelyn Fox. 1985. *Reflections on Gender and Science.* New Haven: Yale University Press.

Keohane, Robert. 1989. "International Relations Theory: Contributions of a Feminist Standpoint." *Millennium: Journal of International Studies* 18(2):2245–54.

Lennon, Kathleen. 1995. "Gender and Knowledge." *Journal of Gender Studies* 4(2):133–43.

Marx, Karl. 1970. "Theses on Feuerbach." In *The German Ideology,* ed. C.J. Arthur. New York: International Publishers.

McDowell, Linda. 1992. "Doing Gender: Feminism, Feminists, and Research Methods in Human Geography." *Transactions of the Institute of British Geographers* 17(4):399–416.

McLennon, Gregor. 1995. "Feminism, Epistemology, and Postmodernism: Reflections on Current Ambivalence." *Sociology: The Journal of the British Sociological Association* 29:391–409.

Mohanty, Chandra. 1992. "Feminist Encounters: Locating the Politics of Experience." In *Destablizing Theory,* ed. Michele Barrett and Ann Phillips. Oxford: Polity Press.

Narayan, Uma. 1989. "The Project of Feminist Epistemology: Perspectives from a Nonwestern Feminist." In *Gender/Body/Knowledge: Feminist Reconstructions of Being and Knowing,* ed. Alison, M. Jaggar and Susan R. Bordo. New Brunswick: Rutgers University Press.

Noddings, Nel. 1990. "Ethics from the Standpoint of Women." In *Theoretical Perspectives on Sexual Difference,* ed. Deborah L. Rhode. New Haven: Yale University Press.

Offen, Karen. 1990. "Feminism and Sexual Difference in Historical Perspective." In *Theoretical Perspectives on Sexual Difference,* ed. Deborah L. Rhode. New Haven: Yale University Press.

Ramazanoglu, Caroline. 1989. "Improving on Sociology: The Problems of Taking a Feminist Standpoint." *Sociology: The Journal of the British Sociological Association* 23(3):427–42.

Rixecker, Stefanie S. 1994. "Expanding the Discursive Context of Policy Design: A Matter of Feminist Standpoint Epistemology." *Policy Sciences* 27(2/3):119–42.

Ruddick, Sarah. 1989. *Maternal Thinking: Toward a Politics of Peace.* New York: Basic Books.

Seller, Anne. 1994. "Should the Feminist Philosopher Stay at Home?" In *Knowing the Difference: Feminist Perspectives in Epistemology,* ed. Kathleen Lennon and Margaret Whitford. New York: Routledge.

Smith, Dorothy. 1990. *Texts, Facts, and Femininity: Exploring the Relations of Ruling.* New York: Routledge.

Spelman, Elizabeth V. 1988. *Inessential Woman: Problems of Exclusion in Feminist Thought.* Boston: Beacon Press.

Swigonski, Mary E. 1994. "The Logic of Feminist Standpoint Theory for Social Work Research." *Social Work: Journal of the National Association for Social Work Research* 39(4):387–93.

Sylvester, Christine. 1994. "Empathetic Cooperation: A Feminist Method for International Relations." *Millennium: Journal of International Studies* 23(2):315–34.

Weeks, Kathi. 1995. "Feminist Standpoint Theories and the Return of Labor." In *Marxism in the Postmodern Age: Confronting the New World Order,* ed. Antonio Callari, Stephen Cullenberg, and Carole Biewener. New York: Guilford Press.

26

The Subsistence Perspective

MARIA MIES
VANDANA SHIVA

... We share common concerns that emerge from an invisible global politics in which women worldwide are enmeshed in their everyday life; and a convergence of thinking arising from our participation in the efforts of women to keep alive the processes that sustain us. These shared thoughts and concerns aim not to demonstrate uniformity and homogeneity but rather a creative transcendence of our differences. There are many reasons for our collaboration. One is to make visible the "other" global processes that are becoming increasingly invisible as a new world order emerges based on the control of people and resources worldwide for the sake of capital accumulation. Another is the optimistic belief that a search for identity and difference will become more significant as a platform for resistance against the dominant global forces of capitalist patriarchy, which simultaneously homogenizes and fragments.

This capitalist-patriarchal perspective interprets difference as hierarchical and uniformity as a prerequisite for equality. Our aim is to go beyond this narrow perspective and to express our diversity and, in different ways, address the inherent inequalities in world structures which permit the North to dominate the South, men to dominate women, and the frenetic plunder of ever more resources for ever more unequally distributed economic gain to dominate nature.

Probably we arrived at these common concerns because our experiences and insights, and the analyses we have formulated, grew out of participation in the women's and ecology movements rather than from within the cocoon of academic research institutions. In recent years we had increasingly been confronted by the same fundamental issues concerning survival and the preservation of life on this planet, not only of women, children and humanity in general, but also of the vast diversity of fauna and flora. In analysing the causes which have led to the destructive tendencies that threaten life on earth we became aware—quite independently—of what we call the capitalist patriarchal world system.

This system emerged, is built upon and maintains itself through the colonization of women, of "foreign" peoples and their lands; and of nature, which it is gradually destroying. As feminists actively seeking women's liberation from male domination, we could not, however, ignore the fact that "modernization" and "development" processes and "progress" were responsible for the

degradation of the natural world. We saw that the impact on women of ecological disasters and deterioration was harder than on men, and also, that everywhere, women were the first to protest against environmental destruction.
As activists in the ecology movements, it became clear to us that science and
technology were not gender neutral; and in common with many other women,
we began to see that the relationship of exploitative dominance between man
and nature, (shaped by reductionist modern science since the 16th century)
and the exploitative and oppressive relationship between men and women that
prevails in most patriarchal societies, even modern industrial ones, were closely
connected....

If the final outcome of the present world system is a general threat to life
on planet earth, then it is crucial to resuscitate and nurture the impulse and
determination to survive, inherent in all living things. A closer examination of
the numerous local struggles against ecological destruction and deterioration,
for example: against atomic power plants in Germany,[1] against chalk mining
and logging in the Himalayas;[2] the activities of the Green Belt Movement in
Kenya;[3] and of Japanese women against food pollution by chemically stimulated,
commercial agriculture and for self-reliant producer-consumer networks;[4] poor
women's efforts in Ecuador to save the mangrove forests as breeding grounds for
fish and shrimp;[5] the battle of thousands of women in the South for better water
management, soil conservation, land use, and maintenance of their survival
base (forests, fuel, fodder) against the industrial interests, confirmed that many
women, worldwide, felt the same anger and anxiety, and the same sense of
responsibility to preserve the bases of life, and to end its destruction. Irrespective
of different racial, ethnic, cultural, or class backgrounds, this common concern
brought women together to forge links in solidarity with other women, people
and even nations. In these processes of action and reflection similar analyses,
concepts and visions also sometimes emerged.

In South-West Germany, peasant women in the Whyl Movement were the
most active in one of the first anti-nuclear power movements in that country.
They established cross-border links with similar movements in Switzerland and
France as well as with other movements in Germany, to intellectuals, students
and to city-dwelling feminists. In this process they became conscious of the
patriarchal men-women relationship; for many women this was the first step
towards their own liberation.[6] When, some years later, two of the movement's
leading women were interviewed they clearly articulated their vision of an alternative society, based not on the model of growth-oriented industrialism and
consumerism but close to what we call the subsistence perspective.[7] Other examples of women's endeavours to overcome social fragmentation and create
solidarity are Lois Gibbs's opposition to the dumping of toxic waste and Medha
Patkar's to the construction of the Narmada dams. Women activists in the USA
have led the campaign against toxic waste dumping, and Lois Gibbs's strenuous
and persistent efforts in opposing toxic waste dumping in the now notorious

Love Canal outrage are well known. As Murray Levine wrote,[8] "If Love Canal has taught Lois Gibbs—and the rest of us—anything, it is that ordinary people become very smart, very quickly when their lives are threatened. They become adept at detecting absurdity, even when it is concealed in bureaucratic and scientific jargon."

In the 1980s toxic dumps began to be sited in areas inhabited by poor and coloured people; today, the strongest resistance against this practice is to be found in these areas. For women fighting against toxic dumping, the issue is not just NIMBY (not in my backyard) but "everyone's backyard" (the title of a newsletter on citizen's action). Joan Sharp, who worked at the Schlage Lock Company in North Carolina USA until the factory was closed to be set up as a maquiladora in Tecate, Mexico, exemplifies this solidarity. In March 1992, then unemployed, she went to Mexico as a representative of Black Workers for Justice in order to give the Mexican workers information on the company and hazardous chemicals which she and others believe caused 30 of her co-workers to die of cancer. The 200 pages of documents she had brought described Schlage's use of toxic chemicals, its contamination of the groundwater, and its failure to provide promised severance pay for production workers. None of the Tecate workers had been aware that Schlage had closed operations in San Francisco in order to take advantage of low wages in the Black Belt South, and then in Mexico.[9] ...

These examples show how the shared concern of countless women worldwide override their differences, and evokes a sense of solidarity that perceives such differences as enriching their experiences and struggles rather than as marking boundaries. . . .

Freedom Versus Emancipation

This effort to create a holistic, all-life embracing cosmology and anthropology, must necessarily imply a concept of freedom different from that used since the Enlightenment.

This involves rejecting the notion that Man's freedom and happiness depend *on an ongoing process of emancipation from nature,* on independence from, and dominance over natural processes by the power of reason and rationality. Socialist utopias were also informed by a concept of freedom that saw man's destiny in his historic march from the "realm of necessity" (the realm of nature), to the "realm of freedom"—the "real" human realm—which entailed transforming nature and natural forces into what was called a "second nature," or culture. According to scientific socialism, the limits of both nature and society are dialectically transcended in this process.

Most feminists also shared this concept of freedom and emancipation, until the beginning of the ecology movement. But the more people began to reflect upon and question why the application of modern science and technology, which has been celebrated as humanity's great liberators, had succeeded only in procuring increasing ecological degradation, the more acutely aware they became of the contradiction between the enlightenment logic of emancipation and the eco-logic of preserving and nurturing natural cycles of regeneration. In 1987, at the congress "Women and Ecology" in Cologne (Germany), Angelika Birk and Irene Stoehr spelt out this contradiction, particularly as it applied to the women's movement which, like many other movements inspired by the Enlightenment ideas, had fastened its hopes on the progress of science and technology, particularly in the area of reproduction, but also of house- and other work. Irene Stoehr pointed out that this concept of emancipation necessarily implied dominance over nature, including human, female nature; and, that ultimately, this dominance relationship was responsible for the ecological destruction we now face. How, then, could women hope to reach both their own and nature's "emancipation" by way of the same logic?[10]

To "catch-up" with the men in their society, as many women still see as the main goal of the feminist movement, particularly those who promote a policy of equalization, implies a demand for a greater, or equal share of what, in the existing paradigm, men take from nature. This, indeed, has to a large extent happened in Western society: modern chemistry, household technology, and pharmacy were proclaimed as women's saviours, because they would "emancipate" them from household drudgery. Today we realize that much environmental pollution and destruction is causally linked to modern household technology. Therefore, can the concept of emancipation be compatible with a concept of preserving the earth as our life base?

... But our critique of the Enlightenment emancipation-logic was impelled not only by an insight into its consequences for women, but also a concern for those victims, who, since the White Man's march towards "the realm of freedom" had paid for this freedom by the denial of their own subjectivity, freedom, and, often, their survival base. As well as women, these include nature and other peoples—the colonized and "naturized"—"opened up" for free exploitation and subordination, transformed into the "others," the "objects," in the process of European (male) "subject's" emancipation from the "realm of necessity."

From the perspective of these victims, the illusory character of this project becomes clear. Because, for them, this means not only, as noted above, the destruction of their survival base and so on but also that ever to attain (through so-called catching-up development) the same material level as those who benefited from this process is impossible. Within a limited planet, there can be no escape from necessity. To find freedom does not involve subjugating or transcending the "realm of necessity," but rather focusing on developing a vision of freedom, happiness, the "good life" within the limits of necessity, of nature. We call this vision the subsistence perspective, because to "transcend" nature can no longer be justified, instead, nature's subsistence potential in all its dimensions and manifestations must be nurtured and conserved. Freedom *within* the realm of necessity can be universalized to all; freedom *from* necessity can be available to only a few. ...

Notes

1. N. Gladitz, *Lieber heute aktiv als morgen radioaktiv* (Berlin: Wagenbach, 1976).
2. V. Shiva, *Staying Alive: Women, Ecology and Survival* (New Delhi: Kali for Women, and London: Zed Books, 1988). V. Shiva, "Fight for Survival" (Interview with Chamun Devi and Itwari Devi), *Illustrated Weekly of India*, November 15 1987.
3. I. Dankelman, and J. Davidson, *Women and Environment in the Third World: Alliance for the Future* (London: Earthscan Publications Ltd., 1988).
4. Paul Ekins, *A New World Order: Grassroots Movements for Global Change* (London and New York: Routledge, 1992).
5. E. Accion Ecologica, Bravo, *Un Ecosistema en peligro: Los bosques de maglar en la costa ecuatoriana.* Quito, n.d.
6. This is based on an interview with Annemarie Sacher and Lore Haag, two of the women leaders of the anti-atomic movement, at Whyl, Kaiserstuhl, S.W. Germany. This was the first of these movements in Germany; it lasted from 1974 to about 1976 when the construction of the nuclear reactor was stopped. For more details see Saral Sarkar, *Green Alternative Politics in West Germany, Vol. I, The New Social Movements* (New Delhi: Promilla Publishers, 1992).
7. Dankelman and Davidson, *Women and Environment.*
8. Murray Levine, *Love Canal: My Story* (Albany, NY: SUNY, 1982), p. xv.
9. *Voices Unidas*, vol. I, no. 2 (1992).
10. A. Birk and I. Stoehr, "Der Fortschritt entläßt seine Tochter," in *Frauen und Ökologie. Gegen den Machbarkeitswahn*, (Köln: Volksblattverlag, 1987).

27

Why Standpoint Matters

ALISON WYLIE

Standpoint theory is an explicitly political as well as social epistemology. Its central and motivating insight is an inversion thesis: those who are subject to structures of domination that systematically marginalize and oppress them may, in fact, be epistemically privileged in some crucial respects. They may know different things, or know some things better than those who are comparatively privileged (socially, politically), by virtue of what they typically experience and how they understand their experience. Feminist standpoint theorists argue that gender is one dimension of social differentiation that may make such a difference epistemically. Their aim is both to understand how the systematic partiality of authoritative knowledge arises—specifically, its androcentrism and sexism—and to account for the constructive contributions made by those working from marginal standpoints (especially feminist standpoints) in countering this partiality.

In application to scientific knowledge, standpoint theory holds the promise of mediating between the extremes generated by protracted debate over the role of values in science. In this it converges on the interests of a good many philosophers of science who are committed to making sense of the social nature of scientific inquiry without capitulating to the kind of constructivist critique that undercuts any normative claim to epistemic privilege or authority.[1] Moreover, it offers a framework for understanding how, far from compromising epistemic integrity, certain kinds of diversity (cultural, racial, gender) may significantly enrich scientific inquiry, a matter of urgent practical and political as well as philosophical concern. Despite this promise, feminist standpoint theory has been marginal to mainstream philosophical analyses of science—indeed, it has been marginal to science studies generally—and it has had an uneasy reception among feminist theorists. My aim is to disentangle what I take to be the promising core of feminist standpoint theory from this conflicted history of debate, and to outline a framework for standpoint analysis of scientific practice that complements some of the most exciting new developments in philosophical science studies.

Contention about Standpoints

Standpoint theory may rank as one of the most controversial theories to have been proposed and debated in the twenty-five to thirty year history of second wave feminist thinking about knowledge and science. Its advocates as much as its critics disagree vehemently about its parentage, its status as a theory, and, crucially, its relevance to current feminist thinking about knowledge. In a special feature on standpoint theory published by *Signs*, Hekman describes standpoint theory as having enjoyed a brief period of influence in the mid-1980s but as having fallen so decisively from favor that, a decade later, it was largely dismissed as a "quaint relic of feminism's less sophisticated past."[2] On her account, standpoint theory was ripe for resuscitation by the late 1990s; it is now being reconstituted by new advocates, revisited by its original proponents, and in Hekman's case (one of the former), heralded as the harbinger of a new feminist paradigm.

Hekman's telling has been sharply contested by those aligned with now canonical examples of standpoint theorizing—Hartsock, Harding, Smith, and Collins, most immediately.[3] The point of departure for much of this discussion is Nancy C. M. Hartsock, "The Feminist Standpoint: Developing the Ground for a Specifically Feminist Historical Materialism," in S. Harding and M. B. Hintikka, eds., *Discovering Reality: Feminist Perspectives on Epistemology, Metaphysics, Methodology, and Philosophy of Science* (Dordrecht: Reidel, 1983); hereafter cited in the text as "Historical Materialism." Hartsock responds to the debate generated by "Historical Materialism" in "Standpoint Theories for the Next Century," in Kenny and Kinsella (eds.), *Politics*, 93–102; hereafter cited in text as "Next Century"; and in "The Feminist Standpoint Revisited," in *The Feminist Standpoint Revisited and Other Essays* (Boulder, Colo.: Westview Press, 1998), 227–48; hereafter cited in text as *Standpoint Revisited*. On some dimensions the differences among her critics are as great as between any of them and Hekman. Some ask whether there is any such thing as "standpoint theory": perhaps it is a reification of Harding's field-defining epistemic categories, an unstable (hypothetical) position that mediates between feminist empiricism and oppositional postmodernism.[4] When specific positions and practices are identified as instances of standpoint theory, the question arises of whether it is really an *epistemic* theory rather than a close-to-the ground feminist methodology; to do social science as a standpoint feminist is to approach inquiry from the perspective of insiders rather than impose on them the external categories of professional social science, a managing bureaucracy, ruling elites.[5] Among those who understand standpoint theory to be a theory of knowledge, there is further disagreement about whether it is chiefly descriptive or normative, aimed at the justification of knowledge claims rather than an account of their production. And there is wide recognition that feminist standpoint theory of all these various kinds has undergone substantial change in the fifteen years it has been actively debated. As Hartsock observes, "standpoint theories must be recognized as essentially contested" ("Next Century," 93).

As fractious as this recent debate has been, however, there are some things on which everyone agrees. Whatever form standpoint theory takes, if it is to be viable it must not imply or assume two distinctive theses with which it is often associated:

> *First,* standpoint theory must not presuppose an *essentialist* definition of the social categories or collectivities in terms of which epistemically relevant standpoints are characterized. *Second,* it must not be aligned with a thesis of *automatic epistemic privilege;* standpoint theorists cannot claim that those who occupy particular standpoints (usually subdominant, oppressed, marginal standpoints) automatically know more, or know better, by virtue of their social, political location.

Feminist standpoint theory of the 1970s and 1980s is often assumed to be a theory about the epistemic properties of a distinctively gendered standpoint: that of women in general, or that defined by feminists who theorize the standpoint of women, where this gendered social location is a biological or psychoanalytic given, as close to an "indifferent" natural kind as a putatively social, "interactive" kind can be (to use Hacking's terminology).[6] The claim attributed to this "women's way of knowing" genre of feminist standpoint theory is that, by virtue of their gender identity, women (or those who critically interrogate this identity) have distinctive forms of knowledge that should be valorized.

It is not clear that anyone who has advocated standpoint theory as a theory of knowledge or research practice has endorsed either the essentialist or the automatic privilege thesis. Hartsock and Smith, for example, were appalled to find their explicitly Marxist arguments construed in essentialist terms (Hartsock, "Truth or Justice," *Standpoint Revisited,* 232; Smith, 1997); the point of insisting that what we know is structured by the social and material conditions of our lives was to throw into relief the contingent, historical nature of what we count as knowledge and focus attention on the processes by which knowledge is produced. Hartsock is no doubt right that early arguments for standpoint theory have been consistently misread because many of the commentators lack grounding in Marxist theory.[7] I would extend this analysis. The systematic and, in this sense, the perverse nature of the misreadings to which Hartsock responds reflect exactly the thesis her critics deny; their social location (if not consciously articulated standpoint—a distinction to which I will return) seems to impose the limitations of categories derived from a dominant individualist ideology. Hartsock, Collins, Harding, and Smith all object to a recurrent tendency to reduce the notion of standpoint to the social location of individuals, a move that is inevitable, I suggest, if it is incomprehensible (to critics) that social structures, institutions, or systemically structured roles and relations could be robust enough to shape what epistemic agents can know. On such assumptions, unless the standpoint-specific capacities of knowers are fixed by natural or quasi-natural forces (e.g., bio-genetic or psychoanalytic processes), standpoints fragment into myriad individual perspectives, and standpoint theory reduces to the relativism of identity politics.

It has to be said that, in her rebuttals to Hekman and various other critics, Hartsock makes little mention of her early use of psychoanalytic theory (object relations theory) to account for how individuals internalize the power relations constitutive of a sexual division of labor (specifically, reproductive labor) and the associated gender roles. If essentialism lurks anywhere it is in this component of her original argument, and it is this that has drawn the sharpest criticism. It was the use of object relations theory to develop feminist theories of science and knowledge that Harding challenged in 1986 when she argued that the epistemic orientation attributed to women could not be a stable or universal effect of psychoanalytic processes set in motion by interactions with female caregivers; the characteristics distinctive of women closely parallel those claimed by the advocates of a pan-African world-view as typical for men as well as women (*The Science Question*, 167–79, 185). But her critique left standing the central and defining (Marxist) insights of standpoint theory as articulated by Hartsock.[8] Indeed, Harding drew attention to structural characteristics of the power relations that constitute marked categories in opposition to (as exclusions from) whatever is normative in a given context—the oppositions between colonial elites and those subject to colonial domination; between men and women/not-men— and she argued that these have powerful, if contingent, material consequences for the lives of those designated "other" in relation to dominant social groups. It is an empirical question exactly what historical processes created these hierarchically structured relations of inequality, and what material conditions, what sociopolitical structures and symbolic or psychological mechanisms, maintain them in the present. But these are precisely the kinds of robust forces of social differentiation that may well make a difference to what epistemic agents embedded in systemic power relations are likely to experience and understand. The processes of infantile socialization described by object relations theory may play an important role but so, too, do the ongoing relations of production and reproduction—the different kinds of wage and sex-affective labor people do throughout their lives—that are at the center of Hartsock's epistemic theory and Smith's sociological practice.

By the early 1990s a number of standpoint theorists and practitioners had explicitly argued that it is this historical and structural reading of standpoint theory that bears further examination; essentialist commitments, if they were ever embraced or immanent, were roundly repudiated.[9] In this case the variants of standpoint theory that have been live options in the last decade need not be saddled be with a commitment to claims of automatic privilege. Like essentialist readings of standpoint theory, I suspect that attributions of automatic privilege persist not because anyone advocates them, but because they are necessary to counter deep-seated anxieties about what follows if strong normative claims of epistemic authority cannot be sustained. Debates about the viability of standpoint theory often seem to be driven by the assumption that, unless standpoint theorists can provide grounds for a new foundationalism, now rendered in social terms, they risk losing any basis for assessing and justifying knowledge claims;

unless standpoints provide special warrant for the knowledge produced by those who occupy them, standpoint theory devolves into a corrosive (now solipsistic) relativism.[10] Hekman's protests that, although standpoint theorists routinely claim that "starting research from the reality of women's lives, preferably those who are also oppressed by race and class, will lead to a more objective account of social reality," in the end, these theorists "offer no argument as to why this is the case" ("Truth and Method," 355). Hekman is dissatisfied with Harding's appeal to the epistemic advantage of standpoints that produce less partial, less distorted, "less false" knowledge ("Truth and Method," 353–55; Harding, 1991, 185-87), and she rejects out of hand Hartsock's references to standpoints that put us in a position to grasp underlying realities obscured by ideological distortion ("Truth and Method," 346; Hartsock, "Historical Materialism," 299). Her objection seems to be that talk of better and worse knowledge can make no sense unless we have a firm grip on notions of truth and objectivity that are robust enough to anchor epistemic justification; standpoint theorists have invoked, but failed to deliver, epistemic foundations.

I believe there is another way of reading the claims central to standpoint theory. Nonfoundationalist, nonessentialist arguments can be given (and have been given) for attributing epistemic advantage to some social locations and standpoints, although they are not likely to be satisfying for those who hanker for the security of ahistorical, translocational foundations. But to get this reading off the ground, a number of key epistemic concepts need to be reframed, and a distinction central to standpoint theory needs reemphasis.

Situated Knowledge versus Standpoint Theory

First, the distinction. A recurrent theme in responses to Hekman, among others, is an insistence that standpoint theory is concerned, not just with the epistemic effects of *social location,* but with both the effects and the emancipatory potential of *standpoints* that are struggled for and achieved, by epistemic agents who are critically aware of the conditions under which knowledge is produced and authorized.[11] Although the importance of standpoints in this second sense is emphasized in these exchanges, I believe that standpoint theorists should concern themselves with the epistemic effects of (systemically defined) social location as well as with fully formed standpoints.

On the first more minimal sense, the point of departure for standpoint analysis is commitment to some form of a *situated knowledge* thesis[12]: social location systematically shapes and limits what we know, including tacit, experiential knowledge as well as explicit understanding, what we take knowledge to be as well as specific epistemic content. What counts as a "social location" is structurally defined. What individuals experience and understand is shaped by their location in a hierarchically structured system of power relations: by the material conditions of their lives, by the relations of production and reproduction that structure their social interactions, and by the conceptual resources they have to represent and interpret these relations.

Standpoint in the sense that particularly interests standpoint theorists is our differential capacity to develop the kind of a standpoint *on* knowledge production that is a "project" (Weeks, 101), a critical consciousness about the nature of our social location and the difference it makes epistemically. Standpoint theory is itself such a project, carried out both through the kinds of social research that take seriously the understanding of insiders—for example, feminist research that starts from women's experience and women's lives (Smith, 1990; Harding, 1991)—and by feminist philosophers who are intent on creating a politically sophisticated, robustly social form of naturalized epistemology and philosophy of science. In either case, what is at stake is the jointly empirical and conceptual question of how power relations inflect knowledge: what systematic limitations are imposed by the social location of different classes or collectivities of knowers, and what potential they have for developing an understanding of this structured epistemic partiality.

On standpoint theory so conceived, it is necessarily an open question what features of location and/or standpoint are relevant to specific epistemic projects. For example, although any location or standpoint that "disappears gender" should be suspect,[13] we cannot assume that gender is uniquely or fundamentally important in structuring our understanding, or that a feminist standpoint will be the key to understanding the power dynamics that shape what we know. The project of developing critical consciousness—a jointly empirical, conceptual, and social-political enterprise—is the only way to answer questions about the epistemic relevance of a standpoint (in either sense) to specific epistemic projects.

But then the normative question reasserts itself: is there any basis for claiming that we should privilege the knowledge produced by those who occupy a particular location or standpoint? Does an analysis of the epistemic effects of social location or achieved standpoint provide a basis for justification or does it reinforce a social constructivism that ultimately gives rise to corrosive relativism? The inversion thesis that underpins most forms of feminist standpoint theory suggests that, when standpoint is taken into account, often the epistemic tables are turned. Those who are economically dispossessed, politically oppressed, and socially marginalized and are therefore likely to be discredited as epistemic agents—for example, as uneducated, uninformed, unreliable—may actually have a capacity, by virtue of their standpoint, to know things that those occupying privileged positions typically do not know, or are invested in not knowing (or, indeed, are invested in systematically ignoring and denying). It is this thesis that Hekman contests when she objects that no argument has been given for attributing greater objectivity to such standpoints.

Epistemic Advantage

The term objectivity (like truth) is so freighted it might be the better part of wisdom to abandon it. But for present purposes, I propose a reconstruction that may be useful in showing what a standpoint theorist can claim about epistemic advantage without embracing essentialism or an automatic privilege thesis.

As Hekman uses the term, objectivity is a property of knowledge claims. Objectivity is also standardly used to refer to conventionally desirable properties of epistemic agents: that they are neutral, dispassionate with regard to a particular subject of inquiry or research project. And sometimes it is used to refer to properties of the objects of knowledge.[14] Objective facts and objective reality are contrasted with ephemeral, subjective constructs; they constitute the "really real," as Lloyd puts it (1996), a broad category of things that exist and that have the properties they have independent of us. Presumably Hacking's "indifferent" kinds are at the core of this category of objects of knowledge (1999, 104–6). As a property of knowledge claims, objectivity seems to designate a loosely defined family of epistemic virtues that we expect will be maximized, in some combination, by the claims we authorize as knowledge. Standard lists, from authors as diverse as Kuhn, Longino (1990), Dupré, and Ereshefsky include, most prominently, a requirement of empirical adequacy that can be construed in at least two ways: as fidelity to a rich body of localized evidence (empirical depth), or as a capacity to "travel" (Haraway) such that the claims in question can be extended to a range of domains or applications (empirical breadth).[15] In addition, requirements of internal coherence, inferential robustness, and consistency with well-established collateral bodies of knowledge, as well as explanatory power and a number of other pragmatic and aesthetic virtues, may be taken as marks of objectivity collectively or individually.

Standpoint theory poses a challenge to any assumption that the neutrality of epistemic agents, objectivity in the second sense, is either a necessary or a sufficient condition for realizing objectivity in the first sense, in the knowledge claims they produce. Under some conditions, for some purposes, observer neutrality—disengagement, strategic affective distance from a subject—may be an advantage in learning crucial facts or grasping the causal dynamics necessary for understanding a subject. But at the same time considerable epistemic advantage may accrue to those who approach inquiry from an interested standpoint, even a standpoint of overtly political engagement. The recent history of feminist contributions to the social and life sciences illustrate how such a standpoint may fruitfully raise standards of empirical adequacy for hitherto unexamined presuppositions, expand the range of hypotheses under consideration in ways that ultimately improve explanatory power and open up new lines of inquiry.[16]

Likewise, there is no reason to assume that the qualities of empirical adequacy, consistency, explanatory probity and the rest cannot be realized, in some combination, in the investigation of objects of knowledge that are not "really real," for example, in the study of social phenomena that are interactive. Certainly objectivity in these cases may be sharply domain-limited; empirically adequate knowledge about an interactive social kind that transforms itself in the course of investigation will not travel very far, but it is no less objective for all that.

This last points to a key feature of the epistemic virtues that figure on any list of objectivity-making properties: they cannot be simultaneously maximized.[17] For example, the commitment to maximize empirical adequacy in understanding a rapidly transmuting interactive kind requires a tradeoff of empirical depth against empirical breadth. Similarly, explanatory power often requires a compromise of localized empirical adequacy, as does any form of idealization.[18] The interpretation of these requirements is open-ended; they are evolving standards of practice. The determination of how one virtue should be weighed against others is, likewise, a matter of ongoing negotiation that can only be settled by reference to the requirements of a specific epistemic project or problem. None of the virtues I have identified as constitutive of objectivity in the first sense are context or practice independent; they are all virtues we maximize for specific purposes. That said, the list I cite consists of epistemic virtues that have proven useful in a very wide range of enterprises—virtually any in which success turns on understanding accurately and in detail what is actually the case in the world in which we act and interact.

If the objectivity Hekman has in mind were understood in this sense—as designating a family of epistemic virtues that should be maximized (in some combination) in the claims we authorize as knowledge—there would be no incongruity in claiming that contingently, with respect to particular epistemic projects, some social locations and standpoints confer epistemic advantage. In particular, some *standpoints* (as opposed to *locations*) have the especially salient advantage that they put the critically conscious knower in a position to grasp the effects of power relations on their own understanding and that of others. The justification that an appeal to standpoint (or location) confers is, then, just that of a nuanced, well-grounded (naturalized) account of how reliable particular kinds of knowledge are likely to be given the social conditions of their production;[19] it consists of an empirically grounded assessment of the limitations of particular kinds of knowers, of how likely they are to be partial, and how likely it is that the knowledge they produce will fail to maximize salient epistemic virtues.

The Advantages of Marginal and Insider-Outsider Standpoints: A Framework for Analysis

When standpoint theorists discuss the kinds of epistemic advantage that may accrue to otherwise disadvantaged knowers, they consider a number of dimensions on which standpoint may make a difference to what we know and how well we know it. These include access to evidence (sometimes including background or collateral evidence); inferential heuristics that confer particular skill in disembedding empirical patterns; an expanded range of interpretive and explanatory hypotheses for making sense of evidence; and, often a condition for the rest, critical dissociation from the taken-for-granteds that underpin authoritative forms of knowledge. What I offer here is the outline of a framework for analysis (jointly empirical and conceptual) of cases in which the differential advantages of standpoint seem to be at play. It is only through the grounded analysis of concrete examples that we are likely to move beyond recurrent controversy about the viability of standpoint theory and delineate, with precision, its potential and limitations.

Consider the first of these elements of advantage, access to evidence. The central insight, which originates in class-based analyses of knowledge production, is that those who negotiate social, legal, and economic institutions from a position of marginality may quite literally see a side of society that can be ignored by those who are comparatively privileged and that is systematically obscured (or inverted) by dominant world-views that legitimate entrenched hierarchies of privilege. This point is illustrated by a recurrent theme in the feminist standpoint literature: that those who do domestic labor (at home or for pay) have access to a range of evidence that is invisible to (or systematically avoided by) those whose privilege includes a presumption that the daily work of maintaining their physical well being and home space will be taken care of by others. As Collins observes, "Afro-American women have long been privy to some of the most intimate secrets of white society,"[20] not only because of the messes they clean up, the garbage they dispose of, or the errands they are sent on, but also because of an asymmetry of recognition that arises when those they clean up after presume them to be epistemically incompetent. It is a staple of fictional accounts, like Barbara Neely's mystery *Blanche on the Lam*,[21] that those presumed ignorant and uninformed may learn a great deal about the lives of the elite when those who employ them assume that "hired hands didn't think, weren't curious, or observant, or capable of drawing even the most obvious conclusions" (*On the Lam*, 185).

But differential access to evidence is rarely an advantage on its own. Standpoint theorists often point to a special inferential acuity, a skill at discerning patterns and connections in the available evidence that goes along with subdominant status. As Narayan describes this, not only do the oppressed "have epistemic privilege when it comes to immediate knowledge of everyday life under oppression,"[22] but their experience also fosters an awareness of the dynamics of oppression that those living lives of relative privilege do not have to develop. Insider-outsiders are alert to "all the details of the ways in which their oppression . . . affects the major and minor details of their social and psychic lives" (36); they grasp subtle manifestations of power dynamics and they make connections between the contexts in which these operate that the privileged have no reason to notice or, indeed, have good reason not to notice. A number of parallels can be drawn with the empirical insights that have been pivotal for the flourishing programs of feminist research that have transformed many fields in the last thirty years. In some cases practitioners who are women and/or feminists have quite literally had privileged access to aspects of cultural life from which their male counterparts were excluded (e.g., in the early ethnographic work on the subsistence contributions of women to "hunter-gatherer" societies). In other cases the evidence that opened up feminist analysis was accessible to all, but its distinctive structure and significance was not recognized until a feminist angle of vision was brought to bear (e.g., the personal letters and diaries studied by feminist historians, the material record of household activities central to feminist analysis in archaeology, or the evidence of gender-differentiated pathways in moral development that has drawn the attention of feminist psychologists).

It is important to recognize that epistemic advantage on these first two dimensions is neither automatic nor all-encompassing. A condition of oppression and marginalization is often unequal access to key epistemic resources: certain kinds of information, the analytic skills acquired through formal education, or a range of theoretical and explanatory tools. As Narayan puts this point, the oppressed may have an intimate knowledge of local power relations that is not matched by an equally robust knowledge of "how their specific form of oppression originated, how it has been maintained and of all the systemic purposes it serves" (Narayan, 36); their evidential advantages may not translate into broader, more incisive explanatory insight.

At the same time, however, one dimension of epistemic advantage that has been especially important to standpoint theorists is the explanatory leverage that may accrue to those who use the resources of a marginal or insider-outsider standpoint to develop a stance of critical dissociation from the authoritative forms of knowledge that constitute a dominant world-view. In Neely's story, it is precisely because Blanche has to know how the world looks from more than one point of view that she sees through the self-serving and often self-deluding epistemic confidence of her employers. In an academic context, Collins describes how the dissonance between what she knows as a Black woman and what she has learned as a sociologist—the assumptions that "traditional sociologists see as normal"—throws into relief the partiality of authoritative sociological knowledge (1991, 49, 51). What Collins draws attention to here is the capacity of standpoint theory to account for the conceptual contributions that insider-outsiders have made to a range of research fields by throwing into relief certain framework assumptions that most practitioners do not even recognize they hold, by drawing attention to unexamined factors that enlarge existing interpretive and explanatory hypotheses, and by generating entirely new research questions. Standpoint theory offers a framework for explaining how it is that, far from automatically compromising the knowledge produced by a research enterprise, objectivity may be substantially improved by certain kinds of situated non-neutrality on the part of practitioners.

Conclusion

To recapitulate: wherever structures of social differentiation make a systematic difference to the kinds of work people do, the social relations they enter, their relative power in these relations, and their self-understanding, it may be relevant to ask what epistemic effects a (collectively defined) social location may have. And whenever commonalities of location and experience give rise to critical (oppositional) consciousness about the effects of social location, it may be possible to identify a distinctive standpoint to which strategic epistemic advantage accrues, particularly in grasping the partiality of a dominant way of thinking, bringing a new angle of vision to bear on old questions and raising new questions for empirical investigation. *Contra* Hekman, arguments can be given (and have been given) for ascribing *contingent* epistemic advantage to sub-dominant standpoints so conceived. These are arguments that demonstrate that objectivity can sometimes be improved and partiality reduced when inquiry is approached from these standpoints, not in an abstract sense measured against an absolute, ahistorical, or transcontextual standard, but with reference to one or another subset of the more homely virtues I have identified as constitutive of objectivity.

Extended to philosophical science studies, standpoint theory complements the social naturalism and pragmatism evident in the proposals for reframing the post-positivist philosophy of science suggested by an increasingly broad spectrum of philosophers of science. Advocates of standpoint theory in the sense outlined here are centrally concerned to understand science as a collective enterprise shaped by the kinds of factors identified by Solomon (2001). They share Longino's commitment to move beyond the rational-social dichotomy that has so deeply structured divergent traditions of science studies (2002), a commitment that, as Rouse and Hacking have argued, directs attention to the practice (rather than the products) of science as it unfolds in socially and polit-ically structured fields of engagement.[23] And they share Kitcher's appreciation of both the need and the potential for reframing ideals of objectivity so that scientific success can be understood in explicitly normative, pragmatic terms (2001). Most important, standpoint theorists recognize that questions about what standpoints make an epistemic difference and what difference they make cannot be settled in the abstract, in advance; they require the second order ap-plication of our best research tools to the business of knowledge production itself. And this is necessarily a problem-specific and open-ended process.

Notes

1. I have in mind four recent monographs that, in quite different ways, make this mediation their central objective: Joseph Rouse, *Engaging Science: How to Understand Its Practices Philosophically* (Ithaca, NY: Cornell University Press, 1996); Helen Longino, *The Fate of Knowledge* (Princeton, NJ: Princeton University Press, 2002); Philip Kitcher, *Science, Truth and Democracy* (Oxford: Oxford University Press, 2001); Miriam Solomon, *Social Empiricism* (Cambridge, MA: MIT Press, 2001).
2. Susan Hekman, "Truth and Method: Feminist Standpoint Theory Revisited," *Signs* 22.2 (1997): 341; hereafter cited in text as "Truth and Method."
3. Collins, Hartsock, Harding, and Smith all published responses that appeared with Hekman's article. Nancy C. M. Hartsock, "Comments On Hekman's 'Truth and Method': Truth or Justice?" *Signs* 22.2 (1997): 367–74; hereafter cited in text as "Truth or Justice." Patricia Hill Collins, "Comment on Hekman's 'Truth and Method': Where's the

Power?" *Signs* 22.2 (1997): 375–81. Sandra Harding, "Comment on Hekman's 'Truth and Method': Whose Standpoint Needs the Regimes of Truth and Reality?" *Signs* 22.2 (1997): 382–91. Dorothy E. Smith, "Comments on Hekman's 'Truth and Method,'" *Signs* 22.2 (1997): 392–98. In the same year a special issue of *Women and Politics* 18.3 (1997) on feminist standpoint theory appeared, edited by Sally J. Kenney and Helen Kinsella. This was subsequently published as *Politics and Feminist Standpoint Theories* (New York: The Haworth Press, 1997); hereafter cited in text as *Politics*. Contributions by Kenney, Welton, and Hirschmann provide useful assessments of the debate generated by standpoint theory.

4. Sandra Harding, *The Science Question in Feminism* (Ithaca, NY: Cornell University Press, 1986), 24–29; hereafter cited in text as *The Science Question*. See also Sandra Harding, *Whose Science? Whose Knowledge? Thinking From Women's Lives* (Ithaca, NY: Cornell University Press, 1991), chapter 5.

5. Dorothy E. Smith, "Women's Perspective as a Radical Critique of Sociology," *Sociological Inquiry* 44 (1974): 7–14; "A Sociology for Women," in J. Sherman and E. T. Beck, eds., *The Prism of Sex: Essays in the Sociology of Knowledge* (Madison: University of Wisconsin Press, 1979), 137–87.

6. Ian Hacking, *The Social Construction of What?* (Cambridge, MA: Harvard University Press, 1999), 100–24.

7. Hartsock, *Standpoint Revisited* (229, 233).

8. This is an argument I developed in a review essay, "The Philosophy of Ambivalence: Sandra Harding on 'The Science Question in Feminism,'" *Canadian Journal of Philosophy*, Supplementary Volume 13 (1987): 59–73.

9. For a review of these developments see Helen E. Longino, "Feminist Standpoint Theory and the Problems of Knowledge," *Signs* 19.1 (1993): 201–12.

10. See, for example, O'Leary's and Hirschmann's contributions to *Politics*; O'Leary addresses relativist worries that arise from a "logic of fragmentation" attributed to standpoint theory (1997, 57), and Hirschmann discusses "universalist" critiques of standpoint theory (1997, 77).

11. Hartsock emphasizes that "a standpoint is not simply an interested position (interpreted as bias) but is interested in the sense of being engaged" ("Historical Materialism," 285); it is a matter of developing an "oppositional consciousness . . . which takes nothing of the dominant culture as self-evidently true" (96–97).

12. Miriam Solomon, "Situatedness and Specificity" (manuscript in possession of the author, 1997).

13. Helen E. Longino, "In Search of Feminist Epistemology," *Monist* 77 (1994): 481.

14. For an elaboration of these distinctions see Elisabeth A. Lloyd, "Objectivity and the Double Standard for Feminist Epistemologies," *Synthese* 104 (1996): 351–81.

15. Helen E. Longino, *Science as Social Knowledge: Values and Objectivity in Scientific Inquiry* (Princeton, NJ: Princeton University Press, 1990). Thomas S. Kuhn, "Objectivity, Values, and Theory Choice," in *The Essential Tension* (Chicago: University of Chicago Press, 1977). John Dupré, *The Disorder of Things: Metaphysical Foundations of the Disunify of Science* (Cambridge, MA: Harvard University Press, 1993). Marc Ereshefsky, "Critical Notice: John Dupré, *The Disorder of Things*," *Canadian Journal of Philosophy* 25.1 (1995): 143–58. Donna J. Haraway, "Situated Knowledges: The Science Question in Feminist and the Privilege of Partial Perspective," in *Simians, Cyborgs, and Women: The Reinvention of Nature* (New York: Routledge, 1991), 183–202.

16. This argument is made with reference to a number of research fields in two recent publications: Londa Schiebinger, *Has Feminism Changed Science?* (Cambridge, MA: Harvard University Press, 1999); Angela N. H. Creager, Elizabeth Lunbeck, and Londa Schiebinger, eds., *Science, Technology, Medicine: The Difference Feminism Has Made* (Chicago: University of Chicago Press, 2001).

17. Longino makes this point with respect to a related list of epistemic virtues (1994, 479).

18. Nancy Cartwright, *How the Laws of Physics Lie* (Oxford: Oxford University Press, 1984); "Capacities and Abstractions," in *Scientific Explanation*, Minnesota Studies in the Philosophy of Science Volume XIII, ed. Philip Kitcher and Wesley C. Salmon (Minneapolis: University of Minnesota Press, 1989), 349–56. William C. Wimsatt, "False Models As Means to Truer Theories," in *Neutral Models in Biology*, ed. M. H. Nitecki and A. Hoffman (Oxford: Oxford University Press, 1987), 23–55. See also Kitcher's use of

"significance graphs" to capture the evolving contextual interests that shape trade-offs between epistemic virtues such as generality, precision, and accuracy (2001, 78–80).

19. This is the form of epistemic advantage Harding claims for critically self-conscious standpoints under the rubric of "strong objectivity," *contra* Hekman's foundationalist interpretation (Harding, 1991); see also Sandra Harding, "Rethinking Standpoint Epistemology: 'What Is Strong Objectivity?'," in Linda Alcoff and Elizabeth Potter, eds., *Feminist Epistemologies* (New York: Routledge, 1993), 49–82.

20. Patricia Hill Collins, "Learning from the Outsider Within," in Mary Margaret Fonow and Judith A. Cook, eds., *Beyond Methodology: Feminist Scholarship as Lived Research* (Bloomington: Indiana University Press, 1991), 35.

21. Barbara Neely, *Blanche on the Lam* (New York: Penguin Books, 1992); hereafter cited in text as *On the Lam*.

22. Uma Narayan, "Working Together Across Difference: Some Considerations on Emotions and Political Practice," *Hypatia* 3.2 (1988): 36.

23. For example, Ian Hacking, "The Self-Vindication of the Laboratory Sciences," in *Science as Practice and Culture*, ed. Andrew Pickering (Chicago: University of Chicago Press, 1992), 29–64.

28

Feminism and the Social Construction of Scientific Knowledge[1]

JOSEPH ROUSE

Feminist science studies and the sociology of scientific knowledge have emerged within the past twenty years as explicit challenges to the epistemological individualism that still predominates within most philosophy of science. The "Strong Programme" for the sociology of scientific knowledge was put forward first to provide distinctively sociological explanations for the diversity of human beliefs about the natural world.[2] Whereas earlier programs in the sociology of knowledge had exempted the natural sciences and mathematics from their purview, and the dominant Mertonian approaches to the sociology of science had confined their studies to scientific institutions, motivations, and organizational norms, the new sociologists proposed to explain the content of scientific knowledge in the same way that they would explain any other system of beliefs and practices. To do otherwise, they often argued, would invoke a scientifically unjustifiable a priori decision to exempt the sciences from empirical sociological investigation. Indeed, they called for a methodological commitment to some form of epistemological relativism to prevent centuries of cultural admiration for and epistemic deference to science from prejudicing sociological inquiry.

Alternative conceptions of scientific knowledge as a social achievement have emerged from recent feminist scholarship. An initial concern of feminist science studies was to examine and criticize the ways in which biological, psychological, and social scientific studies of women and men, and of sex and gender more generally, have been androcentric. The aim was to develop an explicitly feminist *science* alongside feminist transformations of scholarship in the humanities and social sciences. Scientific and philosophical resistance to these initial feminist criticisms of sexism in the guise of science has encouraged more general feminist reconceptions of scientific inquiry that would recognize feminist criticism as a constructive contribution to science.[3] In the resulting reconceptions of the sciences as politically engaged social practices, sex and gender have become aligned with race, colonialism or imperialism, sexual orientation, and other politically significant categories; the concern to challenge sexism specifically has remained a powerful motivation for feminist science studies, but sex and gender are no longer privileged or isolable analytic categories.

In this paper, I compare these two traditions, as challenges to philosophical orthodoxies and as constructive proposals for a *social* understanding of science. In juxtaposing feminism and sociology of science, however, my principal aim is to clarify the significance of feminism for philosophy of science and thereby to contribute to this volume's proposed dialogue. Feminist science studies are often thought to seek an intermediary position between traditional philosophy of science and the sociology of scientific knowledge: whereas the sociologists reject any normative account of the objectivity, rationality, or truth of scientific claims or methods, feminists would revise norms of rationality or objectivity rather than abandon them. I shall challenge this interpretation, despite its familiarity and initial plausibility. The supposedly sharp differences between normative philosophy and descriptive sociology presuppose a shared conception of knowledge, which I characterize as *epistemological.* Feminist scholars, I argue, are developing a different ontology of knowing, whose articulation displays and challenges the continuity between epistemological philosophies and sociologies of science.

Before initiating this comparison, I offer two significant caveats. First, my discussion deliberately overlooks contested issues within the feminist and sociological traditions in order to accentuate some shared conceptions that frame those internal disputes. My aim is not to minimize or suppress the disagreements, which in other contexts remain vital, but only to recognize some interwoven themes connecting otherwise disparate approaches. Some feminist theorists may well dissent from my presentation of these themes, but my hope is that dissenters will still find it useful in clarifying such differences. Even for my purposes, we should recognize that some recent work in the sociological tradition, most notably by Bruno Latour, Leigh Star, Andrew Pickering, Karin Knorr-Cetina, Michael Lynch, and others, challenges orthodox sociology of scientific knowledge in ways that encourage rapprochement with feminist studies of science. Yet the significance of such a rapprochement may also become clearer in light of my contrast between feminist and sociological approaches to scientific knowledge.

The second caveat is that my comparison brackets the most obvious difference between feminist and sociological studies of science, namely that gender and the sex/gender distinction play almost no role in sociologists's empirical case studies and methodological reflections. The absence of sociological attention to gender in science should be surprising, given the importance of sex and gender as social categories, and especially given the historical predominance of men within the sciences and the widespread use of gendered imagery to characterize both science and scientific interpretations of nature. Even if the relative unimportance of sex and gender for understanding science were an outcome of empirical research in sociology, one might expect that this conclusion would be highlighted and supported by extensive argument. No such argument is apparent in the sociological literature, and its absence ought to be regarded *prima facie* as a serious problem for the sociological tradition. Yet despite the importance of this issue, there are good reasons to bracket it for my purposes. Sociologists' inattention to gender, if mistaken, might reflect only a faulty application of their theoretical frameworks; perhaps the frameworks themselves leave ample room for a full appreciation of the significance of gender relations as a social explanans for the content of scientific knowledge. Moreover, bracketing questions of sex and gender can usefully emphasize that feminist science studies are not limited to studies of gender in science. Feminist scholars have called for a much more far-reaching reconception of the sciences as social, political, and cultural practices, a reconception that would thereby *enable* critical studies of gender to occupy a more prominent place in the culture of science.

The differences I shall identify between the sociological and feminist traditions emerge from a background of three important shared themes. First, both traditions understand scientific knowledge as a collective or social achievement. We may still reasonably speak of individuals as knowers, but such attributions of knowledge to individuals are derivative from or dependent upon the social achievement or authorization of knowledge. Second, both traditions argue that important aspects of traditional epistemologies and philosophies of science are not merely false, but ideological. Sociologists of scientific knowledge argue that philosophical explications of the rationality or verisimilitude of scientific methods and practices misconstrue the actual practice of science as revealed by empirical sociological studies and thereby unjustifiably legitimate the cultural and political authority of the sciences. Moreover, they argue, the exceptional or asymmetrical treatment accorded to the sciences by such philosophical accounts obscures important similarities between the sciences and other less authoritative practices and belief systems. Many feminists, meanwhile, have argued that familiar conceptions of scientific knowledge, as achieved or possessed by individuals, as disinterested and apolitical, or as rational and cognitive in ways that exclude the affective and embodied aspects of human experience, have simultaneously served to distort our understanding of science, to rationalize male dominance in science and elsewhere, and to reinforce the alienation or exclusion of many women from effective participation in science.

This insistence upon the ideological character of individualist and rationalizing interpretations of scientific knowledge points to the third common theme between feminist and sociological studies of science: both are politically engaged projects. Political commitment has been more readily apparent in feminism, since feminist science studies have always been projected as part of a larger political and cultural movement to criticize sexism and empower women. Yet beneath the sociologists' frequent insistence upon the need for methodological detachment and a symmetrical treatment of all belief systems has also been a broad political commitment to a humanism that is effectively articulated by Collins and Yearley (1992):

> The effect of SSK has been to show that the apparent independent power of the natural world is granted by human beings in social negotiation. Because the special power and authority of natural scientists comes from their privileged access to an independent realm, putting humans at the center removes the special authority.... Symmetry between the true and the false requires a human-centered universe. (310–11)

Thus, both feminists and sociologists of science argue that important aspects of science are contingent and alterable, even though traditional epistemologies present them as natural and immutable, and that recognizing their contingency makes a political difference.

The Sociology of Scientific Knowledge as Epistemological

From this shared background, however, the two traditions importantly diverge. Many of their differences result from sociologists' commitment to an *epistemological* conception of their project, or so I shall argue, whereas many feminist science studies begin to develop a philosophy of science that rejects an epistemological conception of knowledge. But what do I mean by an "epistemological" understanding of science? The intelligibility of epistemology as a field of study presumes that "knowledge" demarcates a coherent, surveyable domain of inquiry. Michael Williams has recently challenged the commonplace philosophical acceptance of that presumption:

> It is tempting to use "human knowledge" and "our knowledge of the external world" as though it were obvious that such phrases pick out reasonably definite objects of study. But it isn't obvious, or shouldn't be. We can talk of "our knowledge of the world," but do we have any reason to believe that there is a genuine totality here and not just a loose aggregate of more or less unrelated cases? (1991, 102)

The corresponding temptation in philosophy and sociology of science would be to presume that *scientific* knowledge is a "reasonably definite object of study," either on its own or parasitic upon its subsumption within knowledge in general.[4] To see why the program for a sociology of scientific knowledge remains committed to epistemology in this sense (and why most feminist science studies are not), we need to consider the epistemological project in more detail. Williams succinctly summarized the characteristic forms in which this epistemological commitment has been deployed within philosophy:

> The traditional philosophical examination of knowledge ... points to four central ideas: an *assessment* of the *totality* of our knowledge of the world, issuing in a judgment delivered from a distinctively *detached* standpoint, and amounting to a verdict on our claim to have knowledge of an *objective* world. (1991, 22)

Sociologists of scientific knowledge have given a distinctive spin to each of these ideas, but all four remain important to their project.

The ideal of detachment has clearly played a central role in the recent sociological tradition; indeed, sociological criticisms of mainstream philosophy of science often focus upon philosophers' insufficient detachment from the norms and cultural familiarity of the natural sciences. The classic statement of sociologists' conception of an appropriately detached standpoint to study science is David Bloor's programmatic demand that the sociology of scientific knowledge be "impartial with respect to truth or falsity, rationality or irrationality, success or failure, . . . and symmetrical in its style of explanation . . . [of] true and false beliefs" (Bloor, 1991, 7). But relativism has not been the only methodological commitment that has resulted from sociologists' desire for a detached standpoint from which to understand the sciences. Latour and Woolgar deliberately construct their account of Latour's participation in a neuroendocrinology laboratory from the perspective of a relative *stranger* to the culture of science:

> We regard it as instructive to apprehend as strange those aspects of scientific activity which are readily taken for granted. . . . The uncritical acceptance of the concepts and terminology used by some scientists has had the effect of enhancing rather than reducing the mystery which surrounds the doing of science. . . . For us, the dangers of "going native" outweigh the possible advantages of ease of access and rapid establishment of rapport with participants. (1986, 29)

More recently, Collins and Yearley (1992) have suggested an alternative image of detachment from epistemic norms and commitments. The sociologist of science must be able to *alternate* between competing beliefs, methods, and epistemic ideals, understanding each from the "inside" but without the insider's epistemic commitment. Moreover, the sociologist must combine this "promiscuous" epistemic alternation with a "meta-alternation" that also permits the sociologist to accept naively the categories and norms of everyday life and of sociology itself. From Collins' and Yearley's perspective, Latour and Woolgar's methodological estrangement is thus not detached enough—ultimately, what is called for is a disciplinary *antagonism* between natural and sociological realisms:

> We provide a prescription: stand on social things—be social realists—in order to explain natural things. The world is an agonistic field; others will be standing on natural things to explain social things. That is all there is to it. (Collins and Yearley, 1992, 382)

Whichever form of sociological detachment is preferred, the result is to situate the sciences within a larger epistemic *totality*. Claims to scientific knowledge are to be regarded as examples of a more general kind, which can be surveyed and assessed as a whole. Sociologists characterize this more general object of study variously, as beliefs (Barnes, Bloor), order (Latour and Woolgar, Collins, Shapin, and Schaffer), discourse (Gilbert and Mulkay), inscriptions (Latour and

Woolgar), or representation (Woolgar), but underlying these differences is a shared commitment to subsuming the sciences under a more general analytical category. Of course, the new sociologists of science rightly pride themselves on the wealth of detailed case studies that exemplify their methodological and theoretical commitments. Steven Shapin's (1982) prominent review already listed an impressive range of such sociological studies, which has since greatly expanded. Yet the supposed *significance* of these studies is oddly disconnected from their empirically rich particularity. MacKenzie and Barnes recognized this disconnection in reflecting upon the implications of their own study of early twentieth-century controversies between Mendelians and biometricians:

> The general point is not that the goal-directed character of scientific judgment implies its relationship to any particular contingency, or to external factors, or political interests; what is implied is that any such contingency *may* have a bearing on judgment and that contingent sociological factors of some kind *must* have. (1979, 205)

What matters is that all scientific practices and achievements exemplify a more general kind that can be accounted for by appeal to distinctively social contingencies.

These general categories that sociologists of science have used to define their object of inquiry have been perhaps surprisingly continuous with the "semantic ascent" that so often characterizes philosophical reflection upon science. Sociologists, too, have shifted from accounting for scientists' interaction with the world to explaining scientists' beliefs, accounts, inscriptions, or representations, or still further removed, the *content* of their beliefs or representations. Undoubtedly the sociologists have multiple reasons for their semantic ascent. The Strong Programme was explicitly defined in opposition to Mannheim's and Merton's sociological approaches, which had exempted the content of knowledge from sociological study. The sociologists also intended to challenge normative philosophical accounts on their own turf, and that challenge might be facilitated if the contested turf were described commensurably. Finally, a sociology of science needs a sociologically accessible domain. Collins and Yearley emphasize this concern in challenging Michel Callon's (and Bruno Latour's) attempts to recognize natural objects as "actants":

> There is only one way we know of measuring the complicity of scallops [or other natural objects that scientists work with] and that is by appropriate scientific research. If we are really to enter scallop behavior into our explanatory equations, then Callon must demonstrate his [natural] scientific credentials. (1992, 316)

If scientific knowledge can instead be characterized in terms of "collectively accepted systems of belief," consensus, discourse, order, representation, or other forms of mediation, then sociological credentials may regain their relevance. Whatever the reason, however, the new sociology of science defined its domain of inquiry in ways that significantly abstract from and generalize over the diverse forms of scientific practice.

The sociology of scientific knowledge may nevertheless initially seem to diverge from epistemological philosophy of science by rejecting the normative perspective from which philosophers would assess the rationality or verisimilitude of scientific knowledge. Sociologists have hoped to explain why scientists accept some beliefs (representations, accounts, etc.) rather than others, in ways that are carefully severed from whatever justification they might have for accepting those beliefs themselves. As Barnes and Bloor put the point,

> the incidence of all beliefs without exception calls for empirical investigation and must be accounted for by finding the specific, local causes of this credibility. Whether the sociologist evaluates a belief as true or rational, or as false and irrational, he must search for the causes of its credibility. (1982, 23)

But this shift from a classically normative epistemological stance to an empirical and explanatory account is a move within epistemology rather than against it; the sociological accounts thereby make common cause with the increasingly widespread philosophical commitment to *naturalized* epistemology.[5] Moreover, such naturalized (or socialized) accounts of knowledge do not thereby lose all normative force. Explanations of the acceptance or credibility of beliefs may then reinforce or undermine one's own inclination to accept them. Knowing the causes of certain beliefs might well increase confidence in them by displaying reliable causal connections to aspects of their intended objects. Adherents of the Strong Programme's commitment to explanatory symmetry typically go in the opposite direction: they suggest that the causes for the acceptance of scientific beliefs are disconnected from any reason for the analyst to believe them and, hence, that "all beliefs [including scientific beliefs] are on a par with one another with respect to the causes of their credibility" (Barnes and Bloor, 1982, 23). To that extent, the most prominent adherents of the sociology of scientific knowledge do engage in the epistemological project as Williams described it: they assess the totality of scientific beliefs *as* claims to knowledge of an objective world and find them to have no greater (but also no less) justification than any other collectively accepted systems of belief. The new sociology has not abandoned justification; rather, it has engaged in the quite general epistemological project of showing why standard philosophical defenses of the rationality or truth of scientific claims should instead be regarded as *ex post facto* rationalizations. In Latour and Woolgar's words, "'reality' cannot be used to explain why a statement becomes a fact, since it is only after it has become a fact that the effect of reality is obtained" (1986, 180).

The distinctively epistemological character of the new sociology of science can be seen clearly in another way. Despite their rejection of a realist philosophy of science, few of the new sociologists of science espouse a metaphysical anti-realism. Barnes and Bloor are especially clear about this point, for they are metaphysical *realists*. They only insist that truths about the natural world, what-ever those truths are, are useless to explain the diversity of conflicting beliefs about that world. Latour and Woolgar, whose views differ in so many important ways from Barnes's or Bloor's, nevertheless concur in distinguishing sociological from metaphysical anti-realism: "we do not wish to say that facts do not exist or that there is no such thing as reality.... Our point is that 'out-there-ness' is the *consequence* of scientific work rather than its *cause*" (1986, 181–82; N.B. the quotation marks, indicating that the supposed consequence of scientific work is not reality itself, but the *effect* of reality, i.e., what can *count* as reality for social beings like us). The sociologists separate their commitment to an epistemological relativism from a metaphysical anti-realism by arguing that the world's effects upon our beliefs or representations are always socially mediated to an extent that makes beliefs referentially opaque. Social practices, interests, or interactions, and the holistic interconnections among beliefs (and among the concepts in which they are framed and the experimental and observational practices that provide them evidential support) always intervene *between* us and the world, in much the way that strict empiricist anti-realists take *experience* to mediate the world opaquely. The sociologists' commitment to relativism is a nat-ural consequence of conjoining the social mediation of belief or representation with acknowledgement of diverse social practices among humans. Sociological relativism is thus epistemologically parallel to the relativism strict empiricists would presumably accept if there were compelling evidence that human beings differed significantly in their sensory modalities and capacities.

There remains one last revealing feature of the new sociology of science that further displays its continuity with the epistemological tradition. Among David Bloor's four tenets of the Strong Programme is the call for a *reflexive* account of one's own claims to sociological knowledge (Bloor, 1991, 7). Subsequent the-orists in the sociological tradition, most notably Woolgar and Ashmore, argue that neither Bloor nor the ensuing sociological tradition have taken reflexivity seriously enough, while others (Collins and Yearley, 1992) respond that there must be limits upon reflexive criticism if the sociological project is to proceed at all. Yet these disagreements conceal an unexamined presumption that the important question to ask reflexively is epistemological. Bloor makes very clear that what is at stake in reflexivity are internal consistency and completeness: the sociology of scientific knowledge should neither be self-refuting nor should it accept arbitrary limits upon its scope. Woolgar (1988) and Ashmore (1989), by contrast, sometimes characterize their reflexive concern as rhetorical. Yet the central rhetorical problem they pose is that the authoritative authorial voice of sociological narrators and the apparent transparency of their referential prose are in pragmatic contradiction with the explicit content of their "findings" about the social construction of all accounts and representations. Woolgar and Ashmore are far too sophisticated to ask that sociological rhetoric accurately represent the findings it expresses, but they do ask that sociologists adopt literary forms that disrupt and interrogate readers' too easy acceptance of their claims as transparent representations *of* the social construction of scientific knowledge. The "other voices" that Woolgar hopes would be included in sociologists' texts are there not because of their own need to be heard, but only to satisfy the sociologists' need not to be believed too readily. Collins and Yearley object to Woolgar's project primarily because they do, after all, want their own accounts to be believed straightforwardly.

Feminist Reconceptions of Knowing

Feminists' insistence that scientific knowledge is socially constructed appears in a new light when juxtaposed against my subsumption of the sociology of scientific knowledge within the epistemological tradition. Feminist science studies scholars most evidently differ from the new sociologists in their opposition to relativism, their normative stance toward particular scientific claims, and their willingness to retain and employ suitably revised conceptions of evidence, objectivity, and a distinction between belief and knowledge. Yet in many cases, these familiar differences are a consequence of feminist scholars working toward *postepistemological* conceptions of knowledge, evidence, justification, and objectivity, and thereby opposing a framework *shared* by traditional philosophies of science and the new sociologies of scientific knowledge.

There are five ways in which I shall elaborate such feminists' transcendence of epistemology. First, these feminist science studies shift their primary object of study from sociologists' focus upon the semantic "content" of knowledge or belief to a concern with *relationships* among knowers and known. Second, these feminist studies take up a participatory stance toward scientific practices and scientific knowledge rather than trying to explain or assess scientific knowledge as a totality. Third, such feminist science studies have a different temporal orientation than either the sociology or classical philosophy of science as their primary concern is less with the present state of knowledge than its future possibilities. Fourth, many feminist reconstructions of the concept of "objectivity" in science and science studies dissolve any sharp conceptual distinction between epistemic and political criticism, a transformation that also prohibits reducing one category to the other. Finally, some feminists develop a more adequate conception of reflexivity and its epistemic, rhetorical, and political significance for science studies.

My first point concerns the ways many feminists have conceptualized scientific knowledge as an object of study. Feminist science studies have typically worked with a conception of knowledge that is less austere and abstract than the various forms of semantic ascent that characterize much recent philosophy and sociology of science. My claim is not that feminist science studies are an epistemological analogue to an ethics of care,[6] but rather that feminist scholars conceive of "knowing" as concretely situated and as more interactive than representational. Knowledge is not merely a propositional attitude (belief or acceptance) toward some ideal or abstracted propositional content, but a *relationship* between knower and known, a *situation* that guides what knowers do and how the known responds and can be understood. Evelyn Fox Keller pointed clearly in this direction when she suggested that,

> Although scientific theories cannot be understood as faithful reflections of either culture or nature, perhaps they can be understood as good enough reflections of the forms of interaction that speaking and desiring social actors seek to implement with that mute but nonetheless responsive world of actors we call nature. (1992, 95)

Yet even Keller's formulation still preserves an unnecessary vestige of the representational idiom; it would be consistent with her overall argument to omit altogether any talk of "reflections" and to say that theorizing is indispensable to the "forms of interaction" that she takes as central to science.

Undoubtedly this emphasis upon knowledge as a concrete relationship to its intended object gains its centrality and its urgency from initial feminist concern with the human sciences. Feminist theorists saw early on that knowledge claims about women, or about human beings in general, which excluded or diminished the humanity or rationality of women, are not simply *instruments* that could be used to oppress women or justify that oppression, but are integral to patterns of domination. These concerns with scientific knowledge as itself a form of action were reinforced by parallel reflections upon the politics of the human sciences within postcolonialist anthropology, where Western ethnographers' interactions with and writings about the people they study are increasingly seen to embody power and not merely to serve it. Observing, writing, and reading are not merely proposing or accepting the content of certain beliefs but are themselves actions with consequences (one must consider to whom one writes, in what language, available to whom, drawing upon what patterns of interaction, using what narrative conventions and authorial stances, and who is permitted or enabled to respond, with what effects).[7] Yet feminist science theorists apply these lessons more generally. As Donna Haraway noted,

> The agency of people studied itself transforms the entire project of producing social theory, . . . but the same point must apply to the other knowledge projects called sciences. A corollary [for] . . . the sciences as a heterogeneous whole, and not just in the social sciences, is granting the status of agent/actor to the "objects" of the world. Actors come in many wonderful forms. Accounts of a "real" world do not, then, depend on a logic of "discovery," but on a power-charged social relation of conversation. (1991, 198)

Feminist science studies have as a consequence often been explicitly concerned with *different* ways in which knowers might interact with the objects of knowledge. One way of manifesting this concern has been criticism of the sexual politics embedded in some epistemic models and practices. Feminist scholars have directed critical attention, for example, to Bacon's vision of scientific mastery over a feminized nature, to Boyle's articulation of a distinctively masculine modesty as an epistemically constitutive virtue, to molecular biologists' invocation of their project as "a calculated assault on the secret of life," and to the sadism that structured the scientific vision, narrative structure, and experimental practices of Harry Harlow's Wisconsin Primate Laboratory.[8] Lynn Hankinson Nelson reminds us that these issues

> are not about language or mysterious metaphysical agendas. The commitments to linear and hierarchical relationships, to executives and controllers, and to laws that phenomena obey are incorporated in our theories, methodologies, and models, and a commitment to "dominating nature" is incorporated in many of our scientific practices. (1990, 213–14)

Feminists' concern for different ways of knowing have also led to the articulation of possibly more constructive relationships between knowers and knowns. Most familiar, perhaps, are Evelyn Fox Keller's biographical evocation of Barbara McClintock's "feeling for the organism," and many feminist scholars' defense of holistic and interactive explanatory models in various scientific fields.[9] But these projects do not exhaust feminist reconstructions of knowing. Haraway has described her own erotic response to some "rigorously analytical and biotechnical" procedures in cell biology as a "knowing love [that] took shape in quite particular, historical-social intercourse, or 'conversation', among machines, people, other organisms and parts of organisms" (Haraway, 1992a, 71, 72). She has also argued for a feminist reconstrual of vision as an epistemic model:

> The "eyes" made available in modern technological sciences shatter any idea of passive vision; these prosthetic devices show us that all eyes, including our own organic ones, are active perceptual systems, building in translations and specific *ways* of seeing, that is, ways of life. (1991, 190)

Feminist defenses of holistic models, then, are best regarded not as *constitutive* of feminist reconstructions of knowing, but as one specific group of contestable moves within a more widely shared concern to understand knowledge as embedded within specific ways of engaging the world. Thus, Haraway crucially captures this feature of feminist science studies as a critical project: "the point is not new representations, but new *practices*, other forms of life rejoining humans and not-humans" (1992, 87).

Sociologists of scientific knowledge might reasonably object that I have overstated the contrast between the feminist and sociological traditions. After all, most recent constructivist sociologists of science emphasize that scientific knowledge is situated within forms of life, while Shapin and Schaffer's influential sociological reconstruction of seventeenth-century conflicts over experiment perhaps goes further in claiming that "solutions to the problem of knowledge *are* solutions to the problem of social order" (1985, 332, my emphasis). Differences reemerge, however, upon considering the place of feminist and sociological *accounts* of scientific knowledge with respect to the forms of life within which knowing is to be situated. The crucial difference, marking the second of my five main points, is located in the sociologists's aspiration to *explain* the content of scientific knowledge, and the attempt to achieve a *detached* standpoint from which such explanations could be launched. Feminist science studies, by contrast, have generally eschewed detachment and the explanatory project in favor of a participatory stance. Feminist science studies belong to the culture of science, and most feminists have been concerned to have an effect upon scientific knowledge and to legitimate the specific effects they hope to bring about.

Feminists' opposition to the sociologists' explanatory detachment has multiple motivations. Latour and Woolgar's hesitation to "go native" among the scientists, for fear of being taken in, ironically contrasts to feminists' recognition that for women, being taken in*to* science has too often not been an option. Adopting a stance of estrangement or antagonism toward the culture of science would risk *endorsing* an exclusion of feminist concerns from that culture that would dangerously reenact its history of excluding women. A thoroughgoing constructivist detachment from science threatens to be just "one more excuse for not learning any post-Newtonian physics and one more reason to drop the old feminist self-help practices of repairing our own cars (they're just texts anyway, so let the boys have them back)" (Haraway, 1991, 186, my parentheses), along with one more rationalization for those who would take feminist criticism to signify that women do not belong in science.

Perhaps more fundamentally, however, feminists often regard the sociologists' aspiration to a detached and totalizing *explanation* of the content of scientific knowledge to be objectionably androcentric. Feminist theorists have been suspicious of attempts to escape (metaphorically, methodologically, or theoretically) from the concrete particularity of bodies and social relationships.[10] Sociologists of scientific knowledge may initially seem to share feminists's concern and to respond by insisting that knowledge claims are always situated within particular forms of social life. Yet their explanatory aspirations require that these particular forms be surveyable as a totality: as determined by interests, as the outcome of negotiations, or as the manipulation of inscriptions, etc. As Bruno Latour has since put this point, such explanations are attempts to act at a distance and, thereby, to exercise power (1987, ch. 6; 1988). The "strategic position" from which such explanatory abstractions can account for the totality they survey (in this case, for scientific knowledge in its diverse manifestations) is precisely what Nancy Hartsock (1984, 240–47) once critically characterized as the standpoint of abstract masculinity and what other feminists have since characterized as the suppression of differences. It is not simply the desire for "explanatory power" in its dual political and epistemic senses to which feminists object, but the specific connections between this aspiration to explanatory detachment and the androcentrism that feminists have been specifically concerned to criticize.

Feminists have also objected to the specific forms that sociological detachment has taken, for they cannot afford to follow Bloor in his "impartiality to truth and falsity." Whereas the political commitment of the sociology of scientific knowledge has been to challenge the supposedly unjustified cultural hegemony of natural scientific knowledge in general, feminist science studies were initially concerned with the adequacy of particular scientific projects and proposals that are damaging to women. Feminists have been concerned to substitute scientific approaches and accounts that are not harmful, but it matters to them that those proposals provide not merely more congenial beliefs, but more adequate knowledge. Feminists certainly hope to change important aspects of the way the world is, but they want the political struggles on behalf of their utopian aspirations to be responsive to their actual situation, and that calls for more reliable knowledge. A feminist understanding of scientific knowledge thus requires not detachment or neutrality,[11] but a reflective and self-critical participation in the assessment of particular scientific projects and knowledge claims.

The explanatory ambitions of some recent sociologists of scientific knowledge are problematic for feminist science studies for another reason. Sociologists have often aspired to an explanation of scientific knowledge in a very stringent sense that would require the (social) explanans to be independently variable from or constitutive of the explanandum, so that a sociological explanation of the content of scientific knowledge would require that the relevant sociological categories not be dependent upon or interdependent with the categories whose application is to be explained (recall Collins' and Yearley's call, cited above, for sociologists to "stand upon social things to explain natural things"). Yet feminist science studies have neither sought nor provided such independence from the terms of their interpretations. Elizabeth Potter's study of Robert Boyle, for example, does not try to *explain* the content of Boyle's scientific project by reference to a pregiven conception of gender, but instead interprets Boyle's work as itself a linked reformulation of received conceptions of both gender and natural philosophy: Boyle was simultaneously "making gender [and] making science." Haraway has insisted upon the importance of this point more generally, in articulating her "nervousness about the... appropriationist logic of domination built into the nature/culture binarism and its generative lineage, including the sex/gender distinction" (1991, 198) while Butler has trenchantly argued that feminists need to problematize the discursively conditioned experience through which sex and gender emerge as possible categories:

> Whether gender or sex is fixed or free is a function of a discourse which seeks to set certain limits to analysis.... The locus of intractability, whether in "sex" or "gender" or in the very meaning of "construction," provides a clue to what cultural possibilities can or cannot be mobilized through any further analysis. (Butler, 1990, 9)

I shall return to the concern Butler expresses to understand the effects and limits of feminist analysis itself when considering sociological and feminist conceptions of reflexivity.

These differences between feminist and sociological approaches to science are also manifest in their *temporal* orientation, which is my third main point. The sociologists' explanatory project would account for the present state of scientific knowledge as an outcome of a social history and the present social situation. An important aim of the sociological project is to display the contingency of scientific beliefs and practices to counteract the appearance of their natural or rational necessity. The sociology of scientific knowledge does not by itself point toward specific changes in scientific belief or practice, but instead opens a space of contingency within which human agency can be exercised more freely: "scientific choice is in principle irreducible and open, [even though] historically, options are foreclosed according to the opportunities perceived for future practice" (Pickering, 1984, 405). As I noted earlier, the underlying cultural politics of the classical sociology of scientific knowledge is thus a *humanism* that would allow broader scope to human freedom in constructing views of the world and practices within it.

The temporal orientation of feminist science studies is more specifically futural and transformative. The aim of feminist science studies is not to expose scientific knowledge as *in general* contingent and alterable if "we" choose, but rather to show it as in need of alteration in specific respects and as potentially open to changes responsive to that need. Feminist science studies are thus specifically oriented toward a "successor science" in a way that the sociology of scientific knowledge has not been.[12] To some extent, this concern has a specifically utopian dimension that would encourage envisioning new ways of organizing specific scientific fields and the cultural politics in which they are situated.[13]

This difference in orientation emerges especially clearly in contrasting *uses* of a superficially similar rhetorical and argumentative strategy. Both feminists and sociological constructivists frequently display alternatives to well-established historical or contemporary scientific programs, and argue that there was or is no *compelling* epistemological justification for a choice many scientists actually made. Yet when Pickering, for example, argues for the contingency and underdetermination of high-energy physicists' commitment to the Weinberg-Salam model of electroweak interactions in the face of apparently contrary experimental results (1984, esp. ch. 10), the point is emphatically not to advocate the resurrection of the contingently defeated points of view.

Feminists use comparable juxtapositions to quite different ends. When Longino (1990, ch. 7) compares the evidence for and against linear hormonal and neural selectionist explanations of higher brain functions, Keller (1985, ch. 8) argues for the underdetermination by evidence of biologists' preference for pacemaker cell models of aggregation in cellular slime molds, or Haraway (1989, chs. 8, 14, 15) recontextualizes debates over the human evolutionary models of "man-the-hunter" and "woman-the-gatherer," their aims are specifically to encourage reconsideration of the merits of the less dominant view and to show how "one story is not as good as another" (Haraway, 1989, 331). Feminist science studies have been specifically concerned to criticize androcentrism and sexism in the development and acceptance of scientific work,[14] to envision less constraining and differently revealing scientific practices, and to enhance recognition of the contribution feminist inquiry can make to science and the culture of science.

Feminists resurrect ideals and norms of objectivity in the context of this concern to reconstruct science and to secure a place for feminist inquiry in that ongoing reconstruction. This continuing endorsement of objectivity marks the fourth main point of feminist transcendence of epistemology. Yet this endorsement is more often read as an attempt to find an intermediate or compromise position between a strongly internalist claim that scientific knowledge and practice are (or ought to be) fully determined by reason and evidence alone and a thoroughgoing sociological constructivism whose explanations of knowledge as the outcome of interests, ideologies, or the contingencies of social negotiation would leave no rationalist residue.[15] I think feminist science studies are better understood as attempting to rescue a conception of objectivity from the clutches of *both* epistemology and sociology of knowledge. Epistemological accounts of objectivity or rationality have traditionally been surrogates for realism: if objects of knowledge cannot directly ᴿegulate practices of inquiry from "outside," then perhaps the *concern* for objective representation can regulate them from within. The new sociology of science would deny even this last vestige of transcendence, but such denial is only *significant* if one accepts the epistemological framing of the question (Rouse, 1996, Introduction, ch. 7). Feminist science studies would reclaim objectivity not by finding a new route to transcendence of our all too human epistemic limitations but by carefully distinguishing the desire for objectivity from desires for transcendence.

A plausible but mistaken reading of these feminist reconstructions of objectivity might initially characterize them as sociopolitical *rather than* epistemic. The crucial virtue that objectivity would better serve would then be justice rather than truth.[16] The exclusion or marginalization of groups of knowers, whose lives, concerns, or needs are thereby prevented from contributing to the critical assessment of knowledge claims, is after all a characteristic failure of objectivity cited by many feminist theorists, and the objectionable consequence seems to be domination mediated by misrepresentation rather than vice versa. Yet by thus contrasting epistemic to sociopolitical virtues and ends, we risk seriously misunderstanding and understating many feminist theorists' interest in better knowledge. For most feminist theorists of science, knowledge is neither external to nor merely instrumental for justice but is itself a valued end for which justice is integral.

To understand this point, we have to take very seriously my earlier claim that feminist theorists are construing knowledge as multidimensional *relationships* between knowers and knowns, rather than a simple relation of representation and correspondence (or of intertextuality, for those who, like Woolgar

(1988), would deny any transcendence of representation). Moreover, these relationships are overlapping, so that scientific knowing always involves complex interrelations among knowers as well as relations to the proximate object of knowledge.[17] The question is how all parties involved can be accorded what is due them. Representation is a power-charged relation that involves not merely speaking for other people and things but also the power to shape their circumstances. Feminist reconstructions of objectivity are attempts to hold knowers accountable for what they do and to determine to whom and to what they need to be held accountable. These attempts take place with the recognition that inquiry and representation are inevitably partial, perspectival, and interested. The demand for justice cannot be an impossible demand for completeness or equal significance but must instead call for recognition of partiality, openness to criticism and to alternative practices of inquiry and the concerns that motivate them, responsibility for one's actions and position as inquirer and authoritative knower, and accountability for the effects of those actions and that positioning.

This concern to make knowledge more adequately accountable is manifest at multiple levels. Feminist science studies are centrally concerned with questions of evidence, not as a vestige of a theory of confirmation or rational belief but as an aspect of understanding how knowers should be accountable for what they do. Feminist theorists such as Longino (1990, 1992) and Wylie (1996) contextualize questions of evidence and focus upon *how* phenomena come to count as evidence and what they can be evidence *for*, what other assumptions, concerns, and practices play a role in constituting evidential relations, and how we can come to a more adequate critical assessment of evidential relations in their many dimensions. Similarly, Haraway's concern to reconceive vision should be understood as a more richly articulated account of the partiality, activity, malleability, and relationality of seeing and with it a recognition of more complex and far-reaching possibilities for criticism and transformation of what technologies of vision can make evident. In these feminist recontextualizations of seeing and making evident, "the goal of an epistemology and politics of engaged, accountable positioning remains eminently potent; the goal is better accounts of the world, that is, 'science'" (Haraway, 1991, 196). This goal cannot be achieved by subordinating or reducing the epistemic to the political, but instead it requires recognition of how familiar conceptions of *both* "domains" are transformed when their boundaries dissolve.

Feminists' moral-epistemology/epistemic-politics also raise questions about how knowledge claims and practices of inquiry become *significant* and authoritative. For example, not all, or even most, recognized truths about the world count as *scientific* truths. Science as an ongoing practice of inquiry discounts truths that are trivial, marginal, anomalous, arcane, or otherwise "uninteresting" in order to focus resources and attention upon others that are taken to be significantly revealing.[18] Feminist objectivity would incorporate self-critical assessment of judgments about what is interesting or important as well as what is well confirmed. Not surprisingly, for example, feminists see the coupling of an obsessive interest in researching possible sex-linked differences in cognition with an abiding disinterest in research on diseases afflicting women as simultaneously epistemic and political failings. But the critical assessment of scientific significance extends much further than just the exposure of blatant sexism. The feminist quest to hold judgments of scientific significance accountable extends to critical narrative reconstructions of the cultural significance of what is at issue in whole fields of inquiry, as in Keller's (1992) account of the reorientation of biology around a molecular biological quest for "the secret of life" or Haraway's (1989) examination of how Western primatology came to be focused upon questions of origins.

These questions about how knowledge becomes significant are closely related to feminists' critical examination of how knowers are positioned, a further reminder of why knowing is a multidimensional network of relationships from which distinctively epistemic and political judgments cannot be readily disentangled. Feminist assessment of knowledge is directed not merely at what is said on what grounds, but also who gets to speak, who is heard as authoritative, whose concerns and possible responses must be taken into account in constructing knowledge claims, who has access to the material and social resources needed for research, what sustains or compromises these various forms of credibility, and how the resulting authorization of knowers and knowledge changes people's life situation, and constrains or enables their lives. The normative aspirations of feminist science studies are addressed not only to the content of knowledge and justification, but also and inseparably to questions of who knows, with what effects. Yet these aspirations are intertwined without being subordinated to one another. The aim is better knowledge and a better world, together.

This broadening of the normative questions at stake in feminist science studies points to the fifth and final contrast I would draw between feminist science studies and the sociology of scientific knowledge. I maintained earlier that sociological discussions of reflexivity have been guided by epistemological concerns about consistency and completeness. Even Woolgar's and Ashmore's questioning of sociological rhetoric turned out to be focused upon a pragmatic *inconsistency* between what sociologists of science have said and how they have said it. Reflexivity has also incorporated a political dimension for feminist science studies. This contrast does not exempt the rhetoric of science studies from reflexive criticism. Sharon Traweek, for example, criticizes the same rhetorical strategies that concern Woolgar, but to different ends. Traweek notes that, like scientists,

> almost all those writing the newer social studies of science and technology also account for everything and reject all other stories. Almost all these stories, whether about nature, scientists, or science, are narrative leviathans, producing and reproducing all-encompassing stories of cause and effect through the same rhetorical strategies. (1992, 430)

In criticizing such rhetoric, Traweek's concern is not to "interrogate" and defamiliarize representational practices generally. From such a feminist perspective, Woolgar's stories comprise yet another narrative leviathan about how all representations (including his own) are projections of "the Self."[19] Moreover, this conception of "the Self" as encountering only its own constructions is widely recognized in feminist theory as characteristically masculine. For Traweek and other feminist theorists, by contrast, reflexivity discloses partiality and situatedness, not self-enclosure. It exposes the illusion that representation is autonomous and self-projecting; feminists respond that we can never encounter or understand *ourselves* (and especially not "the Self") except through our interactions with others in partially shared surroundings. If rhetoric is always situated, then reflexive concern for one's own authorship cannot remain internal to texts. The textual self-presentation of the author is subject to reflexive criticism only as part of a larger concern for writing and speaking as forms of action. What do these writings and sayings *do*? To whom and about whom are they expressed? In what ways do they allow for and acknowledge, or foreclose and not hear, the responses of those they speak to, about, or past? Above all, to whom are they accountable? Critical reflection upon knowledge claims is thus always both moral/political and epistemological, and feminist reflexivity would reconfigure the *politics* of science and science studies (including the consequences of the knowledges they produce) in reconstructing their rhetoric. Reflexive attention to one's own practices of speaking and writing would encourage a science, and a political engagement with science, that would be appropriately *modest* and self-critical.[20] Such a reflexive science would be attentive to the effects of its own investigations, including the foreclosing of some questions and concerns by its own theoretical categories and experimental practices.[21]

Conclusion

I have been arguing that the contrast between feminist and sociological science studies points toward a *postepistemological* conception of science and scientific knowledge. My aim in this paper, however, has been to clarify the significance of such a postepistemological approach, not to develop the more extensive arguments needed to defend it.[22] Williams's characterization of the epistemological project offers a useful way to summarize the contrast. Feminist science studies as I understand them would abandon the epistemological aspiration to a detached assessment of the totality of knowledge (or scientific knowledge) and its relation to an objective world. The alternative is engaged and self-critical participation in the making and remaking of scientific knowledges of the world we live in. Such participation requires an abiding interest in questions of justification, consistency, clarity, and so forth. These questions now arise more locally, however, while drawing upon more wide-ranging considerations. Thus, what is *at issue* in feminist accounts is not scientific knowledge as a totality, but particular scientific practices, projects, and claims, that are understood as ongoing interactions among knowers and the world known. What is *at stake* in feminist participation in science and science studies is at once better knowledge and a better world.

Notes

1. I am grateful to Lydia Goehr, Jill Morawski, and Lynn Hankinson Nelson for helpful comments on earlier versions of this chapter.
2. I interpret the scope of the Strong Programme broadly; my discussions of the sociology of scientific knowledge will presume that its central adherents are the Edinburgh School (e.g., Barnes, Bloor, Shapin, Edge, MacKenzie, and Pickering), the Bath and York groups (Collins, Pinch, Mulkay, Gilbert, Woolgar, and Yearley), the early sociological ethnographers (Latour and Woolgar, and Knorr-Cetina) and the social history of Shapin and Schaffer.
3. Among the more prominent critical assessments of gender in science are Bleier (1984), Hubbard (1990), Birke (1986), and Fausto-Sterling (1985). My discussion, however, will focus upon the broader feminist reconceptions of science found in Haraway (1989, 1991, 1992a, 1992b), Longino (1989, 1992, 1993), Nelson (1990, 1993), Keller (1985, 1992), Wylie (1991, 1992, 1996), Harding (1986, 1991, 1992), Alcoff and Potter (1993), Potter (forthcoming), or Addelson (1991, 1993).
4. Rouse (1996) argues that the principal research traditions in philosophy of science and sociology of scientific knowledge are committed to epistemology in this sense and develops in much more detail what a nonepistemological philosophy of science might look like.
5. Both naturalized epistemologists and sociologists of scientific knowledge emphasize their break from classical normative epistemology because they seek to explain rather than to justify knowledge. I am emphasizing their underlying continuity in taking "knowledge" to be a theoretically coherent domain that needs to be accounted for as such, whether the account is an explanation or a justification.
6. Some feminist studies of science or other ways of knowing may indeed fit under this heading, for example, Belenky (1986), or the conception of knowledge that Evelyn Fox Keller (1983) attributes to Nobel laureate Barbara McClintock. My point, however, is perhaps best exemplified by theorists like Haraway, for whom feminist reconceptions of how we might engage the world epistemically require *suspicion* of metaphors of organicism, holism, and caring, etc., yet do strongly suggest that new forms of knowledge are as much changes in our *practices* as changes in our beliefs or other representations.
7. Clifford and Marcus (1986), Marcus and Fischer (1986), Rosaldo (1989), among others.
8. On Bacon, Keller (1985, ch. 2); on Boyle, Potter (2001); on the "secret of life," Keller (1992, part II); on Harlow, Haraway (1989, ch. 9).
9. Keller (1983), Longino (1990), Nelson (1990), Hubbard (1990), among others, defend specific holistic, interactive, and/or dialectical models as epistemically and politically preferable to more simplified causal accounts of the same domains.
10. Feminists' concern not to overlook the concrete particularity of bodies and relations does not preclude all generalization or any feminist *theory*. The objection is rather to a specific kind of theoretical detachment that seeks to *overlook* particularity by appeal to free-floating, ahistorical categories. As Fraser and Nicholson (1990) concluded, "[feminist] theory would be explicitly historical, attuned to the cultural specificity of different societies and periods and to that of different groups within societies and periods. [Theoretical] categories would be inflected by temporality, . . . non-universalistic, . . . pragmatic and fallibilistic. It would tailor its methods and categories to the specific task at hand, using multiple categories when appropriate and forswearing the metaphysical comfort of a single feminist method or feminist epistemology" (34–35).
11. See Proctor (1991) and Rouse (1991) on criticisms of recent social constructivist views of science for their detachment and their aspiration to value neutrality, and Harding (1992) and Haraway (1991, ch. 9), on feminist alternatives to neutrality and detachment.
12. I use the phrase "successor science" here more expansively than some feminist theorists do, to denote any transformation of scientific practice or belief motivated by feminist criticism.

13. To some extent, this utopian dimension is present in any feminist imagination of alternative ways of organizing scientific culture and practice that would escape or confront the androcentrism or sexism revealed by feminist criticism. It is perhaps most strikingly manifest, however, in Haraway's explicit use of SF literature (1989, ch. 16; 1991, ch. 10; 1992b) as a way of posing the utopian imaginative task set by feminist science studies.

14. As noted above, scholarship has been identified as specifically "feminist" due to its critical focus upon sexism and androcentrism, but feminist scholars have been as much or more concerned to examine racism, heterosexism, colonialism, and other forms of domination and exclusion, *within* feminist politics as well as elsewhere.

15. McMullin (1992, 22), exemplifies this familiar reading of feminist science studies as "less epistemically radical" than the sociology of scientific knowledge.

16. In recent political philosophy, "justice" is often used to refer only to fair distribution of rights, goods, and obligations; feminists sometimes criticize not merely particular conceptions of justice, but they focus upon justice as the most central political virtue (e.g., Baier, 1987). Here, I use "justice" in a more expansive sense, as a placemarker for whatever criteria or concerns should be used in the moral and political assessment of actions and the institutions and relationships that facilitate or sustain them.

17. Rouse (1987, ch. 7) exemplifies this point in discussing the kinds of disciplines that must be imposed to enable laboratory knowledge and the extension of those disciplines that must accompany the extension of knowledge outside of the local setting of the laboratory.

18. For further discussion, see Elgin (1993), Rouse (1996, ch. 6).

19. Woolgar's own capitalization (1988, 109).

20. Haraway's (1988: chapter 10) discussion of the scientific career of primatologist Alison Jolley provides an illuminating example of how such reflexive modesty might be realized in one very particular setting. Jolley's career and its scientific and cultural setting are unusual in ways that would strongly discourage taking her work as a *model* for politically engaged scientific practice, but it nevertheless illustrates Haraway's conception of a reflexive rhetoric and politics.

21. Butler (1995) thematizes this concern for the contingent limits of one's own theoretical foundations, but for a natural science the concern must certainly be extended to the material practices at laboratories and field sites.

22. In Rouse (1996) I articulate and defend my own approach to a postepistemological philosophy of science, which I take to support and complement the developments in feminist science studies that I characterize here.

References

Addelson, Kathryn Pyne. 1993. "Knowers/Doers and their Moral Problems." In Alcoff and Potter, 1993: 265–94.

————, and Elizabeth Potter. 1991. "Making Knowledge." In Ellen Messer-Davidow and Joan Hartman, eds., *Engendering Knowledge: Feminists in Academe.* Knoxville: University of Tennessee Press, 259–77.

Alcoff, Linda, and Elizabeth Potter, eds. 1993. *Feminist Epistemologies.* New York: Routledge.

Ashmore, Malcolm. 1989. *The Reflexive Thesis: Wrighting Sociology of Scientific Knowledge.* Chicago: University of Chicago Press.

Baier, Annette. 1987. "The Need for More Than Justice." In Marsha Hanen and Kai Nielsen, eds., *Science, Morality and Feminist Theory.* Calgary: University of Calgary Press.

Barnes, Barry, and David Bloor. 1982. "Relativism, Rationalism, and the Sociology of Knowledge." In M. Hollis and S. Lukes, eds., *Rationality and Relativism.* Cambridge: MIT Press.

Belenky, Mary, et al. 1986. *Women's Ways of Knowing.* New York: Basic Books.

Birke, Lynda. 1986. *Women, Feminism, and Biology.* Brighton: Wheatsheaf.

Bleier, Ruth. 1984. *Science and Gender: A Critique of Biology and its Theories on Women.* New York: Pergamon Press.

Bloor, David. 1983. *Wittgenstein: A Social Theory of Knowledge.* New York: Columbia University Press.

————. 1991. *Knowledge and Social Imagery.* 2nd ed. Chicago: University of Chicago Press.

Butler, Judith. 1990. *Gender Trouble.* New York: Routledge.

———. 1995. "Contingent Foundations." In Linda Nicholson, ed., *Feminist Contentions: A Philosophical Exchange.* New York: Routledge.

Clifford, James, and George Marcus. 1986. *Writing Culture: The Poetics and Politics of Ethnography.* Berkeley: University of California Press.

Code, Lorraine. 1991. *What Can She Know?* Ithaca, N.Y.: Cornell University Press.

Collins, Harry. 1992. *Changing Order: Replication and Induction in Scientific Practice.* 2nd ed. Chicago: University of Chicago Press.

———, and Steven Yearley. 1992. "Epistemological Chicken." In Pickering, 1992: 301–26.

Elgin, Catherine. 1993. "Understanding in Art and Science." *Synthese* 95: 13–28.

Fausto-Sterling, Anne. 1985. *Myths of Gender.* New York: Basic Books.

Fraser, Nancy, and Linda Nicholson. 1990. "Social Criticism Without Philosophy: An Encounter Between Feminism and Postmodernism." In Linda Nicholson, ed., *Feminism/Postmodernism.* New York: Routledge: 19–38.

Haraway, Donna. 1989. *Primate Visions: Gender, Race, and Nature in the World of Modern Science.* New York: Routledge.

———. 1991. *Simians, Cyborgs, and Women,* New York: Routledge.

———. 1992a. "Otherworldly Conversations; Terran Topics; Local Terms." *Science as Culture* 3: 64–98.

———. 1992b. "The Promises of Monsters: A Regenerative Politics for Inappropriate/d Others." In Lawrence Grossberg, Cary Nelson, and Paula Treichler, eds., *Cultural Studies.* New York: Routledge: 295–337.

Harding, Sandra. 1986. *The Science Question in Feminism.* Ithaca, N.Y.: Cornell University Press.

———. 1991. *Whose Science? Whose Knowledge?* Ithaca, N.Y.: Cornell University Press.

———. 1992. "After the Neutrality Ideal." *Social Research* 59: 567–88.

Hartsock, Nancy. 1984. *Money, Sex, and Power.* Boston: Northeastern University Press.

Hubbard, Ruth. 1990. *The Politics of Women's Biology.* New Brunswick, N.J.: Rutgers University Press.

Keller, Evelyn Fox. 1983. *A Feeling for the Organism.* San Francisco: W. H. Freeman.

———. 1985. *Reflections on Gender and Science.* New Haven: Yale University Press.

———. 1992. *Secrets of Life, Secrets of Death: Essays on Language, Gender and Science.* New York: Routledge.

Knorr-Cetina, Karin. 1981. *The Manufacture of Knowledge: An Essay on the Constructive and Contextual Nature of Science.* Oxford: Pergamon.

———, and Michael Mulkay. 1983. *Science Observed: Perspectives on the Social Study of Science.* London: Sage.

Latour, Bruno. 1987. *Science in Action.* Cambridge: Harvard University Press.

———. 1988. "The Politics of Explanation: An Alternative." In Steve Woolgar, ed., *Knowledge and Reflexivity.* Beverly Hills: Sage: 155–76.

———, and Steve Woolgar. 1986. *Laboratory Life: The Construction of Scientific Facts,* 2nd ed. Princeton: Princeton University Press.

Longino, Helen. 1989. *Science as Social Knowledge.* Princeton: Princeton University Press.

———. 1992. "Essential Tensions—Phase Two: Feminist, Philosophical, and Social Studies of Science." In McMullin, 1992: 198–216.

———. 1993. "Subjects, Power, and Knowledge: Description and Prescription in Feminist Philosophies of Science." In Alcoff and Potter, 1993: 101–20.

MacKenzie, Donald, and Barry Barnes. 1979. "Scientific Judgment: The Biometry-Mendelism Controversy." In Barry Barnes and Steven Shapin, eds., *Natural Order: Historical Studies of Scientific Culture.* Beverly Hills: Sage.

Marcus, George, and Michael Fisher. 1986. *Anthropology as Cultural Critique.* Chicago: University of Chicago Press.

McMullin, Ernan, ed. 1992. *The Social Dimensions of Science.* Notre Dame, Ind.: University of Notre Dame Press.

Nelson, Lynn Hankinson. 1990. *Who Knows?: From Quine to a Feminist Empiricism.* Philadelphia: Temple University Press.

———. 1993. "Epistemological Communities." In Alcoff and Potter, 1993: 121–60.

Pickering, Andrew. 1984. *Constructing Quarks: A Sociological History of Particle Physics.* Chicago: University of Chicago Press.

———. 1992. *Science as Practice and Culture*. Chicago: University of Chicago Press.

———. 1995. *The Mangle of Practice*. Chicago: University of Chicago Press.

Pinch, Trevor. 1986. *Confronting Nature*. Dordrecht: D. Reidel.

Potter, Elizabeth. Forthcoming. "Making Gender/Making Science." In Bonnie Spanier, ed., *Making a Difference: Feminist Critiques in the Natural Sciences*. Bloomington: Indiana University Press.

Proctor, Robert. 1991. *Value-Free Science? Purity and Power in Modern Knowledge*. Cambridge: Harvard University Press.

Rosaldo, Renato. 1989. *Culture and Truth*. Boston: Beacon Press.

Rouse, Joseph. 1987. *Knowledge and Power: Toward a Political Philosophy of Science*. Ithaca, N.Y.: Cornell University Press.

———. 1991. "Policing Knowledge: Disembodied Policy for Embodied Knowledge." *Inquiry* 34: 353–64.

———. 1996. *Engaging Science: How to Understand its Practices Philosophically*. Ithaca, N.Y.: Cornell University Press.

Shapin, Steven. 1982. "History of Science and Its Sociological Reconstructions." *History of Science* 20: 157–211.

———, and Simon Schaffer. 1985. *Leviathan and the Air-Pump*. Princeton, N.J.: Princeton University Press.

Traweek, Sharon. 1992. "Border Crossings: Narrative Strategies in Science Studies and Among Physicists in Tsukuba Science City, Japan." In Pickering, 1992: 429–65.

Williams, Michael. 1991. *Unnatural Doubts: Epistemological Realism and the Basis of Scepticism*. Oxford: Basil Blackwell.

Woolgar, Steve. 1988. *Science: The Very Idea*. London: Tavistock.

Wylie, Alison. 1991. "Gender Theory and the Archaeological Record: Why Is There No Archaeology of Gender?" In Joan M. Gero and Margaret W. Conkey, eds., *Engendering Archaeology: Women and Prehistory*. Cambridge: Blackwell's: 31–54.

———. 1992. "The Interplay of Evidential Constraints and Political Interests: Recent Archaeological Research on Gender." *American Antiquity* 57: 15–35.

———. 1996. "The Constitution of Archaeological Evidence: Gender Politics and Science." In Peter Galison and David Stump, ed., *The Disunity of Science: Boundaries, Contexts, Power*. Stanford: Stanford University Press.

Index

CPSIA information can be obtained at www.ICGtesting.com
Printed in the USA
LVOW10s0530200514

386458LV00012B/247/P